SHAKESPEARE SURVEY

ADVISORY BOARD

Aspects of *Macbeth*
Aspects of *Othello*
Aspects of *Hamlet*
Aspects of *King Lear*
Aspects of Shakespeare's 'Problem Plays'

SHAKESPEARE SURVEY

AN ANNUAL SURVEY OF
SHAKESPEARIAN STUDY AND PRODUCTION

40

EDITED BY
STANLEY WELLS

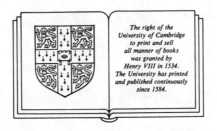

The right of the
University of Cambridge
to print and sell
all manner of books
was granted by
Henry VIII in 1534.
The University has printed
and published continuously
since 1584.

CAMBRIDGE UNIVERSITY PRESS

CAMBRIDGE

NEW YORK   NEW ROCHELLE   MELBOURNE   SYDNEY

Published by the Press Syndicate of the University of Cambridge
The Pitt Building, Trumpington Street, Cambridge CB2 1RP
32 East 57th Street, New York, NY 10022, USA
10 Stamford Road, Oakleigh, Melbourne 3166, Australia

First published 1988

Printed in Great Britain at the University Press, Cambridge

Library of Congress catalogue card number: 49–1639

British Library cataloguing in publication data
Shakespeare survey: an annual survey of
Shakespearian study and production.
40.
1. Shakespeare, William – Societies,
periodicals, etc.
ISBN 0 521 34442 5

201354

CE

EDITOR'S NOTE

Volume 41 of *Shakespeare Survey* (which will be at press by the time this volume appears) will be primarily concerned with 'Shakespearian Stages and Staging'. Volume 42 will be on 'Shakespeare and the Elizabethans', and Volume 43 on '*The Tempest* and After'. Submissions should be addressed to the Editor at The Shakespeare Institute, Church Street, Stratford-upon-Avon, Warwickshire CV37 6HP, to arrive at the latest by 1 September 1988 for Volume 42, and 1 September 1989 for Volume 43. Many articles are considered before the deadline, so those that arrive earlier stand a greater chance of acceptance. Please either enclose return postage (overseas, in International Reply Coupons) or send a non-returnable xerox. A style sheet is available on request. All articles submitted are read by the Editor and by one or more members of the Advisory Board, whose indispensable assistance the Editor gratefully acknowledges.

With this volume we welcome R. S. White as reviewer of Critical Studies.

In attempting to survey the ever-increasing bulk of Shakespeare publications our reviewers have inevitably to exercise some selection. Review copies of books should be addressed to the Editor, as above. We are also very pleased to receive offprints of articles, which help to draw our reviewers' attention to relevant material.

S.W.W.

CONTRIBUTORS

DAME PEGGY ASHCROFT, *London*
ANTOINETTE B. DAUBER, *Buffalo, New York*
MANFRED DRAUDT, *Senior Lecturer in English, University of Vienna*
RICHARD DUTTON, *Senior Lecturer in English Literature, University of Leicester*
MAIK HAMBURGER, *Deutsches Theater, Berlin*
GUY HAMEL, *Associate Professor of English, New College, University of Toronto*
TERENCE HAWKES, *Professor of English, University College, Cardiff*
MACDONALD P. JACKSON, *Associate Professor of English, University of Auckland*
MARTHA RONK LIFSON, *Associate Professor of Comparative Literature, Occidental College, Los Angeles*
CHARLES MAROWITZ, *Malibu, California*
ROBERT S. MIOLA, *Associate Professor of English, Loyola College, Baltimore*
RUTH NEVO, *Professor of English, Hebrew University of Jerusalem*
MARTIN ORKIN, *Senior Lecturer in English, University of the Witwatersrand, Johannesburg*
MARVIN ROSENBERG, *Professor of Dramatic Arts, University of California, Berkeley*
WILLIAM O. SCOTT, *Professor of English, University of Kansas, Lawrence*
NICHOLAS SHRIMPTON, *Fellow of Lady Margaret Hall, Oxford*
GÜNTER WALCH, *Professor of English, Humboldt University, Berlin*
ROGER WARREN, *Lecturer in English, University of Leicester*
R. S. WHITE, *Senior Lecturer in English, University of Newcastle-upon-Tyne*

CONTENTS

ILLUSTRATIONS

ILLUSTRATIONS

RECONSTRUCTING SHAKESPEARE OR HARLOTRY IN BARDOLATRY

CHARLES MAROWITZ

Looking around for a suitable sub-title for this paper I asked a professor of my acquaintance if he could suggest anything and, given the nature of my own Shakespearian rewrites, he said: 'How about *'Tis Pity I'm a Whore?*' I took the liberty of slightly revising that suggestion into the present sub-title. And I don't really think anyone can deny the fact that a good deal of 'harlotry' has insinuated itself into bardolatry. When you have a large, multi-national corporation such as the Shakespeare Industry, it goes without saying that it attracts people of easy virtue, and that's a subject I'll touch on in a moment or two.

As to my credentials, or my lack of them, I have to say that I speak as a professional director – not at all as a scholar or a pedagogue.

A director's relationship to Shakespearian scholarship (Granville-Barker notwithstanding) is very different from an academic's. For the academic, theories, suppositions, and speculations are ends in themselves, and a really solid piece of Shakespearian criticism need only be well argued and well written to join the voluminous tomes of its predecessors. But a director is looking for what in the theatre are called 'playable values' – that is, ideas capable of being translated into concrete dramatic terms. Very often, scholars provide just that, and there is more 'scholarship' on view in classical productions throughout Europe and America than audiences tend to realize. Most directors prefer to play down the fact that many an original theatrical insight can

be traced back, not to a director's leap-of-the-imagination, but to a scholar's dry-as-dust thesis. Three notable and acknowledged lifts immediately spring to mind: Laurence Olivier's Oedipal production of *Hamlet* based on a psychological tract by Ernest Jones (*Hamlet and Oedipus*, 1949), Peter Brook's *King Lear*, and The National Theatre's all-male *As You Like It* – both derived in large part from essays in Jan Kott's *Shakespeare Our Contemporary* (1965).

'Playable values' are not always consistent with literary values. A scholarly insight can make very good sense and be untranslatable in stage-terms. Conversely, a playable value can be brilliantly effective in a *mise-en-scène* and yet not hold up to intellectual scrutiny after the event. A classic in production makes demands that are never called for in the study. And perhaps that's where so much of the trouble lies. And by trouble I mean the traditional animosity that tends to smoulder between the professional theatre and the academic community. There is a factor in Shakespearian production which never enters into the academic study of a text. It's a stubborn factor and a transforming factor and, unfortunately, one that won't go away. I refer of course to the director.

In the nineteenth century, men such as the Duke of Saxe-Meiningen, Henry Irving, and Herbert Beerbohm Tree were closer to chairmen-of-committees than what we, today, call modern directors. They supervised their actors and decided questions of design but they didn't really insinuate a highly personal viewpoint onto their productions. With the advent of Konstantin Stanislavsky in Russia, Augustin Daly in New York, and Max Reinhardt in Germany, the director, armed with a stylistic prerogative and an aesthetic bias, gradually came to the fore. In the 1920s and 1930s in France, with men such as Jacques Copeau, Charles Dullin, Gaston Baty, Louis Jouvet and Jean-Louis Barrault, and in Russia with Nikolai Evreinov, Eugene Vahktanghov and Vsevood Meyerhold, we begin to see the first signs of another kind of director: men who leave their mark on material as much as they do on actors; directors who begin to reveal an attitude to new and established plays which is more pronounced than before. Sometimes, aggressively so.

The emergence of what we would call the modern director coincides *not* with his imposed authority on the physical elements of production, but his intercession with a playwright's ideas. The old autocrat-director controlled his actors; the modern director appropriates to himself those intellectual ingredients usually reserved for the playwright – using the tangible instruments of the stage as a kind of penmanship with which he alters or gives personal connotation to the text of writers both living and dead.

This is most visible in the works of Shakespeare and with directors such as Max Reinhardt, Benno Besson, Giorgio Strehler, Peter Stein, and Peter Brook: men who began to produce resonances in established works which surprised audiences that never imagined the plays dealt with the themes they *now* seemed to be about. So that, for instance, there comes a production of *King Lear* which charts the rise of the bourgeoisie and the gradual disintegration of feudalism, or another production which treats the play as an Oriental fable entirely detached from any historical milieu, or a version in which it's seen as a bleak, apocalyptic vision unfolding in an arid, Beckettian landscape from which God has been banished.

In these instances, and in many others like them, what has changed is the philosophical framework in which the play was originally conceived; the 'spirit' of the work radically re-routed even though the 'letter' remains intact. In short, another 'author' has appeared, and he is saying things different from – sometimes at conflict with – the meanings of the first author, and this interloper is, of course, the modern director; a man who insists on reading his *own* thoughts into those traditionally associated with the author whose work he is communicating.

A director who does *not* proceed in this way, who chains himself to unwavering fidelity to the author and pursues his work in selfless devotion to the 'meaning of the text' is unknowingly abdicating a director's responsibility. Since the only way to express an author's meaning is to filter it through the sensibility of those artists charged with communicating it, 'fidelity' is really a high-sounding word for lack-of-imaginative-output. The director who is committed to putting the play on the stage exactly as it is written is the equivalent of the cook who intends to make the omelette without cracking the eggs. The modern director is the master of the subtext as surely as the author is of the text, and his dominion includes every nuance and allusion transmitted in each moment of the performance. He's not simply a person who imposes order upon artistic subordinates in order to express a writer's meaning, but someone who challenges the assumptions of a work-of-art and uses *mise-en-scène* actively to pit his beliefs against those of the play. Without that confrontation, that sense of challenge, true direction cannot take place, for unless the author's work is engaged on an intellectual level equal to its own the play is merely transplanted from one medium to another – a process which contradicts the definition of the word 'perform' – which means to 'carry on to the finish', to 'accomplish' – to fulfil the cycle of creativity begun by the author.

Having cleared that deck, one can finally get to the subject.

The great Shakespearian pastime has always been, of course, tendency-spotting – the intellectual equivalent of bird-watching – and anyone who's been hard at it has discovered the tendency, for example, towards bigger and more elaborate stage-settings; towards politicizing the histories; towards sexualizing the mixed-gender comedies, etc., etc. But the tendency that interests me most is the separation that's begun to take place between the original plays and works on which they are loosely – sometimes remotely – based. To explain this tendency, I think it's useful to look at the recent TV adaptations of the collected works produced by the BBC. The great lesson of those filmed Shakespearian plays is that, in refusing to allow the material to transform – to adapt itself to a different medium – most of the works were denatured. One could praise *this* performance or *that* scenic idea, but all in all, it produced leaden and inert television viewing. And why? Because the underlying assumption of the exercise was: the plays are so great, all one need do is bring together the best British talent one can find and record them for posterity. It is this high-varnish approach to Shakespeare which is his chiefest foe – the detestable conservative notion that all one ever needs do with 'classics' is preserve them.

One ought to be clear about this.

The bastions that protect William Shakespeare have been established by scholars, critics, teachers, littérateurs – people with a vested interest in language and the furtherance of a literary tradition. It's in their interests that the texts remain sacrosanct – that they're handed down from generation to generation, each providing new insights and new refinements like so many new glosses on an old painting. A process which, judging from the past two hundred years, can go on for at least another five hundred because there will never be a shortage of scholars to point out the semiotic significance of the ass's head in *A Midsummer Night's Dream* or the tallow candle in *Macbeth* or the implications of the syllabus at Wittenberg during the years Hamlet was supposed to have been enrolled there.

In Academe, as I'm sure I needn't tell you, it is considered a step-up-the-ladder to be published in learned journals. It's a help in securing tenure and a fillip towards university advancement. Consequently, the motive for publication is very much like a showcase production for an ambitious actor; a way of strutting his stuff – often at the expense of the material for which that 'stuff' is being 'strutted'. There is very little compulsion behind this kind of Shakespearian scholarship other than scoring points or sticking feathers in one's cap. Often, the writer's underlying aim is merely to catch the attention of a department head or a fund-granting agency. What you might call 'harlotry' in 'bardolatry'. This accounts for the bizarre nature of many of those precious and far-fetched subjects. Then, of course, there is also that peculiar breed of niggling intellectual which actually enjoys picking at the chicken-bones of art in order to re-create a semblance of the whole bird. This breed accounts for many of those microscopic studies of Shakespearian works which seem to be obsessed with every grain, every wart, every follicle to be found in the collected works. They produce the papers that scrutinize the punctuation, the typography, the syntax and the topical allusions of every play. Not only do they not see the trees for the forest, they're often too fascinated by the sap on the bark to even see the trees.

But for people without such obsessions, whose main concern is reconstituting Shakespeare's ideas and finding new ways to dramatically extrapolate them, this myopic preoccupation with the canon seems, more than anything else, like the scrutiny of one chimpanzee fastidiously picking the nits off another.

But to return to Shakespeare and the media. Had the BBC treated the plays as 'material' to be refashioned for a new medium, had they not felt obliged to freeze them for posterity, each one might have been a unique televisual experience without losing the essence of the stage-work on which it was based. A method more successfully practised in motion pictures.

If you do a swift comparison of the early Shakespearian films with the later ones, you find that the biggest single difference is that in the 1930s there was a valiant attempt to stick to the narrative and, as much as possible, to the text, and these are virtually unwatchable today. But from about the 1940s onward, filmmakers were more inclined to abandon the original texts and move off into purely cinematic directions. Which is why, for instance, Olivier's *Richard III* is so much better than Hollywood's *As You Like It* with Elisabeth Bergner, directed by her husband Paul Czinner, or *Romeo and Juliet*, starring a somewhat superannuated Norma Shearer and Leslie Howard. In *Richard III*, Olivier truncated the text, decided on three or four main character-points and then expanded the battle scenes with a kind of inspired, epic filmmaking: the same scenes which on the stage are perfunctorily choreographed duels, usually implausible, and which almost always stop dead the action of the play. What Shakespearian filmmakers discovered was that the more one expanded the cinematic possibilities and the less one felt restricted by the straitjacket of the text, the better the work was realized.

What is it for instance, about Kurosawa's *Ran*, that Japanese director's treatment of *King Lear*, which makes it a reinterpretation of Shakespeare's play and, at the same time, a bold diversion into a completely new work of art? For me, it's the liberty that Kurosawa exercises in following the play wherever, in his own personal imagination, it takes him. And if

the imagination of an artist is rich and resourceful, it leads him to a highly personalized statement on the play's themes which could never have been made without taking the play as its point of departure.

Writing about this film, Jan Kott says:

Kurosawa's greatness lies in his capacity to reveal historical similarity and variance; to find a Shakespearean sense of doom in the other, remote, and apparently alien historical place. He trims the plot to the bone. Hidetora's three sons are all that remains of Lear's three daughters and Gloucester's two sons. Shakespeare added the second plot of Gloucester, Edgar, and Edmund to the old folk tale about three daughters (two vile and one noble). Kurosawa has cut and compressed it. In this Japanese condensation of plot and character, only the eldest wife's son, a substitute for Goneril and Regan, is left in the castle where Hidetora has murdered her entire family. In this samurai epic, it is her drive for vengeance that destroys Hidetora's clan and legacy.[1]

And, discussing the distancing of Shakespeare's play by radically altering its setting, Kott says:

in Shakespeare's dramas, the other place – the other 'historicity' outside Elizabethan England – gives, at the same time, the plays' other universality. And what is more, the place often supplies their other contemporary meanings ... The farther the 'other' setting in Shakespeare's dramas is from Elizabethan England, the less likely it is that the image will match the text. It stops being an illustration and becomes its essence and sign.

Its 'essence' and 'sign' – and the whole assumption of these words is that it's possible to retain a play's essence by changing its 'sign'. Indeed, it is by changing its sign that its essence is both retained and enlarged. It is through a classic's imaginative metamorphosis that its eternal verities shine through. And I would say, the reverse proposition is also true. That by trying to contain those verities in their

[1] Jan Kott, 'The Edo Lear', *New York Review of Books* (24 April 1986), pp. 13–15.

original enclosure they become attenuated and reduced. Because as one generation supplants another, as new ideas force us to test the validity, or at least durability, of the old ones, artists are obliged to verify or nullify what they find in the old works. This 'verification' or 'nullification' is what determines the nature of the new work – and, in an inexplicable way, it often reinforces the integrity of the original.

The advantage that films have over plays is that the medium insists the original material be rethought and then expressed differently. The disadvantage in the theatre is that there's a kind of premium put on some abstract notion called 'fidelity' – which from the standpoint of the purists seems to mean again, make the omelette but don't break the eggs. The only fidelity that cuts any ice in the theatre is a director's fidelity to his personal perceptions about a classic; how well and how truly he can put on stage the visions the play has evoked in his imagination. How much of those visions have to do with him and how much with Shakespeare remains an inexhaustible moot point, and there's nothing to be gained from delving into that one now. The central point, it seems to me, and the one that determines the validity or nullity in the final result is: what added dimensions does the director bring to the original work? If, as is so often the case, a director's imagination falls short of the work he's trying to realize, then he deserves all the calumny that's gleefully heaped upon his head. If he manages to transcend it – and makes something of it that was never expected and never seen before – he has enriched a classic. And if the word classic has any meaning at all it must refer to a work which is able to mean again and perhaps mean something else.

To combat such subversive ideas we have the counterargument succinctly put by Maynard Mack. He writes:

The most obvious result of subtextualizing is that the director and (possibly) actor are encouraged to assume the same level of authority as the author. The sound notion that there is a life to which the words give life can with very little stretching be made to mean that the words the author set down are themselves simply a search for the true play, which the director must intuit in, through, and under them. Once he has done so, the words become to a degree expendable. . . . In the hands of many directors in today's theatre, where the director is a small god, subtext easily becomes a substitute for text and a license for total directorial subjectivity.[2]

For Maynard Mack and others of his ilk, the play is a 'given' and as such, there is a tacit obligation to deliver its original intentions. For contemporary directors, it's an invitation to undergo process, and only when *that* is done can its 'meaning' be understood, and because theatrical process is inextricable from contemporary sensibility, the play is either proven or disproven through the act of interpretation. When Antonin Artaud exclaimed: 'No more masterpieces', he not only meant we must lose our myopic reverence for classics, he also meant the Present, like a Court of Appeal, must confirm or deny the *presumed* greatness of a 'masterwork'. The hard evidence for such an appeal is the director's view of the work as performed by his company and received by his public. Often in such cases, it is the interpreter's vision which is rejected and the masterwork, in all its traditional greatness, which is confirmed. But just as often, it is the artist's metamorphosis of the masterwork that wins the day and when that happens, it *is* the director and his actors – who, in Maynard Mack's words, '*assume the same level of authority as the author*'. To view this as some kind of usurpation of proprietary rights is to misunderstand the nature of dramatic art and its tendency endlessly to reappear in different shapes and forms.

There are basically two assumptions about Shakespearian production. The first, what one

[2] Maynard Mack, *King Lear in Our Time* (Berkeley, 1965; London, 1966), p. 33.

might call the Fundamentalist View, is that if a director cleaves to what the author has written, delves deeper into the complexities of the text and discovers more nuance and more shades of meaning than his predecessors, he has rendered a service to the author and re-established the supremacy of the work. (Many of the Royal Shakespeare Company productions fall into this category.) The second, what one might call the Reform Approach, assumes that an ingenious director, by interpolating ideas of his own often far removed from the ideas traditionally associated with the play, can sometimes produce a *frisson* – or 'alienating effect' – which is so enthralling in itself, people are prepared to forgive the liberties he's taken to achieve it. Set against these two, now fairly standard, practices is what I would call The Quantum Leap Approach to Shakespeare by which an idea, inspired by the text, but not necessarily verifiable in relation to it, creates a work of art that intellectually relocates the original play and bears only the faintest resemblance to its progenitor. There have been a few examples of this kind of work but each so unlike the other that no general definition can as yet be formulated.

Edward Bond's *Lear* is an entirely original work, and yet it still feeds off certain ideas of class and cruelty served up in Shakespeare's original play. Tom Stoppard's *Rosencrantz and Guildenstern Are Dead*, despite its autonomy as a work of art, remains thematically related to *Hamlet* and still operates within the orbit of the original work where, for instance W. S. Gilbert's *Rosencrantz and Guildenstern*, being an out-and-out parody, does not. You could say of Brecht's *Edward II* or *Coriolanus* that they are intensifications of certain aspects of the works on which they're based – but they still derive a lot of their power from the reference point of the original. Whereas, in a work like *The Resistible Rise of Arturo Ui*, although *Richard III* is knocking around somewhere in the background, the play's historical vigour owes more to the author's assembly of con-

temporary political history than it does to The Wars of the Roses.

But much closer to the kinds of transmutations I'm talking about are works such as *Kiss Me Kate* – which can be seen as a brilliant riff on *The Taming of the Shrew*, and *West Side Story* which uses only very general elements from *Romeo and Juliet* (social unrest, family-feuds, etc.) to confront contemporary issues of juvenile delinquency, gang warfare, and ethnic clashes. In a film such as *Forbidden Planet*, a science-fiction movie of the 1950s, one has all the narrative threads and many of the relationships from *The Tempest* without actually treading on any of Shakespeare's turf. Knowledge of the Ur-text here may enhance a film-goer's appreciation but it's just as keen for people who never heard of the original. But all these examples are a little off the mark, for as soon as you have an entirely new wodge of material, a completely different format – that is, a musical form as opposed to straight drama, a movie rather than a theatre piece – you're really in the world of allusion rather than derivation, and given the habits of the Greek and the Roman dramatists, *that* practice is as old as drama itself.

But let's take a play like *The Tempest* for instance. If you consider it in a contemporary frame of mind, it's hard not to be struck with what we today would call its psychological symbolism. Connotations of the Ego and the Id have been read into this play for quite some time now. Now, what is the fable of that play if we remorselessly rethink it along those lines?

In a kind of private sanotorium stuck away in a rustic setting such as Surrey or Hampshire, we encounter a man who suffers from a curious delusion – not unlike Pirandello's Henry IV. He imagines himself shipwrecked on a desert island of which he has become the absolute ruler. Prospero's 'condition' has been brought about by the trauma of having lost his power to his scheming brother Antonio. To avoid the social consequences of that loss and to help him psychologically assimilate it, he creates a fantasy-world, and he peoples it with characters that relate to his condition. There is a good and blameless daughter with whom he strongly identifies. She, like himself, is an Innocent, the antithesis of the scheming, usurping and villainous brother who, unlike Miranda, knows all the ways of the world and how to turn them to his own advantage. There is a 'spirit' that will do his bidding for him; exercise that power which he has lost and, being lost, has to be compensated for with illusions such as Ariel. There is a personification of his own basest nature; that part of him which he recognizes as full of vindictiveness against his wrongdoers and is, at the same time, the deeply suppressed alter-ego of his enlightened and intellectual self. Which not only accounts for Caliban, but explains why he threatens Miranda, that thinly disguised symbol of Prospero's own virtue. And in this fantasy-world, peopled by psychic extensions of his own enemies and ideals, he creates a situation in which he can take revenge against those that have wronged him; can, as all psychotics do in daydreams, 'right the wrongs of the real world' through imaginary actions in his fantasy realm.

However, amidst all this delusion, Prospero is forced to confront his own inadequacies; that in his former position conveniently projected into the guise of the Duke of Milan, he was very ill suited to his job – being more concerned with books and intellectual pursuits than the humdrum business of politics; that, in a sense, being usurped by his brother was not entirely attributable to Antonio's villainy but could, in some way, be blamed on his own lack of qualifications. Which is perhaps why he lays such arduous chores on Ferdinand who is trying to win his daughter's love – that's to say, on a surrogate brother who is trying to prove himself to the virtuous Miranda – that fantasy projection of Prospero himself. And when his delirium has run its full course and he has liberated himself from the irresponsible freedoms he preferred to the duties of his former position *and* confronted the frustrations and aggressions of his own base nature – that is, *freed* his Ariel and *rehabilitated* his Caliban – he is ready to return to the real world; the world in which he must abandon his fantasies and assume his responsibilities. This is why he asks for his 'hat' – that traditional symbol of social respectability, and his 'sword', the practical weapon of defence which, from that point on, will serve him instead of his magical staff. The end of *The Tempest*, like the end of any psychotic delirium, restores the patient to the known world with a greater measure of self-awareness than when he left it.

Now this remorselessly Freudian reading of Shakespeare's play, I would suggest to you, can be played out in a single, contemporary room, in modern dress, with Prospero on a couch and a silent psychiatrist alongside, without any magical or spectacular accoutrements, with a few bits of furniture and some salient bits of modern attire to dramatize our protagonist's voyage from fantasy to reality. It's as valid a reading as setting the play on another planet with all the characters in spacesuits (as has been done in several American university productions), or setting it on a Caribbean island full of characters drawn from a turn-of-the-century naval battalion with Caliban as an insubordinate military lout and Ariel as Prospero's dutiful cabin-boy. For in all these far-fetched extrapolations of Shakespeare's play, there is some unmistakble line, which, stretched as it may be to breaking-point, still connects up to the themes and ideas contained in the original material. The validity or nullity of these far-ranging interpretations depends on the consistency of a director's *mise-en-scène*: how much of a piece he can make of that vision which he sees staring back at him when he gazes into the ruffled pool of Shakespeare's play, *The Tempest*.

In the case of *The Tempest*, we laid a heavy twentieth century net over the play. But there are also ways of reordering a classic's given material from within.

Let's take another example, a play we all know – like *A Midsummer Night's Dream* which itself has gone through quite a few permutations in recent years – and recently transmogrified by Woody Allen in the film: *A Midsummer Night's Sex Comedy*. And if Woody Allen can reinterpret Shakespeare, one wonders with trepidation, is Mel Brooks far behind? We've had dark *Dreams* that emphasized the labyrinth of the forest, and bright *Dreams*, like Peter Brook's magically-Meyerholdian version of 1970 and inevitably, throwbacks to rustic *Dreams* where the nineteenth century version of the play semed to be reasserted with a vengeance. But let's say, based on the sexual mysteries of the work, one chose to interpret it in a decidedly pre-Christian – even decadent – manner, *insinuating* rather than uncovering ideas. According to this reading, the story of the play might run something like this:

Oberon, a vindictive homosexual chieftain who exerts immense authority among his circle of followers in the forest, has tried repeatedly to wrest a beautiful Indian boy from his former lover, now rival, Titania – who is himself a homosexual given to dressing up in women's clothes. Titania's refusal to give up the youth or share him with others (which has been the established sexual convention) has incensed Oberon and caused irremediable friction between both camps.

To wreak the revenge burning in his bosom, Oberon arranges through Puck, not an ethereal sprite at all, but a superannuated and embittered slave, to administer a potent aphrodisiac to Titania which causes him to become sexually obsessed with the first creature he encounters. Because of his immense age and incompetence (as well as the imprecise nature of Oberon's instructions), Puck administers the drug to two of the four refugees who have wandered into the wood to escape arbitrary measures meted out by the State. This causes a series of promiscuous imbroglios, presumably uncharacteristic of the four persons involved.

Eventually, through guile, Oberon manages to appropriate the boy for himself, and Titania, now caught in the spell of the aphrodisiac, becomes enamoured of an amateur actor, one of several rehearsing a play in the forest, who has been transformed into a beast by the vindictive Puck. Having now acquired the coveted youth who is the unquestionable cause of all the play's strife, Oberon takes pity on Titania's condition, releases him from the spell, and the old, sharing homosexual relationship is restored. The wood, transformed into an erotic labyrinth which is what it must be given the proclivities of Oberon and Titania, encourages the lovers to pursue their carnal and licentious desires until Puck lifts their spell. Once returned to Athens, freed from the diabolical influence of the wood and no longer forced into arbitrary bonding, the lovers settle back to enjoy the entertainment laid on for the Duke's wedding, but Puck, in a final act of vindictiveness, upsets the performance of the play, terrorizes the wedding guests and reminds them that despite their heterosexual celebrations, nefarious, anti-social spirits such as himself are the true rulers of the world and characters such as Theseus and Hippolyta only its figureheads.

A preposterous imposition, I can hear some of my listeners muttering to themselves. A travesty of a play that deals with visions of Arcadia and rustic innocence. And yet, as many scholars have conceded, the *Dream is* a play about forbidden fruits – no pun intended; about promiscuity, bestiality, the slaking of carnal appetites, all those irrepressible desires that society firmly represses in order to ensure an orderly perpetuation. Midsummer Night, as the Scandinavians know better than most, is a night of unmitigated revelry in which the most potent sexual and anti-social cravings are released. Shakespeare, being a bourgeois writing for a bourgeois public, had to cloak the expression of these pernicious desires within a framework of 'a dream' to make them acceptable, but it's a thin disguise and the whiff of amorality fairly wafts through the musk and the foliage.

What is love-in-idleness if not an aphrodisiac? 'Idleness' means going nowhere, unproductive, unfruitful – sex for fun and not for procreation. Puck, a character derived from an ancient medieval devil, is the incarnation of our most demonic nature; an old embittered and cruel flunkey who delights in creating confusion and moral disarray. Like a superannuated Ariel, he is Oberon's recidivist – a 'lifer' who, unlike Prospero's sprite, can never have his sentence commuted. He talks about putting a girdle around the earth in forty minutes, but this is empty braggadocio; a pathetic throwback to the alacrity and fleet-footedness he once had but has long lost.

And of course, the amorality of Oberon and Titania is reflected in the surface society in which smug, privileged, upper-middle-class youths play sexual musical-chairs and of which Theseus and Hippolyta are – respectively – the kingpin and queenpin. When they were being themselves – before Puck's nefarious influence was imposed – they 'played at' romance and courtship, blithely circulating from one lover's bed to the other. Demetrius allegedly 'made love' to Helena before becoming besotted with Hermia, and Lysander effortlessly switches to Helena under the influence of a mesmerizing aphrodisiac but, as we know, persons under hypnosis can only perform acts basically consistent with their character. The lure of the wood and the spell of the drug merely release the lust and lechery which were always latent.

Even in the case of the Establishment figures, the scent of amorality is overpowering. Before the present distribution of sexual partners, we are told that Oberon is supposed to have lusted after Hippolyta even as Titania did after Theseus.

The tumult in the world – vividly expressed in Titania's speech 'These are the forgeries of jealousy' etc. – which results from Oberon's feud with Titania, represents the conflict of the ordered universe confounded by the Spirit of Anarchy and its concomitant is untrammelled sexuality. There is an even deeper reverberation; the opposition between heterosexual love and homosexual licence. Oberon, Titania, and their followers represent the homosexual oligarchy which flourished before heterosexuality became the dominant sexual fashion. The phantoms of that older order still cling to the underside of life and though active only under cover of darkness, they manage to exert their influence and project treacheries against the new social order. The carnality, the bestiality, the rustic romps through morally deregulated terrains, the vague sense of orgy and riot which issue from the now forbidden love of man for man constantly subverts the rosy coloured image of heterosexual harmony which was the cover story, not only of Elizabethan theatre but Elizabethan life as well. The *Dream*, like all dreams, is a repression of unacceptable sexual behaviour which, since it could never be stamped out, had to be heavily disguised and, as it were, propagandized out of existence – and Shakespeare's harmonic Christian monogamy was an obvious form of camouflage.

To many, this fanciful view of the sexual politics of *A Midsummer Night's Dream* will seem entirely absurd. And yet every time I read the play, I kept coming back to this beautiful Indian boy and Oberon's fanatical desire to have him. I would propose to you that, fanciful as it may seem, such a scenario can be played out within the textual framework of Shakespeare's play – with virtually nothing to contradict it. As it was, in fact, at the Odense Theatre in Denmark in 1985. And that seems to me to be one of the acid tests of interpretation. If the play cooperates in its own seduction, both director and material are permitted to have their fling. If the play resists, puts up insuperable obstacles or simply *refuses* to play along, obviously, the honourable course is to desist. Although, without meaning to give offence, I should add that on certain occasions, I have known classics to be raped to their everlasting benefit. A few seasons ago The Karamazov Brothers, a travelling juggling-and-vaudeville company, worked over *The Comedy of Errors* to everyone's delectation – and some seasons back in New York, a streetwise version of *The Two Gentlemen of Verona*, full of ethnic vernacular and topical jokes, received some discourteous treatment which didn't altogether go amiss. But whether convoluted within the original work or compounded into an entirely different work, the tendency, as I perceive it, is to scatter Shakespearian seeds into new soil and see what amazing new horticulture will sprout.

It is a notion that the diehards will resist with their last breath but what seems clear to me is: what's essential in the better works of William Shakespeare is a kind of imagery-cum-mythology which has separated itself from the written word and can be dealt with by artists in isolation from the plays that gave it birth. And, by insisting on the preservation of the Shakespearian language, as if the greatness of the plays were memorialized only there, the theatre is denying itself a whole slew of new experiences and new artefacts which can be spawned from the original sources, in exactly the same way that Shakespeare spawned his works from Holinshed, Boccaccio, Kyd, and Belleforest; the future of Shakespearian production lies in abandoning the written works of William Shakespeare and devising new works which are tangential to them, and the stronger and more obsessive the Shakespeare Establishment becomes, the more it will hold back the flow of new dramatic possibilities which transcend what we call, with a deplorable anal-retentiveness, the canon.

PLAYING SHAKESPEARE

PEGGY ASHCROFT[1]

I can only talk about Shakespeare as he came into my life, because I am no scholar – I have no academic knowledge. I was very fortunate that, in the nursery, I was given Lamb's *Tales*, and so I knew the stories and the characters as part of my enjoyment of fairy-tales and romances. Therefore, when I came to read the Shakespeare plays, I found that they were familiar ground: they were about people that I knew, and what fantastic stories! I was very fortunate, too, in that I went to a school where we started reading Shakespeare at about the age of ten. We didn't go in for glossaries and footnotes; we stood up in class and read out the texts; so the characters then started to come alive to us, as they had been alive in my mind. And then I became absolutely addicted to the language. I remember *A Midsummer Night's Dream* as – perhaps naturally – the first play we read. *The Merchant of Venice* was the next, and it positively fired me with a desire to put the play on. I must have been about eleven or twelve when I directed the last scene of *The Merchant of Venice* and we performed it to the school. After that we studied a play in class every year. In addition, in those days we had what we called an elocution class, which was an 'extra'; and there we rehearsed and performed an entire Shakespeare play each year. The first I remember was *As You Like It*, and I was rather bored by playing Celia and very delighted when I achieved Cassius in *Julius Caesar*. Later we did a special, private production of *Henry V* among enthusiasts; and

then we did *The Merchant of Venice* in its entirety, and I played Shylock.

So Shakespeare was the most exciting part of my school life, by far. Admittedly I became passionately interested in Bernard Shaw when I was about thirteen. That, of course, was to me a very puzzling experience in one respect, because I respected Shaw – he taught me so much; he taught me to think and to question things – but then, when he spoke disrespectfully of Shakespeare, I was torn between loyalties!

But my passion for Shakespeare developed, and the first play that I saw in the professional theatre was, again, *The Merchant of Venice*. Since then I have played in it three times. It is rather undervalued nowadays, it seems to me, if not exactly despised. Perhaps it is thought to be boring. I don't think it boring, but a wildly exciting play, if you take it for the truth. Portia must really believe that she is going to deceive them all. It is *make believe*, and then – anything is possible!

So I had a kind of easy introduction to Shakespeare, then, and I feel that perhaps it stood me in good stead, because I never looked on him as being something frightfully difficult. I used to be quite surprised when young actors would come to Stratford with terror

---

[1] This article is based on a conversation, in late November 1986, between Dame Peggy and Inga-Stina Ewbank, which was taped and jointly edited.

that they were going to have to act Shakespeare. That seemed to me extraordinary.

Of course, Shakespeare is special; he is a world of his own. I think he requires intense realism and at the same time he is super-real. So I think actors feel that the great test in playing Shakespeare is that you have to stretch yourself to the limits – that he requires a kind of athleticism, mental and physical. You have to have tremendous control, physically, to carry through the speeches vocally; and you have to have an athleticism of mind, in that you must think the thoughts very quickly. Take five or six lines of Shakespeare: that thought, with all its complications, has to come out as an *immediate* thought. And I think you should use the pause – which actors are very fond of – very sparingly, because otherwise you lose that other thing which you must always bear in mind: the shape, the wonderful shape, of the verse. I also think one danger is ever to make people think about Shakespeare 'poetically'. (As 'poetry', in inverted commas, that is.) The truth is there, and the poetry heightens the truth. Finding the way to make it do that, is what tests you. Of course you can just recite the verse, and it is still wonderful, but if you have to *act* it, to fill it with the psychological truth, with what we call subtext, then this is a more difficult thing to do. It is tiring, but at the same time it develops muscle. It is like what is required of a dancer: your breath is required, your speed of thought, your speed of speech and character of speech, and also control of movement. As in most things, economy is all. But the *size* of what you are doing is also tested, and size is something that we all strive for. We lose it if we reduce Shakespeare to mere colloquialism. It's a matter of finding a way between the colloquial reality of the lines that you speak and the size that the poetry – as opposed to the 'poetical' – requires. The poetry has to have air round it.

I think next to Shakespeare the dramatist who most requires athleticism is Shaw. And, of course, strange as it may seem, Shaw is one of the best teachers of what it takes to speak Shakespeare. Those letters that he wrote to Ellen Terry are absolutely brilliant, and in them he talks about the carrying-through of the thought and not pausing too long or taking too long about it.

I think that my career spans quite an interesting period of Shakespearian playing. At the beginning of the century there had been Beerbohm Tree and Henry Irving – the successful Shakespeare actors of that generation. But their achievement was still in the realm of rhetoric, of speaking the verse very 'beautifully', and of elaborate, realistic settings. I think it was William Poel who really began something new. I never met Poel, but he started the career of Edith Evans with whom I worked when I was very young. He did away with the rhetoric, and with romantic illusions – stage illusion and scenery. It was the speaking, and the character, that he was after. And the speed. I think speed is tremendously important. If I seem to lay emphasis on 'speed', it is speed and agility of thought rather than delivery that I value. We have all suffered from those gabbled speeches which are worse than the slow laborious.

So, in the thirties it was beginning to take shape, this more modern, more psychological and realistic approach to Shakespeare. And of course John Gielgud was wonderful, both as an example of the speaking of Shakespeare and in staging Shakespeare. He followed in Poel's footsteps, and in his first productions at the New Theatre in the thirties, *Hamlet* and *Romeo and Juliet*, he did away with all scenery that had to be changed; the design had to be such that the action could be continuous – as it was played in Shakespeare's own day.

Scholars sometimes ask me whether, when I play Shakespeare, I develop a whole character, or whether I work from scene to scene. This question is easily answered, because the thought of working from scene to scene is, to me, almost absurd. You *have* to have a conception of the character as a *whole* before you would know how to approach any particular scene. If you don't know how your character is going to end, you can't know how to begin it! Certainly an analysis of the structure of the play, knowing the values of each scene, so that you can 'build' a part, knowing when the climaxes have to come, is essential. But the method of acting Shakespeare, basically, is exactly the same as acting any other play where the truth of the *whole*, not just the character, is paramount. I think perhaps we have developed from the earlier Shakespeare companies, where the star actor played the great role and was judged by his interpretations of certain lines. Now we think about the *play* as a whole and what is the interpretation of the director. We may respect or reject that interpretation, but we probably would not be in the production if we did not respect it – at least, I have been fortunate not to have to, on the whole. Though sometimes I think directors do ask things of actors that actors find it very difficult to do!

When I was young, I found the Granville-Barker essays on the Shakespeare plays absolutely marvellous, and so they still seem. He is a perfect guide to the overall conception of each play. But one has to learn by 'doing'. For example, I was very lucky to have the opportunity to play *Romeo and Juliet* three times between the ages of 22 and 28. But it wasn't until the last production, when I had learned something about how I wanted to approach the part, that I felt I achieved the 'fourteen-year-old', and that I realized, for instance, the value of the balcony scene coming straight out of the ballroom scene (even though Romeo has his long soliloquy just before it). Instead of it being what you might be led to think of as a languishing moonlight scene, gazing at the sky, it's a girl who is almost out of breath with excitement, who rushes out into the air. Anyway, that is how I found the way to play the balcony scene, after the third go at it. (The last lines of the ballroom scene:

My only love sprung from my only hate!
Too early seen unknown, and known too
     late!
Prodigious birth of love it is to me,
That I must love a loathed enemy.

And the first lines of the balcony scene:

O Romeo, Romeo! wherefore art thou
     Romeo?
Deny thy father and refuse thy name;

etc.) I was also very fortunate to learn a great deal from the Russian director Komisarjevsky who, of course, did many productions at Stratford, though none that I was in. He taught me to analyse a part, to see it as a whole, and to choose the values of how you were going to portray a character – the very opposite of playing scene by scene. So, one scene has to come from another: it has to be an organic whole.

There is also, in the shaping of a character, the all-important question of the *relation* of one character to another. Legend seems to have it that, at the New Theatre in 1935, I played Juliet with John Gielgud and Laurence Olivier alternating as Romeo and Mercutio but that is not true. They alternated only in that Olivier played Romeo for the first six weeks, and then they changed roles. Alternate nights would, I think, have been extremely difficult. I feel I 'made' the part, rehearsing and playing it with Olivier, so that our interplay was the result of a long working period. John was the director, and the take-over was in some ways – disconcerting! Both actors, I think, excelling in the first version, Olivier as Romeo – a non-pareil – Gielgud as Mercutio.

Every director has his own idea of the overall conception of a play. These days it is often a matter of the so-called updating of Shakespeare that we have become so used to. At times, I think, putting a play in another period can shed a light on it which we might otherwise miss. I was surprised and interested when Trevor Nunn decided that he was going to set *All's Well That Ends Well* at the beginning

1 *The Wars of the Roses* (*Henry VI*). Royal Shakespeare Theatre, 1964. Peggy Ashcroft as young Queen Margaret

2   *Romeo and Juliet*. New Theatre, 1935. Peggy Ashcroft as Juliet

of this century; but his reason for doing it was valid. In a sense, he said, this is very much a play about class. If we think of class in the Elizabethan period, we don't know enough about the subtleties. If we translate it into a more modern period, the various relationships become more meaningful – Helena the paid companion of the Countess; the subtle relationship between the Countess and the 'Clown' becoming 'gardener'; and the difference between the snobbishness of Bertram in his attitude to Helena, etc., and the King's overall dismissal of class – for then we can appreciate them within a context that we know about. This, I think, adds to the audience's appreciation of the play. But – without citing examples – I have seen productions where I have thought that putting the play in a modern period simply didn't make sense at all.

Yet, I shall never forget my first experience of seeing 'Shakespeare in modern dress', as we used to call it then. One of the first in this country was Barry Jackson's production of *Hamlet* at the Birmingham Repertory Theatre, which came to London. I must have been just over sixteen then. I had already seen John Barrymore playing Hamlet, which deeply disappointed me! It was the Renaissance *Hamlet*, but it was also Hamlet with interminable pauses: 'To be . . . . . . or not to be': an example of just what you must *not* do when you speak Shakespeare! But Barry Jackson's modern-dress *Hamlet* was different. I was very interested to find, talking to my old friend George Rylands, director of Gielgud's *Hamlet* in 1945 and of *The Duchess of Malfi* in the same year, that he had the same experience as I did when I saw that production. He said that it brought everything so much closer to him, shedding a new light across the play. And it wasn't filled with drinking cocktails and the silly little gimmicky things of modern life, but we saw people as we know them today, speaking the words – and they spoke them, as I remember, very well and very clearly – in a way that made the characters freshly alive for everyone. I am

sure it would have done any class of sixth-formers an enormous amount of good to see that production. Buzz Goodbody's production at The Other Place, with Ben Kingsley, achieved the same immediacy.

Much Ado About Nothing is a play which, of late, is nearly always done in modern or nineteenth-century dress. I had the opposite experience. I would have loved to play *Much Ado About Nothing* in purely Elizabethan dress, because it feels to me so totally Elizabethan. But in Gielgud's production at Stratford we did it in fifteenth-century costume. It was a wonderfully decorative production, designed by the Spanish designer Mariano Andreu, and visually it had great success. But I didn't feel totally happy – physically – because I felt that the women would not have had the freedom in that period, whereas I felt that the Elizabethan woman was released and much freer.

And this takes me to another question which was put to me by a scholar the other day: do I believe that Shakespeare understood women from inside, from their own point of view? The answer is that I certainly do. I think you could say that he idealized certain aspects of womanhood and girlhood, but I think he understood them very thoroughly. He seems to me to understand every subtlety of women. Think of the range from, say, Juliet, or Ophelia, or Desdemona, to the freedom of Portia, or Rosalind, or Beatrice, and to the maturity of Cleopatra – which is a part incomparable, I think, with any other. And he didn't just create romantic heroines: there is the richness with which he could write the Nurse – one of his most marvellous characterizations – or Mistress Quickly, or Margaret of Anjou. There is the wonderful waywardness and wantonness of Cressida. And there are the independent women: I think that Helena in *All's Well That Ends Well* is the most marvellously *modern* character. I have never played her, alas, and I have never played Cressida. But at least I played the Countess in *All's Well That Ends Well*: it is really a comparatively

3   *The Wars of the Roses (Richard III)*. Royal Shakespeare Theatre, 1963. Peggy Ashcroft as old Queen Margaret

4 *The Duchess of Malfi.* Aldwych Theatre, 1960–61. Peggy Ashcroft as the Duchess

small part, but it is exquisite in what it contains. Shaw, I think, said of the Countess that it was the most wonderfully written old woman's part that he knew. And there are those two fascinating women: Paulina and Emilia, both of whom I have played – two *women* as opposed to his *girls*.

It seems to me amazing that *women* can think of Shakespeare as anti-feminist. Take Desdemona: some people see her as a sort of softy, a milk-and-watery character. I think she has enormous strength – and the courage of the step that she took. She is of course the victim of the play, and perhaps victims are written off when they are not the main protagonist. But she is a wonderfully drawn character – rather the same as Cordelia in her individualism. So I cannot believe that she was drawn by a patriarchal author for a patriarchal audience, suspicious of individualism in women. Those who think so seem to forget that Elizabeth was ruling the country, and was a total individualist. And they seem to forget those many women in Shakespeare – young and old, and sometimes quite minor, like the Duchess of York in *Richard II* – who have tremendous guts and domination. And Portia just wipes the floor with the men!

Playing Margaret of Anjou, as a Shakespearian woman *and* as part of the whole *Wars of the Roses*, in a way sums up all that I have been saying here. What was exciting was that we all felt we were playing in a new play, because *Henry VI* doesn't often come one's way. I had never seen a production of it, and I don't think any of us had. And of course we had the excitement that John Barton and Peter Hall decided to include *Richard III* and so telescoped the three parts of *Henry VI* into two to make a trilogy; possibly we lost a great deal in that, but I think we gained in the drive and in the goal of reaching the climax of *Richard III*. And *Richard III* gained, in a sense, by your knowing about all these terrible people from having seen the *Henrys*. Now, Margaret both changes and stays the same. Her first scene is one of such wonderful comedy; it seemed to me rather like Katherine in *The Taming of the Shrew*. Even the language of the two women is similar in the early wooing scene. But there is already in that scene the treacherous, adventurous, dangerous character that she is going to become later. And she develops, until in *Richard III*, I think, she becomes the embodiment of the curse on the houses of York and Lancaster.

Perhaps I should end on what happens to be one of my favourite – though non-Shakespearian – plays, *The Duchess of Malfi*. I played the Duchess in 1945 and again in 1960; and in the second production, where we played on a very open set, I missed that claustrophobic feeling that we had in 1945 and that I think is so essential to the play. But I didn't feel differently about the Duchess, playing her fifteen years later. I think she is an intensely strong woman. She rebelled against the sexual restraints of her brother and her society; because it would be considered immoral to marry again, and because she would never be allowed to, she did it! In some ways I think she *is* a rather Shakespearian character. Webster's language is different, and you have to learn that afresh. Perhaps you can approach it better if you are used to playing Shakespeare!

TAKE ME TO YOUR LEDA

TERENCE HAWKES

I. CRASH

Let me begin with two voices: 'Give up literary criticism!' – the exasperation of a philosopher – and '*We* are not on trial; it is the system under which we live ... It has broken down everywhere' – the desperation of a politician. Both utterances surfaced in the same year, and the peculiar resonance they retain for modern British ears probably results from the fact that the year was 1929. I open with them because the crisis of 1929–30 and its bitter fruit still finds sufficient parallels in our current situation to make any echoes from its depths somewhat disturbing. On that basis alone it would not be unreasonable to argue that the period marks a genuine watershed in the development of British ideology. In May 1929 a general election had produced the second Labour government (albeit a minority one). Confident, hopeful, even with Ramsay Mac-Donald at its head, it rode full tilt into the great stock market crash of October of that year, inheriting the debacle that MacDonald's words attempt to grapple with: '*We* are not on trial; it is the system under which we live'. The apocalyptic atmosphere was heightened by the ungraspable nature of the breakdown. It was inexplicable, a text impossible to decipher. And when readings were forthcoming, the man and woman in the street found these difficult to understand and very far from re-assuring. As the historian A. J. P. Taylor puts it, this was the year in which a perceptible 'cleavage' opened up between the assumptions of ordinary mortals on the one hand and academic and 'informed' opinion on the other which has lasted almost to the present.[1] Even the great revisionary economists, such as J. M. Keynes, had to accept a recondite specialism forced upon them by the crisis. 'Common sense' – the intellectual stock-in-trade of the ordinary mortal – seemed to have crashed along with the rest of the market.

For a potent emblem of the situation, one in which 'readings' and 'decipherments' are of the very essence, we need of course not so much to 'give up' literary criticism as to take up the nature of its manifestation in the academy, under the aegis of the subject called 'English'. For the period 1929–30 also saw the publication of two of the most influential academic works of our century: G. Wilson Knight's *The Wheel of Fire* and William Empson's *Seven Types of Ambiguity*.

Their fundamental premises could hardly have been more opposed, and if their publication in the same year helps to mark that 'common-sense' divide quite precisely for us, their discussion of a particular Shakespeare play indicates that, in effect, they stand on either side of it. Appropriately, the play is that study of system, trial, and breakdown, *Measure for Measure*.

---

[1] A. J. P. Taylor, *English History 1914–1945* (Oxford, 1965), p. 268. For MacDonald's words see p. 285.

The appeal of Wilson Knight's essay '*Measure for Measure* and the Gospels' in *The Wheel of Fire* can broadly be said to be to the 'ordinary mortal' and the play seems to offer no problems to this kind of common sense. Seen as a wholly reassuring 'unambiguous' text, it apparently embodies a 'deliberate purpose'. That purpose involves the teaching of Christian morality, and Knight refers extensively to a fitting atmosphere 'pervading the play'. He sees the Duke as 'lit at moments with divine suggestion comparable with his almost divine power of foreknowledge and control and wisdom' and speaks of the 'ethical standards of the Gospels' being rooted in the play, with the 'evidently divine' duke 'actually compared' to the 'Supreme power': his 'supernatural authority' making him 'exactly correspondent with Jesus' and 'automatically comparable with Divinity'.[2]

Seven Types of Ambiguity takes exactly the opposite view. Far from presenting the play as unambiguous, it cites a passage from *Measure for Measure* as an instance of ambiguity of the fifth type. This is the sort of ambiguity that denies any dimension of 'exact' correspondence to a text because it 'occurs when the author is discovering his idea in the act of writing'. The result is that the author is 'not holding it all in his mind at once, so that, for instance, there is a simile which applies to nothing exactly, but lies halfway between two things when the author is moving from one to the other'.[3]

The idea of a simile which applies 'to nothing exactly' but which lies 'halfway between two things' is challenging to say the least, and not the least of its challenges is to a common-sense notion of reading. Certainly it raises fundamental questions about 'correspondence' and 'comparability'; about the way language works. Empson makes a point of refusing an obvious lifeline; the one which proposes a domesticated sort of ambiguity that shades into mere complexity, offering the reader two meanings for the price of one. In

fact, he says quite categorically in a subsequent footnote that the fifth type of ambiguity 'does not assert that there would be alternative reactions to the passage when completely grasped, or that the effect necessarily marks a complex but integral state of mind in the author'. No; what it asserts is the absence of the integral and of the coherent; what it marks is the presence of what Empson directly terms 'confusion' and proceeds to describe as a serious and recurrent kind of 'logical disorder'. In short, this type of ambiguity results in nothing less than a complete breakdown of the common sense on which Wilson Knight's idea of 'exact correspondence' rests.

The passage in question involves those lines spoken by Claudio in act 1 in which, replying to Lucio, he admits that his own indictment and his imprisonment come directly

> From too much liberty, my Lucio, liberty;
> As surfeit is the father of much fast,
> So every scope by the immoderate use
> Turns to restraint. Our natures do pursue,
> Like rats that ravin down their proper bane,
> A thirsty evil; and when we drink we die.
>
> (1. 2. 119–24)

Empson's analysis of these lines pinpoints the issue:

Evidently the first idea was that lust itself was the poison; but the word *proper*, introduced as meaning 'suitable for rats', but also having an irrelevant suggestion of 'right and natural' ... produced the grander and less usual image, in which the eating of the poison corresponds to the Fall of Man, and it is drinking water, a healthful and natural human function, which it is intolerable to avoid, and which brings death. By reflection, then, *proper bane* becomes ambiguous, since it is now water as well as poison.[4]

---

[2] G. Wilson Knight, *The Wheel of Fire* (1930), pp. 76, 80–1, 87, 90–1.

[3] William Empson, *Seven Types of Ambiguity* (London, 1930, 1947). See the 3rd edn (Harmondsworth, 1961), p. 184.

[4] Empson, p. 184.

Of course, the case can be pushed further: 'proper bane' is more than merely ambiguous. At stake is a wholesale contradiction between the concept of 'proper' or 'appropriate' and that of 'bane' in the sense of 'harmful', or fundamentally inappropriate. A genuine *aporia* – as we modern literary theorists dextrously term it – looms in the text at this point. Applied to human beings, as it is by the simile, it represents a major challenge to integrity and coherence, well capable of bringing common sense crashing down. '*We* are not on trial' – could it almost be the voice of Claudio we hear?' . . . it is the system under which we live.'

What emerges from this clash of readings of *Measure for Measure* might then form the basis for at least a minor revision of the history of literary criticism in our century. We are accustomed to hearing (and some of us, to making) complaints concerning the depredations wrought by recent and fashionable French ideas upon the settled certainties of Anglo-American critical analysis. Structuralism, post-structuralism, deconstruction, those great disintegrative movements from across the channel, have suborned our youth – and our middle-aged – it is said, by pointing to the supposed chasms that underlie our logic, the contradictions that untune the strings of our meaning, the shifting intellectual sands on which the tents of our literary judgements are pitched. Yet, as we can see, if we read the evidence closely enough, the issues are much more deeply rooted here, go back much further than a few years, and can be located in places much nearer home than Paris or New Haven. Here, in Britain, in the year of crisis, 1929–30, when things have 'broken down everywhere', certain familiar critical battle lines seem quite clearly drawn. And there is not a Frenchman in sight.

2. GOODNIGHT, VIENNA

Of course, *Measure for Measure* is a text that seems frequently to draw pointed commentary to itself. In fact, the persistence and sharpness of the disagreement over it might begin to suggest that the play periodically functions as a cultural arena in which significant ideological conflict takes place.

If that was true in 1929–30, another no less significant example erupted in the following decade, when L. C. Knights's essay, 'The Ambiguity of *Measure for Measure*', appeared in *Scrutiny*, vol. 10, no. 3 (January, 1942), pp. 222–33. Knights begins by voicing what by then had become a recurrent sense of disquiet: 'It is probably true to say that *Measure for Measure* is that play of Shakespeare's which has caused most readers the greatest sense of strain and mental discomfort.' This results, he claims, from an uneasy sense of paradox which prevails throughout; of conflicting 'truths' in the play whose antagonisms the text seems unable or unwilling to resolve.

The perplexity centres on the context of Claudio's supposed offence and in particular on the 'odd and inappropriate' way in which Claudio himself comments upon it. And Knights finally focuses on exactly the lines that concerned Empson: Claudio's response to Lucio's inquiry about the cause of his imprisonment:

> From too much liberty, my Lucio, liberty;
> As surfeit is the father of much fast,
> So every scope by the immoderate use
> Turns to restraint. Our natures do pursue,
> Like rats that ravin down their proper bane,
> A thirsty evil; and when we drink we die.
>
> (1. 2. 119–24)

Drawn, like Empson, to that final simile, Knights concludes that it presents a crucial contradiction. Overtly, it proposes that, in respect of sexuality, human beings behave like rats. Made thirsty when they 'ravin down' poison, they continue to drink it, and so die. However, he goes on, since it is in our 'natures' to be prompted by sexual desire, the 'mere fact of being human' condemns us to 'ravin down', rat-like, that which dooms us. To be aware of this paradox, as human beings irrevocably are, is to confront insoluble dilemmas about the limitations that hedge social behaviour. For it finally raises general and disruptive questions of 'the relations of law and "justice", of individual freedom and social control, of governors and governed' (p. 229).

If the different readings of Wilson Knight and William Empson can be said to reflect some of the tensions of 1929–30, an initial response to L. C. Knights's reading would point out that the ambiguities and social paradoxes at which it worries are precisely those that, by 1942, the pressures of war were forcing to the centre of attention. Issues such as the bombing of civilians, concentration camps, the requirements of military discipline, all combine to place the contradictions and uncertainties of the relation between individual freedom and social control at the head of any agenda, and it is perhaps unsurprising that such a text should be read in this way.[5]

In fact, it may even be somewhat surprising that a dissenting voice should be heard. Yet at the end of Knights's piece in *Scrutiny* we find – dread words – that the author has, he says, 'invited F. R. Leavis to develop his expressed dissent from the above. See the following page.'

Turning to it, we find the essay 'The Greatness of *Measure for Measure*' (pp. 234–47) which Leavis subsequently reprinted in *The Common Pursuit* (1952). Wholly rejecting all of Knights's reservations about the play, Leavis commits himself roundly to the view that it is simply 'one of the very greatest' of Shakespeare's works. He denies the existence of any damaging shortcomings, even to the extent of praising the play's dénouement as a 'consummately right and satisfying fulfilment of the essential design' (p. 243).

Knights, Leavis goes on, has unaccountably made 'heavy weather' of Claudio's lines about the reason for his imprisonment. He can see nothing 'odd' or 'inappropriate' in the simile of the 'rats that ravin down their proper bane', and reminds us that Claudio has committed

what he calls a 'serious offence, not only in the eyes of the law, but in his own eyes' (p. 236). The play presents us, he concludes, with no contradiction, uncertainty, or ambiguity. It does present us with complexity, which is a very different thing. But the central focus of that is not Claudio but Angelo.

In effect, Leavis's determination to scale contradiction and uncertainty down to the level of complexity – for that is what it amounts to – radically shifts the focus of the discussion and significantly re-contextualizes it. Knights's work, we should briefly recall, had come to prominence against a quite specific background: it had acted as the spearhead of the *Scrutiny*-based attack on an older, Oxford-dominated form of Shakespeare criticism represented by the writings of A. C. Bradley. Yet according to Leavis, Knights's essay now seems set to undermine the very principles in whose name that attack had been mounted. The charge must consequently be one of betrayal, or at least of culpable backsliding, for Knights's worried sense of the play's 'unsatisfactoriness' can only be explained, Leavis thunders, 'in terms of that incapacity for dealing with poetic drama, that innocence about the nature of convention and the conventional possibilities of Shakespearean dramatic method and form, which we associate classically with the name of Bradley' (p. 234). That this should come, as he points out, 'from the author of "How Many Children Had Lady Macbeth?"' is the unkindest cut of all.

This 'literary critical' re-focusing comes finally and fully to permeate and to determine Leavis's account of the play. Taking up what we might call the 'law and order' issue, for instance, he briskly dispatches its central features:

---

[5] Cf. Rebecca West, *The Meaning of Treason* (1949), pp. 235 and 238 on the case of the wartime traitor Stoker Rose, whom she casts as Claudio in *Measure for Measure*.

We accept the law as a necessary datum, but that is not to say that we are required to accept it in any abeyance of our critical faculties. On the contrary it is an obvious challenge to judgement, and its necessity is a matter of the total challenge it subserves to our deepest sense of responsibility and our most comprehensive and delicate powers of discrimination. (p. 241)

The key operations recommended here, use of our 'critical faculties', exercise of 'judgement', 'responsibility' and of 'comprehensive and delicate powers of discrimination', are of course exactly those which *Scrutiny* notoriously set out to promote as fundamental to the activity of literary criticism, and the terms signal an immediately recognizable discourse in which they occupy a crucial position.

In short, we might say that Leavis's reading of *Measure for Measure* proves to be concerned less with the objective assessment of an 'essential' play than with a continuing debate about critical method originating from within the *Scrutiny* camp. L. C. Knights's account of the play makes an anguished Claudio the site of struggle and thus the centre of attention. It offers us an Angelo in whom an iron 'self-control' and a 'taut and strained' will prove the cause of Claudio's unhappy situation. It would be over-simple, I suppose, to suggest that, in his account of Angelo, Knights was already nervously sketching the Leavis he knew his essay would have to take on. And I shrink from the bald proposal that he saw himself as a compromised Claudio anxious, despite the evidence, to justify his crime. Perhaps more to the point is the fact that Leavis's account of the play makes Angelo the central figure. And his carefully reasoned sympathy for Angelo incorporates a recognition that the character offers a model with a broad moral application beyond the play. With his comment 'If we don't see ourselves in Angelo, we have taken the play and the moral very imperfectly' (p. 246), sympathy intensifies into an odd kind of identification. Leavis's self-appointed role in *Scrutiny* as Shakespeare's lieutenant, charged with the

strict enforcement of the Bard's meaning in his absence, perhaps reinforces that impression. And it may finally be not entirely mischievous to suggest that within Leavis's Angelo-like perception of the backsliding Claudio who 'has committed a serious offence' for which harsh punishment is due, we might just glimpse the recalcitrant figure of Knights.

At this point, then, the play's location threatens to become wholly Englished: Vienna, we might almost say, seems about to turn into Cambridge.

3. LEGAL FICTION

In one sense, of course, it already had. One of the signal events of that crucial year of 1929–30 had been the re-establishment in Cambridge of the Viennese philosopher Ludwig Wittgenstein. Wittgenstein's return to Cambridge not only marked a significant development in the impact of a particular sort of philosophy, it also signalled a new level of engagement in a battle as old as Plato: that between the rival claims to knowledge advanced by the poet on the one hand and by the philosopher on the other.

In the Cambridge of 1929 the issues were sharply focused. If the sort of philosophy represented by Wittgenstein had in a sense emerged victorious from the defeat of idealism in the early years of the century, the study of 'creative', 'poetic' writing – literature – institutionalized in the new subject English – was also the product of a conflict, but a much bloodier one. In the words of F. L. Lucas,

It was ... in March 1917, while the German armies were falling back to the Hindenberg Line, while Russia was tottering into Revolution and America preparing for war, that at Cambridge members of the Senate met to debate the formation of an English Tripos ... [6]

---

[6] *Cit.* Francis Mulhern, *The Moment of Scrutiny* (1979), pp. 3–4.

Certainly the shape taken by the subject at Cambridge was decisively influenced by that conflict to the extent that philological engagement with the language (a staple of the Oxford and London courses) was rejected as an unwholesome Teutonic pursuit.

F. R. Leavis must unquestionably rank as one of the most forceful proponents of that new School's principles, and his repeated claims on its behalf to a superior kind of knowledge always stressed a principled opposition to the rival claims of philosophy. Few more succinct examples of it are available than his flat declaration: 'philosophers are always weak on language'. Against this may be set what he calls his 'opposing conviction . . . that the fullest use of language is to be found in creative literature, and that a great creative work is a work of original exploratory thought'.

These of course are life-long views, but I have taken the particular expression of them here from an essay written late in Leavis's career. In fact, the essay is devoted to his memories of Wittgenstein.[7] It consists largely of anecdotes and reflections, with a number of them quite firmly located in 1929. One of the most fascinating stories actually records an encounter between the German-speaking philosopher and the new discipline of English literary criticism. Curiously enough, the subject of the discussion was a poem by William Empson. Leavis takes up the story:

He said to me once (it must have been soon after his return to Cambridge): 'Do you know a man called Empson?' I replied: 'No, but I've just come on him in *Cambridge Poetry 1929*, which I've reviewed for *The Cambridge Review*.' 'Is he any good?' 'It's surprising,' I said, 'but there are six poems of his in the book, and they are all poems and very distinctive.' 'What are they like?' asked Wittgenstein. I replied that there was little point in my describing them, since he didn't know enough about English poetry. 'If you like them,' he said, 'you can describe them.' So I started: 'You know Donne?' No, he didn't know Donne. I had been going to say that Empson, I had heard, had come up from Winchester with an award in mathematics and for his Second Part had gone over to English and . . . had read closely Donne's *Songs and Sonnets*, which was a set text. Baulked, I made a few lame observations about the nature of the conceit, and gave up. 'I should like to see his poems,' said Wittgenstein. 'You can,' I answered; 'I'll bring you the book.' 'I'll come round to yours,' he said. He did soon after, and went to the point at once: 'Where's that anthology? Read me his best poem.' The book was handy; opening it, I said, with 'Legal Fictions' [*sic*] before my eyes: 'I don't know whether this is his best poem, but it will do.' When I had read it, Wittgenstein said, 'Explain it!' So I began to do so, taking the first line first. 'Oh! I understand that,' he interrupted, and, looking over my arm at the text, 'But what does this mean?' He pointed two or three lines on. At the third or fourth interruption of the same kind I shut the book, and said, 'I'm not playing.' 'It's perfectly plain that you don't understand the poem in the least,' he said. 'Give me the book.' I complied, and sure enough, without any difficulty, he went through the poem, explaining the analogical structure that I should have explained myself, if he had allowed me.

(pp. 78–9)

Certain aspects of this narrative surely demand our attention. The literary critic's nervous policing of the boundaries of his own newly established discipline is immediately apparent. A mystifying smokescreen at once comes down. The philosopher's initial reconnaissance, which seeks intelligence of Empson's poems, draws withering tracer fire: 'they are all poems and very distinctive'. A patrol probing the nature of this distinction runs into the bayonets of a thin red line: 'I replied that there was little point in my describing them, since he didn't know enough about English poetry.' To the flanking movement of 'If you like them . . . you can describe them' the response is the heavy artillery of condescension: the philosopher would first need to know

---

[7] F. R. Leavis, 'Memories of Wittgenstein', *The Human World*, no. 10 (February 1973), pp. 66–79. The essay is reprinted in F. R. Leavis, *The Critic as Anti-Philosopher*, ed. G. Singh (1982), pp. 129–45.

about Donne, and then about the English syllabus, if not about England (the casual mention of a famous and exclusive English public school threatens escalation of the conflict almost to the level of germ warfare). What possible sanctions can make an impression on the impenetrably foreign? A slightly languid note of *noblesse oblige* tempers the final bugle call: 'I made a few lame observations about the nature of the conceit, and gave up.'

Empson's poem nevertheless proves highly significant in respect of the symbolic dimensions of that skirmish. For 'Legal Fiction' turns out to be a work to which the issues of textual interpretation and of critical reading are themselves central. Its main concern, as its title suggests, is the Law, and the process by which legal texts seem to construct narrative – and fictional – accounts of the status on earth of the human animal:

> Law makes long spokes of the short stakes
>   of men.
> Your well fenced out real estate of mind
> No high flat of the nomad citizen
> Looks over, or train leaves behind.

But despite the narrative constructed by the law and its texts, the poem seems to say, human beings have no essential rights. Their stakes in this world are short, regardless of the lengthy pronouncements ('spokes') of the law. The *real* 'estate' of the mind involves other reaches, both spatial and spiritual. We 'own land in Heaven and Hell' as the poem later puts it and our rights extend 'under and above' those dimensions that the law lamely 'claims' as part of its fiction. In fact, the earth has no permanent continuing centre despite the concentric, wheel-like structure hinted at in that image of 'long spokes'. And beyond that, there lies no 'real' presence or essential central core of individual identity to substantiate the law's demands. In fact,

> Earth's axis varies; your dark central cone
> Wavers, a candle's shadow, at the end.

Wittgenstein's shamingly effortless exposition

of Empson's disturbing, deconstructive thesis – achieved without the benefit of English or of Englishness – clearly carried a threat to which Leavis's efforts at closure and composure represent an uneasy response. That Wittgenstein is here mocking, as philosopher, the practice of one kind of literary criticism emerges clearly enough in his repeated needling of Leavis in the name of just the sort of essentialist reassurances that the poem 'Legal Fiction' itself denies: 'Explain it! . . . Oh! I understand that . . . But what does this mean?'. Leavis's ill-tempered opting-out, 'I'm not playing', paradoxically gives the game away, and can stand as that sort of criticism's evidently ineffectual response to philosophy's upsetting investment in the notion of language 'games'. Against Leavis's dismissive 'philosophers are always weak on language', we must therefore set Wittgenstein's shattering, resonant retort: 'It's perfectly plain that you don't understand the poem in the least . . . Give me the book.'

Throwing off, at this moment, an apparently playful disguise, the returning philosopher suddenly emerges as an authoritative and sternly compelling figure, fully able to command the intricacies of texts about the law, and indeed perfectly capable of demonstrating this to an astonished upstart who, in his absence from the city, has temporarily usurped his powers. If Cambridge *were* Vienna, no Angelo could have been more disconcerted.

4. PUTTING ON SOME ENGLISH

It is hardly necessary to point out that Empson's poem effectively confronts the philosopher and the critic with issues that are central to *Measure for Measure* itself. Both texts deal with the matter of 'legal fiction' in that both rehearse the notion of 'laws' whose unity and coherence proves not permanent, immutable, or God-given, so much as the result of particular and contingent practices of reading.

In the case of Empson, the point is made that the 'real' estate of human beings may be read spiritually ('you own land in Heaven and Hell') as well as materially to a degree that mocks legal pretensions to deal solely in terms of attested 'fact'. In *Measure for Measure*, in the case both of Claudio and Angelo, a differently conceived reading of the law enshrined in the concept of the *sponsalia per verba de praesenti* in the one case or *de futuro* in the other, challenges and problematizes throughout the play the kind of legality on which Angelo bases his reign of terror.[8]

By insisting on the 'letter' of the law in the face of an opposing, older, common-law tradition of oral 'handfast' commitment which could be said to respond to its 'spirit', Angelo commits himself to a reading of the legal text which constructs it as unified, coherent, objective, and distinctive: 'It is the law, not I, condemn your brother' (2. 2. 80). But such a reading of the law can hardly be separated from the 'I' who undertakes it. Indeed, it surreptitiously generates and validates a particular version of that 'I', construed as an individual subject, at the mercy of specific fleshly promptings: appetites which, having determined, the law then proceeds to condemn. As Claudio rightly complains, laws read thus inevitably generate the crimes they punish, producing the paradox of the 'proper bane': that double bind in which what must be avoided proves to be coterminous with what is unavoidable.

Wittgenstein's remarkable performance as an analyst of the 'analogical structure' of Empson's poem might be said to hint, despite Leavis's coolness, at a capacity for higher things. And indeed, without even applying for the necessary visa from Downing College, the philosopher did later proceed to a series of spirited engagements with Shakespeare. In them, the same kind of 'analogical' structures continued to attract his interest. In fact, with an unnerving directness quite alien to the felicitous Arnoldian mode favoured by most true-born English critics, he goes straight, as it were, for the poetic jugular:

Shakespeare's similes are, *in the ordinary sense*, bad. So if they are all the same good – and I don't know whether they are or not – they must be a law to themselves.[9]

By this Wittgenstein seems to mean that both the equivalences proposed by Shakespeare's poetic devices and those analogically put forward by the plays at large (to push his word *Gleichnisse* to its broadest reach) fail to match reality with much precision. That they therefore rank as 'bad' (he uses the uncompromising German word *schlecht*) strikes him as an obvious conclusion, whose only surprising feature is that it doesn't appear to have been reached by everybody. In fact, as he points out, 'a thousand professors of literature' unaccountably share an opposite conviction. This prompts the suggestion that Shakespeare's adequacy in respect of reality, his vaunted 'truth to life' in which we can 'see ourselves' and perhaps even go on to make the peculiar sort of sympathetic identification experienced by Leavis in the case of Angelo, simply isn't relevant: 'you just have to accept him as he is if you are going to be able to admire him properly, in the way you accept nature, a piece of scenery for example, just as it is' (*Culture and Value*, p. 49e).

We should, Wittgenstein seems to be proposing, cease to regard Shakespeare as an individual personality intent on the exact sympathetic reproduction of a 'real' experienced world. We would do better to start thinking of him more as an inanimate feature of our own

---

[8] See Ernest Schanzer, 'The Marriage-Contracts in *Measure for Measure*', *Shakespeare Survey 13* (Cambridge, 1960), pp. 81–9.

[9] Ludwig Wittgenstein, *Culture and Value* (*Vermischte Bemerkungen*), ed. G. H. Von Wright and Heikki Nyman, trans. Peter Winch (Oxford, 1980), p. 49e. My attention was first drawn to this material by George Steiner. See his *Reading Against Shakespeare* (The W. P. Ker Lecture, 1986; Glasgow, 1987).

world, like a mountain, or a piece of scenery, something which is first and foremost simply *there*. The evident 'badness' of his similes (and to his credit, Wittgenstein never abandons that judgement) then poses no problem. We can content ourselves with staring 'in wonder' (p. 84e) at a Bard whose standing is that of a 'spectacular natural phenomenon' rather than a 'human being' (p. 85e).

It is important of course to place Wittgenstein's remarks in context, and when we do so this wholly alien view of Shakespeare takes on a special significance. Most of the comments I have quoted come from notes made during or just after the Second World War. As a Jew, as a former citizen of Vienna, and as a native speaker of German, Wittgenstein would have had a sense of the full horror of those years and the incapacity of language to prove 'exactly correspondent' to it that few of his Cambridge colleagues could have appreciated.

Wittgenstein's personal alienation was by this time virtually total. The issue of his own sexuality may have been a cause of some difficulty, and he was fully estranged from the fundamental precepts of his earlier philosophy. This rather daunting reality is surely part of a range of experience that he finds Shakespeare's plays inadequate to match, and his irritation at the 'thousand professors of literature' who thought otherwise is at least understandable.

One of them, like it or not, must have been F. R. Leavis. For by 1942, as we have seen, a newly professionalized academic literary criticism had been firmly established in Britain under the aegis of the subject called 'English'. In fact, Leavis must have been one of the first teachers at Cambridge actually to have taken a degree in that subject and then to have taught it for a living. Perhaps it is not unreasonable, looking back at his account of *Measure for Measure*, to suggest that it is finally and conclusively determined by a context which, wholly excluding Wittgenstein and his alien philosophical concerns, can be said, in both a literal and a metaphorical way, to put the label 'English' on the play.

I intend here both the American colloquial sense of 'English' as a bias applied, say, to a ball, to cause its path to swerve, and also a British sense of the word which – in a tradition extending from Arnold through Eliot to its climax (and perhaps its conclusion) in Leavis – perceives 'English' as an academic subject wholly unlike any other in that it can be held to function as the sacred repository of the traditions and values of an entire national culture.

In its British context, of course, putting on 'English' in this way not only excludes a Teutonic Wittgenstein and satisfactorily confirms an irredeemable 'weakness' in respect of language. It also excludes, in a process of systematic, even purposive, alienation, numerous native-born British people (Welsh, Scottish, Irish) – to say nothing of those whose inherited Englishness regrettably falls beyond the Cambridge pale. But perhaps the time seemed ripe. In 1942, the year of Leavis's *Scrutiny* piece on *Measure for Measure*, English was less than twenty-five years old at Cambridge, but *Scrutiny* was exactly ten. In the very next issue of the journal, that anniversary was celebrated with an Angelo-like commitment to the rigorous and combative prosecution of the battle for an English 'ideal of civilization'.[10]

However, implacable adversaries lay in wait. In December 1942 the Beveridge Report appeared, with its commitment to a new ideal of social democracy and the welfare state. In the same year R. A. Butler was appointed to the Ministry of Education and began the work which was to lead to the famous Butler Education Act two years later. By opening up the grammar schools and ultimately the universities to large sections of the population hitherto denied those benefits (a development which the novelist Evelyn Waugh later char-

---

[10] *Scrutiny*, 10, no. 4 (April 1942), 328.

acterized as the awarding of 'degrees to the deserving poor') this would prove a major instrument in the ultimate betrayal, in Leavis's terms, of the embattled English culture whose defender *Scrutiny* had claimed to be. Indeed, in the subsequent years in *Scrutiny*'s pages we can follow Denys Thompson as he gloomily rummages for metaphors that might correspond to a sense of national collapse treacherously engineered by alien forces. If the harsh yoke of equal opportunity was going to be imposed on the island race by a vengeful enemy from within (the Labour government, no less) then – Thompson finally lights upon the *mot juste* – a whole set of ancient moral and political principles would find themselves 'pearlharboured' as a result.[11]

5. SWANSONG

Since I stand before you as a child of the Butler Education Act, my person and my paper ample evidence of the appalling catastrophe it generated, you may permit me to smile – perhaps inscrutably – at that. (I might even whisper 'Tora! Tora! Tora!') Let me go on to suggest, from the vantage point of forty years on, that Leavis's 'Englished' account of *Measure for Measure* has possibly found itself overtaken by a peculiarly English fate: has been 'dunkirked', if you like, by elements also from within, with Cambridge playing its by now traditional subversive role. I am speaking not of the shades of Burgess and Maclean, Philby and Blunt – all of whom passed through Cambridge in these years – but of the implications of the work of that no less subversive pair Empson and Wittgenstein.

Wittgenstein's interest in Empson was certainly reciprocated. In fact, Empson once slyly arranged for Wittgenstein to make a curious personal appearance in a poem of his called 'This last pain':

'What is conceivable can happen too',
Said Wittgenstein, who had not dreamt of you. . . .

If we wanted to pin down the sort of game Wittgenstein was playing with Leavis, this perhaps offers a clue. Truth, these lines seem to imply, is a matter of projection as much as perception. It is conceived, not found: made by the mind, not discovered by it. A world of objective, un-processed, uninterpreted 'reality' is not and never has been available to us. Whatever is conceivable can happen because the conceivable constitutes the condition and the limit of our perception and awareness. It is a principle as old as Vico, to which the term *verum factum* applies: that which we regard as true is that which we have ourselves made. In this poem, Empson appears not only to accept that state of affairs. He even counsels that we should, whatever disappointment may be involved, nevertheless make it the basis of a life-style: we should, as he puts it in the same poem, 'learn a style from a despair'.

For Wittgenstein, the doctrine of *verum factum* had its implications for literary language, as it did for life-style, and we might suspect that these lurk, again memorialized for us in Leavis's account, within a classic peremptory injunction with which on one occasion he confronted the dumbfounded critic. It is the challenge with which we began: 'once', says Leavis, 'he came to me and, without any prelude, said "Give up literary criticism"'.[12]

Leavis's uncharacteristic response – silence – is garnished in the telling with a good deal of defensive *esprit de l'escalier* whose purpose seems once more to be the policing of boundaries: 'I abstained from retorting, "Give up philosophy, Wittgenstein!" largely because that would have meant telling him that he had been listening to the talk of a dominant coterie, and ought to be ashamed of supposing that Keynes, his friends and their *protégés* were the

[11] *Scrutiny*, 13, no. 3 (Autumn–Winter 1945), 234. See also vol. 12, no. 3 (Summer 1944), 222–7 and vol. 13, no. 1 (Spring 1945), 72–3.

[12] Leavis, *art. cit.* p. 72.

cultural élite they took themselves to be.' But even as it turns in disgust from the academic, specialized and non-commonsensical world of such as Keynes, that response sadly misses the point.

The point is surely that to Wittgenstein the sort of literary criticism which Leavis was coming to represent at that time seemed an obvious blind alley. It might as well be given up, for what Wittgenstein means by literary criticism here is the sort of thing he can already do perfectly well – to Leavis's surprise, when he 'explains' the 'analogical structure' of Empson's poem.

Wittgenstein's value to us lies precisely in the fact that his vision is a distinctive, un-English, alien one. He subscribes, as we have seen, to none of those assumptions about Shakespeare's essential 'greatness' or 'truth to life' that constitute the inheritance of the English or the preference of the Anglophile. His encounters with the Bard are profitably 'outlandish': they take place beyond the barbed wire of that 'English' front line behind which most of us crouch. And his comments make manifest a position with whose implications we are only relatively recently – in Britain – coming to terms. That is, that to the un-involved, alienated eye, no text offers values or meanings that exist as essential features of itself. Shakespeare's plays are not essentially this or essentially that, or essentially anything. They are, to take up Wittgenstein's metaphor, far more like natural phenomena, mountain ranges, pieces of scenery, out of which we *make* truth, value, 'greatness', this or that, in accordance with our various purposes. Like the words of which they are composed, the plays have no essential meanings, only uses.

If Wittgenstein's thinking thus urges us to 'give up' the idea that language 'represents' an essential reality to which 'explanation' can open the door, it demands by implication that we cease to 'divinize' the universe, as Richard Rorty has recently put it, by the presupposition of an ultimate, divinely authenticated

reality that can finally be thus revealed.[13] In respect of literary texts made out of language, one sort of criticism can be said to have long since arrogated to itself a similar 'divinizing' function, its central presupposition a God-like author whose hidden meaning remains to be revealed or 'explained' by a priestly critic.

The notion of Shakespeare as a sort of disguised Duke-like deity, inseminating his Viennese subjects with eternal truths brought ultimately to birth by the practised ministrations of a midwife Angelo-style literary critic is not of course an uncommon one, and part of my point is that it lurks undetected as an animating force in a good many twentieth-century accounts of Shakespeare – in particular those of Wilson Knight and F. R. Leavis to which I have been referring. Knowing analysts among you will already have detected an oddly mixed metaphor here deriving partly from *Measure for Measure*, but mostly from the ancient figure of Zeus who, disguising himself as a Swan, rapes the beauteous Leda. She, Yeats tells us, lacking the services of a literary critic, remained unfortunately ignorant of the true import both of the impregnating act and of its outcome.

But perhaps we should be less condescending, less dismissive than Yeats of Leda's potential as a positive, not to say resistant element in an arrangement whose fundamental opposition cries out in any case to be unpicked. The over-simple disposition of active and passive roles presupposed by it should at least alert us to the possibility that its main function is to generate and sustain the demeaning relationship which it purports only to describe. For the truth is that such an opposition – which makes no allowance for Leda's non-compliance or principled oppugnancy – is like most others not immutable, absolute, or permanent, and we have *Measure for Measure* to

---

[13] Richard Rorty, 'The Contingency of Language,' *London Review of Books*, 8, no. 7 (17 April 1986), 3–6.

remind us of that: a play whose very title hints at the potential for swivelling or turning contained in every conceptual polarity, and whose narrative gives ample evidence of its always possible occurrence. As every liberty slithers towards imprisonment, as every 'scope' turns into restraint, Claudio's account of the condition he terms our 'proper bane' must bring to mind the permanency of the impermanence that involves us all: of that perpetual swivelling motion in which opposites are continuously open to be de-polarized, re-aligned, with the sense they purport to weave accordingly unravelled to a degree that makes the straightforward communication of pre-packaged, coherent, and unified 'meaning' seem an impossible project.

To abandon the project is of course to reject the notion of an essential, given, even God-given 'meaning' for any play and to bring seriously into question the model of a coherence-generating one-way transaction in which the writer's work supposedly deals, and in whose name his Zeus-like (and inevitably male) fertilization of the Leda-reader takes place. As Empson shows when, at his most deconstructive, he is prepared to read a Shakespearian simile as fundamentally incoherent, and as Wittgenstein demonstrates when, similarly disposed, he is prepared to read Shakespeare's similes as 'bad', those roles need at least to be problematized. They might even be reversed. In short, the reader can, should, and, some might say, always does resist the writer, reject his avian advance, throw off his feathered embrace, and take the initiative in making the text mean.

Does this suggest that in 1929–30, that year of crisis, we find ourselves confronted by the end of one notion of the literary process, its swan-song, perhaps, in the mellifluous pages of *The Wheel of Fire*? And at the same time, do the spiky, uncomfortable sentences of *Seven Types of Ambiguity* ring in the new – the song of Leda in which no Zeus is good Zeus?

Of course, 1929–30 is certainly an obvious candidate to be the Year Of The Reader. It saw, after all, the publication of another major work of literary criticism, one in which, for the first time in the Anglo-American tradition, the reader achieved pride of place: I. A. Richards's *Practical Criticism*. Also, I have said that there was not a Frenchman in sight, but that is only partly true (or a case of *verum in parte factum*). In the same year, in the French colony of Algeria, the wife of the local rabbi gave birth to a son. He was to be called Jacques, and his family name was Derrida.

Nevertheless, more than fifty years on the central issues still seem to await resolution, at least in the English-speaking world. Where does the initiative finally lie? With the writer or with the reader? And whose side are we ultimately on: that of Zeus and the Swan, or that of mere mortals and of Leda? It seems that in order to give up one sort of literary criticism it is always necessary to embrace an alternative. If we wish Leda to become our leader we can hardly hope to remain, as the French might say, *du côté de chez Swan*.

SIGN THEORY AND SHAKESPEARE

MARVIN ROSENBERG

You will follow my proposals more easily if you begin by acting one line of Shakespeare. You can do it sitting down. The line is Ophelia's. Women readers will do it naturally; and men can remember that only they would have been allowed to act the part in Shakespeare's time.

Ophelia, deeply troubled, rushes to her father, to describe Hamlet's silent, distracted visit to her closet:

> He took me by the wrist, and held me hard;
> Then goes he to the length of all his arm,
> And, with his other hand thus o'er his brow,
> He falls to such perusal of my face
> As 'a would draw it.   (2.1.87–91)

The line I am after is: 'And with his other hand thus o'er his brow . . . ' How 'o'er his brow'? What did he do with his hand? Think about this for a moment, be the distraught Ophelia. Then, please, say the line with accompanying action:

> And with his other hand thus o'er his brow . . . .

What you do, of course, is make a sign – a sign Shakespeare required to give an idea of Ophelia's image of Hamlet's distraction. Your sign will be your unique reflection of an emotional state. In a search among the reviews at the Colindale library, my wife, Mary, and I found Tom Taylor's observation of 1873 that Ophelia's usual gesture in the theatre was 'as if to shade the eyes from the light'.[1] Taylor preferred the hand 'pressed hard on the fore-head' – a considerable difference: one gesture directed mainly outward, the other inward.

Herein is the basic problem with sign theory, 'semiotics', when it confronts the theatre. Actors' gestures are creative, and may widely differ. But at least since Aristotle, thinkers who like to classify have tried to codify the acting art. Most recently semioticists are making the effort and are running into trouble. A number of essays and books have been written; they all come up against the individuality of the artist, which refuses to be pigeon-holed. However, there are semiotic-related techniques that might make a comparable approach very useful to Shakespeare scholarship. Shakespeare's work must stand as an ultimate test of any semiotic analysis of the theatrical art, because no other playwright obtained so much creative collaboration from the artists of the theatre – his actors, his sign-makers.

The theatre speaks in a visual and aural language that is the most primitive of human sign-systems: the gestures and sounds of the body. Words are arbitrary noises we use to name things. When the body talks, it is the thing itself. Except in stylized drama, or cross-sex impersonations, the man intended on the stage to personate a man is a man. The woman is a woman. Each, like Edgar, is a poor (nowadays sometimes bare) forked animal making

---

[1] *Observer*, 4 May 1873.

33

its sounds and motions in a meaningfully physical language.

It is a language susceptible to the multiple levels of art. The sensitive face, hands, and body of a great actor can reflect many layers of emotion and thought, conscious and subconscious. Surface disguise can instantly dimension relationships. Thus Rosalind, dressed as a man, pretends to be the girl she is. We observe momentary slips back into her maiden sexuality that the lovesick Orlando misses, as she covers it with signals to us of braggadocio. That she was really a man-actor in Shakespeare's time made Chinese boxes of the role. Iago's earnest honesty is more physical than verbal: his body signs must have such sincerity as to fool even us, if we did not know. Then there is the ambiguity of the art itself – it is made of 'actions that a man might play'.

By what magic of representation does the actor become the character? In *Hamlet* the First Player weeps for Hecuba, and a moment later is himself again – is First Player. Cordelia weeps for Lear, and remains Cordelia until her end – until she rises from death a moment later to bow as the actress. The histrionic vocabulary of our bodies has an almost infinite variety.

Semiotics has tried to deal with it by breaking it down into components, along with other aspects of theatre art – as in the catalogue of theatrical sign systems proposed by Tadeusc Kowzan, and enlarged by Keir Elam.[2] It is extensive, but the essential dimension missing, as in so much of the writing on theatre semiotics, is the elusive contribution of the living artist – the actor. The actor's shared, physical experience of humanity remains the core of theatre, its instruments his body, face, voice, and personality. Traditional semiotics tries to pigeon-hole even these mediums. Horace long ago insisted on a specific decorum of signs – stage dress and behaviour – for standard dramatic types. Some students of the Elizabethan period assumed – wrongly – that then

great actors played roles following typical fixed gestural patterns – by analogy with postures in manuals of oratory.[3] In the eighteenth and nineteenth centuries, actors' manuals did appear with rules for expressing emotion on the stage. In Garrick's time, for instance, a book called *The Art of Speaking* gave these signs for fear – a prescription thought to match Garrick's own posture and speech as Hamlet when he saw the ghost:

Opens very wide the *eyes and mouth* . . . . lifts up the open *hands*, the fingers together, to the height of the breast, so that the palms face the dreaded object, as shields opposed against it. One *foot* is drawn *back* against the other, so that the *body* seems *shrinking* from the danger, and putting itself in a posture for *flight* . . . . The voice is weak and trembling.[4]

If this were the one and only physical image of fear an actor could project, the task of theatre semiotics would be much easier. The image could be coded as a fixed sign. But actors of genius, like writers of genius, will not submit to such mechanization: they stretch their physical vocabularies towards new limits.

Can a semiotic study of Shakespeare's plays help us to record its possibilities as well as its structure? Consider a promising model proposed by Keir Elam, that indicates both the strengths and weaknesses of the approach. Elam applies his technique to the first eighty lines of *Hamlet*.[5] He charts eighteen columns, with symbols for classifications such as speaker, listener, referents to time, space, and human and non-human context, content, cultural codes, themes and thematic echoes. Several columns are devoted to the complexities of language: its forms of address, as greetings, directives, commands, questions, assertions, negations, and so on. Elam also has pictographs: to note instances of seeing and

---

[2] See Keir Elam, *The Semiotics of Theatre and Drama* (1980), p. 50.
[3] See Marvin Rosenberg, 'Elizabethan Actors, Men or Marionettes', *PMLA*, 69 (1954), pp. 915–27.
[4] James Burgh (?), *The Art of Speaking* (1761).
[5] Elam, pp. 185ff.

hearing, an eye and an ear; lips for the act of speaking; human stick figures for references to the body and its movement; a heart for emotional states; a tiny cloud to represent cerebration, ideas.

Elam carefully marks, line by line, the relevant symbols. In some cases, a quick look down a column can be suggestive of the first scene's verbal patterns. One widely accepted idea of *Hamlet*'s language is that it is essentially interrogatory; though Robert Hapgood, in an excellent essay, has shown how often the speech is also in the imperative mood.[6] Elam seems to confirm Hapgood. The exclamation mark symbols outnumber the question marks; and Elam has intelligently used *both* a question mark *and* an exclamation for a line like Francisco's 'Who's there?' when he challenges Horatio's approach. This is indeed a line that commands as well as demands. Here Elam's technique is at its best, dealing in the dimensions of semantics. But he is operating in the semiotics of text, not of theatre. He tells us about the structure of the language, but almost nothing about the gestural language that accompanies it. The essence of Shakespeare's play is its emotional and ideational content, and how its words are expressed in voice and action. Elam finds just four notations for emotion. First, when Francisco says, '´Tis bitter cold, / And I am sick at heart'; no other until Horatio's 'It harrows me with fear and wonder'; then Marcellus, about the Ghost, 'It is offended'; finally, 'How now, Horatio! You tremble and look pale.' These are indeed emotional moments; but so is every other moment in the scene. There is not one where the three men are not in a highly charged state; a faithful notational system could only at best indicate structural variations in the atmosphere of fear and wonder as the playwright manipulates the responses of his audience. In subsequent drafts Elam might note these subtle variations; but he would still be making a textual rather than theatrical study. In nothing does this show more than in his notations for the body in movement. There are exactly three: when Bernardo says, 'Sit down awhile', when Horatio, 'Well, sit we down', and finally, Marcellus, 'Good now, sit down.' There are certainly meanings in these text-ordered sitting downs: but in fact they are indexes to temporary oases of relative *non-movement* in a scene sometimes almost frenetic with the signs of men restless with dread, sentinels challenging mortals and the supernatural, retreats in terror, desperate pleas for communication, a flitting ghost. Again, Elam, a skilled critic, might surely, by close attention to all implied action, fill out his chart with more comprehensive probabilities of movement; even so, the essential element of creative possibility, of inspired gestural illumination of the text, would still be missing.

Is there any methodical way to approach such inspiration? Suppose we begin with this axiom: all significant visual-aural actions in great drama are *character-derived signs*. To account for such signs we need to begin with the most thorough possible perception of the characters who make them. We humanists tend to approach characters by intuiting, from our own learning and experience, what their motives and meaning must be. If, as Hazlitt said, we are all Hamlet, then we know all about who he is – if we know all about who we are. We may call on Freud, or Marx, or other specialists to help us intuit. Semiotics, on the other hand, is a kind of social science: can its techniques help us to study the characters and the signs they manifest?

One helpful model is the essay by Elemer Hankiss from Hungary, on '*Hamlet* in the light of communication theory'.[7] Hankiss arranged

---

6 Robert Hapgood, '*Hamlet* and its Thematic Modes of Speech', *Perspectives on Hamlet*, ed. W. G. Holzberger and P. B. Waldeck (Lewisburg and London, 1975), pp. 29–47.

7 Elemér Hankiss, 'Shakespeare's *Hamlet*: The Tragedy in the Light of Communication Theory', *Acta Litteraria Academiae Scientiarum Hungaricae*, vol. 12, nos. 3–4 (1970), 297–312.

for some sixty subjects to experience the play, then asked them to note essential qualities of the characters. For Prince Hamlet's 'personality channel', as Hankiss called it, from hundreds of suggestions he winnowed out eighteen central concepts – as inner division, wit, strength of mind, weakness of will, suspicion, disgust, longing for death, for truth, for integrity, irony, melancholy, loneliness, madness. He provides a valuable cluster of character signs.

I have proceeded differently. I began with one of the psychologists' standard personality assessment forms. I enlarged its list of descriptives to take into account the human qualities in extremity of tragic characters, partly drawing key adjectives and adverbs from critical interpretations and theatre reviews. Going down the list marking Hamlet's characteristics is very instructive – so complex is his identity that almost any adjective could fit. The trouble with such an inventory is that it establishes only a temporary profile of a personality. A tragic hero, under continuous stress, often reflects what Norman Rabkin calls 'complementarity'.[8] The hero experiences not only many impulses, but often opposing impulses simultaneously – he (or she) is strong *and* weak, loves *and* hates, struggles between sanity and madness. So I adapted my personality inventory to an instrument called the Osgood differential; I listed polar qualities at the ends of ten-point spectrums.[9] On these scales can be marked the relative intensity of dialectic qualities, or even the presence of both. But the method was still incomplete. While a living person could be profiled on such an inventory for a given time, tragic characters move through time, and change radically. I am working on the instrument so that such changes can be graphed as well.

Still, there would be a missing dimension. My instrument helpfully collects character indications for the theoretical Hamlet of the text; but he is not necessarily the Hamlet Shakespeare created for the theatre. *That*

Hamlet must depend on *who* is playing Hamlet, with his distinctive temperament, physique, and intellectual and emotional gestalts. Which of Hamlet's many qualities and impulses will different actors emphasize, which subdue? How much subtext – and what kind – will resonate beneath speech and action? I have used the metaphor 'polyphony' to suggest the dynamic, fluid shifting of character tones in developing tragic roles: as Hamlet, a Gielgud, for instance, would stress the sensitivity; an Olivier, the strength; a McKellen, the madness. And they would adjust the other notes, harmonious and dissonant, into their distinctive wholes. Each new Hamlet's gestural-aural language will differ in mood, rhythm, and passion. In their very differences will reside, often, the illuminations they bring to the playwright's text. Have we not all sometimes sensed a line of Shakespeare's suddenly bathed in the light of an unexpected acting gesture? An intonation of voice? Do we not hope for such illuminating signs when we set out to see Shakespeare's plays?

Let me remind you of such a moment that many of us have seen. In the Russian *Othello* movie, remember when Othello first asks Desdemona for the handkerchief, knowing from Iago that she does not have it. The language is terse. Desdemona has asked Othello to see Cassio. He, upset:

Othello.
        I have a salt and sorry rheum offends me;
        Lend me thy handkerchief.
Desdemona.   Here, my lord.
Othello.
        That which I gave you.
Desdemona.   I have it not about me.
                      (3.3.49–51)

---

[8] Norman Rabkin, *Shakespeare and the Common Understanding* (1953), pp. 20ff.
[9] Charles Osgood, G. Suci, and Percy Tannenbaum, *The Measurement of Meaning* (Champaign, 1957).

He asks for it, she doesn't have it; he is angry. The verbal language seems to deny any opportunity for interruption. But in the film, when Desdemona said 'Here, my lord' as she reached for the substitute handkerchief, and he understood that she had it, such a blissful look came upon Othello's face. 'Love could not be greater' was the sign. He hugged her to him, in relief and happiness. The actor let us see for a moment how much his life turned on her. Then, of course, he saw the substitute, and his frustration was terrible. If it was not done that way at the Globe, I think Shakespeare would have liked it to be.

In the acting of great plays like Shakespeare's, that allow for seemingly endless creative discovery, great actors themselves learn to be surprised by new insights in performance. Over the many years that Gielgud played Hamlet, his interpretation changed and deepened; and still he learned more when, later in his career, he directed Richard Burton. In an illuminating moment, the two discussed the possibility that when Burton spoke the soliloquy at the end of act 2, he might stab the throne, at 'O, vengeance', with the prop-sword left behind by the Player. Though much of the stage business for the play was set, Burton wanted room left for inspiration; he said, 'I wouldn't want to rely on a prop, John, in case I change my mind in performance.'

In this ever-new playwright/actor collaboration, if the actor's share is so inspirational and variable, can any semiotic methodology encompass his nuclear part of Shakespeare's sign system? It is apparently impossible; but I would like to propose a practical hypothesis. Suppose we do our best to store, in a data bank of the sort Louis Marder of *Shakespeare Newsletter* encourages, acting profiles of distinguished performances of the great roles. For contemporary staging we should be able to draw on film and television, records and videotapes. For past performances, and for contemporary ones not filmed, we would seek deposits of reviews, interviews and personal reports. Increasingly, Shakespeare scholars, following the path of Arthur Colby Sprague, who showed us the importance of recording acting signs, are recognizing how this kind of knowledge can enrich textual studies of Shakespeare's plays. We can all thank the colleagues in this pursuit whose work is most helpful to us. Again, I don't think we can classify in detail all the kinds of physical signs we would record; but I would like to suggest some groupings at increasingly complex levels of ambiguity.

1. First, there is the primary matter of stage appearance. I don't mean here the accompaniments of set design and technical theatre. They are relatively easily codable: even such mobile elements as Craig's screens and Svoboda's powered columns and fluid light systems can be defined. These mechanical and electronic marvels are not themselves capable of improvising – not yet, at least, though who knows what robotic miracles technology may some day create. I agree with Pavis' proposal that to reconstruct fully 'a performance-text, every possible piece of information . . . should be provided'. By all means the programmable, inanimate phenomena that support and illuminate performance can be usefully recorded. But I am primarily concerned with dramatic character that half-creates itself upon the stage through the medium of the actor's semi-autonomous signs.

I think initially, then, of the actor's – or actress's – appearance: the simple biological presentation – the physique and its personality signs – such qualities of strength, weakness, pride, submission, costume, rank, etc. These are especially significant in terms of the visual and sensed relationship with other personae. Take Hamlet again. At the primary level, a very young Hamlet, for audiences used to mature ones, can revolutionize the gestalt, as Wilson Barrett did in 1884. If Hamlet's mother seems very young, as Olivier's did in the film, her relations with both son and new husband will carry special maternal and sexual – and currently Oedipal – signals. If, as sometimes happens, Claudius seems noticeably younger than Gertrude, the wife for some thirty years of his older brother, something particular may be signalled about the impulses behind her attraction, his ambition, and their incest. Physical irregularities can stir special responses. A Richard III who skips on crutches, as we saw one do recently, evokes a particular web of responses. Othello's skin may go from tawny to black, arousing topical varieties of racial sensitivity. In *The Winter's Tale*, how pregnant will Hermione look, and how will it affect her relation to Polixenes?

2. More ambiguous, equally dependent on the actor, are the occasional character signs that Shakespeare worked into his speeches. Thus the terrified Desdemona asks Othello:

> ... why gnaw you so your nether lip?
>
> (5.2.46)

So we know the actor was projecting a familiar expression – an expression so apparently simple that it seems the kind an old actor's manual might have canonized – 'bite nether lip to show your anger'. Now that a whole discipline, kinesics, has developed to study body language, encouraged by the work of Ray Birdwhistel and of Jurgen Ruesch and Weldon Kees[10] in the nineteen fifties, such gesture-classifying has attained the status of a social science. In drama, a gesture like this is only the tip of an emotional iceberg that may vary enormously in depth and complexity. Some three hundred years after *Othello* Eugene O'Neill, in a stage direction in *The Hairy Ape*, has Mildred Douglas 'biting her lip angrily'. Mildred Douglas is a cardboard character who nearly runs out of emotions with her anger; Othello is tragic and dangerous – and polyphonic. Given this simple lip-gnawing action, one Othello, say Edwin Booth, with a greater veneer of civilization upon him, would be more restrained, more inward, more mixed with dread and apprehension than would the

more bull-like, insecure Paul Robeson, or the anguished, titanic Salvini.

3. Even more ambiguity attaches to stage directions that stipulate an action, but leave its specifics vague. Thus Ophelia, describing Hamlet's tortured, torturing invasion of her room, remembers among others of his gestures:

> thrice his head thus waving up and down.
>
> (2.1.93)

Thus – how? Does she show once how he nodded? Three times? Why not try this one too? In my workshops, actresses have head-waved a half-dozen different ways. Kozintsev's Ophelia almost bent from the waist. What will Ophelia's action reflect of her own fears and anxieties? What of Hamlet's agony? His recognition of something intolerable? His bitterness over shedding an emotional relationship? His playacting? Will the gesture, again, reflect primarily what he saw in her, or what he was feeling?

4. At a further level of ambiguity still, Shakespeare sometimes demands of his actors the most subtle of physical expression, but leaves open its precise mode: thus Lady Macbeth says,

> Your face, my thane, is as a book where men
> May read strange matters.   (1.5.59–60)

There may be as many such facial books as there are Macbeths, as each individual actor reflects in his features a characteristic polyphony of impulse and idea. Shakespeare knew that a great actor's face could, by itself, reflect the human mystery of conflicting emotions and thoughts; and he demanded – and surely obtained – the full range. When Burbage played Macbeth, the legend his Lady – and the audience – saw in his face was unique and

---

10 Ray L. Birdwhistel, *Kinesis and Context: Essays on Body Movement Communication* (Harmondsworth, 1971). Jurgen Ruesch and Weldon Kees, *Nonverbal Communication* (Berkeley, 1956).

probably deepened in complexity and power from performance to performance. Macbeth can only escape presenting his conflict-torn face to us if he turns his back, so that the audience has to imagine what his Lady saw. This is a clever way of sustaining mystery, but at the loss of the experience of acute inner struggle at a pivotal moment that Shakespeare delights in. Still, it is material for our file, as all gestural, spatial, relationships must be.

5. Still less definable signs must be accounted for. Performances need to be scrutinized for the many wordless moments of crisis and climax. Shakespeare is a master of silences; as in the rare, marvellous moment he stipulates in *Coriolanus*, when Volumnia has begged her son to spare Rome and he agonizes over his decision. The familiar stage direction demands that his troubled felt life be mirrored in his face for a long moment:

He holds her by the hand, silent. (5.3.182)

Some of these mute moments are unmistakable, as in the classic recognition scenes: as at the instants when Lear, Macbeth, Othello understand how they have been misled and betrayed. Even beyond such evident moments, actors sensitive to Shakespeare's meanings have punctuated other pivotal climaxes, less obvious from textual reading, that need to be recorded.

Think of *The Winter's Tale* again. Unless, as Quiller-Couch thought, Shakespeare simply made 'a piece of impossible implausibility', Leontes must be able to make physically meaningful his sudden paranoid jealousy.[11] Will it seem a kind of emotional explosion that might happen to anybody? Or will he prepare for it with some sign of subtextual characterization? Perhaps reveal, before his outbreak, hints of a psyche close to the razor's edge? A masked, polite rigidity? A dangerously soft mildness? We saw McKellen prepare his Leontes at Stratford several years ago: his hands made fists as he playfully, as it were, pummelled his boy, his friend, his wife.

Something in him was waiting to explode. Leontes will say that he is 'a feather for each wind that blows'. Will showing this be enough? And if we are given no sense of vulnerability in Leontes, will the alternative be a sensuality in Hermione so flagrant that Leontes may understandably be suspicious? How will any manifest character flaw in either reflect on the relationship among all three? Shakespeare demanded much from his actors' physical imagery here.

6. We must track all the unstipulated physical manifestations of the individual actors' total conceptions: like Macready's Macbeth, never free from his oppressive awareness of a hovering supernatural; Irving's Lear, touched from the first with madness, all his gestures slightly oblique; Salvini's Othello, the volcanic subtext seemingly superbly under control, hinted in the senate scene, momentarily glimpsed at the Cyprus riot, later erupting fiercely – but the dimension always latent in his massive movements.

7. What is true of the actor's unforeseeable inspired gestures, is also true of the actor's creative voicing. One of the most ambiguous of all drama's one-word speeches is Cordelia's 'Nothing'. Out of what conflict of impulses, among them filial love, filial rebellion, sibling rivalry, injured ego, familial stubbornness, the need to appear worthy in France's eyes, will the actress find her emotional emphases for this word? What form of transcription, short of full description or recorded sight-sound, can preserve for us old Lear's fearful cry as he enters in the last scene? 'Howl, howl, howl, howl' the text says; to most theatre Lears it is not a word at all, but a naked wail. How translate, except in a variable system, the animal ululation that the four letters represent, as different actors have been heard to voice them: a quiet sobbing, by a Japanese Lear, a

---

[11] *The Winter's Tale*, eds. J. Dover Wilson and Arthur Quiller-Couch (Cambridge, 1931), p. xiv.

deep baying (Redgrave), the wail of a wolf (Krauss, the German), a command to attendants (Mikhoels, the Russian), a mourning dog (Cobb, the American), an accusation against the universe (Scofield).

A true study of Shakespeare will have to accept the actor's innovative, even improvisatory contribution to the art form. It will have to try to record every distinctive acting characterization. It will describe every significant gesture and sound and subtext of these characterizations. We will not pretend to an absolute precision, because we are dealing with an artistic process, but we will try to have the same patience in cataloguing truly significant samples as any taxonomist since Aristotle. We will never be through, because as time goes on, new actors of genius will always find new ways of rediscovering Shakespeare's language. But as we proceed, relating the theatrical characterizations to semiotic breakdowns of the text, seeking correspondences between the verbal and non-verbal elements, we may achieve a deeper perception of the sign systems of the great plays, and of drama itself.[12]

---

[12] I am now collecting actors' signs that have illuminated Hamlet. If any readers can tell me of any moments in the theatre when a gesture, a grimace, a voicing, a stage business have illuminated the text, I will be most grateful to receive the information at Department of Dramatic Art, University of California, Berkeley, California 94720, USA.

TIME IN 'RICHARD III'

GUY HAMEL

My approach to my subject is oblique. It seems to me useful, at the cost of a brief delay, in arguing for something of an emblematic reading of *Richard III*, to illustrate Shakespeare's use of emblem-like properties in a work of small compass – a sonnet. Moreover, the model I have chosen serves itself as an emblem of the play.

The ostensible occasion of Shakespeare's Sonnet 77 ('Thy glass will shew thee how thy beauties wear') is the presentation as a gift of a commonplace book.[1] The sonnet refers to three objects that bear emblematically on time: a mirror, a sundial, the book that the poem accompanies. The glass will reveal the signs of ageing, the dial will show the passage of the minutes, the blank leaves of the book will through time register the thoughts that will be committed to them. No sooner is the moralizing possibility of the objects raised in the first quatrain than the book becomes a gloss upon itself. The remaining lines express the 'learning' that the book will record. The wrinkles that the glass will show must inevitably remind the addressee of graves. The irresistible 'shady stealth' of the dial must inescapably bring to mind 'Time's thievish progress to eternity'. What may be rescued from oblivion are the thoughts that, written down, survive to generate afresh new thoughts. However, the victory over time is qualified. Richard II discovers when he reviews his 'still-breeding thoughts' that 'no thought is contented' and that all thought tends to the conclusion that no

man can be 'pleas'd, till he be eas'd / With being nothing' (5.5.8, 11, 40–41).[2] The sense of impermanence, restlessness, and constraint to be found in Richard's condition insinuates itself into the sonnet. However often the diarist reviews his entries, those visits are circumscribed by his lifespan. They have no finality except the *terminus ad quem* of death. The certainty that marks both the processes recorded by the glass and the dial and the reminders of mortality linked to these processes attaches itself to the book. The 'learning' it must inescapably set down refers to death as well as to victory over time. The diarist *must* note the intimations of mortality not only in the glass and dial but in the recollection of dead

---

1
    Thy glass will shew thee how thy beauties wear,
    Thy dial how thy precious minutes waste,
    The vacant leaves thy mind's imprint will bear,
    And of this book this learning mayst thou taste:
    The wrinkles which thy glass will truly show
    Of mouthèd graves will give thee memory;
    Thou by thy dial's shady stealth mayst know
    Time's thievish progress to eternity;
    Look what thy memory cannot contain
    Commit to these waste blanks, and thou shalt find
    Those children nurs'd, deliver'd from thy brain,
    To take a new acquaintance of thy mind.
      These offices so oft as thou wilt look
      Shall profit thee and much enrich thy book.
The text is that of *Shakespeare's Sonnets*, eds, W. G. Ingram and Theodore Redpath (1964).
2 All references to Shakespeare's plays are to *The Riverside Shakespeare*, ed. G. Blakemore Evans (Boston, 1974).

thoughts that are of the past no matter how revivified.

Other conditions affecting this sonnet further complicate its commentary upon time. For one matter, the poem is self-referential. The instabilities it claims for the addressee's thoughts apply to the poem itself and to the rest of the Sonnets. They may be read repeatedly in order to generate new thoughts. The variety of interpretations to which the Sonnets have been subjected warrants the claim that what seems fixed on the written page may 'take a new acquaintance'. I do not think one forces the reading to find in the poem the irony so marked in the shifting perspective of the Sonnets. This verse expresses simultaneously the triumphant authority that a living thought has over mortality and the inevitable victory that death will claim over all mortals.

The relation of the poem to its context raises a second of the conditions that qualify Sonnet 77. The poem by celebrating the timeless quality of what the addressee will write recalls the claims for the immortality of his own verse that the poet makes repeatedly elsewhere. Shakespeare, in fact, manages a witty extension of a conceit that in the Sonnets is exploited in what seems every manner possible: the addressee himself will vindicate the principle by which the poet has advanced the worth of his praise. Moreover, the image of thoughts as 'children nurs'd, deliver'd from thy brain' brings to mind the claim in the first of the Sonnets that procreation is a means to 'repair' what time seeks to 'ruinate' and by such means to conquer death. That argument seems, insofar as the fiction of the sequence may be trusted, simply to give way to other topics – or strategies; and there is no reason to feel that the metaphoric children are a better buffer against mortality than the real ones.

Time is both a process and a constant. In Shakespeare's comedies, to generalize extravagantly, the two conditions are sympathetic. The wearying routines of what Rosalind terms the 'workaday world' lead somehow to what Duke Orsino calls 'golden time'. For the comic Shakespeare as for William Blake 'eternity is in love with the productions of time'. Touchstone expresses the depressing limitation of the workaday perspective untouched by a transcending vision of eternity when he looks at his dial – the same as that of Sonnet 77 – and moralizes that ten o'clock was once nine o'clock and will be eleven and so 'from hour to hour, we rot and rot' (2.7.27). Jaques, who reflects on this scene, seems incapable of appreciating any function of time except that by which rotting hourly we are brought from puking infancy to 'second childishness, and mere oblivion' (2.7.165). His view represents an anti-comic pessimism that in each of Shakespeare's comedies receives some form of expression and of challenge. Rosalind recognizes the relativity of time – 'who Time ambles withal, who Time trots withal, who Time gallops withal, and who he stands still withal' (3.2.309–311). Though quite indirectly she intimates the comic closure announced in Hymen's song:

> Then is there mirth in heaven,
> When earthly things made even
>   Atone together.   (5.4.108–110)

In the tragedies the protagonist often regards himself as dominated by the experience of time. He views time as an inexorable and vicious dimension within which he is trapped. The concept finds its expression in powerful physical images that generate some of Shakespeare's most vivid and most familiar lines. Othello fears that he has become a 'fixed figure for the time of scorn / To point his slow unmoving finger at' (4.2.54–55). For Hamlet 'The time is out of joint' (1.5.188), the uses of the world 'weary, stale, flat, and unprofitable' (1.2.133). It is only the cowardice of conscience and the 'dread of something after death' that make us 'bear the whips and scorns of time' (3.1.77, 69). Macbeth views with intolerable anguish the 'petty pace' with which each tomorrow creeps 'To the last syllable of recorded time' (5.5.20–21). Time as a constant is not as in the comedies the sympathetic extension of the earthbound impulses that sanctions those impulses. It is either the incremental horror of Macbeth's tomorrows or an alternative dimension that liberates the hero from that horror. Eternity in this latter sense is the condition which Cleopatra's 'immortal longings' anticipate, the rest to which guardian angels sing Hamlet. It is most eloquently expressed through Lear's vision of a place where he and Cordelia may wear out 'packs and sects of great ones, / That ebb and flow by th' moon' and take upon themselves 'the mystery of things' as if they were 'God's spies' (5.3.16–19).

Time is, of course, a special preoccupation of the history plays. *Richard III* opens with a soliloquy in which Gloucester complains of his estrangement from the 'time of peace' and ends with an address in which Richmond prays that his heirs will 'Enrich the time to come with smooth-fac'd peace'. Between these speeches we are to a notable degree kept well informed about the passage of time. Gloucester's opening words mark the ascendance of the day's sun as well as of the Sun/Son of York. The sequence of the days following is carefully established by the dialogue. It is early morning when on his death day Clarence greets the Keeper and the night of that day when King Edward dies. Again it is morning when the citizens meet to discuss the consequences of the King's death. We are told of the three days needed for Prince Edward to reach London; and young Edward arrives early enough that, after he has been sent to lodge in the Tower, Gloucester and Buckingham may arrange to 'sup betimes' in order to 'digest' their 'complots' unhurriedly (3.1.199–200). The next morning Hastings is awakened 'Upon the stroke of four' (3.2.5), and events move with sufficient haste for him to be beheaded before Gloucester's dinner hour. The execution done, Buckingham is sent to the Guildhall to win support for the Lord Protector, promising to return 'towards three or four a' clock' (3.5.101). Before the end of that day Gloucester has arranged to be crowned on the morrow. Coronation day begins with the dawn assembly of the women. It is 'Upon the stroke of ten' that Buckingham is dismissed (4.2.112). The murder of the princes is ordered and accomplished in time for Richard to hear the details 'at after-supper' (4.3.31). The last action of the play – the Battle of Bosworth Field – begins with Richmond's observation that it is nightfall. When Richard meets with his officers to make late preparations for battle, he is told that 'It's supper time, my lord, / It's nine a' clock' (5.3.47–48). His men are to 'Stir with the lark to-morrow' and to ensure that Stanley's regiment is in place 'Before sunrising' (5.3.56, 61). Northumberland, it is reported, was seen 'about cock-shut time' (5.3.70). Richard wakes from his dream at 'dead midnight' (5.3.180); the last preparations are settled by Richmond 'Upon the stroke of four' (5.3.235). The hour sounds one last time in Richard's camp in a manner that represents an unresolved bit of stage business. The clock strikes offstage and Richard calls for someone to 'Tell the clock there' but the text records no answer (5.3.276). Whatever decision a director makes – my own is that in these parallel scenes we hear the same 'stroke of four' that Richmond has noted – the audience is, again, asked to take notice of the time.

A lengthened temporal context is provided by a sequence of references and images that bring us from the robust sun of glorious summer described in Gloucester's opening soliloquy to the autumnal closure of his last days. Margaret's choric remark as Richard falters is that 'prosperity begins to mellow / And drop into the rotten mouth of death' (4.4.1–2). Richmond's very first speech in the play promises his followers the end of a tyranny that has 'spoil'd your summer fields and fruitful vines', and he vows 'To reap the harvest of perpetual peace' (5.2.8, 15). On the eve of Bosworth 'The weary sun' is said to have made 'a golden set' (5.3.19).

Of course, it is not only in this play or in history plays that the time at which events happen is observed or that a seasonal frame of reference contains the action. Near his end Macbeth finds himself 'fall'n into the sear, the yellow leaf' (5.3.23). Nevertheless, there are two observations one might make about the treatment of time in *Richard III*. The first is that, however casually the time is noted, the dates – as we all recall from having swotted for exams – have a special significance. Simply, matters have implications beyond their meaning for those immediately involved in them. It is such a sense of the general importance and memorable significance of what has happened that leads Henry V to remark that Englishmen will 'to the ending of the world' honour the feast of Crispin Crispian (*Henry V*, 4.3.58). With much the same impulse Buckingham notes that the day of his death and – unhistorically – of Bosworth Field is All Souls' Day.

My second observation is that the sequence of these rushed and compressed hours in *Richard III*, though they mark the deaths of nobles and of princes and though they witness great dynastic changes, are related to the common terms of the natural order of diurnal events and to the homeliest incidents in a humble quotidian routine: men survey their troops at 'cock-shut time' and plan to rise with the lark to do battle. This play of historically significant time against the common pattern of the hours and the seasons is a factor to which I shall return.

For those caught in the tumultuous events depicted by the play the future is uncertain. The citizens of London 'fear' the times as 'giddy' and 'troublous' and made intelligible only by the most general of formulas: 'Woe to that land that's govern'd by a child' (2.3.5, 9, 11). Such principles are not only inadequate to explain events satisfactorily but they conform

depressingly to that tendency in folk wisdom to prefer bad news:

> When great leaves fall, then winter is at hand;
> When the sun sets, who doth not look for night?
> Untimely storms makes men expect a dearth.
>
> (2.3.33–35)

The last of these cautionary dicta is especially appropriate for my purpose: 'untimely' events are direful.

Within the play the more significant attempts to make sense of events are presented by those who express time as a constant. Elizabeth, foreseeing the consequences of Gloucester's actions against her house, sees '(as in a map) the end of all' (2.4.54). The 'map' she intends may be an astrological chart – a depiction of the relations, propitious and inauspicious, of the heavenly bodies at a precise moment. The prophetic nature of her vision suggests such an interpretation. But it may equally be a terrestrial map. One should bring to mind those Renaissance representations of the world that show the hemispheres between scenes of the Creation or the Fall at the top and of the Last Judgement at the bottom. Well into Shakespeare's time the earth remains a physical domain fixed by temporal termini. The 'maps' of Donne's 'Good Morrow' have a 'declining west'.

The other principal interpretation of time is that given by Margaret through her Hammurabian catalogue of equivalents.

> Thy Edward he is dead, that kill'd my Edward;
> Thy other Edward dead, to quit my Edward.
>
> (4.4.63–64)

Surely no ordinary member of the audience is able to identify as the catalogue goes by all the characters who figure in Margaret's summary. That very fact emphasizes the sheer extent of the carnage and the terrifying and obsessive perseverance of Margaret as an accountant. For Margaret the cancellations she notes represent the dynamic measures that operate the wheel of fortune. She has witnessed figure after figure 'heav'd a-high, to be hurl'd down below' (4.4.86). There is no doubt of the authority with which Margaret is invested within the play. A clutch of victims on their way to execution attest to the accuracy of her fatal prophecies. But one may question whether or not Margaret's vision of history is expressed by the play itself. Her notion that to every *quo* there is *quid* is given a sardonic parody in Richard's proposition to Elizabeth that he can cancel his wrongs to her by marrying her daughter:

If I did take the kingdom from your sons,
To make amends I'll give it to your daughter;
If I have kill'd the issue of your womb,
To quicken your increase, I will beget
Mine issue of your blood upon your daughter.

(4.4.294–8)

I do not see that the parody is much more heinous than the scheme it mocks. Margaret's perspective is limited. Witness to the early events of the Wars of the Roses, she can in these later days recognize what *Henry IV*'s Warwick calls 'the hatch and brood of time' (*2 Henry IV*, 3.1.86). The principles she invokes – nemesis, the wheel of fortune, cause and effect – may be within her terms valid without being, beyond those terms, sufficient. It is in order to subject *Richard III* to a wider scheme that I now wish to draw upon 'Thy glass will shew thee how thy beauties wear.'

The conditions of the theatre invite quite precise links with the objects presented in Shakespeare's sonnet. We all know that, as Hamlet tells us, the purpose of playing is 'to hold as 'twere the mirror up to nature' (3.2.21–22). Our contemplation of our own nature in the mirror is not passive. Some of us, as Gloucester notes, 'court an amorous looking-glass' (1.1.15). As the sonnet states, we check to see how the wrinkles are getting on. We note our approximation to standards of beauty, fashion, and decency. The consequence of theatrical reflection is, Hamlet continues, 'to show . . . the very age and body of the time his form and pressure' (3.2.22–4) –

that is, to show some such shape or configuration as Elizabeth represents in the 'map' of time. But such forms are expressed for dramatic as for human figures in relation to some concept of prefiguration. Hamlet's metaphor was originally applied to comedy. In his expression of it the conceit seems to apply particularly to history: 'to show . . . the very age and body of the time his form and pressure'. Such tales of kings as this play relates have been thought of as mirrors for magistrates. Certainly, in the image there are implications of the tragic. The context of Hamlet's statement is a tragedy – his own as well as that of Gonzago. Marlowe's Prologue informs us that we are to view Tamburlaine's exploits in a 'tragic glass'. Our active function as viewers is to make comprehensive sense of events, and we do so according to patterns created or assumed. All the models I have mentioned – comical, historical, tragical – are, as later I hope to show, involved in *Richard III* as the bases of our active formulation of the play.

The stage is a mirror. It is, to turn to the second object of the sonnet, a sundial. That is, the physical features of the stage reveal through their lengthening shadows the passage of time. The notion may seem fanciful and forced in the extreme. I do think, however, that our experience of plays in the contrived and artificial conditions of the modern theatre makes us insensitive to the effects of presentation under the open sky. Anyone who has watched the shade of the grandstand creep across a playing field or viewed theatrical presentations outdoors will acknowledge that one does indeed notice how shadows mark the passage of time. I have remarked on the striking persistence with which in *Richard III* we are informed of the hour at which events happen. At each instance members of the audience must reset their assumptions about the fictional time against their awareness – so much sharper than we can realize as viewers of lighting effects – of the course of their own actual day. We are given three dimensions of time. The first is our own temporal context within what Doctor Faustus in his last soliloquy calls with terrifying poignancy 'a natural day'. The passage of that time is marked by the players as gnomons. Does not Gloucester twice ask us to spy his shadow in the sun? The second dimension is created by the dramatic compression that makes the morning hour of one scene become some twenty minutes later the dawning of another day.

The immediacy with which the audience knows its own time has, it seems to me, two consequences. The constant adjustment required to define the actual sun as a morning sun or a setting sun or as not being there at all – or, under a clouded and threatening sky, as shining when it wasn't – must, no matter how much the conventions became a matter of reflex, have drawn attention to the play as artefact. The independence of fictional time as a separate dimension is perhaps more strongly affirmed than we realize. Secondly, those homely and frequent references in *Richard III* to 'after-supper' and 'cock-shut time' and the like reinforce the validity of the 'natural day' and of workaday events as a normative matrix. Our concept of what is 'untimely' depends upon the moral sanction we give to events thought of as belonging to the order of time. Anne mourns 'Th' untimely fall of virtuous Lancaster' (1.2.4). Margaret includes in the inventory of Richard's victims Hastings, Rivers, Vaughan, Grey, all 'Untimely smoth'red in their dusky graves' (4.4.70). Richard's untimely birth marks him as estranged from the moral order expressed by 'natural' time. His identity as the enemy of time is most explicitly presented when Richard, repulsed by Elizabeth in his attempt to find something unsullied by which he may take his oath, tries to swear by 'The time to come' and is told the future is compromised, 'Misus'd ere us'd, by times ill-us'd o'erpast' (4.4.396).

The third dimension to add to natural time and fictional time is that sought by the characters as they attempt to find a pattern that will 'map' time. The relation of these three conditions – actual time, fictional time, historical time – is, I believe, suggested by the third point of analogical comparison with Sonnet 77.

The clearest equivalent to the self-referential element in 'Thy glass will shew thee' is the discussion of history introduced by the Prince of Wales when he questions Buckingham about the tradition that Julius Caesar built the Tower of London. In a conversation that has no trace in the sources Edward asks if the ascription is 'upon record, or else reported / Successively from age to age' (3.1.72–73). Assured by Buckingham that the claim is based 'upon record', the Prince remarks that even if it

> were not regist'red,
> ... the truth should live from age to age,
> As 'twere retail'd to all posterity,
> Even to the general all-ending day.
>
> (3.1.75–78)

Edward's faith is touching and it is appropriate to his youth; but it finds no support in Shakespeare's play. There is a historical document in *Richard III*: a Scrivener enters bearing an indictment of Hastings. As he points out, the original and the fair copy have taken eleven hours each to write out; and the initiation of the inquiry is less than five hours past. Though the fraud is, as the Scrivener says, 'palpable', there is no one with the courage to challenge the deceit. One may wonder what, lacking a like caveat, posterity might make of such a document. As for the reports passed from generation to generation, to impugn the reliability of gossip seems hardly necessary. Sir Philip Sidney dismisses the pretensions of historians with the gibe that their 'greatest authorities are built upon the notable foundation of hearsay'.[3] *2 Henry IV* is opened by

---

[3] *A Defence of Poetry*, ed. J. A. Van Dorsten (Oxford, 1966; repr. 1973), p. 30.

Rumour as the personification of the 'continual slanders' and 'false reports' that men retail with the same confidence as they do the truth. In that play Rumour stands as the informing agent of history.

How, then, is the truth to be known and told? The answer is both complex and indeterminate. One kind of truth – observance of chronicled detail – we may dismiss at once. Shakespeare allows himself his usual freedom to manipulate the order of events. Richmond's two expeditions are conflated into one. If we date the action by Edward's death and Richard's accession, the play opens in 1483 and two principals, Clarence and Margaret, are already dead. But Shakespeare's slapdash indifference to historical exactitude is well enough admitted for the point hardly to need extensive documentation. The truth to which Shakespeare as historian is committed does not depend upon fidelity to the record.

Shakespeare's contemporaries echo approvingly the view of Cicero that, in the words of one Elizabethan translator, 'history [is] the witnes of tymes, and light of veritie'.[4] Hannah Arendt reminds us that originally the *histor* or witness was both an eyewitness and a witness of witnesses – a judge who examines the evidence provided by direct observers. The historian, according to a view that Aristotle shares, belongs to the same category as the poet. Both translate *praxis* and *lexis*, action and speech, in *poiesis*.[5] It is in this larger sense of a more detached witness whose task is active and creative that we are to understand Shakespeare's expression of the verity of history. To explore this larger concept of truth I turn to the last of the considerations I applied to Sonnet 77 – the appeal to context.

The immediate application is to the body of the histories. Each play, as we well recognize, is enlarged by its connection to all the others. The mere repetition of incidents and themes – usurpation, loyalty, betrayal, legitimacy, misrule – provides a network of cross-references that illuminates and qualifies any one instance.

The patterns are constantly enforced and elaborated within the plays: the Buckingham of *Henry VIII* regards himself as a duplicate of the Buckingham of *Richard III*. The occurrences are so numerous that one example may stand for them all. The emphasis upon pattern dissolves the constraints of chronology. A configuration that relates the two Buckinghams and joins to them, for example, Humphrey of Gloucester from *2 Henry VI* and Lord Scroop from *Henry V* is spatial, map-like. Moreover, once we involve the whole, no inner perspective has authority. Seen from the viewpoint of *Henry V*, Hal's victories are vindications of his royalty; seen from the viewpoint of *Henry VI*, they are ironically empty. A comprehensive or final perspective can only be implied. It is, after all, divine and timeless.

Many of the persons in the histories claim the ultimate sanction provided by access to the divine outlook – that is, they assume God's approval; but such characters tend to cancel one another. 'In God's name', says the usurping Bolingbroke, 'I'll ascend the regal throne' (*Richard II*, 4.1.113). To the Bishop of Carlisle, who hears the words, they are blasphemy against 'the figure of God's majesty' (4.1.125). Margaret of Anjou has been taken as an accurate expositor for *Richard III* because she articulates the scheme of retributive justice that governs its action. These are the words that mark her acknowledgement that the pattern she champions is accomplished:

> O upright, just, and true-disposing God,
> How do I thank thee that this carnal cur
> Preys on the issue of his mother's body.
>
> (4.4.55–57)

I believe we may say flatly that the God pleasing to Margaret is not the God who

---

[4] John Daus, *A famous cronicle of oure time called Sleidanes commentaries* (1560), p. 471; cited in *OED*, s.v. 'time', *sb.* 1.3.

[5] *Between Past and Future* (Cleveland, 1954; repr. 1963), pp. 44–5, 229.

presides over all time in Shakespeare's vision of history. A providential order is, as I said, implied, not pronounced. To my mind the import of a divine order rests on a set of unstated relations that are, as much as one word may describe them, typological, and is intimated by a felt presence of a narration of time that is ideal and apocalyptic. To try another formulation, I assume that Shakespeare's frame of reference and conceptual scheme are very like Spenser's.

There is still a larger context to consider for *Richard III* and that is the one established by the entire canon of Shakespeare's works. So enlarging our field, we are brought again to comedy and tragedy. Certainly, *Richard III* in a number of its internal references touches upon motifs and incidental effects that are associated primarily with comedy and tragedy. Richard is treated by his mother to a personal version of his progress through the ages of man:

> A grievous burthen was thy birth to me,
> Tetchy and wayward was thy infancy;
> Thy school-days frightful, desp'rate, wild, and
>   furious,
> Thy prime of manhood daring, bold, and
>   venturous;
> Thy age confirm'd, proud, subtle, sly, and
>   bloody.   (4.4.168–72)

Jaques' version of man's life, though reductive, is tempered by his own indulgent pleasure in his melancholy and is finally set aside – though not finally discounted – by the presiding authority of Hymen. Elizabeth's account is definitive: Richard is monstrous. The suggestions of tragedy are made principally through the theatrical references and images that appear prominently in *Richard III*. These echo the 'great stage of fools' in *King Lear* and the 'poor player' in *Macbeth*. In *Richard III* Elizabeth's elevation to the throne is 'The flattering index of a direful pageant' (4.4.85). The Queen's intemperate response to the death of Edward is a 'scene of rude impatience' that extends itself to become 'an act of tragic violence' (2.2.38–9). Margaret sees

herself as the 'induction' to a play that will prove 'bitter, black, and tragical' (4.4.5, 7). But, although such references have their place in determining the texture of the play, there are larger generic considerations that affect the character of the play as a whole. To put the matter bluntly, the play has two endings.

In Richard's soliloquy when he wakes on the eve of Bosworth, he assumes a tragic dimension from which Shakespeare has until then excluded him. The facile declaration he makes at the beginning of the play that he is 'determined to prove a villain' (1.1.30) becomes the fearful realization that 'I am a villain' (5.3.191). At the close of *3 Henry VI* he asserts with blind self-assurance, 'I am my self alone' (5.6.83). In his last soliloquy he mourns at the recognition that 'there is no creature loves me' (5.3.200). The implications of 'creature', touching not only compass but also the benign origin of life, stress the dreadful extent of Richard's isolation. The figure who has seemed to control time proves its victim. It is the appropriate extension of this new stature given to Richard that he should in his oration to his troops recapture the command and energy of his earlier presence. And his last moment of defiance as he once more possesses the stage crying out the phrase that became a by-word in Shakespeare's own day corroborates his tragic grandeur.

The conclusion of *Richard III* is emphatically comic. The death of the tyrant is not only the prelude to a renewed order under a restored lineage, as it is in *Macbeth*. The triumph extends itself into time. Richmond promises a future of 'smiling plenty, and fair prosperous days' (5.5.34). Accord is to be achieved and symbolized by a wedding that is pledged by 'sacrament' and that through its 'fair conjunction' heals a 'divided' realm (5.5.18, 20, 27).

The prominence that each definition, tragic and comic, is given in *Richard III* means that each modifies – perhaps diminishes – the other. The tragic anguish of Richard's 'I shall despair' is countered by the potential magnitude of

Richmond's victory. The comfortable assurance expressed by Richmond that the world is now a healthy place seems an anticlimactic admission that the realm under its new management has been given over to the virtuous second rate.

Tragic and comic definitions may, however, be thought of as subordinate to the ruling generic considerations, which are historical. Richard's death has dynastic as well as tragic implications. It is an event in a very large pattern that requires the tyrant's defeat. Shakespeare at the close of his comedies complies – tacitly, obliquely, inferentially, and with some degree of caution, but nevertheless complies – with the formula that enjoins the lovers to live happily ever after. We know that this bridegroom in his historical rather than fictional character becomes the capable but distrustful, mean-spirited, and miserly Henry VII and that the sacramental union he promises is a piece of political expediency if not of political fraud.

And yet history is not the final consideration. Truth, we are told, is the daughter of Time. The proverb does not indicate the length of the gestation period before the daughter comes forth. It is, I am afraid, infinite. To apply fictional forms to events in time – to schematize history – is to respect the coherence of Providence. However, the play as an artefact has the same status as one of the friend's notations in his commonplace book – fixed as a point in the flux of time, like one of Krapp's first tapes, indefinite in its susceptibility to a new understanding. We should not undervalue the independent integrity of the work or its holding power against time. We remember the Feast of Crispian much less because of Henry's victory at Agincourt than because of Shakespeare's celebration of that victory. We should also respect Shakespeare's recognition that the word is not impervious to mutability. To those with an emblematic or hieroglyphical bent of mind – a category that I should think probably contains all writers of the early seventeenth century (not even excluding Francis Bacon) – the limitations of truth are acceptable because the possibilities of understanding are limitless. The shape of time is comic. Segments viewed from an internal perspective may be tragic; and even if a comic expression adumbrates the process of divine comedy, it does so sketchily, imperfectly, uncertainly in the shadowed world in which we see through a glass darkly.

NEW CONCEPTS OF STAGING
'A MIDSUMMER NIGHT'S DREAM'[1]

MAIK HAMBURGER

The majority of Shakespeare productions in the German Democratic Republic in the 1960s explored what might broadly be termed public or socio-political aspects of the plays. This did not necessarily imply uniform or reductionist interpretations; there were indeed in that decade a number of notable stagings of Shakespeare, revolving around such features as power structures and struggles for political power, the Renaissance ethic as an (unrealized) humanist ideal or the aristocratic and the plebeian experience of historical processes. The most striking productions, those that made their mark in theatrical life, were stagings of tragedies or histories, in which self-fulfilment of the individual was equated with a political objective of some kind, whether the achievement or retention of power or a change in the social system.

At the turn of the 1970s a shift of interest began to make itself felt. People who had experienced the upheavals of war and social restratification gradually became aware that in all probability no more social eruption would occur within their lifetime. This implied a basic change of perspective. Themes involving questions of individual happiness, of personal self-fulfilment within a given social structure, began to gain significance. Plays like *Romeo and Juliet* and *A Midsummer Night's Dream* were now seen to meet newly conceived needs in the theatre. It was at this juncture that Halle and Magdeburg (both considerable industrial cities with large, well-established theatres), came up with productions of *A Midsummer Night's Dream* that broke new ground and in many respects set the standard for this play for the next decade.

For all their differences, these stagings of *A Midsummer Night's Dream* were successful on two counts: first, they finally broke away from the romantic illusionism of the Reinhardt productions; and second, by laying bare tensions and contradictions within the play that had been glossed over by the traditional *Bildungstheater* as well as by socio-political interpretations, they were able to address present-day problems and arouse the interest of a younger generation for whom Shakespeare had been no more than a school subject.

It should be said that that first item represented no mean achievement. Max Reinhardt's production of *A Midsummer Night's Dream* at the beginning of the century integrated the music of Mendelssohn-Bartholdy and the Romantic translation of August Wilhelm von Schlegel into a masterpiece of luscious illusionism. This staging (with its successors, revivals, and films up to the 1930s) had built up a legendary reputation that was ever present to haunt directors producing this play in Germany. The two productions discussed

[1] This article is a modified and updated version of a paper contributed to the seminar 'Current Trends in Non-English Shakespearian Performance' at the World Shakespeare Congress, Stratford-upon-Avon, August 1981.

5　*A Midsummer Night's Dream*. Landestheater Halle, 1971. The Bergomask, Act 5

here, no doubt stimulated by Peter Brook's version of 1970 (itself a legend by now), were the first in the GDR to steer fully clear of the Reinhardt model.

The staging of *A Midsummer Night's Dream* at the Landestheater Halle directed by Christoph Schroth has as its basic concept the struggle of the individual for freedom as reflected in all its complexity in the three planes of the play.[2] It asserts the *relative* contradictoriness of the three worlds (court/fairies/mechanicals) as well as their *fundamental* unity. The state of Athens is seen as a rigid, closed, intact society that curtails human potentialities. A young couple defy authority to fight for their love. The girl is prepared to go to her death rather than give up her claims to self-fulfilment in the union with her lover. The fate

of the lovers could become as tragic as in *Romeo and Juliet* were it not for the intervention of the midsummer night and its strange occurrences.

The wood is regarded as a mythologically alienated, distorted reflection of the Athenian court, opening up vistas of utopian anticipation. Court rigidity gives way to lawlessness, to the freedom of uninhibited passion. This change is scenically depicted by a simple but impressive device: strips of white cloth initially hung in vertical rows to suggest the

---

[2] William Shakespeare, *Ein Mittsommernachtstraum, A Midsummer Night's Dream*, Deutsch von Maik Hamburger, Musik Reiner Bredemeyer, Erstaufführung, Regie Christoph Schroth, Ausstattung Liliane el Hachemi. Premiere, 8 May 1971.

ordered array of Greek pillars are then brought into disorder to present the jungle of tree-trunks through which the Athenians stagger as in a labyrinth. The direct repression exerted by society is now in abeyance, but the anarchy that breaks out suggests that these Athenians are as yet incapable of existing in freedom. Oberon has to assume the protective function of the law to prevent the young bloods from killing each other.

The story of Theseus and Hippolyta is also continued in the wood in the guise of Oberon and Titania; thus the doubling of these parts indicates the continuity of behaviour patterns. The subjugation of the Amazon by Theseus is resumed in the subjection of Titania by Oberon. Freed from court conventions, the struggle for male domination becomes naked and brutal. However, Theseus/Oberon and Hippolyta/Titania are conscious that their affairs are not just their private concerns. Monarchs, be it in Athens or in Fairyland, have a responsibility to their realms and are not free to determine their partnerships. In the end, Titania and Hippolyta accept their situation in deference to political necessity in order to restore harmony to nature and to the state.

The production succeeds in building up an atmosphere of a 'dream', of events simultaneously real and unreal, without recourse to the kind of beguiling illusion Brecht was apt to dismiss contemptuously as 'witchcraft'. It achieves this by acting out to the utmost the extremes of human behaviour in extremely diverging environments, a spectacle visually supported by the skilful use of costumes in the fairy world, of multi-coloured cloaks handled with great dexterity. Oberon and Titania are, of course, not just doubles of their mortal counterparts, they are King and Queen of the Fairies in their own right; their immortality is taken as the ability to realize all human potentialities; they have the capacity to harbour all emotions ranging from the cruellest hatred to the tenderest love and the deepest compassion.

The harmony reached at the Athenian court in act 5 is qualified by the reactions of the courtiers to the performance of Pyramus and Thisbe. The mechanicals (depicted with sympathy and humour throughout) unwittingly present the young couples with a replica of their own predicament of act 1 and are laughed at for their pains. The lovers are now fully re-integrated into the patriarchal state and scoff at notions of human equality and freedom to love.

For this production, a new translation was commissioned from the present writer. To justify this, the director and his team argued that Schlegel's romantic-poetic translation (a merit and a valuable quality) levelled out the social problems, did not differentiate between the variegated planes, and did not clearly show the nodal points of the action. Other existing translations were rejected for similar reasons. The new translation attempted to grasp Shakespeare's language as *theatre text* that must have a physical meaning to actors, that allows the attitudes of the characters to be conveyed by the physical qualities inherent in their speech.[3] It follows the verse and rhyme forms of the original (as did Schlegel) although many present-day translators eliminate at least the rhyme, maintaining that it puts the German text under too great a formal pressure.

The production of *A Midsummer Night's Dream* directed by Werner Freese at the Bühnen der Stadt Magdeburg, also using the Hamburger translation, can be summarized in a shorter space.[4] According to the programme notes, the theme of the play here is 'not harmony but the overcoming of disharmony'.

---

[3] Cf. my attempt to explore this dimension in '*Gestus* and the Popular Theatre', *Science & Society*, 41, no. 1 (Spring 1977), 36–42.

[4] William Shakespeare, *Ein Sommernachtstraum*, Deutsch von Maik Hamburger, Regie Werner Freese, Ausstattung Frank Borisch, Helga Borisch. Musik Thomas Natschinski, Felix Mendelssohn-Bartholdy. Premiere, 2 October 1971.

6 *A Midsummer Night's Dream*. Bühnen der Stadt Magdeburg, 1971. The Lovers in the Wood, Act 2:
Hermia (Silvia Löhken), Lysander (Klaus-Rudolf Weber), Demetrius (Berndt Stübner), and Helena (Evelyn Cron)

The significance of this staging does not, however, lie in a closely reasoned concept but rather in its original, spirited use of choreography as a theatrical idiom to reflect the behaviour and attitude of young people of the day. In many respects the Brook staging served as a model that was used with discretion.

Modernism and dynamics are the keynotes of this production. The wood is represented by colourfully enamelled metal structures resembling huge pieces of jewellery brought into motion by the revolving stage; an impressive spectacle is produced by the lavish use of technical devices, a kaleidoscopic interplay of stage and lighting effects and by strong musical accents; the composer Thomas Natschinski is one of the leading writers of

dance music. The actors, in clothes based on hippie dress but heightened to a point where they again resemble historical costumes, throw themselves full of abandon and with considerable acrobatic skill into the task of expressing the action of the play in predominantly physical terms with particular emphasis on the sexual aspect. The erotic urge is regarded as chief motivation in this production, and all relations are seen basically as relations between man and woman. As one critic points out, this places all characters on one 'human' level, and indeed the objection could be raised that the production makes scarcely any distinction between the various planes of Shakespeare's comedy. Exception could also be taken to the crudity with which erotic acts are depicted and to a certain modern slickness that occasionally glosses over the play's contours. It is equally characteristic of the striking features and of the questionable aspects of this production that more than most stagings of Shakespeare at the time or since, it aroused the immediate interest of teenage audiences. But it also impressed more mature spectators by its high-spirited approach to Shakespeare and by the sheer artistry and vitality of the acting.

The following years saw numerous interesting stagings of *A Midsummer Night's Dream*, notably by Klaus-Dieter Kirst in 1974 in Dresden and by Klaus Fiedler in 1976 in the small town of Rudolstadt, using the modern translation of Erich Fried. It is worth noting that of 16 productions of the comedy from 1971 to 1978, 11 made use of modern translations (one each by Erich Fried and Rudolf Schaller and the rest by Hamburger).

Then in 1980, after an abstinence of 25 years, Berlin brought out two productions of *A Midsummer Night's Dream* almost simultaneously. Both stagings adopted exceptional positions in their interpretations. It was as though the Berlin theatres had been biding their time in order to brush aside all conventions and traditions that weighed upon this play.

Alexander Lang's staging at the Deutsches Theater, the house where Reinhardt had once mounted his productions, sets up an antitype to the Reinhardt model.[5] Lang's attitude to the romantic staging and its successors is summed up (by himself) in the quotation:

> For, as a surfeit of the sweetest things
> The deepest loathing to the stomach brings;
> Or as the heresies that men do leave
> Are hated most of those they did deceive.
> (*A Midsummer Night's Dream*, 2.2.136–9)[6]

Lang's aversion to all 'sweet' interpretations makes him concentrate with relentless consistency on all that is bitter in the play. His concept is, of course, not mere contrariness towards a one-time dominant theatrical model; it is a reaction to the all-too-common practice, in works of art and in official communication generally, of 'sugaring over' the problems and contradictions apparent in social reality; a reaction characteristic of the present post-war generation in the GDR.

The whole play is enacted in a room on the stage confined by three reddish walls looking like panels of creased paper, with two apertures at the back for entrances and exits. At the start, all the characters wake up from a sleep and dance, singing a German rendering of 'Sumer is icumen in'. The production contains a number of references to the mythological rites of expelling winter and welcoming summer; but it does not show much confidence in the summer that is to come. The hopes and illusions of youth have been jettisoned before the play starts. Theseus, in white furs, full of ennui, is seen fondling Hippolyta in a bored kind of way, he gives judgement indifferently on the tiresome quarrel between Egeus and his daughter, and finally sends Hermia on her way with a lazy slap on the bottom.

The lovers are driven to each other by an irresistible impulse that appears to derive more from the frustrations of a midlife crisis than from pristine love. Played by actors in their thirties accoutred in carefully designed casual wear, these lovers have no hopes for the future. Lysander's suggested flight to the woods is a last resort rather than a proposal for a new beginning. Hermia's vow to follow him comes as a droned-out ritual instead of enthusiastic consent. The programme notes quote Elias Canetti:

Melancholy begins when the escape transmutations (*Fluchtverwandlungen*) are finished and are all felt to

---

5 William Shakespeare, *Sommernachtstraum*, in der Übersetzung von Johann Joachim Eschenburg 1775, Regie Alexander Lang, Bühne Gero Troike, Kostüme Heiko Zolchow und Heide Brambach. Premiere, 12 April 1980.

6 Quotations are from the new Arden Shakespeare, edited by Harold F. Brooks (1979).

7 *A Midsummer Night's Dream*. Deutsches Theater Berlin, 1980. Act 3, Scene 2: Demetrius (Dieter Mann),
Helena (Margit Bendokat), Lysander (Roman Kaminski), and Hermia (Simone v. Zglinicki)

be futile . . . can one no longer escape. One cannot transmute into anything. Everything one has tried was in vain.

In the wood – no change of scenery – the aggressiveness of the lovers reaches new dimensions. Demetrius drives away Helena with karate blows and Lysander makes frantic grabs at Helena's lap: the 'object' of love is directly assailed. The aggression is exacerbated by the drug love-in-idleness which is here translated as *Lieb-im-Wahnsinn*, i.e. love-in-madness. The juice is administered forcibly like chloroform and the patient struggles impotently until he succumbs to its effects. The machinations of Puck and Oberon are not regarded as a benign attempt to help the lovers sort out their problems but as an unwarranted manipulation by means of drugs. Lang argues: 'A doctor is not permitted to do that today without the consent of his patient.'

After a while the unseen forces in the wood act like a narcotic on all four lovers. Their experiences recede totally into the realm of their imagination. When Puck incites Demetrius and Lysander to fight, the action merely takes place in the minds of the lovers; all four stand in a bemused group with intertwined arms, swaying back and forth as they mumble their lines intoxicatedly.

Nature here caricatures the neuroses of modern civilization. Titania is a mundane Marilyn Monroe with high heels and a blond wig. Oberon in a black plastic coat represents total man, dominant indeed, but painfully

8 *A Midsummer Night's Dream.* Deutsches Theater Berlin, 1980. The Mechanicals Rehearsing:
Flute (Horst Weinheimer), Bottom (Dietrich Körner), and Quince (Ralph Borgwardt)

aware of the suffering one is forced to inflict to exert one's will; he achieves a richness of characterization surpassing that of the other figures, being faintly reminiscent of Marlon Brando in one of his self-torturing roles. The fairies, wearing dilapidated top hats, are a mixture of *fin de siècle* decadence and Freudian sex symbols. For her love affair with Bottom, Titania abandons her role, throwing away the wig and finding her true self in the arms of the ass. On awakening, she does not recoil from the beast; on the contrary, she is extremely reluctant to face harsh reality and parts from her animal lover with every sign of regret.

There is nothing genial about Peter Quince and his company either. They are depicted (in *Biedermeier* costume) as a group of professional actors at rehearsal: irritable, weary, occasionally rising to a bit of stale drollery, as when Flute, rehearsing the part of Thisbe and simulating a bosom with enormous rubber balls, is supplied with a vagina by Snout jamming his dented trilby between his legs. Quince as director and *Intendant* of the troupe is over-taxed from the start, doubling up with nervous stomach trouble and boxing Bottom's ears, who promptly retaliates.

In the last act of Lang's staging the projected *taedium vitae* prevails over the production itself, which begins to show signs of petering out. The Interlude is reeled off by uninterested professionals acting before an inattentive audience. Lysander and Demetrius, instead of watching the play, lie listlessly on top of their respective fiancées as though robbed of all energy by their adventures in the woods. The Bergomask dance and the blessing are replaced by a sixteenth-century song expelling the winter, sung by the whole company, who then lie down again to sleep.

This stark production of *A Midsummer Night's Dream* is about the loss of human relations, about man threatened by manipulation and loss of identity, about people helplessly entangled in a mesh of uncontrollable internal and external forces. When Brook worked on *A Midsummer Night's Dream* he told his actors to look for the 'secret play', the 'white magic' that was at the centre of his comedy. It would probably be correct to say that at the centre of Lang's production there was a good deal of black magic.

No doubt this courageous and fascinating piece of work gives us a one-eyed view of the play, which is supported by the text version used. Lang went back beyond the Romantics to a text attributed to Johann Joachim Eschenburg which is, in fact, an incomplete translation by the poet Christoph Martin Wieland revised by Eschenburg for publication in 1775. It is an uncouth, jejune text that quite fails to capture the lyrical qualities of Shakespeare's play. Written at a time when blank verse was just being discovered for the German drama and before the great classic verse plays had appeared (Lessing's *Nathan der Weise* 1779, Goethe's *Iphigenie* 1787, Schiller's *Wallenstein* 1798), its iambic pentameters are clumsy and it ignores such features as the use of verse for heightened emotional temperature (in Shakespeare, rhyme significantly sets in with Hermia's vow and on the word 'love': 'By the simplicity of Venus' doves / By that which knitteth souls and prospers loves' 1.1.171–2). It is worth noting that Eschenburg, dissatisfied with that version, undertook a new translation some twenty years later (1798–1806), then already in competition with Schlegel. Insofar as the director was not primarily out for the elegance of form and the musicality of the

play, the rough-hewn translation chosen was suited to his purpose.

In spite of or perhaps because of its intense one-sided emphasis, it is an extraordinarily compelling performance that is still (in 1986) playing to full houses. The marked, occasionally self-conscious style of this production is based more on ritual than on musicality. The critics were, on the whole, much impressed by this *tour de force*, although one writer complained that Shakespeare was being acted as though he were Strindberg or Wedekind and another remarked that what Lang needed but obviously did not have 'would be a new *A Midsummer Night's Dream*'. It may be noted in passing that this year Lang directed both parts of *Dance of Death* as his first actual Strindberg.

A few months later, the Maxim Gorki Theater Berlin presented its version of *A Midsummer Night's Dream* directed by Thomas Langhoff.[7] Langhoff's approach is lighthearted, nimble, and unencumbered by tradition rather than critical of it. Langhoff does not feel any need to counteract the Reinhardt model: what impressed him in the Reinhardt film was the reckless montage of elements derived from the most varied styles and traditions. He admits the influence of Brook both directly and through the mediation of other productions, for instance that of Dieter Dorn in Munich.

Under Langhoff's direction the traditional opulence of scenery and music is turned into an opulence of theatrical action. He emphasizes from the start the popular component of the play: in front of a backdrop representing a whitewashed brick wall with graffiti and the legend 'Salve Theseus' inscribed upon it there is a bustle of activity as a number of workmen

---

[7] *Ein Sommernachtstraum (A Midsummer Night's Dream)*, von William Shakespeare, Deutsch von August Wilhelm Schlegel, Bühnenfassung des Maxim Gorki Theaters, Regie: Thomas Langhoff, Ausstattung: Henning Schaller, Musik: Uwe Hilprecht. Premiere, 1 and 2 October 1980.

sweep the stage, hang up flags, and roll out a red carpet as though they were preparing Athens for a Mayday parade. The workmen – the mechanicals, as it turns out – are present as spectators during the opening scene, sitting on scaffolding along the auditorium walls.

Theseus is shown as a benevolent playboy-king who likes things to go smoothly. He makes every effort to put Hippolyta at her ease and gets really annoyed when Hermia resists his attempts to reach a compromise with Egeus: this kind of obstinacy is unusual and uncalled-for in his state. Indeed, the youngsters – the men in initialled T-shirts, the women in white dresses and sneakers – are quite ordinary, 'nice' young people who would not dream of questioning the existing order. But, Langhoff maintains, love is something that always disturbs regular life; it is a beautiful madness that disavows all ties to regular institutions. The mere fact of being thwarted in her love brings Hermia into total conflict with a state that is actually not at all rigoristic but quite humane and livable-in. The total break away from convention already takes place in Athens and the wood merely provides the environment for the love-madness to soar to its full height.

Already in Athens the lovers hurl themselves into each other's arms, roll on the floor, and fill the stage with uninhibited physical action. In an impressive transformation from Athens to the wood, the brick wall crumbles away to reveal a wide open space bounded by yellow silk. This is the wood, whose main features are a floor that gives way under people's feet and various traps and trip-ropes set up by a malicious Puck. Here the love-madness of the two couples runs fully amok. Indulging in perilous callisthenics, the actors run, jump, wrestle, roll, wallow, and chase each other at breakneck speed. One is not surprised to learn that the actors did an hour of yoga gymnastics before rehearsals each day to acquire a sense of physical freedom and co-ordination. The juice of the flower (here trans-

lated as Lieb-im-Wahn – love in delusion) causes a zigzag of attraction and revulsion that brings the lovers to the extreme limits of their emotive (and physical) capacities.

Oberon and Titania (doubled with Theseus and Hippolyta) are also a love-mad couple whose falling-out brings all nature into disorder. Titania's retinue consists of figures from erotic nightmares: a dwarf with wings and a plastic penis, a fairy-tale grandmother with spectacles and swinging breasts, a muscular man with a pair of antlers sprouting from his thighs, a high-heeled pin-up girl in petticoats. This interpretation, Langhoff explains, goes back to erotic connotations concealed in the names of the elves in the original myths. For the mechanicals, too, the central theme is love; not only as the subject of their play: it is love of art, of the theatre, that lifts them out of their humdrum lives and gives them a chance to transcend their everyday civil existence. They are shown as solid, self-confident workmen who have done their day's job and now come with lunch-bags, thermos flasks, and beer bottles to indulge in their amateur dramatics.

In the last act the youngsters fall into line again because they are, in effect, married couples; love has given way to institutionalized union and the motive for revolt has vanished. Celebrating their engagements with champagne, they are not merely derisive of the Interlude, they actually interfere with the performance and harass the mechanicals to such a degree that there is almost an exchange of blows. Chastened by this incident, the mechanicals, in a state of fear, drop all false theatricality and perform the tragedy of Pyramus and Thisbe with such natural intensity of feeling that even the blasé court audience is moved to silence.

Langhoff started out with the Schlegel translation, partly because, as he states, this text had been imprinted on his mind since childhood. Becoming aware of numerous disturbing archaisms and inadequacies during the course

9 *A Midsummer Night's Dream*. Maxim Gorki Theater Berlin, 1980. Titania (Monika Lennartz), centre left, and her retinue

of work, he then undertook a considerable amount of adaptation, so that in the end the lines spoken are something of a farrago in which classical German and improvised doggerel ('... durchsichtige Helena / Durch deinen Busen seh ich ins Herz dir ja') exist side by side. Formal aspects such as rhyme are largely ignored. It is characteristic of the attitude to the text that the incantations accompanying the application of the juice are spoken in English, guttural and incomprehensible, which is just good for a laugh. The text is treated as a libretto for action. The word-music, the evocative qualities of the language have substantially disappeared except where they have been transmuted into the medium of physical action. The verse is sloppily spoken;

this may partially be due to lack of poetic theatre practice, as the Maxim Gorki Theater normally specializes in modern prose drama; still, it seems significant that the director should have devoted so much time to yoga training but apparently none to training verse elocution.

The picture we get of GDR stagings of *A Midsummer Night's Dream* is that in the 1970s, theatres were interested in problems of social harmony and dissonance seen both historically and with contemporary connotations.[8] They

---

[8] The problems of tensions between the historical and actual dimensions of Shakespeare's drama had, of course, been treated before that. See in particular: Robert Weimann, 'Shakespeare on the Stage: Past Sig-

interpreted the comedy as a metaphorical exploration of relations between the individual and a historically determined, patriarchal society. They predominantly used modern translations profiting from the Brechtian concept of *Gestus* in a stage language that tried to revitalize the acting qualities of Shakespeare's speech as against the more literary bent of older versions.

In the Berlin stagings in 1980 the pendulum has swung to the other extreme. The productions concentrate on (very different) immediate, contemporary aspects of the play and largely disregard its historical origin. On the other hand they show considerable pre-occupation with the mythological background of *A Midsummer Night's Dream*. The radically subjective interpretations highlight the predicament of the individual at the mercy of unseen manipulatory forces in one staging and human passion as an elementary force that renders all social ties irrelevant in the other. These productions are certainly one-sided (and, in a sense, complementary) but each brings out powerful contemporary aspects of the play that had hitherto been insufficiently observed and each makes a very immediate impact on audiences. It could be argued that this directness again has something Shakespearian about it. The translations used – Eschenburg (Wieland) and a free adaptation of Schlegel – may be open to charges of eclecticism but they provide lines pliable to the needs of the director without claiming the attention a text of greater artistic coherence would have done. Shakespeare's text does not seem to possess an intrinsic value for the directors; it

seems as though both of them mistrusted the suggestive power of words, possibly as an over-reaction to certain traditional productions of classical drama largely compounded of rhetoric and elocution.

Conceptional features shared by all four productions are a critical emphasis on the element of male domination and a scepticism towards the harmonious ending of the play.

Although a number of imaginative stagings of *A Midsummer Night's Dream* have been seen in the GDR since, there was no new concept that might be considered to have superseded the Berlin productions; none to equal these in power and intensity and, at the same time, give us a greater share of the richness of Shakespeare's play. Alexander Lang, questioned by the present writer, regards his elucidation of the dark side of the comedy as still valid and feels no compulsion to re-direct it today, nor does he feel that his production of Strindberg's *Dance of Death* has in any way undercut his concept of *A Midsummer Night's Dream*. Thomas Langhoff, however, feels that, having liberated the comedy from the weight of German interpretativeness, he would now be able to vitalize other facets of the drama. What fascinates him are the royalty and passion of the mythological-magical figures of Titania and Oberon, and he would, in a new production, explore the question as to whether there are elements of such beings still alive somewhere in man today.

---

nificance and Present Meaning', *Shakespeare Survey 20* (1967), 113–20. Weimann adduces two stagings of *Hamlet* in the GDR from the 1960s.

'HENRY V' AS WORKING-HOUSE OF IDEOLOGY

GÜNTER WALCH

Among the features specific to the text of *Henry V* its apparent property of giving rise to particularly acrimonious division of opinion has often been noted. To say that there are two camps sharply opposing each other is indeed almost a commonplace of critical literature, the one camp fervently applauding what they see as a panegyric upon, indeed a rousing celebration of, 'the mirror of all Christian Kings'[1] and most successful English monarch of all the histories; and the followers of the other camp deriding with no less conviction the exaltation of a machiavellian conqueror in a rapacious and, after all, senseless war. Little wonder, then, that in 1939 Mark Van Doren should have thought even Shakespeare's genius baffled *vis-à-vis* such hopeless material;[2] that E. M. W. Tillyard should have considered *Henry V*, remarkably enough at the time of the Second World War, a dramatic failure on account of its puerile patriotism and lack of form;[3] or that Moody E. Prior should consider the play 'a theatrically handsome fulfillment of an obligation, performed with skill but without deep conviction'.[4] Puzzled by such an unprecedented attack of Tudor apologetics suffered by an author almost simultaneously engaged in composing *Julius Caesar* (1599) and *Hamlet* (1599–1601), scholars have since suggested readings of the text assuming either that 'the play is full of ironies, most of which challenge the legend, well-established at the time the play was written, of Henry the "mirror of all Christian Kings"'[5] or of dis-

parate presentations co-existing in unbridgeable contradiction: Henry as ideal ruler *and* brutal conqueror for instance;[6] or as a politically strong monarch *and* weak human being;[7] or Harry as model ruler saddled with a nation sadly deficient in moral virtue,[8] to give just a few examples.

I am not quarrelling with interpretations of this kind which add inscriptions which can enhance our understanding of the text. But one of the things that seem to have happened in the process of an intensifying search for implicit ironies is that the dramatic character of the protagonist has dwindled in stature. He has been reduced even from Hazlitt's 'amiable

---

1 1, Chorus, l. 6. All references to *Henry V* (henceforth in the text) follow The Arden Shakespeare, edited by J. H. Walter (1954).

2 Cf. Mark Van Doren, *Shakespeare* (New York, 1939), p. 179. For a brief summary of divergent criticism of *Henry V* see my 'Tudor-Legende und Geschichtsbewegung in *The Life of King Henry V*: Zur Rezeptionslenkung durch den Chorus', *Shakespeare-Jahrbuch* (East) 122 (1986), pp. 37f, notes 2–17.

3 E. M. W. Tillyard, *Shakespeare's History Plays* (1944), pp. 304–314.

4 Moody E. Prior, *The Drama of Power. Studies in Shakespeare's History Plays* (Evanston, 1973), p. 341.

5 John Wilders, *The Lost Garden. A View of Shakespeare's English and Roman History Plays* (1978), p. 141.

6 Valentina P. Komarova, '*Heinrich V* und das Problem des idealen Herrschers', *Shakespeare-Jahrbuch* (East) 115 (1979), pp. 98–116.

7 W. L. Godshalk, 'Henry V's Politics of Non-Responsibility', *Cahiers Élisabéthains*, 17 (1980), 11.

8 Prior, p. 272.

monster' to a rather commonplace person, at times intensely unpleasant, occasionally a neurotic, compulsively circumnavigating the pressures of having to make decisions,[9] and so forth.

I'd better say at this point that this is not my view of the protagonist, not the image suggested to me by the text, and even less by its representations on the stage. For on the stage the young king appears to have a knack of capturing audiences by his youthful and intelligent vitality even against their will, as it were, in spite of all reservations, triumphing sometimes over directors whose sympathy he does not seem to enjoy. In fact, Harry on the stage seems to wrest sympathies from audiences understandably reluctant to embrace the ideological tenets, the Tudor orthodoxies, and above all the warmongering with which he must be associated. From that derives the point I wish to make. As Robert Egan has shown, negative as well as positive reactions to the text have, encouraged by the Chorus, usually been produced by identifying both the central character and the play as a whole with the ideological material represented in it.[10] But that is just what the text carefully sets out to avoid. That is why the general poststructuralist objection to all representation as establishing or reinforcing authority can be seen not to apply: Shakespeare does not reinforce authority by re-presenting or re-writing or inscribing in the text an interpretation of an historical personage agreed upon in advance. As I shall argue, the dramatist does far more in the text than write a pageant, at best ambiguous – but ambiguity will not solve our problem – , about the audience's favourite ruler. He creates, through his text, the score for a theatricalization of that material, and in the process turns the text – if I may vary one of the Chorus's invigorating appeals to our imagination – into a 'quick forge and working-house' (5, Chorus, l. 23) of ideology.

The history of *Henry V* in the theatre and the other more recent mass media shows distinctly, more clearly perhaps than is the case with most Shakespearian plays, that the play's reputation has depended heavily on its political and ideological contexts. Since the Second World War theatres in many countries seem to have been somewhat wary of a text that in times of national crisis was put to superbly efficient use as a patriotic morale booster. Sir Laurence Olivier's war-time film, naturally always referred to in this connection, demonstrates this kind of significant use of the text, always keeping in mind some 1700 lines cut and others added by the filmmakers.

I am not quarrelling over violations of some presumed sanctity of the play's text, let alone of a text with a single fixed meaning. I share the interest in the text as an interest in the history of social uses of – in this case – dramatic material, uses without exception historically and socially specific. And I also believe that texts cannot be reduced to successive inscriptions during the course of history, but that accounts of the moment of the original production of a text, although rightly no longer privileged, are far from irrelevant.[11] *Henry V* is so pertinent to that kind of historical approach because it is not only, like all art, ideological in the sense of generally being part of the process of social consciousness. This text is rather special among Shakespeare's works in parading, or even flaunting, the ideology – in the narrower sense of the term – re-presented in it. This is the major function of 1.2, with the state's top dignitaries engaged in ideological preparation for the war against France. Thus

[9] Cf. Godshalk, *passim*.

[10] Robert Egan, 'A Muse of Fire: *Henry V* in the Light of *Tamburlaine*', in *Modern Language Quarterly*, 29 (1968), p. 15. Egan does not, however, follow up his own conclusions but reduces his analysis to another opposition of the kind mentioned before, that of conqueror and human being; cf. p. 19.

[11] Cf. Francis Barker and Peter Hulme, 'Nymphs and reapers heavily vanish: the discursive con-text of *The Tempest*', in *Alternative Shakespeares*, ed. John Drakakis (1985), p. 193.

the scene offers a rich choice of official thinking, culminating, first, in Canterbury's famous legalistic dispensation, and, second and even closer to the heart of authority, in the same speaker's no less renowned sermon on the commonwealth of the honey-bees, the lesson of which had been so well rehearsed by Shakespeare's audience in a lifetime of church attendance.

Although it would now be probably harder than it used to be to find romantic believers in Shakespeare's unqualified acceptance of the doctrine of Order and Degree and absolute ideological Obedience, the actual aesthetic significance of the dramatist's inclusion of such weighty contemporary ideological material is still widely underrated. Canterbury's disappearance from the play after that scene may tell us that he has done the job assigned to him within the plot, but certainly not that the rest of the play is unconcerned with ideology. On the contrary, concern with the consequences of, and the historical problems inherent in, the doctrine placed so obtrusively in the text, and all it stands for, is central to the play as a whole.

That this concern was felt to be disturbing or at least irritating may be inferred from 'the apparent modesty of its early success'[12] in striking contrast to much later exhilarating celebrations of the hero and hence of the play. A look at what the very first social uses of the text have to tell us can be quite revealing, even allowing for its somewhat hypothetical character. For if we do not confine ourselves to considering only the practical side of the genesis of the First Quarto of 1600 as 'a cut form of the play used by the company for a reduced cast on tour in the provinces',[13] but also, as the editor of the new Oxford edition suggests and as I think we should, the ideological quality of those cuts, we can indeed see that nearly all 'difficulty in the way of an unambiguous patriotic interpretation of Henry and his war'[14] have been removed: all references to the Church's mixed motives for, and

its financial support of, the war; to Henry's personal responsibility for Falstaff's fate; to motives beyond bribery for the conspiracy against Henry; to Henry's 'savage ultimatum' and the devastation wreaked by him on France; MacMorris and some of the choruses.[15] In other words, it was not only that the touring company had to make shift with its casting. Profiting from the experience of the play's original performances, we may assume, they also saw to it that technically necessary textual reductions were employed to make the text less recalcitrant to meeting the conventional audience expectations of a dashing hero confirming their own superiority.

That recalcitrance is not restricted to isolated passages but deeply structures the text as a whole. To give at least an indication of this, I shall isolate the character of the Chorus as a means which, although behaving in a deceptively epic way as a character, can be shown, I believe, to have an essential dramatic function within the context of the work. This consists in playing with the audience's conventional expectations in a number of intricate ways. The Chorus titillates those expectations nurtured by the illustrious 'gentles all' (Prologue, ll. 8, 11) in the abjectly decried 'cockpit', but raised also by previous triumphs prepared by Shakespeare's 'rough and all-unable pen' (Epilogue, l. 1) for 'this unworthy scaffold' (Prologue, l. 10) which are then fulfilled grudgingly or not at all. The Chorus as Prologue promises battle scenes the grandeur of which the audience will have to use their 'imaginary forces' (Prologue, l. 18) to enjoy properly, while the gentles remember very well previous battles – Bosworth Field, Angiers, Shrewsbury – 'Which oft our stage hath shown' (Epilogue, l. 13) so magnificently. The

[12] *Henry V*, ed. Gary Taylor, *The Oxford Shakespeare* (Oxford, 1982), p. 12.

[13] Walter, p. xxxv.

[14] Taylor, p. 12.

[15] For the details see Taylor, pp. 12, 20.

Chorus conjures up, or deplores the absence of, a super-cinemascopic verisimilitude the humble author and his platform stage never dreamt of supplying, or indeed had any need of. The Chorus thus theatricalizes the whole problem of representation on the Elizabethan stage, only to use what is in effect a brilliant defence of Shakespeare's non-naturalistic aesthetic to lead the audience into assuming, from their previous experience and expectation, that they know very well what they can expect to see happening on the stage. In a puzzling way, they are both confirmed in this – as far as the manner of representation is concerned – and disappointed, concerning the matter of representation. Thus, for instance, while the 'Muse of fire', the 'casques' and the 'proud hoofs' of Agincourt are invoked by the Prologue, in contrast to previous history plays this one does not show us a single actual battle scene. The only scene set during the battle has the cowardly and greedy clown Pistol taking an equally scared Frenchman prisoner, a parody of heroic combat.

We are gradually made aware, by the way the Chorus operates, that he cannot be relied upon to be always talking of what is actually represented on the stage. On somewhat closer scrutiny, he does not seem to be operating innocently 'as a peculiar feature, connecting and explaining the action as it proceeds' at all, as he was thought to do by Charles Kean[16] and a majority, it seems, of scholars since. In fact, the Chorus seems quite far from 'describing and connecting the quick succession of events, the rapid changes of locality; and the elucidating passages which might otherwise appear confused or incongruous ...'[17] We are made to stumble on such incongruity, created rather than elucidated by the Chorus, when the very first dialogue opens, and when after the Prologue's eulogy the very first line deals, not with patriotism, as we've been promised by the Prologue, but with ecclesiastic financial transactions, something nowhere hinted at in the Chorus. Equally, we certainly do not see

the French 'Shake in their fear', even though evidently they should, and our expectations of seeing 'this grace of kings' (2, Chorus, ll. 14, 28) foil the heinous attempt on his life by the conspirators, whose sole motive he says is money (although 'crowns' – 'crowns imperial, crowns and coronets' are given prominence as 'Promis'd' to Harry's 'English Mercuries' earlier on in the same Chorus; II, Chorus, ll. 7–11), our expectations are at least delayed because we are first introduced to the down-and-out Cheapside gang. About these, however, and the common soldiers so prominent in the play, the Chorus is conspicuously silent. They are mentioned only once, collectively, 'mean and gentle all', presumably flattered as joint recipients of 'A little touch of Harry in the night' (4, Chorus, ll. 45, 47), obviously for propaganda purposes. Again, contradicting 4, Chorus's announcement of a forth-going Harry 'Walking from watch to watch, from tent to tent' visiting and cheering up 'all his host' (ll. 30–33), Harry is actually shown as rather isolated throughout all the acts except the last. At least in the Folio text he does not approach the soldiers. They approach him, and what follows is the long, tortuous discussion, verbal fighting within his own camp taking the place of armed combat in that of the enemy. In the Quarto text, the dialogue has been changed drastically.[18] Here, Henry does approach the soldiers and speaks to them first, reversing the Folio situation and thus bringing it into line both with the Chorus and with audience expectations based on it and on Prince Hal's behaviour of yore. Just as 2,

---

[16] Charles Kean (ed.), *Shakespeare's Play of 'King Henry the Fifth'*, *Arranged for Representation at The Princess's Theatre, with Historical and Explanatory Notes*. As first performed on Monday, March 28, 1859 (n.d.), p. vi.

[17] John William Cole, *The Life and Theatrical Times of Charles Kean, F.S.A. Including a summary of The English Stage for the Last Fifty Years, and a Detailed Account of the Management of the Princess's Theatre from 1850 to 1859*. 2 vols (1859), vol. 2, p. 342.

[18] Cf. Taylor, p. 43.

Chorus ('honour's thought / Reigns solely in the breast of every man', ll. 3–4), 3, Chorus, also announces the splendid readiness of the whole nation to achieve heroic deeds of war ('For who is he, whose chin is but enrich'd / With one appearing hair, that will not follow / These cull'd and choice-drawn cavaliers to France?' ll. 22–4). But we are made aware of a majority back home in England safely tucked up in bed.

The function of the Chorus cannot, then, possibly be confined to the epic one of providing information. The information provided by him is, in the first place, for the most part superfluous, for we learn nothing from it about the plot, about Harry and his world that we do not learn much better from the dialogues. Since 2, Chorus eagerly tells us how the traitor scene will end, obviously the structure and meaning of the events are meant to be more important than their mere course (the verdicts had been drawn up *before* the trial in any case).

This interpretative dimension of the Chorus has been appreciated both on the stage, for example by Mrs Kean's representation of the Chorus as Clio, the muse of history, but operating typically as 'the presiding charm'[19] of the play; and in Eamon Grennan's description a few years ago of the Chorus as a commissioned historiographer who shows his royal subject making history.[20] But if he is a historiographer, he is characteristically not merely recording events. He is bent on presenting his subject, the king, in the most glaringly idealized colours, and his war invariably in the rosiest of tones. He is much more than a functional epic device, neutral observer and reporter. He is a deeply involved maker of ideology. And while he is intent on convincing us that Harry is achieving the great victory virtually single-handed, and that with God's assistance he is thus making history as a Great Man of History, we are made to understand, through the different components of the complete play's text, that Henry, just as his histori-

ographer and propagandist, is actually busy creating his, Harry's, legend.

The Chorus in *Henry V* is thus, in my understanding of the play, not a later addition, but indispensable to its functioning. The Chorus is an integral part of Shakespeare's strategy not in spite of his information being unreliable, but because it is unreliable, and because what he does not tell us is more important than what he does tell us. Shakespeare thus creates a unique dramatic structure in his last history play in order to do something completely different from what he had been doing in his previous histories. The genetic context with *Julius Caesar* and *Hamlet*, which now appears anything but a *non sequitur* on the part of Shakespeare, can actually further our understanding of the play's relation to the other histories, in particular to *Richard II*. By this new structure, by emphasizing not the events but the functioning of ideology, the conspicuously ancient theatrical device is made to ask, through the means of its art, completely new and shocking questions concerning the function of the monarch himself ('O hard condition! / Twin-born with greatness'; 'thou idol ceremony', 4.1.239–40, 246). By showing the young king not shining in the world of the Chorus' creation but living in the world of history Henry becomes a complex character. Moreover, the play's questions are addressed to problems concerning the nature of history, its motivating forces and the ideological function of its representation. The

---

[19] Cole, vol. 2, p. 342. Also quoted by Taylor, p. 57. Kean considered the idea of casting his wife as a female Chorus, which set a trend in productions of the play in England, very frankly and practically as 'an opportunity . . . to Mrs. Charles Kean, which the play does not otherwise supply, of participating in this, the concluding revival of her husband's management' of the Princess's Theatre. See Kean, p. vi.

[20] Eamon Grennan, ' "This Story Shall the Good Man Teach His Son": *Henry V* and the Art of History', *Papers on Language and Literature*, 15 (1979), 370–82.

Chorus can make the Elizabethan audience aware of the political significance of these questions by highlighting the discrepancies between the orthodox historical legend perpetuated by those in power and the ideology connected with it on the one hand, and the actual movement of history on the other, and thus shows the official ideology up for what it has become: an illusion effectively used as an instrument of power.

SHAKESPEARE AND HIS SOURCES: OBSERVATIONS ON THE CRITICAL HISTORY OF 'JULIUS CAESAR'

ROBERT S. MIOLA

Conspicuous in my title, the term 'source' is today highly problematic. Critics now understand 'source' variously and employ as well many different terms in its place. These terms, each one rich in its own embedded metaphors and critical implications, embody conflicting notions about what a source is and about how it functions. Our tacit acceptance of these conflicts has resulted in radical redefinition of sources and a revaluation of their relations to texts. To illustrate such changes, this essay will examine the critical history of *Julius Caesar*, a play that bears a close and complex relationship to a long-established specific source, North's Plutarch. The issues raised in this discussion should be pertinent, however, to less established sources, the tragedies of Seneca, let us say, and, of course, to other plays.

'Source', from the Old French 'sors', derives from 'sourdre', 'to rise or spring'. A source is a 'support'; 'the act of rising on the wing'; 'the fountain-head or origin of a river or stream'; 'the chief or prime cause *of* something of a non-material or abstract character'.[1] A work of art then may rise from a source and leave it behind or it may flow from a source, existing in poised and dynamic tension, ever dependent on the source for its being. We often speak of tracing things to their sources, assuming then that there are connecting lines always present and discernible. This assumption, a venerable tenet of literary criticism, still appears today. Tobin's recent book, for example, traces

Apuleius' influence on Shakespeare along the lines of verbal echo and coincidence.[2] The implicit idea here is that the source is a book open on the desk or in the mind of the author; it appears as a direct, verbal, and visible presence in the text.

The vagaries of the modern critical lexicon suggest alternative possibilities to this conception of source. For their authoritative works John W. Velz and Leo Salingar choose the term 'tradition'.[3] Both intend 'tradition' to be broader and more capacious than source; to include, on the one hand, 'the devious paths by which the Renaissance found access to the classics', and, on the other, 'underlying conventions'. The word 'tradition', an adaptation of the Latin 'traditio', means 'the action of handing over'; 'a giving up, surrender'; 'a delivery'. 'Tradition' may be a gift graciously handed down or over, or something reluc-

---

[1] *The Oxford English Dictionary*, s.v. 'Source'. Unless otherwise noted, all definitions below derive from this dictionary.

[2] J. J. M. Tobin, *Shakespeare's Favorite Novel: A Study of 'The Golden Ass' as Prime Source* (Lanham, Maryland, 1984).

[3] John W. Velz, *Shakespeare and the Classical Tradition: A Critical Guide to the Commentary, 1660–1960* (Minneapolis, 1968); Leo Salingar, *Shakespeare and the Traditions of Comedy* (Cambridge, 1974). The first quotation below belongs to Velz, p. ix, the second to Salingar, p. ix. It is a pleasure to acknowledge here general indebtedness to Velz, who first drew my attention to some of Shakespeare's various ways with Plutarch.

tantly surrendered; it may take the form of static condition or dynamic action. Ernest Klein complicates matters by exploring etymology further: '*Tradition* is a scholarly formation and represents a doublet of *treason*.'[4] Tradition can be a betrayal.

We may also consider 'background'. John Erskine Hankins calls his book *Backgrounds of Shakespeare's Thought* because he believes that 'one cannot always pinpoint the particular book from which Shakespeare derived an image or idea'.[5] According to this rationale, 'background' is less precise and delimiting than 'source,' a term more tolerant of intermediation, more open to possibility. Theatrical in origin, the word denotes the ground behind the 'chief objects of contemplation'. The word 'background' assumes that an object is visibly (if not conspicuously) present and stands in a relationship that is spatial, usually static, and possibly incidental. The book is not necessarily open on the desk then, but can be closed on the shelf. Another popular term, 'antecedent', ultimately from the Latin 'antecedere', changes the spatial reference to the temporal. An 'antecedent' is 'a thing or circumstance which goes before or precedes in time or order.' 'Antecedent' is more strongly causal than 'background' (witness its use in logic and grammar), and less certainly visible. It is, in fact, similar to another old-fashioned term resuscitated recently by Harold Bloom – 'precursor'.[6]

Also of long-standing popularity, the word 'influence' usually signifies a cause less direct than 'source' and secondary in significance. Witness its use in the *Shakespeare Variorum Handbook*:

At the discretion of the editor the appendix on sources may include a section on general influences, such as the work of other playwrights, theatrical fashions, literary traditions and modes, and intellectual or historical milieu. If it is included at all the discussion should be kept distinctly a subordinate part of the appendix.[7]

Leaving aside for now the tantalizing possibilities of 'fashions', 'modes', and 'milieu', (this last term figuring significantly in Roland Mushat Frye's learned *The Renaissance Hamlet*),[8] we may observe that 'influence' means literally the 'action or fact of flowing in' and originally denoted an astrological emanation. Its history emphasizes efficacy and importance as well as secrecy, invisibility, and insensibility.

At present, other words confound with their implications and perplex with their possibilities. 'Origin,' chosen by Emrys Jones and Ann Thompson for their books,[9] is ultimately from the Latin 'oriri', 'to arise', and means 'the act of arising or springing from something'. Jones uses the term broadly to refer to the 'whole complex of literary passages' that Shakespeare's mind reverts to when he is writing with great power. Shakespearian moments, then, arise from complex origins, not from single open or shut books. Another term, 'heritage', appearing notably in books by Willard Farnham and Glynne Wickham,[10] signifies 'that which has been or may be inherited', that 'which devolves by right of inheritance'. 'Origin' (like 'source') is flight, 'heritage' is property. The one term suggests the primeval chaos of the cosmos and the mysterious act of creation, of ordering by a supernal intelligence; the other, more mundanely, suggests a tangible legacy bequeathed in due sequence from one party to another.

---

[4] *A Comprehensive Etymological Dictionary of the English Language*, 2 vols (Amsterdam, 1966–7), s.v. 'tradition'.

[5] (Hamden, Conn., 1978), p. 9.

[6] *A Map of Misreading* (New York, 1975).

[7] Richard Hosley, Richard Knowles, and Ruth McGugan, *Shakespeare Variorum Handbook: A Manual of Editorial Practice* (New York, 1971), p. 101.

[8] (Princeton, 1984).

[9] Emrys Jones, *The Origins of Shakespeare* (Oxford, 1977). The quotation below is on p. 21. Ann Thompson, *Shakespeare's Chaucer: A Study in Literary Origins* (Liverpool, 1978).

[10] Willard Farnham, *The Medieval Heritage of Elizabethan Tragedy* (Berkeley, 1936); Glynne Wickham, *Shakespeare's Dramatic Heritage* (1969).

Recent critical discussion has introduced new terms. Meditating on Milton, John Hollander has engagingly written on the Echo allegorical, schematic, metaphorical, and metaleptic.[11] 'Subtext' is now popular – a term that removes the source from above (influence) and from behind (background) to locate it below the text, changing the metaphorical field of reference to the earth or garden. The student of sources, then, does not trace lines of transmission or perceive spatial or temporal relations, but searches for underground pools and digs up roots. Usually the text above little resembles the subtext below and the relationship between the two is not always so nutritive as the embedded metaphors imply. At times the text defies the subtext, breaks free of its constraints, and opposes it in silent struggle. A related and equally current term is 'context'. This term eliminates the distance between text and source; it places the source in the fabric of the text, despatializes and detemporalizes the relationship, and fuses the separate identities into one. Certain new historicists, of course, deny the possibility of distinguishing, even theoretically, between text and context. For them, both are competing signifiers in a continuous social and institutional discourse.

The most elusive of these terms in critical parlance, one which Geoffrey Bullough employs in his thorough and useful compendium, is 'analogue'.[12] An 'analogue' is 'a representative in different circumstances or situation; something performing a corresponding part'. 'Ana-logos': the 'word', 'up, in place or time, back, again, anew'. 'Analogue', then, posits the vaguest of relations between text and source. It is a source from which nothing flows, a tradition not handed over, an invisible background, a stationary origin, a still influence, an unclaimed heritage, a silent echo, an absent subtext and context. Perhaps St John the Evangelist originally wrote, 'In the beginning was the analogue.'

My purpose here is not to deconstruct, but rather to expose the assumptions implicit in

our language. These assumptions are crucial because they determine what constitutes a source and what kind of evidence for sources is valid. If one assumes, traditionally, that a text flows from its 'source', then one posits a direct and immediate relationship between the two. Accordingly, verbal echoes and repetitions become significant as proofs of relationship. If one assumes, as many now do, that a text can derive from a source indirectly or obliquely (source as tradition, background, etc.), then other kinds of evidence become important: scenic form, thematic figuration, rhetorical strategy, structural parallelism, ideational or imagistic concatenation.[13] Accordingly, there will be a decreased emphasis on verbal iteration. One's initial often unconscious choice of terms, assumptions, and metaphors will determine to a large degree conclusions both about what a source is and how it functions. The initial choice will also dispose the critic to one side of the spectrum that ranges between nugatory reminiscence and purposeful imitation. It will also, perforce, involve one in the ongoing debate about the nature of a text. And it will affect materially final evaluation of a work, its originality and achievement.

The critical history of *Julius Caesar* well illustrates the significance of initial assumptions about sources, of one's choice of terms and embedded metaphors. From early times onward, this play's relations to Plutarch have been a subject of discussion and debate. Our recently expanded understanding of sources

---

[11] *The Figure of Echo: A Mode of Allusion in Milton and After* (Berkeley, 1981).

[12] *Narrative and Dramatic Sources of Shakespeare*, 8 vols (1957–75).

[13] On scenic form see Emrys Jones, *Scenic Form in Shakespeare* (Oxford, 1971); James E. Hirsh, *The Structure of Shakespearean Scenes* (New Haven and London, 1981); on concatenation see John W. Velz, '*Sir Thomas More* and the Shakespeare Canon: Two Approaches,' revised from a paper delivered at the Shakespeare Association of America meeting, Ashland, Oregon, 1983 (forthcoming).

has had four specific effects on this controversy: it has prompted 1. the revaluation of North's Plutarch as source; 2. the consideration of source as background or influence; 3. the discovery of source as subtext; 4. the introduction of new texts as sources.

A significant trend in the early critical history of *Julius Caesar* registers disappointment in what is perceived as excessive reliance on Plutarch. Witness Nicholas Rowe, for example:

For the last two [Brutus and Antony] especially, you find 'em exactly as they are describ'd by *Plutarch*, from whom certainly *Shakspear* copy'd 'em. He has indeed follow'd his Original pretty close, and taken in several little Incidents that might have been spar'd in a Play.[14]

Likewise, Samuel Johnson wrote, Shakespeare's 'adherence to the real story, and to *Roman* manners seems to have impeded the natural vigour of his genius'; he found the play 'somewhat cold and unaffecting'.[15] These complaints gather force and echo throughout the nineteenth and early twentieth centuries. The judgements of Gervinus, Trench, Stapfer, and Sidgwick, for example, are typical.[16] Wondering about Shakespeare's uncharacteristic fidelity to a source, many pointed to consequent faults in historical accuracy or artistic design. A notorious example of the former fault is Shakespeare's transcription of North's mistake regarding Caesar's bequest of lands 'On this side Tiber' (3.2.249).[17] Noting that the original Greek signified just the opposite, the other side of the Tiber, Richard Farmer demonstrated Shakespeare's use of North's translation and mocked his classical learning.[18] An example of the other kind of fault, that of artistic design, appears to be the curious incident of Young Cato's death, inserted into a busy sequence of battle scenes (5.4.1–8). Young Cato braves the enemy and dies in less than ten lines and the rapidity and repetition of the lines veer precariously close to the comic.

Today such faults are no faults at all. Since the important labours of M. W. Mac-Callum,[19] critics are much more likely to emphasize Shakespeare's creative departures from Plutarch, his reworking of historical incident into tragic drama. Shakespeare's 'error' concerning the Tiber, a prime example of close and uncritical copying, is largely forgotten, and most consider the once popular search for such inconsistencies a pedantic version of Trivial Pursuits. And to some, at least, Shakespeare's portrayal of Young Cato seems now deft and assured. Granville-Barker finds a 'touch of romance' in the death, and Traversi believes that the 'parody of vain self-assertion' signals the doom fast overtaking the conspiracy.[20] The incident suggests to the modern eye, ever alert for irony, the inadequacy of Roman egotism, the delusive and dangerous nature of Roman concern

---

14 *Works*, 6 vols (1709), vol. 1, pp. xxx–xxxi. First, I believe, to suggest North's translation as source was John Dennis in a letter to *The Spectator*, 6 February 1711, reprinted by Brian Vickers (ed.), *Shakespeare: The Critical Heritage*, 6 vols (1974–81), vol. 2, pp. 286–7. Anticipating modern developments, some early critics praised Shakespeare's creative adaptation of Plutarch: Edward Capell (1768), James Beattie (1776), and the author of an unsigned essay in *Lounger's Miscellany* (1789), Vickers, vol. 5, p. 321; vol. 6, pp. 155–6; vol. 6, pp. 500–5.

15 *Plays*, 8 vols (London, 1765), vol. 7, p. 102.

16 G. G. Gervinus, *Shakespeare Commentaries*, trans F. E. Bunnètt (1883), p. 699; Richard Chenevix Trench, *Plutarch: His Life, His Lives and His Morals – Four Lectures* (1873), pp. 51–2; Paul Stapfer, *Shakespeare and Classical Antiquity*, trans. Emily J. Carey (1880), p. 8; Henry Sidgwick, *Miscellaneous Essays and Addresses* (1904), p. 103.

17 For all citations to Shakespeare I have used *The Riverside Shakespeare*, edited by G. Blakemore Evans (Boston, 1974).

18 *An Essay on the Learning of Shakespeare* (Cambridge, 1767), p. 11.

19 *Shakespeare's Roman Plays and Their Background* (1910; repr. 1967).

20 Harley Granville-Barker, *Prefaces to Shakespeare*, 4 vols. (1946, repr. Princeton, 1963), vol. 2, p. 211; Derek Traversi, *Shakespeare: The Roman Plays* (Stanford 1963), pp. 73–4.

(especially Brutus') for honour, name, and fame.

Broadened understanding of sources and of the oblique ways in which they shape texts has also prompted consideration of Plutarch as 'background' or 'influence'. Passages in Plutarch sometimes retain no verbal markers in *Julius Caesar*, but shape powerfully character and theme.[21] One such passage, first noted by W. Warde Fowler,[22] occurs at the end of Plutarch's Caesar:

But his great prosperitie and good fortune that favoured him all his life time, did continue afterwards in the revenge of his death, pursuing the murtherers both by sea and land, till they had not left a man more to be executed. (volume 5, p. 70)

Herein are two seminal conceptions for Shakespeare, particularly for acts 4 and 5: the notion that Caesar (or a part of him) lives on after death; the idea that Roman history works like a revenge tragedy. Commenting on the mistranslation of 'daemon' as 'great prosperitie and good fortune', J. A. K. Thomson declares that this passage, 'gives the clue to Shakespeare's play'.[23] Plutarch's 'daemon' becomes the spirit of Caesar who haunts Brutus and who turns the conspirators' swords in their own proper entrails.

Another example of Plutarch as 'background' or 'influence' is the passage relating Cassius' Epicurean opinion of spirits:

In our secte, Brutus, we have an opinion, that we doe not always feele, or see, that which we suppose we doe both see and feele: but that our senses beeing credulous, and therefore easily abused (when they are idle and unoccupied in their owne objects) are induced to imagine they see and conjecture that, which they in truth doe not. For, our minde is quicke and cunning to worke (without eyther cause or matter) any thinge in the imagination whatsoever. And therefore the imagination is resembled to claye, and the minde to the potter: who without any other cause than his fancie and pleasure, chaungeth it into what facion and forme he will. And this doth the diversitie of our dreames shewe unto us. For our imagination doth uppon a small

fancie growe from conceit to conceit, altering both in passions and formes of thinges imagined. For the minde of man is ever occupied, and that continuall moving is nothing but an imagination.

(volume 6, p. 218)

No direct parallel to this speech exists in the play, of course, though there are numerous half-echoes and hints of it. Surprised at the neglect of this passage, D. J. Palmer asserts its great importance for the tragedy as a whole.[24] And he is right. For Plutarch here succinctly and powerfully expresses the pervasive scepticism found in *Julius Caesar*, that concern with the unreliability of the senses, the uncertainty of judgement, and the dubious process of fashioning verities. Liberated from the narrow criteria of verbal iteration, critics now observe the larger yet more subtle influence of Plutarch on the play.

The changes in critical thinking have also led to the discovery of North's Plutarch as subtext. The distinguishing characteristic here is denial of the source in ways that differ from simple addition (e.g., the character of Lucius) or omission (most of Caesar's early career). *Julius Caesar*, as many have begun to note, asserts its independence from North's Plutarch by the aggressive rearrangement of transference; that is, by the switching of characters and the reattribution of personal traits. In Plutarch, for example, Caesar suspects those 'leane and whitely faced fellowes' (volume 6, p. 188), Brutus and Cassius, not just Cassius (cf. volume 5, p. 64; volume 6, p. 12). Moreover, the conflict about leading the right wing actually occurs between Brutus and Cassius:

---

21 All references below to Plutarch are cited to George Wyndham (ed.), *Plutarch's Lives of the Noble Grecians and Romans Englished by Sir Thomas North, Anno 1579*, 6 vols (1895–6). In this edition volume 5 contains 'The Life of Iulius Caesar', and volume 6, 'The Life of Marcus Antonius', and 'The Life of Marcus Brutus'.
22 *Roman Essays and Interpretations* (Oxford, 1920), p. 270.
23 *Shakespeare and the Classics* (1952), p. 195.
24 'Tragic Error in *Julius Caesar*', *Shakespeare Quarterly*, 21 (1970), 399–409, p. 401.

Then Brutus prayed Cassius he might have the leading of the right winge, the which men thought was farre meeter for Cassius: both bicause he was the elder man, and also for that he had the better experience. But yet Cassius gave it him.

(volume 6, p. 222)

In Shakespeare's play this incident becomes a taut and pointed exchange between Antony and Octavius, one which foreshadows their future discord and Antony's eventual fall (5.1.16–20). Others have remarked that Shakespeare transfers from Antony to Brutus the proposal for Caesar's funeral rites and a love of music – two attractive touches.[25] He transfers from the Roman people at large to Cinna at Cassius' direction the petitions urging Brutus to action. And, most significantly, the concern for appearances everywhere evident in Plutarch's demagogic Caesar Shakespeare partly transfers to Brutus, who spares Antony not because the murder would be dishonest and there was yet hope of change in him, as in Plutarch (volume 6, p. 198), but because the killing would 'seem too bloody' (2.1.162).

Sometimes the text challenges the subtext more directly; Julius Caesar, as MacCallum observed, occasionally contradicts North's Plutarch outright.[26] Plutarch's Brutus visits Caius Ligarius whereas Shakespeare's receives him. By all accounts, Caesar was a powerful swimmer; Plutarch tells the story of his leaping into the sea with several books to outswim a boat of hostile Egyptians (volume 5, p. 51). Yet Shakespeare's Cassius depicts Caesar as a weak swimmer who nearly drowned in the 'troubled Tiber' (1.2.100ff). Plutarch's Casca cries out in Greek at the moment of the assassination (volume 5, p. 67), but Shakespeare's Casca cannot understand Cicero's Greek speech (1.2.181–4). Caesar tries to read Artemidorus' bill of warning but cannot because of the crowd (volume 5, p. 66); Shakespeare's Caesar, in a significant and self-conscious gesture of largesse, refuses to con-

sider it: 'What touches us ourself shall be last serv'd' (3.1.8). Plutarch's Cassius gives Brutus a third of his money (volume 6, p. 211); Shakespeare's denies Brutus gold (4.3.70). And Plutarch's Cassius, a recent editor notes, would at times 'jest too brodely' (volume 6, p. 210), while the Cassius in the play is 'austere, critical, and unconvivial'.[27] The text flows from the fountainhead but also back and against it.

Finally, recent changes in critical thinking have led to the introduction of new texts as sources – a direct result of decreased emphasis on verbal iteration.[28] Critics now hunt for verbal and non-verbal signs of meaningful if submerged presence. Some, who go the old route, argue that such presence derives from a reading, remembering, and forgetting by the author. Others take a new route, the way of Biagio Conti with Virgil, for example, and argue that such presence is an encoded form in the text implicit in genre and in language itself.[29] The source is not, then, a book on the desk, on the shelf, above or below the author; it is in the text as it is being written. Another related possibility is that there is no source book at all but merely a phantom Ur-text, an assemblage of conspicuous generic features and conventions that exists in the minds of an

---

25 For the first see Arthur Humphreys (ed.), Julius Caesar, The Oxford Shakespeare (Oxford, 1984), p. 18; for the second, Jean-Marie Maguin, 'Preface to a Critical Approach to Julius Caesar, with a Chronological Catalogue of Shakespeare's Borrowings from North's Plutarch', Cahiers Élisabéthains, 4 (1973), 15–49, p. 28.

26 MacCallum, pp. 198ff.

27 Humphreys, p. 11.

28 This critical development may owe something to Kenneth Muir's demonstrations of 'polygenesis' several decades ago: 'Portents in Hamlet', Notes and Queries, 193 (1948), 54–5; 'Menenius's Fable', Notes and Queries, 198 (1953), 240–2; 'Pyramus and Thisbe: A Study in Shakespeare's Method', Shakespeare Quarterly, 5 (1954), 141–53; 'Shakespeare Among the Commonplaces', Review of English Studies, NS 10 (1959), 283–9.

29 Gian Biagio Conti, The Rhetoric of Imitation, trans. Charles Segal (Ithaca, 1986).

audience rather than in a single material text.[30] By whichever route taken, North's Plutarch, once regarded as the sole and preemptively powerful source, now finds itself in very mixed company. Critics have proposed as sources a variety of figures, texts, and movements: Euripides, Seneca, Cicero, Livy, Virgil, St Augustine, Marlowe, contemporary religious polemic, the tyrannicide debate, and Counter-Renaissance scepticism, to name only the most interesting.[31] The accumulated weight and subtlety of the argumentation impresses and often persuades. But, more important, the critics here represented subscribe to an expanded notion of the source. Many do not seek out the fountainhead at all, but search instead the deep and perilous waters of intertextual *écriture*.

At present, criticism characterizes the relationship between source and text to be complex and often contradictory. Paradoxically, this characterization finds some support in the old doctrine of *imitatio*, so dominant in the creative activity of the Renaissance. In fact, the relationship between Shakespeare's plays and sources might well be considered *sub specie imitationis*, as a kind of imitation. Sometimes Renaissance imitation proceeded by way of iteration, echo, or copying, complete with visible and intentional markers. Other times, and more often, it proceeded by way of subtle imitation, *ut intelligi simile queat potius quam dici*, in Petrarch's phrase, 'so that the likeness may be felt rather than defined'.[32] Such is clearly the case with Shakespeare's use of Plutarch as influence or background. Art historians, who may have some things to teach literary critics in such matters, have frequently noted this sort of influence in the Renaissance and have called it 'assimilation'.[33] What is more, Renaissance *imitatio* also furnishes many examples of source denial, a phenomenon labelled 'eristic' imitation by one prominent authority, 'dialectical' by another.[34] Shakespeare's use of Plutarch as subtext clearly qualifies as this sort of transaction. Once again, Renaissance art supplies

interesting parallels. Often a painter or sculptor denied his model by practising the

[30] Working from this perspective, Alan C. Dessen has explored Shakespeare's relations to neglected medieval drama in *Shakespeare and the Late Moral Plays* (Lincoln, Nebraska, and London, 1986).

[31] (Euripides) Jones, *Origins*, pp. 108–18; (Seneca) Robert Ornstein, 'Seneca and the Political Drama of *Julius Caesar*', *Journal of English and Germanic Philology*, 57 (1958), 51–6, John W. Velz, 'Clemency, Will, and Just Cause in *Julius Caesar*', *Shakespeare Survey 22* (1969), 109–118, pp. 112–13; (Cicero) Marvin L. Vawter, ' "Division 'tween Our Souls": Shakespeare's Stoic Brutus', *Shakespeare Studies*, 7 (1974), 173–95, and also his ' "After Their Fashion": Cicero and Brutus in *Julius Caesar*', *Shakespeare Studies*, 9 (1976), 205–19; (Livy) Ronald Berman, 'A Note on the Motives of Marcus Brutus', *Shakespeare Quarterly*, 23 (1972), 197–200; (Virgil in the heroic tradition) Reuben A. Brower, *Hero & Saint: Shakespeare and the Graeco-Roman Heroic Tradition* (New York and Oxford, 1971), pp. 217–38; (Virgil) Robert S. Miola, *Shakespeare's Rome* (New York and Cambridge, 1983), pp. 76–115; (St Augustine) J. L. Simmons, *Shakespeare's Pagan World: The Roman Tragedies* (Charlottesville, 1973), pp. 65–108; (Marlowe) Harry Morgan Ayres, 'Shakespeare's *Julius Caesar* in the Light of Some Other Versions', *PMLA*, 25 (1910), 183–227, pp. 221ff, Nicholas Brooke, 'Marlowe as Provocative Agent in Shakespeare's Early Plays', *Shakespeare Survey 14* (1961), 34–44, pp. 42–4; (religious polemic) David Kaula, ' "Let Us Be Sacrificers": Religious Motifs in *Julius Caesar*', *Shakespeare Studies*, 14 (1981), 197–214; (tyrannicide debate) Robert S. Miola, '*Julius Caesar* and the Tyrannicide Debate', *Renaissance Quarterly*, 38 (1985), 271–89; (scepticism) Joseph S. M. J. Chang, '*Julius Caesar* in the Light of Renaissance Historiography', *Journal of English and Germanic Philology*, 69 (1970), 63–71, Julian C. Rice, '*Julius Caesar* and the Judgment of the Senses', *Studies in English Literature*, 13 (1973), 238–55.

[32] I quote from Thomas M. Greene, *The Light in Troy: Imitation and Discovery in Renaissance Poetry* (New Haven and London, 1982), p. 95.

[33] See E. H. Gombrich, 'The Style *All'Antica*: Imitation and Assimilation', in *The Renaissance and Mannerism: Studies in Western Art: Acts of the Twentieth International Congress of the History of Art*, ed. Ida E. Rubin, et al., 2 (Princeton, 1963), 31–41, pp. 36–7. For a more general discussion see Goran Hermerén, *Influence in Art and Literature* (Princeton, 1975).

[34] See Greene, pp. 43f, and G. W. Pigman, III, 'Versions of Imitation in the Renaissance', *Renaissance Quarterly*, 33 (1980), 1–32.

visual equivalent of transference, usually called 'reversal', that is, the turning of figures around or the switching of their places. Such positional variations appear notably in the work of Giulio Romano, 'that rare Italian master' (*The Winter's Tale* 5.2.97). Writ large, manifesting itself in various forms, and expanded into an intercultural *machia*, eristic or dialectical imitation characterizes much Renaissance art and literature. Lorenzo Ghiberti in his Baptistery doors, for example, transforms a fallen and

crumpled warrior into the awakening Adam, a serene and sensual Venus into the sorrowful and tragic Eve.[35] And in his next Roman play Shakespeare will transform Plutarch's ageing voluptuaries into immortal lovers, Antony and Cleopatra.

---

[35] On Ghiberti see Benjamin Rowland, Jr, *The Classical Tradition in Western Art* (Cambridge, Mass., 1963), pp. 159–60.

THE SPECULATIVE EYE: PROBLEMATIC SELF-KNOWLEDGE IN 'JULIUS CAESAR'

WILLIAM O. SCOTT

Terry Eagleton began his early book on *Shakespeare and Society* by quoting from Ulysses' effort to draw Achilles into action in act 3, scene 3 of *Troilus and Cressida*; at Ulysses' urging, Achilles remarked on the notion that we see ourselves only by reflection:

> The beauty that is borne here in the face
> The bearer knows not, but commends itself
> To others' eyes . . .
> For speculation turns not to itself
> Till it hath travel'd and is mirror'd there
> Where it may see itself

and Ulysses continued,

> no man is the lord of anything,
> Though in and of him there be much
>   consisting,
> Till he communicate his parts to others
> (3.3.103–11, 115–17)[1]

Eagleton read these words as saying that 'uncommunicated qualities don't have any real existence at all; a man is not simply known to others through communication, he can only know his own experience by putting it in a communicable form' and that 'a man who contracts out of public life is contracting out of reality'. He did not discuss the parallel and in some ways more challenging exchange when Cassius tries to recruit Brutus for his conspiracy in act 1, scene 2 of *Julius Caesar*:

Cassius.
  Tell me, good Brutus, can you see your face?

Brutus.
  No, Cassius, for the eye sees not itself
  But by reflection, by some other things.
Cassius.
  'Tis just.
  And it is very much lamented, Brutus,
  That you have no such mirrors as will turn
  Your hidden worthiness into your eye,
  That you might see your shadow. I have heard
  Where many of the best respect in Rome,
  Except immortal Caesar, speaking of Brutus
  And groaning underneath this age's yoke,
  Have wish'd that noble Brutus had his eyes.
  (1.2.51–62)

Though Ulysses certainly has his own purposes in his scene, Cassius is even more obvious in pursuing self-interested objectives, and these call in doubt his claim to speak for society in interpreting Brutus. Thus Cassius' questioning is in turn questionable though it is not cancelled. In the development of modern literary theory too, critiques of both individual experience and social authority have made each seem increasingly complex and unstable; in a revisionary spirit one might now reread into Eagleton's early views something like Mikhail Bakhtin's proclamation of an open-

---

[1] *Shakespeare and Society* (1967), pp. 13–14. I have quoted more from *Troilus* than Eagleton did and have used, as throughout, the *Complete Works*, ed. David Bevington, 3rd edn (Glenview, 1980). I gratefully acknowledge the assistance of the University of Kansas General Research Fund grant 3439–0038.

ended polyphony of voices in the novel.[2] But there were doubts too in Shakespeare's own time about the individual's access to private experience of selfhood that have been overlooked, and in some sort postmodernism may actually stimulate a recovery of the past.

First, though, it is helpful to clarify the occasion of Brutus' and Cassius' dialogue. Brutus has reported the Soothsayer's warning to Caesar about the ides of March and has expressed a desire to withdraw from Caesar's ceremony; Cassius next complains of Brutus' recent pensiveness. The prophecy may be as powerful a stimulus as the witches' greetings to Macbeth, though it is addressed to neither of them and though for the moment Brutus may resemble a Banquo more than a Macbeth. Its eventual impact on Brutus is shown when, having decided on Caesar's death, he checks the calendar (2.1.40). Along with the potentially related question whether to join Caesar in the ritual by which he seeks an heir, the prophecy creates a good moment for Cassius to sound out Brutus.

These are political matters, and Brutus too is doubtless aware of their public nature, which probably underlies the verbal sparring on both sides. But he chooses to define his response as a solely personal one:

> If I have veil'd my look,
> I turn the trouble of my countenance
> Merely upon myself. Vexed I am
> Of late with passions of some difference,
> Conceptions only proper to myself,
> Which give some soil, perhaps, to my
>   behaviors.
> But let not therefore my good friends be
>   griev'd –
> Among which number, Cassius, be you one –
> Nor construe any further my neglect,
> Than that poor Brutus, with himself at war,
> Forgets the shows of love to other men.
>
> (1.2.37–47)[3]

Cassius' reply, which depends on the analogy with the eye's inability to see the face in response to Brutus' claim to turn inward, does not so much question the basis of personal qualities in the individual (as Ulysses' and Achilles' discussion does) as it denies the privileged status of Brutus' assertion of self-knowledge. The power to determine what Brutus may become (ironically a similar issue to Brutus' later deliberations about Caesar) resolves first into the power to perceive what he is now.

The claim of a uniquely privileged self-knowledge was by no means secure in Shakespeare's time, despite the impressions we are likely to form from popular moral tags. Evidence lies at hand in some of the most widely read authors, including sources or parallels that have been named for the passages in *Julius Caesar* and *Troilus and Cressida*.[4] Perhaps the simplest is Cicero's raising of a doubt in his *Tusculan Disputations*; he interprets the command of Apollo's oracle at Delphi, 'Know

---

[2] The example of Bakhtin is not casual: the view quoted from Eagleton resembles the thesis in *Marxism and the Philosophy of Language*, published under the name of V. N. Volosinov but argued to be Bakhtin's by Katerina Clark and Michael Holquist, *Mikhail Bakhtin* (Cambridge, Mass., 1984), pp. 160, 166. Without naming titles, Eagleton describes Raymond Williams, to whom his early book is dedicated, as a long-time enthusiast of Volosinov – *The Function of Criticism* (1984), p. 109. Bakhtin's views on the novel are expressed in *Problems of Dostoevsky's Poetics* and *The Dialogic Imagination*. Eagleton cites both the *Marxism* book and Bakhtin's book on Rabelais in *William Shakespeare* (Oxford, 1986), p. 106.

[3] His flight into privacy is well discussed by Jonathan Goldberg, *James I and the Politics of Literature* (Baltimore, 1983), pp. 170–1.

[4] There are discussions in the Oxford, Arden, and Cambridge editions of *Julius Caesar*, and the New Variorum edition of *Troilus and Cressida*. Sources for wording and ideas are discussed by Gary Taylor, '*Musophilus, Nosce Teipsum,* and *Julius Caesar*', *Notes and Queries*, NS 31 (June, 1984), 191–5. The ideas about eyes and reflections are treated as proverbial in Morris Palmer Tilley, *A Dictionary of the Proverbs in England in the Sixteenth and Seventeenth Centuries* (Ann Arbor, 1950), and R. W. Dent, *Shakespeare's Proverbial Language* (Berkeley, 1981), E231a and 232. There is much information on writings about self-knowledge in Rolf Soellner, *Shakespeare's Patterns of Self-Knowledge* (Columbus, 1972).

thyself', to mean 'Know thy soul' (I.52), and reasons as follows:

> the soule is not able in this bodye to see him selfe. No more is the eye whyche although he seeth all other thinges, yet (that whiche is one of the leaste) can not discerne his owne shape. But admit that the soule can not consider him selfe: howebeit perhaps he may. His operacions, as quyckenes of inuention, sure remembraunce, continuance and swiftnes of motion, it doth wel ynoughe perceyue. And these be greate, yea heauenlye, yea euerlastinge thinges.
>
> (I.67)[5]

There is a gap here, however Cicero may try to reduce it, between knowledge of the soul directly and knowledge merely through its actions. Human self-knowledge also suffers from comparison with divine self-intuition, as in the Neoplatonic meditations (with citations from Plotinus) of Philippe de Mornay's *Woorke concerning the trewnesse of the Christian Religion*: the discursively-reasoning human subject has a hard time knowing 'his owne Soule by the power of his Soule . . . For the maner of his discourse is but to proceede from kynd to kynd, and to passe from one reason to another. But on the contrary part, his mynd seeth not it selfe, but onely turneth into it selfe. . . .' In contrast, God's self-intuition yields 'a reflexion backe againe to it self, as a face doth in a Lookingglasse. . . . And whereas wee comprehend not our selves; that commeth of the darknesse and lumpishnesse of our flesh, which maketh us unlike our selves.'[6] Several difficulties are raised by Marcantonio Zimara, whose *Problemata* appeared in British editions of the pseudo-Aristotelian work of that name; he questions whether self-knowledge can be attained only by 'a reflexed action': 'to reflect and looke vnto himselfe, is a token that we are separated from the flesh. For he who would know himselfe, should be drawne from sensible affections, and how hard this is, no man is ignorant. Or is it because a man liueth by vnderstanding? But the vnderstanding of a man cannot conceiue himselfe, but after the vnderstanding of another, and this is very hard.'[7] Showing through the precise philosophical content of these difficulties is the notion that for a variety of reasons the discrepancies between knower and known hinder full self-knowledge; but if self-knowledge is merely of externals, it is only as certain as other knowledge. In Brutus' case an interested party directs the other knowledge and tries to weaken the status of self-knowledge.

The instabilities in *Julius Caesar* find closer analogues among critiques of self-knowledge that invoke a radical scepticism (even with a fideistic aim) towards all human knowledge. These involve a turning of statements that restrict knowledge back on their own origins to show that the mind is trapped in its own self-limitations and self-descriptions; though the play does not go so far in general statement, we may wish, for a start, to turn Cassius' words back on him and ask what mirror shows him himself, and how accurately. A world made up of selves each determined by all the others would not be simple or stable. Though he does not raise questions of this last sort, Sir John Davies gives a sharp critique in *Nosce Teipsum* of the problems of reflexive knowledge (however necessary it

---

5 *Those fyue qvestions, which Marke Tullye Cicero, disputed in his manor of Tuscalanum*, trans. John Dolman (1561), E6v–E7. Perhaps Cicero is influenced by Plato's distinction in *1 Alcibiades* (another source which has been claimed for Shakespeare), 132E–133E, between the soul itself and qualities or things which merely belong to the person.

6 Trans. Sir Philip Sidney, *Prose Works of Sir Philip Sidney*, ed. Albert Feuillerat (1912; repr. Cambridge, 1962), vol. 3, 252, 264–5; other references include 266, 270–1, and 296 (Plotinus).

7 *Problemes*, in *The Problemes of Aristotle* (Edinburgh, 1595), G5–G5v. Zimara's work appeared with Aristotle in at least the Latin edition of 1583 and the English ones of 1595 and 1597. He is mentioned as raising problems about self-knowledge in the oft-printed annotations by Claudius Minoes on Andrea Alciati's *Emblemata* (Emblem CLXXXVII, 'Submouendam ignorantiam'). He was very well known as a commentator on Aristotle and Averroës.

may be). The stanzas that are usually cited to parallel Shakespeare are these:

> Is it because the minde is like the eye,
>   (Through which it gathers knowledge by
>   degrees)
>   Whose rayes reflect not, but spread
>   outwardly,
>   Not seeing it selfe, when other things it
>   sees?
>
> No doubtlesse: for the minde can backward
>   cast
>   Upon her selfe her understanding light;
>   But she is so corrupt, and so defac't,
>   As her owne image doth her selfe affright.[8]
>
> (lines 105–12)

This corruption of the mind is explained better by Davies's retelling of the fall of Adam and Eve: the 'Spirit of lies' tempted them by suggesting 'That they were blind, because they saw not Ill', and their first act of self-knowledge was of the evil they had just learned to do (lines 13–24) in order to know. Self-knowledge was tainted from the start, and even now we are mocked by Socrates, Democritus, and the Delphic oracle (the devil's continuing triumph):

> For this, the wisest of all Morall men,
>   Said *he knew nought, but that he nought did
>   know*;
>   And the great mocking Maister, mockt not
>   then,
>   When he said, *Truth was buried deepe below.*
>
> For how may we to other things attaine?
>   When none of us his owne soule understands?
>   For which the Divell mockes our curious
>   braine,
>   When *know thy selfe*, his oracle commands.
>
> (lines 77–84)

The powers of human and diabolic knowledge combine only to show us how little we know of ourselves and to taunt us with the impossible. In a related passage Du Bartas (who says in another place that 'as the Eye perceaves / All but it selfe, even so our Soule conceaves / All

save her owne selfes Essence') tells that before the Fall,

> Mankind was then a thousand fold more wise
> Then now, blind error had not bleard his eyes,
> With mists which make th'*Athenian Sage*
>   suppose
> That *nought he knowes, save this, that nought he
>   knowes.*
> That even light *Pirrhons* wavering fantasies
> Reave him the skill his unskill to agnize.
> And th'*Abderite*, within a well obscure
> As deep as darke, the truth of things
>   immure.[9]

Socrates and Democritus are here joined as critics of the limits of knowledge by Pyrrho, spokesman for a radically sceptical school: he would disallow as being dogmatic even the one point of knowledge claimed by Socrates. But then he would have to refrain from actually asserting universal doubt, because that assertion, too, being a positive statement, would contradict its own principle; thus it is that his 'fantasies / Reave him the skill his unskill to agnize' ('la fantasque inconstance / Luy oste le sçavoir de sçavoir l'ignorance').[10] The weakened human reason strikes at itself by the very power of language through which it

---

8 *Poems*, ed. Robert Krueger (Oxford, 1975), p. 9 (ll. 105–12). Other pertinent passages include ll. 185–8 and 761–4. J. L. Simmons says that this first-quoted passage 'shows the incoherence of the image when pursued too far on the literal level' – *Shakespeare's Pagan World* (Charlottesville, 1973), p. 96.

9 Guillaume de Saluste, Sieur du Bartas, *The Divine Weeks and Works*, trans. Josuah Sylvester, ed. Susan Snyder (Oxford, 1979), vol. I, 283, 323–4 (I.vi.773–5; II.i. 'Eden' 261–8). His knowledge of Greek philosophy is evident in 'Le Triomfe de la foi', Chant Second.

10 The French is quoted from *Works*, ed. Urban Tigner Holmes, Jr, John Coriden Lyons, and Robert White Linker (Chapel Hill, 1940), vol. III, 8 (ll. 229–30). Pyrrhonian scepticism is described by Diogenes Laertius (IX.61f.) and by Sextus Empiricus, *Outlines of Pyrrhonism*. In I.14 Sextus discusses the statements such as 'All things are false' which cancel themselves out in the manner of the liar paradox, my next topic.

must operate. In the form of a single statement rather than a general philosophical position, a model for such self-undermining would be the liar paradox, 'This very sentence is false', which refers to itself so as to seem false if true, and true if false. There is good reason to think that Shakespeare knew this paradox from Thomas Wilson's *The Rule of Reason* (1553 or later edition).[11] Though there is nothing in *Julius Caesar* like the content of this paradox or these sceptical views, there are major occasions when the text is at war with itself in this fashion (even if the war is undeclared as in Cassius' mirror concept which simply invites other applications). Self-reference generates highly productive conflicts, especially when the reference is to the action as itself a play.

In a play which throws so much open to interpretation – the meaning of dreams, comparison of rhetorical skills to motivate political reactions – it is fitting that Cicero complains that 'men may construe things after their fashion, / Clean from the purpose of the things themselves' (1.3.34–5). But it may still be questioned whether things do have a purpose that can be specified as Cicero seems to assume. Though he did not use it in the play, Shakespeare had before him in Plutarch's *Life of Brutus* a view, propounded by Cassius as Epicurean philosophy, which gives a broad scope to subjectivity:

In our secte, Brutus, we have an opinion, that we doe not alwayes feele, or see, that which we suppose we doe both see and feele: but that our senses beeing credulous, and therefore easily abused (when they are idle and unoccupied in their owne objects) are induced to imagine they see and conjecture that, which they in truth doe not. For, our minde is quicke and cunning to worke (without eyther cause or matter) any thinge in the imagination whatsoever.

But yet there is a further cause of this in you. For you being by nature given to melancholick discoursing, and of late continually occupied: your wittes and sences having bene overlabored, doe easilier yeelde to such imaginations.[12]

If Brutus is as melancholic as Cassius says here, there is another basis for considering that 'cause or matter' is absent. Timothy Bright finds absence of an object characteristic of melancholy:

The reason is because, they measure all outward accidents, by that they finde of discontentment within: not that the humor that discontenteth is any instrument of passion, or carieth with it faculty to be displeased: but because it disquieteth the body, and giueth discontentment to nature, it is occasion why displeasures are made great: and where there is no cause, nature troubled within, faireth as greatly displeased with that which outwardly should not displease. . . .[13]

The melancholic's self-perception would be especially problematic and circular, for the perceptions on which it depends would be themselves conditioned strongly by the self as perceiver. All these circumstances invite manipulation of appearances by Cassius, Caesar, and in remarkable ways Brutus. The situation has a notable effect on the individualistic politics of the play, well described by A. W. Bell-

---

[11] The relevant passage from Wilson is in the edition by Richard S. Sprague (Northridge, 1972), pp. 216–17, where Epimenides the Cretan, describing Cretans as liars, self-referentially undercuts his own statement. I have given reasons for Wilson's pertinence and have applied the paradox critically to Shakespeare's plays in two articles in *Shakespeare Quarterly*: 'The Paradox of Timon's Self-Cursing', 35 (1984), 290–304; and 'Macbeth's – And Our – Self-Equivocations', 37 (1986), 160–74.

[12] *Narrative and Dramatic Sources of Shakespeare*, ed. Geoffrey Bullough (1964), vol. 5, p. 116. This, along with the speech by Cicero, is cited by D. J. Palmer, 'The Self-Awareness of the Tragic Hero', in *Shakespearian Tragedy*, ed. David Palmer and Malcolm Bradbury, Stratford-upon-Avon Studies 20 (1984), p. 138.

[13] *A Treatise of Melancholie* (1586), facsimile ed. Hardin Craig (New York, 1940), p. 96. Brutus is discussed as melancholic by W. Nicholas Knight, 'Brutus' Motivation and Melancholy', *Upstart Crow*, 5 (Fall 1984), 108–24. Though the description is just, Brutus seems, for reasons which will appear, to be more self-conscious and perhaps therefore less pathological than Knight describes.

ringer: 'The cross-assessments and counter-estimates, the generalisations on men and their worth, are not mere constructions of ambiguous "characters" on Shakespeare's part, but fall essentially into a dialectic of suspicion.'[14] Suspicion is doubtless a more honest fulfilment of Cassius' proposal that persons evaluate each other than the portrayal of it that he gives to Brutus.

For these several reasons given or implied by the various writers, self-knowledge, either direct or reflected, is problematic: the otherness of the soul as object of knowledge from the consciousness-in-a-body that is to do the knowing, the imperfectness of reflection in an imperfect being, the difficulty of modelling knowledge to oneself after knowledge of others, the tendency of self-limiting descriptions of oneself to reflect back on the means and degree to which they are known, and the relativity of the perceptions by which one might judge oneself (including especially their dependence on that very same self). To these can be added a comment by Elizabeth Freund on the passage in *Troilus and Cressida* which lays open the connection with paradoxical self-reference:

The drift of the text Ulysses is so 'rapt in' concerns a perennial philosophical and literary critical topos: we cannot step outside our own minds and must rely on reflection, echo, and mirroring otherness to constitute us. The 'eye', organ of sight, cannot see itself but by reflection; the 'I' cannot know itself with any immediacy, but must loop along strange courses of speculative mirroring which prohibit it from ever coinciding with itself. Achilles remains unperturbed by the prospect of a strange loop which puts in question the very existence of himself as subject, and he persists in believing that 'speculation' (eyesight, insight, consciousness, the self) does eventually – even if indirectly – rise into view. But Ulysses pursues the more radical conclusion, that no man can ever be in full possession of himself, and continues to attack and undercut Achilles' confident self-possession until, by the end of the scene, Achilles is no longer so sure that he can see himself.[15]

Self-knowledge involves self-reference, and in both processes the subject and object fail to coincide. To introduce another person as mediator of self-knowledge is to compound the discrepancy, especially if that person is duplicitous as, for instance, Cassius is. Yet (to continue the application to Brutus and Cassius) after Cassius had shown Brutus a reflection, the situation might not be as much in his control as he thought or wished, if Brutus could in turn adjust his self-image to his own perceptions of Cassius. (Mirrors can reflect reciprocally, though Cassius takes care not to say so.) Trusting though Brutus is, something of the dialectic of suspicion might operate. But Brutus would not be in control either, for self-knowledge would presumably change him, especially to the degree that it involved something alien introduced by Cassius. For this reason, even if he could perceive a good deal about particular strategies of his own and Cassius' at particular moments, Brutus would really never be able to coincide fully with himself in self-knowledge, view himself from an 'absolute' or unchanging position outside his interaction with Cassius. He

---

[14] A. W. Bellringer, '*Julius Caesar*: Room Enough', *Critical Quarterly*, 12 (1970), 31–48; rpr. in *Shakespeare's Wide and Universal Stage*, ed. C. B. Cox and D. J. Palmer (Manchester, 1984), pp. 146–163; p. 152.

[15] ' "Ariachne's Broken Woof": the Rhetoric of Citation in *Troilus and Cressida*', in *Shakespeare and the Question of Theory*, ed. Patricia Parker and Geoffrey Hartman (New York, 1985), pp. 28–9. 'Strange loops' are discussed in relation to the self-reference of the liar paradox by Douglas Hofstadter, *Gödel, Escher, Bach* (New York, 1979). In *Gadamer's Hermeneutics* (New Haven, 1985), Joel C. Weinsheimer applies Gödel's reasoning about self-reference in mathematical axioms to the claims of Hegelian self-knowledge (as an explanation of Gadamer's views): self-knowledge, though it may be true, must be incomplete (as it is, given the nature of language) or else potentially paradoxical (pp. 37–59). William R. Brashear discusses the implications for tragedy of noncorrespondence of knower and known according to Schopenhauer, Nietzsche, and Spengler in *The Gorgon's Head* (Athens, Georgia, 1977), pp. 1–26.

could never make an absolute, accurate statement of self-knowledge that would be definitive, even for that moment.

Thus, although in a large sense self-knowledge and its relation to knowledge of others must be questioned, Brutus may well have a keen eye for Cassius' immediate strategies.[16] In the second scene he responds not directly to Cassius' offer to be a mirror but rather to the obvious political implications in his report of 'many of the best respect in Rome, / Except immortal Caesar, speaking of Brutus / And groaning underneath this age's yoke'; Brutus replies, 'Into what dangers would you lead me, Cassius' (1.2.59–61, 63). Anyone who can then discuss whether Caesar's crowning is to be feared (a slip of the tongue that may be calculated) and can desire that Cassius might impart to him 'aught toward the general good' has a fair idea of what he expects to hear. He keeps his counsel about what he does hear, the obvious envy by Cassius of the Caesar whom Brutus professes to love well, yet he shows not only awareness of Cassius' purpose but some acceptance: 'What you would work me to, I have some aim' (1.2.163). Brutus is thus a willing collaborator in being manipulated; but if self-knowledge alone is problematic, compounded with self-management and collusion it is doubly or trebly so.

Brutus' soliloquy in the orchard sounds most natural not as isolated self-reflection but as meditation conditioned by an internal dialogue with an imagined other, someone like Cassius:

> It *must be* by his death. And, for *my* part,
> I know no personal cause to spurn at him,
> But for the general. He would be crown'd.
> How that might change his nature, there's the
>   question.
> It is the bright day that brings forth the adder,
> And that craves wary walking. Crown him
>   that,
> And then I *grant* we put a sting in him
> That at his will he may do danger with.

> Th' abuse of greatness is when it disjoins
> Remorse from power. And, to *speak truth* of
>   Caesar,
> I have not known when his affections sway'd
> More than his reason. But 'tis a common
>   proof
> That lowliness is young ambition's ladder,
> Whereto the climber-upward turns his face;
> But when he once attains the upmost round,
> He then unto the ladder turns his back,
> Looks in the clouds, scorning the base degrees
> By which he did ascend. So Caesar may.
> Then, lest he may, prevent.   (2.1.10–28)

My italics mark the clearest signs of dialogic response. Brutus begins with what seems like a conclusion;[17] but he would have been brought to that point as if by an unheard voice letting him reach the decision himself. Death is no new concept to him in these deliberations, and the word needs no emphasis; the change is rather in the assertion of will signalled by the verbs. Brutus next defines himself in contrast to the unheard other by his lack of personal animus and his ability to speak truly of Caesar, yet he must concede decisively that Caesar would be crowned and that crowning puts a sting in him. Brutus carries on this persuasion by the imagined other-in-himself through flagrantly rhetorical means: by application of abstract principles to individual cases, and by argument from analogy.[18] Although these arts

---

[16] His awareness of Cassius' doings is discussed by Camille Wells Slights, *The Casuistical Tradition* (Princeton, 1981), p. 83.

[17] Palmer, p. 136. He also says of Brutus that 'The sequence of his speeches progresses inwards, revealing a disordered judgement' – and perhaps, one might add, a strange loop.

[18] Slights, pp. 82–91 (with emphasis, however, on a casuistical rather than rhetorical tradition); Gayle Greene, 'The Language of Brutus' Soliloquy: Similitude and Self-Deception in Shakespeare's *Julius Caesar*', in *Humanitas: Essays in Honor of Ralph Ross*, ed. Quincy Howe, Jr (Claremont, 1977), pp. 74–86. The rhetorical emphasis in the play is justly described by Anne Barton, '*Julius Caesar* and *Coriolanus*: Shakespeare's Roman World of Words', in *Shakespeare's Craft*, ed. Philip H.

are ultimately directed against himself, they are at first weapons in a constant mental skirmish with the idea of Cassius' influence.

Brutus' final direction in this speech seems all the more an artful self-manipulation:

> And, since the quarrel
> Will bear no color for the thing he is,
> Fashion it thus: that what he is, augmented,
> Would run to these and these extremities.
> And therefore think him as a serpent's egg
> Which, hatch'd, would, as his kind, grow
>   mischievous,
> And kill him in the shell.   (lines 28–34)

But A. D. Nuttall rightly puts the emphasis instead on the abstract argument Brutus is pursuing (again, one might add, a more understandable activity if it serves an internal polemic): Nuttall paraphrases 'Fashion it thus' as 'Let's try the argument this way.'[19] His final point, though, is that even if the argument is not itself an attempt by Brutus to dictate a motive to himself, it eventually may become that: 'the proper corruption of moral abstraction is diabolical cynicism'. Surely it is here that self-delusion takes place: though Brutus has consciously cultivated an imagined debate, the dispute does not really establish by rational inquiry what would be sufficient motive for killing Caesar, but rather it becomes itself that motive. Process usurps over substance, and mental staging impinges on overt action. The rhetorical quality of Roman culture (reproduced in Elizabethan education) projects itself into dramatic imagining, and this dramatic pre-enactment in turn governs the act of assassination that will be staged for us. Brutus' self-consciousness thus generates its own self-altering self-reference, a metadrama that rewrites his internal drama and thereby shapes the overt one that we see.

Brutus acknowledges the decisiveness of his commitment though he feels its cost:

> Since Cassius first did whet me against
>   Caesar,
> I have not slept.

Between the acting of a dreadful thing
And the first motion, all the interim is
Like a phantasma, or a hideous dream.
The Genius and the mortal instruments
Are then in council; and the state of man,
Like to a little kingdom, suffers then
The nature of an insurrection.   (lines 61–9)

In this he is like Macbeth, but he himself is the dagger of the mind, to be held by another. He well knows and accepts that he has been whetted by Cassius.[20] He seems to view his suffering not as a warning to turn back but quite the contrary, as a goading to take relief in action. By the end of the scene images of sickness are being converted to frenzied activity through an effort of will: Portia's wound to Brutus' prayer that he may be worthy of her in conspiracy, and Ligarius' probably feigned sickness to companionship in the exploit.

If Brutus' attitude seems strangely self-detached, it befits not only the knowing paradox of self-imaging through others but an ironic distancing from the shows of Caesar's politics. The tone is set by Casca as he describes the display that incited the rebels, Caesar's refusal of a crown:

I can as well be hang'd as tell the manner of it. It was mere foolery; I did not mark it. I saw Mark Antony offer him a crown – yet 'twas not a crown neither, 'twas one of these coronets – and, as I told you, he

---

Highfill, Jr (Carbondale, 1982), pp. 24–47, and by James R. Siemon, *Shakespearean Iconoclasm* (Berkeley, 1985), pp. 153–66. Constitution of an individual through the words of another is a subject of Pierre Spriet, 'Amour et politique: le discours de l'autre dans *Julius Caesar*', *Coriolan* (Travaux de l'Université de Toulouse-Le Mirail, Série B, Tome 5, 1984), pp. 227–39.

19 *A New Mimesis* (1983), p. 108. Perhaps Brutus' mind is almost running ahead to a justifying speech he would make in the Forum; the outline has a heading 'Extremities', though the subtopics are as yet unspecified.

20 The note on l. 61 by the Oxford editor, Arthur Humphreys, partially agrees with this interpretation; but I do not think the implications of 'whet' are unconscious for Brutus.

put it by once; but, for all that, to my thinking, he would fain have had it. Then he offer'd it to him again; then he put it by again; but, to my thinking, he was very loath to lay his fingers off it.

If the tag-rag people did not clap him and hiss him, according as he pleas'd and displeas'd them, as they use to do the players in the theatre, I am no true man.

. . . when he perceiv'd the common herd was glad he refus'd the crown, he pluck'd me ope his doublet and offer'd them his throat to cut. An I had been a man of any occupation, if I would not have taken him at a word, I would I might go to hell among the rogues.　(1.2.235–42, 258–61, 263–8)

Caesar, like Richard III appearing between two bishops to reject an offer of the throne (*Richard III*, 3.7), has mastered the art of the political feeler, which allows him to claim credit now for refusing what he most wants but which also prepares for eventual acceptance. For the more knowing, the performance is, if need be, a transparent ruse that coerces with the force of political prophecy; its effect is to be like the Scrivener's response to another of Richard's stratagems, 'Who is so gross / That cannot see this palpable device? / Yet who so bold but says he sees it not?' (3.6.10–12). As if displaying humility, Caesar also makes an offer to the crowd (like Richard reversing the hostility of Lady Anne) of his undefended body: but again he tries to intimidate possible rebels by showing how safe he is. Almost to foreshadow the assassination, Casca thinks of taking literally this offer that was not meant so; the cynical display is an occasion for a cynical reaction. He looks on Caesar's show with an unwilling suspension of disbelief. Brutus' response too is jaded: where public life is lie and show, and is at least half meant to be known as such, it is paradoxically likely (and not unknown in our own time) that he should willingly connive at distorting his image of himself to prepare for action. And as audience we are yet more directly touched by Casca's gibe at playgoers: powerless to alter a famous event of history and wanting the fictive-

historical show to go on however bloody, we anticipate with the eagerness of tragic audiences for dramatic irony a more literal enactment of Caesar's open-doublet gesture.

The conspiracy can rise to an acceptable claim of nobility only by an effort of will, and Brutus at once sets out to achieve it. As if to ennoble the deed by style and theatricality he sets high standards for the conspirators:

> do not stain
> The even virtue of our enterprise,
> Nor th' insuppressive mettle of our spirits,
> To think that or our cause or our
> 　　performance
> Did need an oath . . .
>
> O, that we then could come by Caesar's
> 　　spirit,
> And not dismember Caesar! But, alas,
> Caesar must bleed for it. And, gentle friends,
> Let's kill him boldly, but not wrathfully;
> Let's carve him as a dish fit for the gods,
> Not hew him as a carcass fit for hounds.
>
> Let not our looks put on our purposes,
> But bear it as our Roman actors do,
> With untir'd spirits and formal constancy.
> 　　　　(2.1.132–6, 169–74, 225–7)

As critics have said, he tries himself to write a tragedy in which the act of killing Caesar is purified.[21] The artifice of such writing, evidenced by the resistance of fact and eventually by the course of the play, is as clear in its self-undermining as a liar paradox.

As the conspirators finally enact their sanctified bloody deed, they at once look forward to future performances which already for us carry their own belying:

Brutus.

　　Stoop, Romans, stoop,

---

21 Sigurd Burkhardt, *Shakespearean Meanings* (Princeton, 1968), pp. 7–8; Nicholas Brooke, *Shakespeare's Early Tragedies* (1968), pp. 152–3; Lawrence Danson, *Tragic Alphabet* (New Haven, 1974), pp. 56–67 (the latter two critics with emphasis on the failure of purification). An earlier treatment of ritual and counter-ritual is Brents Stirling, *Unity in Shakespearian Tragedy* (New York, 1956), pp. 44–53.

And let us bathe our hands in Caesar's blood
Up to the elbows, and besmear our swords.
Then walk we forth, even to the market-place,
And, waving our red weapons o'er our heads,
Let's all cry, 'Peace, freedom, and liberty!'
Cassius.
Stoop, then, and wash. [*They bathe their hands and weapons.*] How many ages hence
Shall this our lofty scene be acted over
In states unborn and accents yet unknown!
Brutus.
How many times shall Caesar bleed in sport,
That now on Pompey's basis lies along
No worthier than the dust!
Cassius.
So oft as that shall be,
So often shall the knot of us be call'd
The men that gave their country liberty.

(3.1.105–19)

The spectacle of stage blood, so popular in Shakespeare's time, reinforces the word-picturing,[22] but at the same time it both corrupts the verbal purification that Brutus sought and reminds us, the tragic spectators, of our thirst for gore. Moreover, in the contrast between the play that the characters thought they were staging for posterity and the way we actually judge the outcome we see how 'history denies their dreams'.[23] Here is a truer action of the mirror than in Cassius' pretensions to represent Brutus: all the characters on stage have their being only as we the audience judge them, but they are in turn a mirror held up to disclose and determine for us our own nature. We see that Caesar bleeds in the sport now played by his jubilant killers, but we know that they themselves will bleed. And are those future tragedies, which are called sport by an actor in the present tragedy, any more or less sportive as entertainment than what we see at the moment? There is moreover no reassuring distinction between reality and its enactment either present or future, since all that we see is staged and our own existence is paradoxically drawn into that staging by the metadramatic mirror. And what is our own sportive nature if we behold in the mirror the expected and desired tragic bloodbath?

More positively, the mental force exerted by Brutus to make his deed other than it is can be viewed as poetic. Probably the word 'sport' is only coincidence, but a comment by Plutarch as he prepares to discuss Alexander the Great puts importance on the smallest mental activity and, somewhat like Cassius, compares the image of the face:

the noblest deedes doe not alwayes shew mens vertues and vices, but oftentimes a light occasion, a word, or some sporte makes mens naturall dispositions and maners appeare more plaine, then the famous battells wonne, wherein are slaine tenne thowsande men, or the great armies, or cities wonne by siege or assault. For like as painters or drawers of pictures, which make no accompt of other partes of the bodie, do take the resemblaunces of the face and favor of the countenance, in the which consisteth the judgement of their maners and disposition: even so they must geve us leave to seeke out the signes and tokens of the minde only, and thereby shewe the life of either of them, referring you unto others to wryte the warres, battells, and other great thinges they did.[24]

Here is almost a challenge to the dramatist to project an internal life into history imaginatively. The imaginative poetic power or 'phantasie' is to George Puttenham a mirror, though there are both false and true glasses: 'And this phantasie may be resembled to a glasse as hath bene sayd, whereof there be many tempers and manner of makinges, as the *perspectiues* doe acknowledge, for some be false glasses and shew thinges otherwise than they

---

22 Maurice Charney, *Shakespeare's Roman Plays* (Cambridge, Mass., 1961), p. 51.

23 Thomas F. Van Laan, *Role-Playing in Shakespeare* (Toronto, 1978), p. 160.

24 *Plutarch's Lives*, trans. Sir Thomas North, ed. George Wyndham, Tudor Translations (1895), vol. 4, p. 298. Reuben A. Brower, *Hero & Saint* (Oxford, 1971), p. 207, remarks on Plutarch's failure to follow his precept.

be in deede, and others right as they be in deede. . . . '[25] These ambivalent notions are put to their hardest test in tragedy where the images are hard to distinguish and where the characters make their choices knowing the difficulties.

The outcome of the deed is foreshadowed almost as soon as Antony comes upon the bloody scene. At once he seems overcome with grief, but he does not lose control of himself:

> O mighty Caesar! Dost thou lie so low?
> Are all thy conquests, glories, triumphs, spoils,
> Shrunk to this little measure? Fare thee well. –
> I know not, gentlemen, what you intend,
> Who else must be let blood, who else is rank;
> If I myself, there is no hour so fit
> As Caesar's death's hour, nor no instrument
> Of half that worth as those your swords, made rich
> With the most noble blood of all this world.
> I do beseech ye, if you bear me hard,
> Now, whilst your purpled hands do reek and smoke,
> Fulfill your pleasure.   (3.1.149–60)

His feelings may well be sincere, but if they are they also serve a politic purpose by making him seem trustworthy in any possible deal with the conspirators.[26] He actually repeats Caesar's gesture in the coronation episode of putting himself at the others' mercy, though not as a show of strength; yet the conspirators are in fact in a weak position, for they must treat him gently if they are to prove themselves in their own minds (or at least in Brutus' mind) not to be butchers. He places an important proviso on any compact he might make with them:

> *Antony.*
> Friends am I with you all, and love you all,
> Upon this hope, that you shall give me reasons
> Why and wherein Caesar was dangerous.

> *Brutus.*
> Or else were this a savage spectacle.
> Our reasons are so full of good regard
> That were you, Antony, the son of Caesar,
> You should be satisfied.   (lines 221–7)

He thus manages to reduce Brutus' project of justifying the death to a condition for a political bargain (an empty one, since Antony has already privately made up his mind). Of course it will also become a public rhetorical contest in the Forum, and that major concession Antony arranges at once, while a show of fairness is still uppermost in Brutus' mind. The old cynical politics of Caesar still live in Antony's somewhat calculated emotional shows and in his purposes which are meant to be partly divined. Antony also knows something like the craftiness of Cassius' mirror tactics: the image of himself he shows to Brutus, or allows him to discover in half-hidden purposes, will minister to the image that Brutus wants to have of himself as sanctified killer.

The triumph of Antony's funeral oration is even more the triumph of the Caesarian politics of show, along with the rhetoric that mirrors and serves them. Again he trots out the display of Caesar's refusing the crown to establish what was always its crudest meaning, and he is obvious in his use of irony and rhetorical question, and also of litotes or perhaps occupatio:[27]

---

[25] *The Arte of English Poesie*, ed. Gladys Doidge Willcock and Alice Walker (Cambridge, 1936), p. 19. This passage is cited by Palmer, p. 139. The element of deceit in figurative language according to Puttenham is discussed by Inga-Stina Ewbank, 'Shakespeare's Liars' (British Academy Shakespeare Lecture, 1983), *Proceedings of the British Academy*, 69 (1983), p. 166.

[26] Alessandro Serpieri, 'Reading the Signs: towards a Semiotics of Shakespearean Drama', in *Alternative Shakespeares*, ed. John Drakakis (1985), p. 129. He also notices (p. 134) that Antony's soliloquy revealing his stratagem (ll. 255–76) parallels one by Cassius after he has worked on Brutus (1.2.308–22).

[27] Serpieri discusses litotes, paralepsis (occupatio), and negation among Antony's techniques (p. 133).

> You all did see that on the Lupercal
> I thrice presented him a kingly crown,
> Which he did thrice refuse. Was this
>   ambition?
> Yet Brutus says he was ambitious,
> And, sure, he is an honorable man.
> I speak not to disprove what Brutus spoke,
> But here I am to speak what I do know.
>
> (3.2.97–103)

The heavyhandedness of his rhetoric and its contrast with our subtler assessments of character produce opposite effects on us and on the plebeians (though they have been, and remain, parodies of the theatre audience). The result is well described by Nicholas Brooke:

His repulsive 'Friends, Romans, countrymen' speech is an exhibition of the destruction of reason by rhetoric; the continuous play on 'Brutus is an honourable man' becomes unbearable in its insistence – to us – on its truth, at the same time that it is used to enforce – on the crowd – the belief that it is not true.   (p. 157)

Almost the same divergence occurs in the beginning of his speech:

> I come to bury Caesar, not to praise him.
> The evil that men do lives after them;
> The good is oft interred with their bones.
> So let it be with Caesar.   (lines 76–9)

Though his statement of intention seems straightforward to his hearers in the Forum at the time, he means them to discover gradually his purpose of actually praising Caesar and to congratulate themselves on their sagacity in sharing in his rhetoric (his tactics of flattery might parody Cassius' initial handling of Brutus). Thus too the crowd would come to perceive a 'good' that ought to live after Caesar, first when his will is read and then when they resolve to avenge his death. For us, who know Antony's resolve that 'Caesar's spirit, ranging for revenge, / With Ate by his side come hot from hell, / Shall in these confines with a monarch's voice / Cry "Havoc!" and let slip the dogs of war' (3.1.271–4), the intended effect of his speech

sounds more like one of the evils living after Caesar. Somewhat like Cassius, Antony projects to his auditors the images he desires them to have of Caesar and themselves (and of course Brutus and the rest), partly by their planned divining of his not-so-hidden meaning. Behind all this there is another art hidden from them in his deeper purposes; if they knew of it, they might not be moved as they are, but one cynically suspects that they would nonetheless. Meanwhile, on the less consoling metadramatic level, the plebeians who execute and partly mirror Antony's intention are parodic versions of us.

In the abstract, as well as in the practical examples displayed by Antony, verbal irony is an especially paradoxical intertwining of notions of truth and falsity. Irony is transparent dissimulation, and its transparency is what distinguishes it from lying; the irony must at once be apparent to the initiated reader. Yet it could be said that a text must be always already understood by the reader in order to be comprehended at all, and this oddity would seem to be especially the case with ironic texts. Further, to the extent that a text contains a signal of its irony, that signal destroys in literalism the irony it displays, so that an ideal irony would dispense altogether with signals.[28] From this viewpoint, irony almost makes the liar paradox, with its overt statement that undoes itself by self-reference, seem unproblematic by comparison. In this play, though, there are multiple levels of paradox which are latent as irony is, and they are all the more hidden when they seem to have disclosed something of themselves. The half-open political moves and the staged disclosures of character (one's own or someone else's) are reversed by what remains for the time hidden;

---

[28] These points about irony are made by Beda Allemann, 'De l'ironie en tant que principe littéraire', *Poétique*, 36 (November, 1978), 388–96. He does not draw a comparison to the liar paradox.

yet events become overt enough in the end for Brutus and Cassius, and therefore us.

Metadramatically too we would like to see and refer to or mirror ourselves in the best qualities of Brutus, especially his self-description, which seems to be our way into his character and into the whole play. But Brutus all but self-consciously turns his best into a great mistake; and apart from that the play continually forces us to compare ourselves and the world we know with characters and situations that are less than perceptive and ideal. Whether through Renaissance puzzlings about the limits and difficulty of self-knowledge, the traditional liar paradox, Cassius' disingenuous notions about mirrors, the metadramatic vision of tragedy as a blood sport, or some more modern problematics, we may have to concede that like Brutus we did not always already know and therefore never will, can never complete the task without paradox, nor indeed begin. Yet these statements themselves claim that *Julius Caesar* has shown Brutus and us a great deal.

LEARNING BY TALKING:
CONVERSATION IN 'AS YOU LIKE IT'

MARTHA RONK LIFSON

Just before the marriage celebration in *As You Like It* while Rosalind is off stage changing into her wedding dress, Touchstone delivers a long set piece on various sorts of lies used in quarrels and duels. He ends with, 'Your If is the only peacemaker. Much virtue in If' (5.4.102–3). Immediately, Rosalind and Celia return with Hymen who pronounces a vision of marriage as an aspect of cosmic harmony; and in rhyme:

> Then is there mirth in heaven
> When earthly things made even
> > Atone together.　　　(5.4.108–10)[1]

In this paper I propose to examine the virtues of 'supposing', of 'if' especially as it defines and frames the conversations between Rosalind and Orlando, but also and by extension as it stands for the importance of some deceit to work out the complexities of conversation and sexuality between the lovers, and to bring the play to its happy conclusion.[2] The sort of habit of mind which the play encourages and which I wish to describe by focusing on this word 'if' is the habit of mind that allows for comedy and romance; for example, if it is possible for such a place as Arden to exist, perhaps it is also possible to bridge the gap between an ideal of some sort and the 'real world' of the play, and to bring some of the one into the other. Or, if spring comes again each year, so might one rediscover a lost child, a lost innocence, a lapsed generosity. If two people can learn to converse in complex and

various ways, perhaps convention itself – which returns powerfully at the end of *As You Like It* – will mean something different. Moreover, such a habit of mind also encourages a kind of mental slippage that positions and re-positions various items in relation to one another: one aspect of a character with another aspect, one character and another, this lover and that, on stage and off stage, life and theatre ('all the world's a stage'), passion and civility, childhood and maturity, male and female, clichéd expressions of love and expressions of love. It implies a way of knowing oneself, others, the world.

Obviously this is not the only Shakespearian play to operate in this way, but *As You Like It* does, it seems to me, draw particular attention to what happens as a result of such complex comparisons and ways of imagining, and to effect analogies between what happens between Rosalind and Orlando and the larger world of the play and the larger world itself. Many critics have noted that *As You Like It* is a

---

[1] All references to the play are to the Signet Classic Shakespeare edition, *As You Like It*, edited by Albert Gilman (1963; New York, rpt. 1972 in *The Complete Signet Classic Shakespeare*).

[2] I here agree with and am indebted to several pages in David Young's book on pastoral: 'I cannot help but think that the atmosphere of artifice and hypothesis is also engendered by the remarkably extensive use of "if" in *As You like It*, as though the grammar that most suited a world like this one was conditional.' *The Heart's Forest* (New Haven, 1972), p. 46 and pp. 46–50.

play filled with references to education and that Rosalind educates Orlando in order to render him worthy of her, that she offers him a sense of humorous perspective.[3] What interests me is what in its most exact form they teach each other; what and in what ways they engage in a discussion that is educative; and what it is about this mode that allows them and us to believe in the ending of comedy.

The sort of learning that goes on for both Orlando and Rosalind is not the learning of rules or precepts for a happy marriage, or even the learning of a sort of wit necessary to get on with another person, but something about exchange, the exchange that occurs in conversation and that makes change possible. Orlando changes because he learns about imagining in a different way from the ways in which his neglected childhood has allowed him; but also Rosalind, who has had a neglected childhood as well, without a mother and father to teach and protect her, changes. In this final scene of the play while she is off stage for a short period of time (becoming as much of a woman as disguising skirts will allow a male actor to become),[4] Touchstone continues to teach both the audience on stage with him and the one in the theatre about the value of lying, not only as a pretty game, but also as protecting and promoting life. What interests me then is the relationship between lying as a falsehood and lying as a form of necessary and earned illusion; that is, how deceit might foster belief and how verbal lying might lead to the ceremonial coupling of two lovers lying down in a marriage bed. At the end of the play Touchstone's disquisition on lies is followed immediately by the arrival of Hymen, a clearly theatrical and illusory figure whose appearance has disturbed some readers of the play. But it seems to me that the close proximity of Touchstone's speech and Hymen's startling arrival makes an unavoidable argument for a relationship between supposing and believing that is at the heart of the play.

Obviously, I am not speaking of the sorts of lies which one finds in the tragedies, lies designed as by Iago to entrap and destroy Othello, or public lies which one experiences daily as destructive, repugnant. Rather, I am interested in lies which are playful as well as edgy perhaps, and which open up possibilities to minds which might otherwise be enclosed, narcissistic, narrow. Appropriately it is the clown, the artificial figure who is outside social norms, who is most insistent on the value of pretence. Touchstone's presence in the play signals the need for ways of shifting perspective and even 'lying' a bit (so long as one avoids the 'lie direct') for the sake of greater social and human value: peace – to which can also be added harmony, marriage and the relationship of both to the larger cosmos. I will examine two aspects of clever supposing in the play: first as demonstrating new habits of mind for Rosalind and Orlando, habits specifically dependent on rhetoric, and secondly as disguising and revealing their sexual desire for one another. The way in which the rhetorical action moves parallels the process of psychosexual growth for Orlando and Rosalind, and at the end witty conversation is dropped for a ceremony of marriage.

I

Before examining the scenes between them in Arden, however, I want to backtrack a bit and describe the lovers as they first appear in the play. In his speeches to both Adam and Oliver, Orlando reveals himself to be justifiably unhappy, denied his rightful place and education, and also a bit ponderous and narcissistic

---

[3] Cf. Jay L. Halio, Introduction, *Twentieth Century Interpretations of 'As You Like It'* (Englewood Cliffs, 1968); Clara Claiborne Park, 'As We Like It', in *The Woman's Part*, eds. Carolyn Lenz, Gayle Greene and Carol Neely (Urbana, 1980).

[4] Madelon (Gohlke) Sprengnether, 'Representing Femininity in *Antony and Cleopatra*', paper delivered at the PAPC Conference, Vancouver, 11 November 1984.

as one who has been isolated might tend to be. At the outset of the play, he says that he has been denied language and human society; in Arden he finds both and thus educated is able to move out from himself and towards love. Unlike Malvolio in *Twelfth Night* who never abandons his narcissism, Orlando changes.[5]

What stands out in Orlando's early character is that he is reduced to a physical existence: he wrestles with his brother, wrestles with Charles, and uses images for himself of animals, large rude ones that plough the land. It is as if at the outset Orlando is a large animal still growing larger and more awkward – an adolescent. 'I', he says, 'gain nothing under him but growth, for the which his animals on his dunghills are as much bound to him as I' (1.1.13–15). When he speaks in order to describe his lack of good habits and speech, he does so either in prose or with great difficulty. Before the heavenly Rosalind, he finds himself tongue-tied by his own desire and unable to thank her for the chain she has given him – she has entangled his tongue and more:

> Can I not say 'I thank you'? My better parts
> Are all thrown down, and that which here
>   stands up
> Is but a quintain, a mere lifeless block.
>
> (1.2.245–7)

Later in the play Rosalind mocks Jaques who argues that it is good to be sad and say nothing, by responding, 'Why then, 'tis good to be a post' (4.1.9). Both lovers, using the same image, thus acknowledge the need for conversation not only to increase pleasure and to get to know another person, but also to be more than a physical item, to be fully alive and human. Protesting against the way in which he has been brought up to be merely physical, Orlando announces that the spirit of his father has begun working in him, that is, that some new, non-physical aspect of his being has come alive. Moreover, when Oliver slanders their father, Orlando turns on him and attacks his throat and mouth, a significant gesture

indicting both the power of speech and Orlando's own lack of a proper tongue to respond and to hark himself as an equal: 'Wert thou not my brother, I would not take this hand from thy throat till this other had pulled out thy tongue' (1.1.59–61). The way in which his father's spirit will come to operate will be by his finding a tongue and a way of talking. He abandons physical wrestling to wrestle with words.

Rosalind too comes to adulthood by means of language. As Ganymede, she takes to herself the verbal power of her father who is praised for his ability to find 'tongues in trees, books in the running brooks, / Sermons in stones, and good in everything' (2.1.16–17). Ironically, although the Duke believes he is commending the rigours of unmediated nature, his followers rightly see that his vision is utopian and highly mediated. What he does off-to-the side is to create, even as Rosalind creates, a sophisticated linguistic community in which gaps between people are bridged by intelligent insight into the multiple meanings of words: 'happy is your grace / That can translate the stubbornness of fortune / Into so quiet and so sweet a style' (2.1.18–20). But Rosalind who is outside this community must act as parent towards herself as well as towards Orlando, and must create language, including the language of love, without adult help. Ingeniously, she invents an uncle, and pretends (as pretender to the throne) to a kind of magical verbal power which this initial deceit renders possible: 'But indeed an old religious uncle of mine taught me to speak' (3.2.342–3).

To explain the sorts of manoeuvres that go on between Rosalind and Orlando, once they reach Arden, however, it is not enough to say that they talk, although of course they do, with affection and wit. Their conversations are

---

[5] Richard A. Lanham, *The Motives of Eloquence* (New Haven, 1976), p. 48: 'To really love another, one must face the profoundly disorienting properties of language, of human society.'

both possible and fruitful because of certain artificialities of place and time and language. The lovers are bracketed off from the larger social world, specifically from the responsibilities of gender and adulthood; Rosalind will pretend to be a boy, living in a cote in a literary pastoral forest, and Orlando will pretend to court this boy as his Rosalind[6]; and they will speak better to one another because of the contrived falsity of the situation (not unlike a classroom or the situation described in a popular song, 'If I loved you').

The self-knowledge they both come to is dependent on their acceding to deceitfulness as a concept and as a mode of behaviour. First of all, Rosalind lets Orlando into the secrets of how to manipulate and quibble with language, offering it not as a mode of truth, but in its playful and even contradictory guises: as a medium of exchange, as something that can be stylistically altered, as a means of conveying deep feeling, as sententious, sharp, bountiful, cruel. The examples Rosalind provides are important models for Orlando to imitate, and even more importantly, together they suggest the possibility of change itself.

Rosalind also offers direct lessons in punning and shifting of verbal perspective, lessons especially necessary for one who needs to enlarge his image of himself by seeing himself from several outside points of view, not as Oliver saw him, as the stupid, bad child, but as a romantic male viewed with good humour as well as with mocking humour. Frequently, in education or psychotherapy, the voice of 'the other' is provided by another person.[7] As the one who counters Orlando's rigid position, Rosalind immediately questions his first assertion – that he is head-over-heels in love:

There is none of my uncle's marks upon you. He taught me to know a man in love; in which cage of rushes I am sure you are not prisoner. (3.2.367–9)

In its most extreme form, such direct contradiction might create a destructive splintering of the self, but here – done in the spirit of play and acceptance – it simply allows Orlando to come to see himself more clearly.

Since it is 'Rosalind' about whom each of the lovers presents quite a fixed view, one can focus on her as a central idea in order to see more exactly how each revises and extends the original pictures, and thereby also revises and extends his or her self-image. Moreover, although it is rigidity that Bergson finds comic, I would suggest that it is the experience of oscillation between fixed extremes that produces comic pleasure, a crucial education in flexibility, and an antidote to anger, the sort of anger and self-pity that trap both Orlando and Rosalind earlier in the play.[8] With each other's help and with the help of Touchstone, both learn to see themselves more broadly, more loosely, and more foolishly. By talking to each other and by exchanging their differing versions of how to view 'Rosalind', each learns flexibility, an important quality in the creation of character and of relationship, particularly the sort of relationship necessary for marriage. It is like watching a static picture come alive ('All the pictures fairest lined / Are but black to Rosalind'); both Rosalind and Orlando come to learn that loving a human being is more complex and interesting than loving a picture,

---

6 Young, pp. 38–72.

7 Cf. Leo Kovar, 'The Purist of Self-Deception', *Salmagundi*, 29 (1975), 43: 'It is said often that we know ourselves least well. The greeting by a friend becomes then: "You're fine, how am I?" While this can be no more than a half-truth – the inviolable privacy of our thinking insures this – it serves to point to a more satisfying conclusion, that it takes at least two to know one. Knowledge of self is a knowledge by selves, a composite of perspectives of which my own is unique but not alone.'

8 Sigmund Freud, *Jokes and Their Relation to the Unconscious*, ed. James Strachey (New York, 1963), p. 231: 'And indeed the small contributions of humour that we produce ourselves are as a rule made at the cost of anger – instead of getting angry.'

as Phebe, say, loves the picture of man in Ganymede.

In the process of defining 'Rosalind', Orlando's clichéd poems form a necessary and initial pole. First of all they provide Touchstone with ample opportunity for bawdy parody, a corrective for extreme adoration and for the simplistic portrait of Rosalind in the poems themselves. The 'if' is the 'if' of animal desire, as good a peacemaker for lovers, Touchstone might argue, as hedging – as in 'your If is the only peacemaker'. He also reminds us here, as he does throughout the play, that love must include a recognition of the body:

> If a hart do lack a hind,
> Let him seek out Rosalind.
> If a cat will after kind
> So be sure will Rosalind.
> Wintred garments must be lined,
> So must slender Rosalind. (3.2.100–5)

Orlando's poems about 'Rosalind' establish an ideal, albeit bookish, necessary to the playful exchanges that follow. They establish a position which is essential to the lovers and to their relationship: Rosalind and Orlando adore and idolize one another. Without these poems as background and without Rosalind's own outbursts of heartfelt emotion, the tone of the conversations in Arden could be abrasive. More importantly, the poems establish a position (reified like a picture, since they are written and posted) which demands a response. From Rosalind's responses, Orlando will learn to converse with a human being with ideas and ways of expression all her own, instead of talking to himself in poems or in maxims passed down from others: 'Why should this a desert be? / For it is unpeopled? No. / Tongues I'll hang on every tree / That shall civil sayings show' (3.2.125–8). He will learn to speak to a particular woman instead of creating her in generalities or cut out of the pieces of other mythic women: 'Thus Rosalind of many parts / By heavenly synod was devised, / Of many faces, eyes and hearts' (3.2.149–51). In the right context, which of course Arden is, Orlando's poems initiate conversation, and without conversation, each lover would be talking to him/herself, locked into the narcissism that stands behind unchallenged adoration.

Moreover, by referring to these poetic efforts, we can mark Orlando's improvement in civility and humour, if not in essential nobility, by his changed manner of talk, by his attempts at wit, by increasingly clear descriptions he gives of his Rosalind. He does not abandon artifice, but rather becomes more accomplished at it, speaking later in the play in blank verse:

Orlando. Good day and happiness, dear Rosalind.
Jaques. Nay then, God b'wi'you, an you talk in
  blank verse. (4.1.28–30)

Here Jaques draws attention to Orlando's artificial mode of speaking just as – to the contrary – he seems to have hit upon a true and natural way of talking: gracious, simple, unpretentious. Jaques emphasizes what I would also emphasize, that Orlando's greeting is carefully 'feigned' to be most true, a good act on Orlando's part (well-rehearsed, most feigning), rather than a bad (clumsy, spontaneous, clichéd). As Orlando gains in civility and assurance he nevertheless clings to the original descriptions he gives in the poems, presented now, however, in clear language. Thus in spite of Rosalind's picture of 'Rosalind' as fickle and wayward, he insists 'Virtue is no horn-maker, and my Rosalind is virtuous' (4.1.60–1). To him she is virtuous, sweet, desirable. Orlando's clear descriptions are not simply correctives to his fumbling attempts at verse, nor are they simply naive assumptions; they are as true and as necessary to the construction of her character, their love, and the ending of the play, as her ironic words about women and herself. His so-called clichéd, conventional view is a necessary addition to Rosalind's version in order to extend and complicate character, in order to make static description dramatic, a flat character round.

Rosalind complicates the original picture of 'Rosalind' in her own way. Although both lovers clearly need to learn to speak and to each other, and although both are in analogous, 'female' positions – without power, stripped of rank and status, fearful of the dangers around them, dazed by love – Rosalind is the one who must most clearly establish her identity before marriage while she has the chance. Thus, while Orlando keeps referring to '*my* Rosalind', Rosalind/Ganymede uses her verbal wit to insist that she is Rosalind, 'his' but also her own:

I will be more jealous of thee than a Barbary cock-pigeon . . . *I will* weep for nothing . . . *I will* do that when you are disposed to be merry; *I will* laugh like a hyen, and that when thou art inclined to sleep.

(4.1.145–52, my emphases)

Then, later, by setting up a picture of a false wife, she establishes that she can imagine herself even as a broad comic figure (a Wife of Bath) as well as a boy as well as a marriageable girl, i.e. complex, but most importantly that she can and does imagine differently from Orlando, and that any definition of 'Rosalind' must remain as flexible as possible, as required not only by marriage, but also by life – referred to in its various stages throughout the play:

Orlando. But will my Rosalind do so?
Rosalind. By my life, she will do as I do.
Orlando. O, but she is wise.
Rosalind. Or else she could not have the wit to do this; the wiser, the waywarder. (4.1.153–7)

Assuming that these sorts of observations about the situation in *As You Like It* bring us closer to what is going on in Arden, perhaps we can better understand why the conversations there focus on deception, not only of gender and role, but also the hiding of one attitude behind another, of positioning one way of being behind and then before another way. Even the coming and going on and off stage is a way of juggling positions, of escap-

ing from role and returning to it. Such movement, obviously central to theatre, also helps to account, in stage terms, for change in character, as it provides a time gap between one appearance and another. The slipping and jostling of these is what accounts – although this may seem contradictory – for our sense that what is happening between the two is somehow real and sincere. It is not so much that they return to their initial roles and to the 'real' court at the end that convinces us, but rather the very nature of their discourse. It is a way of claiming as full a presentation of character, relationship, and desire as language can create. The shifts between sincerity and falsity, and between one attitude and another, provide a sense of inner being, of a character fully capable of love and marriage. When Orlando says that he wishes he could make Rosalind believe that he loves, he is speaking to a complex figure who responds in a wonderfully complex way. Her charting of various positions based on the roles she has taken and her use of multiple pronouns maps out a full and 'true-to-life' character.

Me believe it? You may as soon make her that you love believe it, which I warrant she is apter to do than to confess she does; that is one of the points in the which women still give the lie to their consciences. (3.2.384–8)

The period of duplicity in Arden serves as a developmental stage for Rosalind and Orlando, a necessary period of trying on modes of behaviour and speech in order to come to know who one is. One's sense of the rightness of the end of *As You Like It* is dependent on the lovers' confessions of fearing duplicity. What they come to be at the end of the play is what they always were, but fuller, more complete.

During this time spent in Arden, not only do Rosalind and Orlando practise duplicity of various sorts, they practise the most artificial of forms as set out in Renaissance books of rhetoric, and by so doing prepare themselves for adulthood and marriage. Even in the manner of those commoners who would educate themselves for better places in the world, so Rosalind and Orlando take it upon themselves to prepare for the social positions which indeed they assume at the end of the play. They both speak 'by the book', and yet ironically, because of this pretence, arrive at a naturalness and ease.

Texts of rhetoric began appearing in English as early as 1529, and all of them signalled the interest in discourse pervasive in the period, and the importance that both king and peasant seem to have attached to the written word.[9] In the verbal exchange between one person and another, Renaissance thinkers saw the expression of both passion and reason, that which raised man above the beasts: according to Henry Peacham, speech is the 'key of conceptions, whereby we open the secreates of our harts, & declare our thought to others, and herein it is that we do so far . . . excell all other creatures, in that we haue the gifte of speech and reason, and not they'.[10] By following such teaching therefore, Orlando can leave his solely physical existence behind him.

In *The Tudor Play of Mind*, a book about Elizabethan drama preceding Shakespeare, Joel Altman argues that the rhetorical training which Renaissance students received, a training that conditioned them to argue *in utramque partem*, on both sides of the question, produced a drama that was not didactic, but questioning: 'the plays functioned as media of intellectual and emotional exploration for minds that were accustomed to examine the many sides of a given theme, to entertain opposing ideals, and by so exercising the understanding, to move toward some fuller apprehension of truth than could be discerned only through the total action of the drama. Thus the experience of the play was the thing.'[11] It is this sort of drama, following quite specific models, in which Rosalind and Orlando engage, arguing, contradicting one another, exchanging perceptions, preparing for marriage.[12]

According to Elizabethans, the faculty chiefly employed in rhetorical practices was invention, which in the Ciceronian tradition was considered most important, since it supplied matter for discourse and enlarged one's understanding.[13] Rosalind's particular mode of speaking with Orlando specifically demonstrates inventiveness. By this I mean in part simply that her words are abundant; she elaborates on whatever she has begun, and in so doing does what Erasmus's text *De Copia* trained schoolboys to do – enlarges small

---

[9] Marion Trousdale, *Shakespeare and the Rhetoricians* (Chapel Hill, 1982), pp. 22–3.

[10] Henry Peacham, *The Garden of Eloquence* (1577), sig. Aiir, quoted by Jane Donawerth, *Shakespeare and the Sixteenth-Century Study of Language* (Urbana, 1984), p. 20.

[11] Joel Altman, *The Tudor Play of Mind* (Los Angeles, 1978), p. 6: 'The corollary', he adds, 'of this hypothesis is that such an experience was, in some measure, set apart from that of private life, so as to provide a leisured *otium* wherein the auditor was freed to discover or to recall – and then to contemplate – ideas and feelings not always accessible or expressible in the life of a hierarchical Christian society.' What interests me is the way in which this links the *otium* of drama to the *otium* of pastoral.

[12] Altman also provides an interesting example from Lorich's edition of the *Progymnasmata* in which one thesis is given to support a particular proposition and a counter-thesis is given to oppose it. On the topic of marriage, the first proposition praises its cultivation of courageous, righteous, and temperate men; the *contradictio*, however, notes that marriage is a source of misfortune; in just such a back and forth manner do Rosalind and Orlando discuss marriage, husbands, and wives.

[13] Altman, p. 50; cf. also Lanham, p. 2 and Wilbur Howell, *Logic and Rhetoric in England, 1500–1700* (New York, 1961), p. 151. In his sixteenth-century manual of rhetoric, Thomas Wilson defines invention in a way that includes both truth and falsehood, and describes quite accurately the sort of mode that Rosalind uses: 'The finding out of apte matter, called otherwise Inuencion, is a searchyng out of the thynges true, or thynges likely, the whiche maie rasonably sette furth a matter, and make it appere probable', *The Art of Rhetorique* (1533), intro. Robert Bowers (reproduced in facsimile, Gainesville, Florida, 1962), p. 18.

matter with a multitude of rich words by a variety of means; providing details, causal principles, descriptions, digressions, arguments, comparisons and so forth. In her long speech on how men have not died for love, then, Rosalind follows a common formula, moving from a general statement (no man ever died in a love cause) to a multitude of specific examples, and thus educates Orlando not only about love itself, but also about the possibilities (including, again, the possibility of lying) for linguistic and human change:

The poor world is almost six thousand years old, and in all this time there was not any man died in his own person, videlicet, in a love cause. Troilus had his brains dashed out with a Grecian club; yet he did what he could to die before, and he is one of the patterns of love. Leander, he would have lived many a fair year though Hero had turned nun, if it had not been for a hot midsummer night; for, good youth, he went but forth to wash him in the Hellespont, and being taken with the cramp, was drowned; and the foolish chroniclers of that age found it was "Hero of Sestos." But these are all lies.

(4.1.91–103)

Such amplitude, equated as it was with both pleasure and wisdom, was to the age its own aesthetic justification.[14] But verbal jousting seems also to have been seen as a pleasure because of the highly charged mixture of deceit and truth, and because of the ardent competition involved. In his handbook of rhetoric, Puttenham speaks of the pleasure one can get by dissembling in language, whether by means of figures of speech or tone or allegorical devices; Castiglione notes that the well-educated courtier should create witty pleasure by flavouring his comments with deceit; and in her book on Renaissance rhetoric, Marion Trousdale describes linguistic pleasure again as dependent on the pleasures of deceit:

Poetic pleasure arises from strangeness, but more importantly it arises from deceit. Not only is it pleasant to be aware of the ways in which figures of language are transgressions of daily speech, but it is particularly pleasant to have to work a little at

deciphering the rational base from which the trope originated.[15]

What is pleasurable and riveting in the conversations between Rosalind and Orlando is also the alternating and unpredictable use of truth and deceit, especially as we know that they love and trust one another. The lovers are bonded by their mutual creation of and participation in a highly artificial and fragile world of language, constructed with vast amounts of energy, both mental and sexual.

Such elaboration also functions throughout the Renaissance and in this particular play as a kind of transformation which can signal even larger transformations, as the variations of figures of speech change dull language into the splendid, the mundane into the marvellous.[16] Castiglione, for example, draws attention to the way in which verbal facility can lead to something significant and strange, even as *As You Like It* moves from verbal wit to the unexpected appearance of a god: 'But since these punning witticisms are very sharp, in that a man takes words in a sense different from that in which everyone else takes them, they seem, as I have said, to cause marvel rather than laughter'.[17] In *As You Like It* the idea of change which this change in language

---

[14] Trousdale, p. 43.

[15] Trousdale, pp. 178–9; Richard Puttenham, *The Arte of English Poesie* (1589; reproduced in facsimile Kent, Ohio, 1906), pp. 205–6; Castiglione, *The Courtier*, trans. Charles Singleton (Garden City, 1959), pp. 178–9. I would also tentatively suggest the following ironic truth which I have observed in literature as well as life: one is more true (full, complex, at ease, open to sexuality, faithful) to one to whom one has said: 'I am not true.' In Shakespeare, for example, Sonnet 110 begins, 'Alas, 'tis true I have gone here and there / And made myself a motley to the view', and ends, 'Then give me welcome, next my heaven the best / Even to thy pure and most most loving breast.' The confession seems to lead to and to help create the release and ease (almost divine, the poet suggests) at the end.

[16] Trousdale, p. 83.

[17] Castiglione, p. 157.

portends is dramatized when Orlando encounters his wicked brother threatened by a lioness. Instead of withdrawing as one might expect and as he does twice, he changes his mind and saves Oliver who is immediately converted: ''Twas I', Oliver explains to Rosalind, 'But 'tis not I. I do not shame / To tell you what I was, since my conversion / So sweetly tastes, being the thing I am' (4.3.134–6). Given this faith in language, one understands Rosalind's efforts as efforts in language that reach for larger and more significant transformations, not only of character, but of the world itself.

In one of their most important conversations Rosalind and Orlando directly discuss the Ciceronian ideal of inventing new matter and hence new relationship. Her speech provides a key to my understanding of the play, linking as it does both oration and kissing, and marks a transition from concerns of language to concerns of sexuality in the second half of my paper. Rosalind is quite clear about the purposes of *inventio*. When *oral* contact is refused, a lover can turn to *oratio*:

Rosalind. . . . Very good orators, when they are out, they will spit; and for lovers, lacking – God warn us! – matter, the cleanliest shift is to kiss.
Orlando. How if the kiss be denied?
Rosalind. Then she puts you to entreaty, and there begins new matter.　　　　　(4.1.72–7)

To have things to say, they continue, 'keeps a man in his suit', i.e. both continuing his entreaty and inside his clothes. The close relationship between sexuality and language is here made explicit: witty talk keeps passion contained at least for the nonce; and serves as a kind of erotic foreplay that repression and/or denial helps to engender.[18] Thus denial is necessary not only so that Rosalind can protect her honesty, as she goes on to say, but also so that the process of getting to know one another can continue. Both costume and talk are used to keep desire under control, both perhaps most necessary when passion is especially strong.[19] Initially Rosalind takes on

her costume because she is venturing into a sexually dangerous world with Celia, one that she clearly wants and is ready for, even though in terms of the play she is forced into the forest by the figure of the 'father'. Technically, it is the bad father who puts her in such a vulnerable position, but she wouldn't be in such a position were it not for the absence of her own father. Despite these plot devices, however, what is most important is that going to Arden enacts her desire to be near the one she loves. In describing her, Celia refers both to her costume and most pointedly to her erotic desire: 'You have simply misused our sex in your love-prate. We must have your doublet and hose plucked over your head, and show the world what the bird hath done to her own nest' (4.2.199–202). Rosalind has feigned a boy's part in order to enact the specifically genital desires of her 'nest', and Celia draws attention to Rosalind's desire to reveal her nakedness even as she covers it over with clothes and wit.

Discussing the artifice of poetry rather than costume in relation to sexuality, Touchstone says to Audrey: 'the truest poetry is the most feigning, and lovers are given to poetry, and what they swear in poetry may be said as lovers they do feign' (3.3.18–21). What Touchstone means in the context of seduction and what the lines mean for Rosalind and Orlando are obviously not the same. Yet both couples face a similar tension between the artificial and the natural, and throughout the play poetry is both contrasted with the 'natural' (that which Touchstone and Audrey help define as fleshly, sexy, animalistic, slut-

---

18　Freud, *Jokes and Their Relation to the Unconscious*, p. 150.

19　Describing the rhetorical self at the centre of Ovid's *Ars Amatoria*, Richard Lanham makes remarks that are useful in thinking about Rosalind or indeed Orlando: 'In the world of the *Ars* self and purpose seem to vary not concomitantly, as we usually think – character is destiny – but inversely. The more we want to do something, the more we must relinquish the self that wants it. The wanting self becomes an actor . . .' (p. 9).

tish) and identified with it. Thus, one of the things one understands about what Touchstone says is that in order to enact his desire – to couple like a beast – he must disguise his desire behind courtship, the recitation of verse, even marriage. Like Rosalind described by Celia, in order to get what he wants, he must use pretence. The truest poetry is most feigning because it uses the most deceit to contain the greatest desire.

II

In her conversations about and with Orlando, Rosalind returns again and again to the topic of deceit as something that belongs specifically to the relationship between men and women. Speaking to Celia about how late Orlando is in coming to court 'her', she describes him alternately as false and as true (3.4) – even his hair, she finds, is 'of the dissembling color' and also 'of a good color' (3.4.7 and 10). Again and again she reminds Orlando that women cannot be trusted, that they are giddy and false. In both examples Rosalind displays a sort of nervousness about her lover's faithfulness and even about her own. And, although both are true and no doubt suspect as much, Rosalind helps to make truth possible by facing squarely its opposite. Moreover, she uses language not only to express her qualms, but also (if unconsciously) to reveal another (half-repressed) concern. Language in *As You Like It* is being used then in a second important way, to display and hide sexual desires.

In the central exchange between Rosalind and Orlando in 4.1, Rosalind declares that the wiser the woman, the waywarder; that she would prefer to be wooed by a snail because 'he brings his destiny with him'; that because he is so 'good' she will have 'twenty such'. She presents a picture of a wife going off to a neighbour's bed. Most importantly, she carefully distinguishes between maids and wives, the differences providing the basis for her own

fears and for what she must therefore explore in her conversations with Orlando:

Maids are May when they are maids, but the sky changes when they are wives. I will be more jealous of thee than a Barbary cock-pigeon over his hen, more clamorous than a parrot against rain, more newfangled than an ape, more giddy in my desires than a monkey. I will weep for nothing, like Diana in the fountain, and I will do that when you are disposed to be merry; I will laugh like a hyen, and that when thou art inclined to sleep.

(4.1.144–52)

I read these speeches not only as Rosalind's debunking of Orlando's naive idealism, but also as ways for her to express and thus relieve her own anxieties about giving up being a kind of Diana (as chaste huntress) in order to be a wife. Her language also indicates that she fears being animal even as Orlando feared being an animal at the outset of the play; both look with some trepidation at their own passions and at the distance one must travel between now and then, between before and after 'possession', to use Rosalind's word. When Rosalind insists that Orlando emend his desire to possess her 'for ever and a day' to 'a day', is she not wishing, if only for the moment, that they could stay as they are, courting one another, that time would not move forwards? In her exchanges with him she rushes and then pulls back, wants to marry immediately and fears the future, cannot be apart from him for two hours, yet still wants to be as free and independent as her own agile wit:

Make the doors upon a woman's wit, and it will out at the casement; shut that, and 'twill out at the keynole; stop that, 'twill fly with the smoke out at the chimney. (4.1.157–60)

Such talk also conveys something of what Rosalind is: not not virtuous (Orlando insists on his Rosalind's virtue and of course we trust it as well), but also someone for whom such wanton behaviour can be imagined, and who is like the women in her stories – a woman with passion that can hardly be contained. As

Freud suggests in his chapter on dream symbols in *The Interpretation of Dreams*, 'there is no need to name explicitly the key that unlocks the room'.[20] Several of Shakespeare's tragedies illustrate how crucial it is that a husband know this before marriage; Othello, for example, is driven mad by the image in his mind and his bed of the divine Desdemona who, as she says, wants simply to live with him (and be in bed with him) because she loves him: 'That I did love the Moor to live with him'.[21] He wants her to remain a storybook figure even as he remains a storybook soldier: pretty images in love with one another's minds. The two-backed beast (as distorted an image as that may be, *because* it is only an image) which Iago presents to Brabantio is also for Othello an image that drives him to madness, murder, and suicide. It is therefore essential to the ending of *As You Like It* that Orlando know something of Rosalind's desires, that words be used to extend and complicate pictures.

Albeit that Rosalind protects herself and her sexuality by her disguise – and she is explicit about the need for disguises in the forest since she and Celia are maids and fearful – she also uses it to explore her own growing sexuality; and since she is without a family to keep her safe and also to educate her, she takes on this education with Celia and then with Orlando, moving from the safety and narcissism of a same-sex relationship, also characterized by love, mutuality, twinning, witty conversations about deception, to a heterosexual relationship. Although Celia cannot quite, in spite of her well-intentioned efforts, break Rosalind's bond with her father, Orlando can. 'But what talk we of fathers', Rosalind says to Celia in the forest, 'when there is such a man as Orlando' (3.4.36–7). When we first see Rosalind, however, she is sad and cannot forget her banished father: 'Unless you could teach me to forget a banished father, you must not learn me how to remember any extraordinary pleasure' (1.2.3–6). Nor can she, as Celia suggests,

use her love for Celia to exchange the father present for the one missing. What she can do is begin the practice of what she continues to do throughout the play – suspend one way of feeling in order to focus on and encourage another. This exercise teaches her about her own strength of mind, allows her to explore aspects of herself which are hidden from immediate view, and lets her explore her own maidenly desires and fears.[22]

In the forest of Arden Rosalind continues her self-education; by the use of a witty pretence she can use the time allotted her to come to know herself. It has often been noted that *As You Like It* is filled with references to time and that the green world stops time.[23] Conveniently, for the young lovers, time stops at just the right moment, and the play presents but one of the seven ages Jaques describes: an extended and suspended period of adolescent introspection and conversation. Given such an opportunity to talk and to consider things from a variety of points of view, Rosalind begins this endeavour by playing at deception, aptly by talking first with Celia about the deceitful goddess Fortune and deceit in love:

Celia. . . . but love no man in good earnest, nor no further in sport neither than with safety of a pure blush thou mayst in honor come off again.

(1.2.25–8)

Pretence is described as important here, as it is later on in Arden to protect a maiden's honour and to keep wits in motion, actions which in

---

[20] Sigmund Freud, *The Interpretation of Dreams*, ed. James Strachey (New York, 1965), p. 389.

[21] For an excellent discussion along these lines see Carol Thomas Neely, 'Women and Men in *Othello*', in *The Woman's Part*, eds. Carolyn Lenz, Gayle Greene and Carol Neely (Urbana, 1980).

[22] Cf. Carole McKewin, 'Counsels of Gall and Grace', in *The Woman's Part*.

[23] Cf. Jay L. Halio, 'No Clock in the Forest', *Twentieth Century Interpretations of 'As You Like It'*, ed. Jay L. Halio (Englewood Cliffs, N.J., 1968), pp. 88–98.

this play are closely intertwined. Wit, as Freud describes it in *Jokes and Their Relation to the Unconscious*, is a kind of 'word-disguise', akin to other modes of disguise in the play, a way of drawing attention away from 'exposure' by puns or sound or the form of a particular expression.

Repression of sexuality (or, more complexly, denial and avowal) is, as Freud suggests, one of the major sources for jokes; and 'double-dealing' (sense in nonsense) is essential since as a technique it draws attention both to what is being said or done on the surface and what is hidden, if only scarcely hidden, from view. In using such language then, the speaker can have things two ways at once.

For jokes do not, like dreams, create compromises; they do not evade the inhibition, but they insist on maintaining play with words or with nonsense unaltered. They restrict themselves, however, to a choice of occasions in which this play or nonsense can at the same time appear allowable (in jests) or sensible (in jokes), thanks to the ambiguity of words and the multiplicity of conceptual relations. Nothing distinguishes jokes more clearly from all other physical structures than this double-sidedness and this duplicity in speech.[24]

In his discussion Freud makes two points useful for consideration here: one, that jokes, unlike dreams, are social – that they create relationship since no one is content to have made a joke on his own. Thus, like the rest of their efforts, the specifically sexual wit between Orlando and Rosalind in *As You Like It* creates relationship, and prepares them for the more serious relationship of marriage towards which they are headed. Secondly, Freud argues that witty jokes both suppress and release repressed tendencies towards aggression or the obscene:

The motive force for the production of innocent jokes is not infrequently an ambitious urge to show one's cleverness, to display oneself – an instinct that may be equated with exhibitionism in the sexual field. The presence of numerous inhibited instincts, whose suppression has retained a certain degree of instability, will provide the most favourable disposition for the production of tendentious jokes.[25]

Even before Rosalind reaches the forest, her conversations with Celia in act I reveal her skill at constructing witty jokes, often around issues of gender, and their mutual interest in deceit, both the deceptive disguises which they take on for protection, and the added deception of boy actors dressed as young women; when Touchstone calls them to swear by their beards that he is a knave, Celia replies, 'By our beards, if we had them, thou art' (1.2.72). Thus she gestures towards that which they are pointedly not talking about while they are talking in a sporting way about knavery and Touchstone's story of a deceitful knight who didn't worry about losing his honour – an obvious, if differently defined, concern for Rosalind and Celia – because he didn't have any.

One must suspect that Orlando also, like Celia, 'knows' that something is being repressed, set aside, when he talks to Ganymede; he is after all suspicious of her accent from the first, and, as he tells her father at the end, 'Methought he was a brother to your daughter' (5.4.29). Would he have entered into such a contract with Ganymede without feeling something akin to what he felt before in the presence of Rosalind? Would the conversations be so charged without some knowledge on his part? Why does he join in the chorus with the other lovers at the end and call forth Rosalind's startled remark: 'Why do you speak too, "Why blame you me to love you?"' (5.2.105–6). In explaining a somewhat similar situation, why Henry Fonda as Charles might utter the same words of romantic nonsense that he has uttered earlier in *The Lady Eve* to Jean, Stanley Cavell remarks:

I do not, of course, claim that he does know or believe they are the same, that he is having to do

---

24 Freud, *Jokes and Their Relation to the Unconscious*, p. 172.
25 Freud, *Jokes and Their Relation to the Unconscious*, pp. 143 and 221–2.

with just one woman. But we have had continued evidence that he is in a trance . . . and the fact of the matter is that he is saying his words to the same woman. What he says to Jean at the end is hard to deny: 'It would never have happened except she looked so exactly like you.'[26]

What Rosalind is doing as she speaks to both Celia and Orlando is diverting attention from her real focus: the male she longs for (father and then Orlando), and her own sexuality, a repression that is extended like a long adolescence as she plays the saucy lackey. Indeed, at one point, she equates wit and female desire, responding to Orlando (who perhaps already sees what is coming), as he introduces a word for desire, 'will':

Orlando. A man that had a wife with such a wit, he might say, "Wit, whither wilt?"
Rosalind. Nay, you might keep that check for it till you met your wife's wit going to your neighbor's bed.   (4.1.161–5)

Rosalind thus uses façades until time runs out and no one likes what is going on any more. Part of the reason indeed that wit dominates the conversations between Rosalind and Orlando is that they are putting off their return to reality for as long as possible; as Freud notes, college students who are attempting to hang on to childhood as long as possible while the realities of the world press in on them are those most enamoured of wit and jokes. They too are caught, in pleasurable discomfort, in an extended adolescence, doing – as the title of our play suggests – what they like. The critic David Young describes the title, *As You Like It*, as a 'kind of warning against categorical judgments. Pastoral is not always true or always false or always anything: it is as you like it.'[27] I agree with this description, but also find that this state in which all the characters have been suspended and in which shifting is the nature of the world is one that finally wears thin. The characters are ready to stop living in a pastoral world of deceit and supposing, and so Rosalind promises Orlando: 'I will weary

you then no longer with idle talking' (5.2.51–2). It is time to give up shifting, time for men and women to couple. Yet without the experience of doubt and witty talk and various sorts of lying, love and marriage would not mean what they come to mean at the end of the play.

The woman Rosalind changes into at the end of *As You Like It* while Touchstone rants about formal lies is not the same, although she is, of course, the same as she was at the outset when Orlando first fell in love with her; nor is Orlando the same. The two of them have been through the educating realm of the forest and have already crossed one another; thus Hymen can assert: 'You and you no cross shall part' (5.4.131). Because they have exchanged words, Rosalind can exhort Orlando to 'Keep you your word' (5.4.19). If Hymen represents faith, such an apparition is a giddy vision akin to falling in love at first sight, but unlike this initial love, love here at the end is not 'too soon'. The truth of their initial meeting is still operative, but the magic which Hymen represents is different from the magic which initially draws Rosalind and Orlando together. Rosalind has indoctrinated Orlando into the magic of artifice, as a way of bonding them sexually and as educative rhetoric. In the final chapter of *Of Ornament*, Puttenham (like Sidney) urges the good poet to dissemble, and finally praises the strange and miraculous effects of poetry; his movement from particular rhetorical devices to the beautiful and strange, and from the poetry of sudden inspiration to that which is worked over and meditated on, is paralleled by the treatment of love in *As You Like It*.

I read Hymen's appearance then as the visible manifestation of the lovers' choosing of a particular kind of lie, an illusion which does not deny the awful truths of reality, but which

---

[26] Stanley Cavell, *Pursuits of Happiness* (Cambridge, Mass., 1981), p. 61.
[27] Young, p. 58.

rather extends the necessity for illusions into another realm. Hymen's appearance marks the transition from playful lying (also serious, however) to responsible illusion, recognized and sanctioned by a larger public world. The god seems to stand for the illusion and poetry necessary to bless, effect, contain, and represent a natural truth. Pretence and illusion are therefore necessary, the play argues, to get at truth or to sound most like it, which in a play so devoted to rhetoric may be close to the same thing. Yet the ending makes clear that the higher 'illusion' is that of Hymen, as feigning is replaced by faining, a glad choosing of marriage. In an article in a special issue of *Salmagundi* devoted to the issue of lying, Michael Beldoch discusses belief as a form of lying in a way I find useful to an understanding of the end of *As You Like It*. He notes that in *The Future of an Illusion* especially, but throughout his work as a whole as well, Freud shows that illusions – beliefs – are derived from human wishes: 'Beliefs exist to "correct" reality, and to the extent that reality is – or represents – the truth, or is at least the source of the truth, beliefs are necessarily a variant of lies.' He continues:

I appreciate that to describe belief as a form of lying offends not only common usage but also what many would consider a minimum of tact and good taste. But we have already moved in this discussion beyond consideration of those conscious lies of every day, those politically motivated and carefully advertised lies of simple avarice and greed. We are talking about those motivated self-deceptions which run closer to the heart of the human dilemma, those issues that arise from the paradox of our consciousness, from the conscious knowledge that much of what is most central in our lives lies beyond the awareness of our consciousness.[28]

Thus I would suggest that Hymen's appearance signals not the return to reality, although of course the lovers will return to court, but a different kind of illusion, larger in scope and more conscious. It is not so much that the old illusions of Arden and the pastoral world are

wrong, as that with the passage of time they are no longer as true; what I want to say is that time alters the nature of any illusion, even so good and useful a one as theirs has been, and that a new responsibility marks the difference between adolescent lying and adult belief. Although what the two lovers have weathered together doesn't necessarily prepare them for the trials of marriage, it does count for something that they have tried to know things painful as well as joyful, that they have experienced the various seasons of the mind.

What they have at the end is hard-won, dependent on an experience of duplicity and even pain. Orlando is actually wounded by a lioness in Arden, and Rosalind swoons at the sight of his 'bloody napkin'. Orlando is a man and has displayed his manly wrestler's courage again; Rosalind, as Oliver mocks, is not a man – she lacks a man's heart and more. And the bloody napkin is emblematic of the woman she is (or would be *if*), even as the appealing lines she utters as she revives, and recalls her female nature and desire for return: 'I would I were at home' (4.3.160). Enough has become enough.

Thus at the end of *As You Like It* things are returned to 'normal' and again by means of language. As Touchstone says: 'All these you may avoid but the Lie Direct, and you may avoid that too, with an If.' Rosalind and Orlando have not quarrelled or come to the sort of arguments that Touchstone is describing here, but they have wrangled and played with concepts of lying and deceit. But now it is time to acknowledge that pre-tence has become the present tense:

Duke Senior.
  If there be truth in sight, you are my daughter.
Orlando.
  If there be truth in sight, you are my Rosalind.
(5.4.118–19)

---

[28] Michael Beldoch, 'Unconscious Lies, Unconscious Truths: Psychoanalytic Observations', *Salmagundi*, p. 143.

Since Touchstone recites his speech about the various sorts of lies on stage while Rosalind is off stage, and since these two areas are inextricably related, I would argue that Touchstone's words about beards and lies serve as a kind of incantatory description of what is going on for Rosalind: she is changing. The direct lie is that 'she' is still a 'he' but any distress over this can be avoided, as Touchstone points out, by 'if' and imagination. So too for the ending of the play; the vision at the end is a bit of wishful thinking, a 'supposition' or 'if', i.e. if things can go as we have seen for four and a half acts, and if one can imagine private conversations as the basis for public ceremony, then such endings and happiness can and will necessarily follow. If the lovers don't lie directly and with malice, but rely instead on banter, the exchanges which they have already practised in the forest, and their obvious sexual attraction for one another (lying as in lying down), the play will provide what we all like.

The epilogue reintroduces the suggestive wit of Arden, when Rosalind returns in her guise as boy actor: 'If I were a woman, I would kiss as many of you as had beards that pleased me.' It is appropriate that this remark comes at the end to remind the audience that the oscillation between play and stasis is ongoing (wit bridging here a second gap, here between theatre and life) and of the necessity of deceit for so good a play as this one, and of the entire 'as if' that has ruled while the play was in motion:

Dramatic worlds are hypothetical ('as if') constructs, that is, they are recognized by the audience as counterfactual (i.e. non-real) states of affairs but are embodied as if in progress in the actual here and now. The spectator will conventionally interpret all stage doings in light of this general 'as if' rule.[29]

Dissembling wit is one technique for having things at least two ways at once; so for a man dressed as a woman, so for courtship in the forest of Arden, so for theatre. This play educates its characters and its audience in the value of 'if'.

---

[29] Keir Elam, *The Semiotics of Theatre and Drama* (New York, 1980), p. 102.

'MEASURE FOR MEASURE':
MIRROR FOR MIRROR

RUTH NEVO

Mirror on mirror mirrored is all the show.
W. B. Yeats, *The Statues*

The anomalies of *Measure for Measure* which have caused it to be regarded as the paradigmatic 'problem play' spring from its swerve away from Whetstone's *Promos and Cassandra*.[1] In the source play Cassandra, the sister of Andrugio, the young man condemned to death, is no devout novice in an austerely ascetic order, and therefore there is no barrier to her marriage with Promos, the Corrupt Magistrate, who has fallen in love with her, when matters are set right by the Beneficent Ruler in the end. There is no Mariana, no bed-trick, no plethora of severed heads – one (somewhat mangled and unrecognizable) serves perfectly adequately to provide for the deception of Promos and the escape of Andrugio – and no absconding Duke, setter-up of the delinquent Deputy in the first place. What has been gained, is the question that suggests itself, by the additional complications?

The Duke, watching events from the wings, returns in time to prevent the death of Claudio – the fatal error which would actualize the play's tragic potential – by having recourse to the repertoire of means whereby comedy, for its own eudaemonic ends, evades, circumvents, or surmounts the threats and dangers incipient in initial situations. But these 'theatregrams' as such modular manoeuvres have been called[2] – benign deception or imposture, clownish interlopers or intermediaries, disguises and unmaskings – give rise to as many problems on the level of characterization as they solve at the level of plot.

If Isabella herself (like Rosalind or Viola) had been the initiator of some disguise-device (the bed-trick itself, even, like Helena in *All's Well That Ends Well*) to capture, educate or test a lover, we can quite easily imagine *Measure for Measure* turned into a Shakespearian festive comedy, or comedy of maturation, in which there is space for courtship however disguised or dissimulated, in which obstructive follies are played out, recognized for what they are, and exorcized in time for the wedding celebrations which symbolize fulfilment, harmony and cohesion, individual, familial and social. But in *Measure for Measure* this is not the case. What *Measure for Measure* offers us instead of courtship is the further anomaly of an Isabella totally unprepared for betrothal to the Duke, and his extraordinary behaviour to her: not only does he calumniate her in the trial scene, but he also torments her by withholding the information that her brother is alive. Instead of the wisdom-generating foolery of courtship in disguise, as in the prototypical festive comedies, which *Measure for Measure* resembles in its contrivances, we have a depraved attempt at seduction by a defecting Deputy,

---

[1] On the play's sources see J. W. Lever, the new Arden edition (1965), pp. xxxv–xliv.
[2] Louis George Clubb, 'Shakespeare's Comedy and Late Cinquecento Mixed Genres', in *Shakespearean Comedy*, ed. Maurice Charney (New York, 1980), pp. 133–5.

and a punitive pre-marital ordeal imposed by a devious Duke. This too perhaps can be seen as a process of maturation, but it is certainly a departure from comic protocol which requires elucidation. It will occupy us later on.

Isabella passes the Duke's endurance test with the Christian charity of her appeal on Angelo's behalf. But the speech in which she pleads for Angelo's life is perhaps the most intractable anomaly in the whole play. 'Look, if it please you, on this man condemn'd / As if my brother liv'd' (5.1.444–5) she says.[3] What can we make of this appeal to make-believe? If it is construed as a praiseworthy flexibility, a moral tolerance, acquired in the crucible of her harrowing experiences, what do we then make of two subsequent *non sequiturs* which defeat the intelligence even as special pleading? Her first argument: her brother did what he did, and so received 'but justice' (5.1.448), sounds remarkably like a reiteration of the narrow legalism she espouses at the beginning of her first interview with Angelo. Her second makes a mockery of consistent reasoning. Angelo, she says, did not manage to do what he intended (to her, that is), and was an honest man before he fell into temptation. That Angelo did commit, if not in fact as it turns out, yet in intent, belief, and full consciousness of the moral import of his deeds, at least three serious felonies – extortion, fornication and breach of promise – is thus digested by this once ardently evangelical Puritan moralist.

Is the point of the changes then to advance bad faith as a moral target? Is the play a mockery of ineffectual rulers, pharisaical Puritanism, 'Love-lacking vestals, and self-loving nuns' (*Venus and Adonis*, 752)? When Isabella says to the Duke 'I have spirit to do any thing that appears not foul in the truth of my spirit' (3.1.205–7) she speaks as an arch-Puritan, and she is not, overtly, mocked. But the 'truth' of Isabella's spirit can be, and has been, subjected to very sceptical scrutiny indeed. The satirical interpretation of *Measure for Measure* makes of Pompey Bum, simply 'a poor fellow that

would live' (2.1.223), the uncrowned anti-heroic hero of the play, and the two main protagonists, not to mention the Duke, egotistical hypocrites. And this, for our cynical and disillusioned age, has proved a possible and popular reading. Nevertheless I would wish to challenge it, if only because our feelings are engaged in the tense conflict that develops in the first half of the play in a way not entirely consonant with the aims of satire, or of Bakhtinian carnivalesque.

In 3.1 a tragic plot which up to this point has been fully developed and is progressing at full speed is abruptly truncated. Both actors and audiences must struggle to readjust to the transformation in tone, mood, mode, pace, and style which takes place at 3.1.153 and is emphatically marked by the mid-scene shift from supple blank verse to sententious prose. We have just entertained a spectacle of high drama, of suspense, temptation, cross-purposes and cross-motivations, of a conflict of wills, intentions, desires and dilemmas, at the very edge of disaster and for the highest stakes. The unfolding of the tragic conflict has put at risk Claudio's life and his sister's survival. The play's predicating scenes have made it abundantly clear that whether Isabella rescues her brother, at the cost of her honour and the violation of her virginity, or does not, the consequences in either case would be drastic for her psychic integrity or well-being. Hers is an impossible choice precisely because whichever of the alternatives she chooses must involve her in unbearable guilt. On the one hand are the goals and values to which she most passionately aspires, on the other the needs and affections to which she is most deeply attached. And Claudio, a young man easily browbeaten by authority into believing himself in the wrong, but whose immediately preceding speech, 'Ay, but to die ...'

---

[3] All quotations from Shakespeare's plays and poems are taken from The Riverside Shakespeare, edited by G. Blakemore Evans (Boston, 1974).

(3.1.117 ff) has revealed the exposed nerve of a sensitivity unprotected by internalized conventions and consolations, must choose between the ego-ideal of honour and the primal terror of death.

At 3.1.151, with Isabella and her brother at the very pitch of their reciprocal crisis, the disguised Duke enters, calls Isabella aside, and asks her to 'Vouchsafe a word, young sister, but one word.' If she might dispense with her leisure, he would have some speech with her, which might prove beneficial to herself. This young sister, in a state which can only be described as hysterical in its unconstrained violent passion, has just repudiated her loved brother and consigned him to his death. Yet she replies with a bland composure that must baffle the most accomplished histrionic art. She hasn't as a matter of fact, she says, any superfluous leisure, is indeed rather busy, but will attend him all the same.

We have ringing in our ears at this moment not only

> O you beast!
> O faithless coward! O dishonest wretch!
> Wilt thou be made a man out of my vice?
> (3.1.135–7)

> Die, perish! Might but my bending down
> Reprieve thee from thy fate, it should proceed.
> I'll pray a thousand prayers for thy death,
> No word to save thee   (ll. 143–6)

but also the impassioned evangelical eloquence of

> Alas, alas!
> Why, all the souls that were were forfeit once,
> And He that might the vantage best have took
> Found out the remedy. How would you be
> If He, which is the top of judgment, should
> But judge you as you are? O, think on that,
> And mercy then will breathe within your lips,
> Like man new made.   (2.2.72–9)

The transition is staggering. We are required totally to shift our mental set. We must either suppose Isabella to possess superhuman powers of recovery and composure, or her

author to possess superhuman criteria of dramatic plausibility. And nothing in the sequences which follow seems to be able to restore or fulfil the kinds of expectation generated, or the kinds of reality-testing invited, by acts 1 and 2, or to absorb the energies that have been enlisted and released. In terms of generic models of expectation, therefore, *Measure for Measure* is disorienting. It apparently changes its generic mind in midstream. It cracks in half in the middle, like Humpty Dumpty, and, it seems, not all the king's horses and all the king's men have really been able to put it together again. We must content ourselves with the critical consensus that it is, at best, a 'flawed masterpiece' (Lever, p. xcvii), product of an interim period (variously described and accounted for) in the dramatist's *œuvre*, or we must seek other questions to ask.

The critical consensus has been indeed that the life drains out of the play with the return of the fantastical Duke to take over the management of affairs. The Duke is a stage device, it is said, the characters henceforth mere puppets. And mechanical lifelessness is felt to characterize the second part even when due regard is paid to the possibility that the 'close blend of tragic and comic elements [is] so carefully patterned as to suggest a conscious experiment in the new medium of tragicomedy' (Lever, p. xcvii) which had become popular at the turn of the century.[4] Anne Barton, in her admirably succinct account of the play's difficulties in the Riverside edition (1974, pp. 545–9), suggests that the Duke, conducting events towards the canonical happy ending, parallels Shakespeare himself as comic dramatist. 'There is something forced and blatantly fictional about the Duke's ultimate disposition of people and events', she says. 'The Duke refuses to admit

---

[4] Battista Guarini, *Compendio della Poesia Tragicomica* (1601), quoted in Lever (1965). See also Marvin T. Herrick, *Tragicomedy: Its Origin and Development in Italy, France and England* (Urbana, 1955), and Rosalie L. Colie, *Shakespeare's Living Art* (Princeton, 1974).

failure, but Shakespeare seems perversely to stress the hollowness, in a sense the falsehood, of the happy ending of this comedy ... an ending which is that of fairy tale: conventional, suspect in its very tidiness, full of psychological gaps and illogicalities', and thus, she suggests, 'appears to embody some of the problems of a Shakespeare now seemingly disillusioned with the art of comedy which, in the past, had served him so well'. Richard Wheeler, who consistently reads Shakespeare through the lens of the plays, turns to depth psychology rather than to self-reflexivity in his account of the parallel between author and persona. Shakespeare attempts, he says, 'to distance himself from conflict through the characterization of Vincentio ... [using] Angelo as a scapegoat who suffers in his person the consequences of a conflict Vincentio is thereby spared'. This has the effect, however, of leaving Vincentio 'a shadowy figure' in a 'kind of allegorical no-man's-land'.[5]

I would like to propose a further look at the alleged 'hollowness', at the 'psychological gaps and illogicalities', at the play's 'allegorical no-man's-land' perceived by these shrewd critics. My guiding assumption is that it is precisely such features of discourse that reveal, while they veil, the unconscious of the text, and guide us towards the inner dimensions of the experience the text represents. 'The textual unconscious', says André Green, 'is present in the text's thematic articulations, its brutal silences, its shifts of tone, and especially in [its] blemishes, incongruities, and neglected details.'[6] 'An unconscious process is evident within a highly integrated verbal field', says David Gordon, precisely when 'its coherence is flawed in certain ways'.[7] I believe it possible to put Humpty Dumpty together again, and to point to a kind of 'life' in the second part which a different interrogation of the play might discover, if we allow ourselves to be responsive not only to the bewitching eloquence of Shakespearian dialogue but to what Jacques Lacan has called 'the "unsaid" that lies

in the holes of the discourse'[8] – in its 'hollows', gaps, and flaws. As a first step in such an interrogation let us turn to the shadowy Duke.

We are accustomed to structuring our responses around the pivot of a single main protagonist, a dominant centre of consciousness, the persona whose fate is presented as being of most importance; the person whose story is being told. Such a figure has not proved easy to distinguish in *Measure for Measure* because of the split in the play which makes the manipulating, providential Duke at first a possible 'centre of consciousness', then an absentee, and finally a mere puppet-master and not entirely in control at that. Meredith Skura proposes the notion that the Duke represents an absconding or withdrawing ego-figure, in whose absence the super-ego representatives – Angelo and Isabella – and the id figures of the Viennese underworld play out their disastrously conflicting roles until his return reintegrates a psychic whole. Shakespeare, she says, is Freud's predecessor in the anthropomorphization of the parts of the mind. 'In the comedies and romances, Shakespeare dramatizes Freud's optimistic dictum, "Where id was, there shall ego become" ... Certainly a play like *Measure for Measure* suggests a kind of analytic self-scrutiny, as the Duke, like the analysand's "observing ego", withdraws from the action to oversee the battle between upright Angelo and the low life in the stews.'[9] This is a promising launching pad but it proves reductively schematic.

5 Richard P. Wheeler, *Shakespeare's Development and the Problem Comedies* (Berkeley, 1981), pp. 133–9, *passim*.

6 André Green, 'The Double and the Absent', in Alan Roland (ed.), *Psychoanalysis, Creativity and Literature* (New York, 1978), p. 285.

7 David J. Gordon, 'Literature and Repression', in J. H. Smith, ed., *The Literary Freud* (New Haven, 1980), p. 183.

8 Jacques Lacan, *Écrits*, trans. Alan Sheridan (New York, 1977), p. 93.

9 Meredith Ann Skura, *The Literary Use of the Psychoanalytic Process* (New Haven, 1981), pp. 35, 36.

Angelo's central conflict is not with the stews. Superego and id are so simplistically dichotomized as to deprive Freud's heuristic fictions of hermeneutic value.

Skura's final summation of the play is therefore disappointing; it does not address the play's formal discontinuity, and it conflates the experiences of all the central characters in a single overarching, and truistic, moral theme. 'The primary subject of the play, I would suggest,' she says, 'is the difficulty of growing up – the problem of learning how to move away from self to other; from adolescent ideal to adult, compromised human realities; from a "life removed" without issue to some more fruitful exchange' (264).

But the germ of her idea of the Duke as an observing ego can be made to bear fruit if we integrate it with a feature of the play's dramaturgy which has drawn the attention of critics of many persuasions, not necessarily psychoanalytic. I refer to the prominence and quantity of doubling, or 'decomposition',[10] in *Measure for Measure*.

The Duke, as Walter Lever points out, appoints not one but two deputies: Angelo and Escalus; the one temperate, merciful, tolerant, moderate: 'Let us be keen, and rather cut a little, / Than fall, and bruise to death' (2.1.5–6); the other 'A man of stricture and firm abstinence' (1.3.12), who 'scarce confesses / That his blood flows; or that his appetite / Is more to bread than stone' (1.3.51–3), and who can think only disjunctively: the law must either be a terror or it becomes a mere scarecrow (2.1.1.). These polarities are exhibited in action in the case of Elbow versus Pompey which threatens to last out a night in Russia (2.1.134 ff), though few audiences, delighting in the inimitable Shakespearian comic consternations, would wish it a moment shorter. Angelo, who hasn't the patience to sit it out, wishes them all whipped, regardless; Escalus, patiently attempting to ferret out at least the nature of the offence, threatens to 'prove a shrewd Caesar' to Pompey should he appear

before him again, but lets him off with a scolding, warns Froth of the error of his ways, and tactfully sets about to institute improvements in the manpower situation of the constabulary. It is an object lesson in the difference between a punitive repression of unruly human impulse and a wise, reparative, tolerant management of the errors and frailties of the flesh. 'Mortality and mercy' (1.1.44) as the Duke puts it (notice the significant replacement of 'justice' by 'mortality'), making Angelo the single repository of mediation between the terms of that formidable dichotomy. What we are invited to see, however, is that the Duke splits himself into these two representatives. Escalus is a part of himself which he now repudiates, for reasons which Escalus dutifully repeats:

> Mercy is not itself, that oft looks so;
> Pardon is still the nurse of second woe
>
> (2.1.283–4)

while Angelo is the other part of himself, exhibiting in its purity the asceticism which the Duke admires, but about which he seems equivocal.

> No; Holy father, throw away that thought;
> Believe not that the dribbling dart of love
> Can pierce a complete bosom.   (1.3.1–3)

This is the Duke's denial of the implied suggestion that he is in flight from love, or in pursuit of love in his request for a friar's habit. A 'dribbling' dart is a feebly falling arrow.[11] A

---

[10] See Robert Rogers, *A Psychoanalytic Study of the Double in Literature* (Detroit, 1970) for an account of 'decomposition' – the splitting, doubling, and multiplication of literary characters. Rogers agrees with the view that the play dramatizes the 'endopsychic conflicts' of the Duke, but his interpretation of the play differs considerably from mine. It is a 'comic exorcism of sexual guilt', he says (p. 23). Anton Ehrenzweig, *The Hidden Order of Art* (Berkeley, 1967) refers to decomposition in art as 'de-differentiation'. Psychoanalytic theory deals extensively with the phenomenon in its real-life manifestations.

[11] See Lever, p. 19 for explication of the unusual epithet.

'complete' bosom is presumably an impenetrable one. But would the 'complete' bosom withstand a dart that didn't dribble? The denial, in the form of a double negation, therefore puts the invulnerability it affirms into question. Lucio's slanderous 'darts', it will be recalled, do succeed in piercing the Duke's equanimity later on in the play. I am not suggesting the existence of a clandestine romance in the Duke's life; only that Angelo's Puritanical cast of character is continuous with a tendency in the Duke himself, from which he is partly disassociated and partly identified. Note the consonance of Angelo's rejection of permissiveness in rule:

> We must not make a scarecrow of the law,
> Setting it up to fear the birds of prey,
> And let it keep one shape, till custom make it
> Their perch and not their terror   (2.1.1–4)

with his:

> Now, as fond fathers,
> Having bound up the threat'ning twigs of
> birch,
> Only to stick it in their children's sight
> For terror, not to use, in time the rod
> [Becomes] more mock'd than fear'd.
> (1.3.23–7)

The Duke's quandary, therefore, is projected in the two deputies who are his doubles in that they represent the two halves of his split personality. But this complex persona proliferates further splits. He himself is alternately hermit and ruler, representative of the 'life removed' and the life of office, by way of a role, the Friar's, which, *vis-à-vis* Isabella, is indeterminately father/brother and alternately harshly disciplinarian and tenderly supportive. His bed-trick stratagem is the 'Escalus' counterpart to Angelo's monstrous proposal; his repudiation of Isabella as false witness (5.1.241–5) actualizes Angelo's 'Who will believe thee, Isabel?' (2.4.154). Further, 'Be absolute for death' (3.1.5) and 'Ay, but to die' (3.1.117), antithetical extremities of response to death, dramatize a mythopoeic contest

between death-wish and pleasure principle, but also suggest the fractured halves of a psychic wholeness or integrity not evident in Vienna save at brute base: in Pompey, or in Barnardine, who are beyond good and evil, and in the crucial figure of Juliet. Even Lucio, as Lever suggestively observes (p. xcvi), is an alter ego, in the first part enacting a practical providence as go-between, in the second externalizing the scoffing self-denigration of a spirit deeply divided ' 'twixt will and will not' (2.2.33), between giving and withholding, permitting and forbidding, mortal fallibility and omnipotence.

It is my contention that *Measure for Measure* repeats and reiterates its situations, doubles and redoubles its personae – the Duke and his proxies, but also, as we shall see, Angelo and Isabella; Angelo and Claudio; Isabella, her cousin Juliet, her substitute Mariana; Barnardine, obstinately alive and Ragozin fortuitously dead; the pregnant wife (or common-law wife or punk) of Elbow, Claudio, and Lucio; because that is the way the play works through, and divulges, the fantasies which energize it. It is a masterly study of repression, and of the repressed, and of its Hydra-headed return.

If the characterizations and confrontations of Angelo and Isabella are any indication, post-psychoanalytic wisdom can add little to Shakespeare's where the portrayal of repression and its vicissitudes is concerned.

Consider Isabella's first interview with Angelo. She begins with a disavowal of the extenuation she has come to plead which identifies her position with Angelo's:

> There is a vice that most I do abhor,
> And most desire should meet the blow of
> justice;
> For which I would not plead, but that I must;
> For which I must not plead, but that I am
> At war 'twixt will and will not.   (2.2.29–33)

She needs, quite conspicuously, to be egged on to her persuasive task by Lucio. She is hardly on her brother's side. When, however, she warms to the theme of mercy, and is provoked to her best efforts by the inflexibility of her opponent, she exhibits a powerful, scornful eloquence:

> O, it is excellent
> To have a giant's strength; but it is tyrannous
> To use it like a giant.
>   . . . man, proud man,
> Dress'd in a little brief authority,
> Most ignorant of what he's most assur'd
> (His glassy essence), like an angry ape
> Plays such fantastic tricks before high heaven
> As makes the angels weep; who, with our
>   spleens,
> Would all themselves laugh mortal.
>   (ll. 107–9, 117–23)

Lucio, delighted, records the effect of her vehemence upon the silent Angelo: 'O, to him, to him, wench! he will relent. / He's coming; I perceive't' (ll. 124–5). What does Lucio perceive? The bawdy innuendo is characteristic of Lucio, but that should not blind us to its objective justification. For it is evidently at this point, during Angelo's momentary silence, that the 'snowbroth' of his blood begins to melt, his defences to weaken. Is it, ironically, the defiance of authority that is subtly seductive for so compulsively authoritative a figure? Or her resistance to him, her independence, her, if you will, unfeminine aggressiveness that confuses, and rouses him?

When he next speaks he is defensive: 'Why do you put these sayings upon me?' (ll. 133). And her reply is more telling than she knows:

> Go to your bosom,
> Knock there, and ask your heart what it doth
>   know
> That's like my brother's fault. If it confess
> A natural guiltiness such as is his,
> Let it not sound a thought upon your tongue
> Against my brother's life.   (ll. 136–41)

It is upon an entirely universal guiltiness – original sin – that she bases her plea for charitable forgiveness, but her ardour is perhaps convincing just because of a degree of self-knowledge on her own part, to which we shall return. Angelo's punning aside records the glimpsed possibility of a shared sensuality:

> She speaks, and 'tis
> Such sense that my sense breeds with it
>   (ll. 141–2)

almost as if she were an accomplice in his overthrow.

And then, in all innocence, but with uncannily timely complicity, Isabella produces her trump card: 'Hark how I'll bribe you. Good my lord, turn back' (ll. 145). His startled 'How? bribe me?' betrays his guilty thoughts.

> Not with fond sicles of the tested gold,
> Or stones . . .
>   but with true prayers
>   (ll. 149–51)

is Isabella's reply. 'You had marr'd all else', Lucio wryly, and rightly, remarks. But what would we hear in that slightly odd sequence of syllables if we can imagine a hearing as sexually sensitized as Angelo's has become?

Isabella is totally unaware of the temptation she constitutes for him, of the desire she arouses in him; it is as if the language she uses insidiously traps her, or betrays her. Even her 'mercy then will breathe within your lips, / Like man new made' (ll. 78–9), overtly biblical-prophetic, is surreptitiously sexual or procreative. But the fact that she does not know, or does not allow herself to know, that she is sexually attractive, does not alter the unconscious magnetism subtly dramatized in this scene.

Angelo's defensive armour has depended upon the degradation of women. In his view of women as strumpets, sex can be, and has been, disassociated from tenderness and from respect, from ideals and values. Sex is defilement, defecation:

> Having waste ground enough,
> Shall we desire to raze the sanctuary
> And pitch our evils there?[12]   (ll. 169–71)

---

[12] For the defecatory meaning of 'evils' see Lever, p. 50.

or corruption:

> but it is I
> That, lying by the violet in the sun,
> Do as the carrion does, not as the flow'r.
>
> (ll. 164–6)[13]

It is therefore shattering for him to feel desire for a woman who represents his own conscious ascetic ideal. For a moment he attempts to put the blame upon her, as temptress. But this is an escape his Puritan conscience cannot use. So he falls back upon the Devil: 'O cunning enemy, that to catch a saint / With saints dost bait thy hook! ... Never could the strumpet, / ... / Once stir my temper; but this virtuous maid / Subdues me quite' (ll. 179–86, *passim*). But it is surely not simply because she is a 'saint' that he is erotically aroused – she is not behaving quite like a saint at this moment – but because she is courageously, passionately, resisting him, standing up to him, challenging his omnipotence, challenging his masculinity.[14] Hating his own weakness, unnerved by the breach in his defences, he must in effect deny what in a less conflicted personality would have been gladly acceptable, and available, as love: 'What, do I love her / That I desire to hear her speak again? / And feast upon her eyes?' (ll. 176–8). His perverse, self-tormenting and self-justifying, punitive response is therefore to degrade her, to make of her the prostitute he sees in all women. And this is his strategy in the second seduction scene.

When we next see Angelo he is in a state of nervous agitation and acute self-division. He, the snow-broth man, has become vibrantly aware of his body:

> heaven in my mouth,
> As if I did but only chew his name,
> And in my heart the strong and swelling evil
> Of my conception. (2.4.4–7)

This is language as powerful, and as powerfully displaced as Macbeth's choked excitement as he contemplates murder. And like Macbeth he too embraces his 'evil' as his own

identity: 'Blood, thou art blood / Let's write "good angel" on the devil's horn, / 'Tis not the devil's crest' (ll. 15–17).

The change in Angelo in the second scene with Isabella is dramatic. Sexual equivocation is no longer inadvertent. Isabella has 'come to know your pleasure' (l. 31). 'That you might know it, would much better please me / Than to demand what 'tis' is his sardonic aside. (ll. 32–3). Her 'Like man new made' (2.2.79) re-echoes in his 'It were as good / To pardon him that hath from nature stol'n / A man already made' (2.4.42–4). But he is tense, nervous, over-anxious enough to (nearly) give his game away too soon (ll. 57–60). We note the reversal of the situation. In the first scene her suit was to him, for mercy, to redeem her brother. Now the tables are turned: his suit is to her, for 'charity', to redeem her brother. For a while they are at cross-purposes. The 'charity in sin' (l. 63) that he has in mind has not penetrated her consciousness.

> That I do beg his life, if it be sin,
> Heaven let me bear it! You granting of my
>   suit,
> If that be sin, I'll make it my morn-prayer
> To have it added to the faults of mine,
> And nothing of your answer. (ll. 69–73)

Her impenetrable innocence irritates him since it is the very thing he must debase if he is to have his way. He moves to the attack therefore:

> Your sense pursues not mine. Either you
>   are ignorant,
> Or seem so [craftily]; (ll. 74–5)

impeaches her humility:

> Thus wisdom wishes to appear most bright
> When it doth tax itself; as these black masks
> Proclaim an enshield beauty ten times louder
> Than beauty could, displayed. (ll. 78–81)

---

[13] Cf. *Hamlet*, 2.2.183.

[14] Cf. Empson's view that it is her coldness that excites him, *The Structure of Complex Words* (1952), p. 274.

And returns to his hypothetical case: were there

> No earthly mean to save him, but that either
> You must lay down the treasures of your body
>   . . . or else to let him suffer –
> What would you do? (ll. 95–8)

Let us return at this point to Isabella, caught, like her adversary double, in the compulsions of a sexual repression no less exigent than his. The portrait of Isabella is complex, and we shall have to go back over the play's tracks, to the moment when Isabella first hears that her brother is in prison, in order to unfold its development.

Lucio's opening announcement, that Claudio is in prison for that for which he should have been rewarded, namely getting his friend with child, is hardly a suitable ploy for the persuasion of a novice of St Clare's. Properly reproved for it, he changes tack, abjures 'lapwing' jesting, assures Isabella that he holds her 'a thing enskied, and sainted, . . . an immortal spirit' (1.4.34–5), and, when his 'sincerity' is still put in question – 'You do blaspheme the good in mocking me' (ll. 38) – repeats his information in a very different register:

> Your brother and his lover have embrac'd.
> As those that feed grow full, as blossoming
>   time
> That from the seedness the bare fallow brings
> To teeming foison, even so her plenteous
>   womb
> Expresseth his full tilth and husbandry.
> (ll. 40–4)

The speech has been much discussed on account of the contrast between its celebration of sexuality, of a beneficent fertility and plenitude shared by man and 'great creating nature', shared by man and woman ('As those that feed grow full' is indeterminately applicable to either of the lovers, and enlists the satisfactions of primal nourishment to intensify those of mature sex) and the sordid sexuality both of the 'suburbs' of Vienna, and of the cynical gallants (chief of whom is Lucio himself) of scene 1. The speech is usually glossed as a reflection of a festive Shakespearian mood, now in eclipse. But I think it important to perceive it in context as a part of Lucio's cunning rhetoric, of his attempt to win Isabella over to the rescue mission he is about to propose to her. The point is important because her immediate, spontaneous response, 'O, let him marry her' (ll. 49), is surely an indication that his words can reach her, perhaps even strike a chord. Her response reflects more than simply the Elizabethan understanding of the legal situation of common-law wives.[15] As Walter Lever puts it, ' "Someone with child by him? My cousin Juliet?" is not the response of a novice, but of a typically frank-spoken Renaissance . . . Rosalind or Portia' (p. xxvi). And there is more to be gleaned from this initial dialogue. Juliet, it seems, is not really Isabella's cousin, but 'Adoptedly, as school-maids change[16] their names / By vain though apt affection' (ll. 47–8); Juliet is Isabella's alter ego, or imagined twin, much in the manner of Hermia and Helena, those twinned 'double cherries' of *A Midsummer Night's Dream*. Juliet then, is the woman in Isabella which Isabella, choosing chastity to God, has not chosen to be; Juliet represents the deeply repressed sensuality from which she defends herself by the compulsive perfectionism of her demand for 'a more strict restraint' even than her particularly severe order requires (ll. 3–5). We recall 'the prone and speechless dialect, / Such as move men' – sex-appeal, in the unvarnished dialect of another age – to which her brother refers (1.2.183–4), and upon which he pins his hopes for the persuasion of the Deputy, more, it seems, than upon her 'prosperous art' of 'reason and discourse'.

---

[15] On common-law wives see Lever, pp. liii–liv. See also A. D. Nuttall, '*Measure for Measure*: The Bed-Trick', *Shakespeare Survey 28* (1975) for discussion of Jacobean attitudes to marriage.

[16] 'Exchange' according to the Riverside gloss.

We need to consider more closely the complex sexuality of Isabella. I press the point because I think Isabella is misconceived very often. She slips too easily into reductive stereotypes of frigidity, hypocrisy, or egoism, whereas what the drama articulates is the breakdown of a passionate and sensual nature heroically idealizing a spiritually sanctified abnegation.

Challenged by Angelo's 'What would you do?' (2.4.98) her immediate response is to imagine a martyrdom willingly embraced. But it is in erotically masochistic terms that she pictures martyrdom:

> As much for my poor brother as myself:
> That is, were I under the terms of death,
> Th' impression of keen whips I'ld wear as
> rubies,
> And strip myself to death, as to a bed
> That longing have been sick for, ere I'ld yield
> My body up to shame. (2.4.99–104)

This vision of martyrdom is a cherished idea, not an anticipated actuality, for she has not yet caught the drift of Angelo's probings. And it enables us to see that what surfaces under the pressure of Angelo's 'temptation' is a deep-seated fear, not of sex as such, and not of sin – she knows as well as Angelo that 'compelled sins' are not blameworthy,[17] and that chastity is a state of the soul, not the body – but of the breakdown of her fragile ideology of a desexualized, an alternative ecstasy.

When Isabella, desperate and frightened, flies to her brother to tell him of the monstrous proposal, she is seeking not so much to reconcile him to his fate as to confirm her own decision, to receive authority for it, to have him say something like 'You have done well, my child', and then to embrace him in a loving reciprocal sacrifice – a Christianized *liebestod* of souls. She says

> I'll to my brother.
> Though he hath fall'n by prompture of the
> blood,
> Yet hath he in him such a mind of honor

> That had he twenty heads to tender down
> On twenty bloody blocks, he'ld yield them
> up,
> Before his sister should her body stoop
> To such abhorr'd pollution. (ll. 177–83)

But why tell him, after all? Why torment him with her own anguish? Why does she force him to endure the same agonizing decision that she has been forced to undergo, if not out of her great need for a supporting, confirming, justifying response from him? And she is in deep fear that she will not receive it, as her initial testing of him shows (3.1.64–80). When he does respond with 'Thou shalt not do't' (ll. 102) she is overwhelmingly relieved and cries out in loving magnanimity

> O, were it but my life,
> I'd throw it down for your deliverance
> As frankly as a pin. (ll. 103–5)

This announcement (I am not questioning the genuineness of the feeling) is dramatically ironic, since the sacrifice that one is not asked for invariably appears preferable to the one that is demanded, a point neatly underlined by Claudio's laconic 'Thanks, dear Isabel'. And it precipitates in Claudio the very natural thoughts about the relativity of values which follow (ll. 110–17). As the dialogue proceeds, Isabella becomes more and more alarmed until, when finally faced with Claudio's plea 'Sweet sister, let me live' (ll. 132), and with his morally impeccable argument – her own, at an earlier point, to Angelo (2.4.65–6):

> What sin you do to save a brother's life,
> Nature dispenses with the deed so far,
> That it becomes a virtue (3.1.133–4)

she breaks down in panic-stricken, hysterical repudiation. And her outburst is extremely revealing.

> O you beast!
> O faithless coward! O dishonest wretch!

---

[17] In the sources the woman is always blameless.

Wilt thou be made a man out of my vice?
Is't not a kind of incest, to take life
From thine own sister's shame? What should
   I think?
Heaven shield my mother play'd my father fair!
For such a warped slip of wilderness
Ne'er issu'd from his blood.   (ll. 135–42)

Wheeler, quoting Eric Partridge's *Shake-speare's Bawdy*, points out that 'vice' is an 'anatomical pun'.[18] But we hardly need the image of closing, or opening thighs to alert us to the distraught condensation in Isabella's words; the expression (once more) 'to be made a man out of' and 'to take life from', on either side of the strange question, 'Is't not a kind of incest' make the implicit metaphor an indeterminate composite of birth and intercourse. It is a grotesque figuration which has the nightmarish, revelatory disorder of an imagination under great stress. Isabella defends herself against horror by disowning Claudio, while the displacement of shame – the shame of yielding to Angelo, the shame of Claudio's demand, the shame of her rejection of him – from brother/sister relationships to a hypothetical parental lapse allows her rage an outlet. The passion with which she turns upon him with

Die, perish! Might but my bending down
Reprieve thee from thy fate, it should
   proceed.
I'll pray a thousand prayers for thy death,
No word to save thee   (3.1.143–6)

can surely only be due to the massive energy which has been required to batten down a powerful desire. The play thus allows us to gauge the anguish Angelo's attempted seduction produces in her, and to understand her need for the armour-plated 'More than our brother is our chastity' (2.4.185). But the more we understand her frantic repudiation of her brother, her defensive, panic-stricken rage, the collapse of her heroic self-control:

O fie, fie fie!
Thy sin's not accidental, but a trade.

Mercy to thee would prove itself a bawd,
'Tis best that thou diest quickly   (3.1.147–50)

the less will we be able to understand or accommodate her response to the bed-trick proposal.

The bed-trick is the crux of the matter. Technically it is the 'well-tied knot' which, in Renaissance theory of tragicomedy, must mediate between extreme peril and happy solution. It even provides an extra bonus: a happy solution for a jilted lady we haven't yet become acquainted with, and who does not appear in any of the sources. But the substitution of Mariana for Isabella in Angelo's bed turns out to be the most baffling of all the play's anomalies. Claudio got Juliet with child when she was 'fast' his 'wife' (1.2.147) by common-law statute, which accepted betrothal contracts as binding, and pregnancy as still more so. The canonical solemnizing of ceremony had been postponed, not unreasonably, in real-life Elizabethan terms, till the dowry was forthcoming. Angelo, on the other hand, had broken off his betrothal contract with Mariana because her dowry had been lost at sea with her brother who was bringing it to her; and he will not, so far as he knows, be sleeping with a fiancée but raping a ransom hostage. Neatly, the bed-trick makes Angelo do exactly what he sentenced Claudio to death for, but in circumstances morally far more blackening to his character. Isabella's ready acceptance of the Duke's plan, therefore, strains credibility. The bed-trick foils both the sets of generic expectations which are entangled in *Measure for Measure*: it prevents the tragic outcome the play prepares for, but it does not mediate a harmonizing comic resolution. So far from being a knot which binds the 'serious' with the 'comic order of things' (Guarini, in Lever p. lxi), it has been felt to be the chief stumbling block which breaks the play into two incommensurable, disrelated and dissonant parts.

---

[18] Wheeler, p. 111.

But Humpty Dumpty might be put together again. I want to propose a reading
which might do this, for audiences in our
time, alert to subtexts, to the oneiric, the sub-
terranean in discourse, to what can be meant,
what can be read, and what language can be up
to. It has, I believe, the additional advantage of
being, conceivably, presentable in the
theatre.[19] Certainly in the cinema, with the aid
of a director as gifted and dextrous as Alain
Resnais, for example. I have in mind the
remarkable film *Providence*, in which, it will be
recalled, a dying author projects his own
anxieties, paranoias, obsessions, guilts
through a reconstruction, or construction, or
interpretation, or imagination of his family
circle. In the film fictional 'real' people play
fictional imaginary roles, in circumstances
invented by the fictional waking dreamer–
narrator; characters split and coalesce, plays
embed themselves within plays in infinite
regression, and fact and fantasy shift and inter-
penetrate, mask each other and mock each
other in a bewildering and enthralling phantas-
magoria of the interior life.

My hypothesis is simple: let us suppose that
from the moment in 3.1 when the Duke comes
forward and draws Isabella aside, when the
play changes gear, as it were, in every respect:
tone, style, diction, direction, the play can be
read as the replay – only this time with escape
possible – in Isabella's wishful fantasy, of the
traumatic events that are happening to her, and
in which she is so terribly trapped. To pursue
the cinematic analogy: let us imagine a frozen
still of faces and gestures at a moment of high
drama, break, pause, and, while that representation stops, another reel continues to unwind,
with flashbacks, reminiscence – it is often done
– gradually taking the place of the original
image as that fades out. Isabella's trauma
meshes with the Duke's proposal to produce a
wish-fulfilment dream sequence, in which the
fantasy of escape is shot through by what
Freud calls 'counter-dreams' of pain and
punishment. Read in this way, moreover, act

4, as we shall see, would correspond to Shakespeare's preceding explorations and discoveries in the forms of comic catharsis.

The replay is first of all, structural. Where
the first part moves from Lucio's plea to
Isabella for help, through the monstrous proposal, to Isabella's threat to expose Angelo,
and her flight to her brother, the second part
moves from the Duke's offer of help, through
the actualization of the monstrous proposal, to
the exposure scenes of act 5 and the reunion of
Isabella with her brother. Moreover, the
fatherly Friar steps into Isabella's life, with his
remedy, just at the moment when her own (as
she had hoped) fatherly brother had desper-
ately let her down.

This in itself is disarming, and promotive of
a willingness to be swayed by him. But there
are deeper reasons for her 'content'. Mariana is
Isabella's double in a sense more profound than
that of mere technical substitution. She is, I
suggest, her deeply wished-for double, in a
situation that is, as has already been noted, the
replica of her brother's with Juliet.

Juliet, as was observed, is the Isabella
Isabella the novice has chosen not to be;
Mariana is the woman Isabella the extortion
victim has chosen not to be. But if Mariana to
Angelo is the equivalent of Juliet to Claudio,
an equivalence the Duke's explanation brings
out, then the bed-trick substitution can offer to
Isabella the occasion for a repressed wish-
fulfilment fantasy. We recall the warmth of her
feelings for Claudio, and we recall her outburst
when she repudiates him: 'Is't not a kind of

---

19 In a recent RSC production Isabella and Mariana were
dressed alike, and indeed looked rather alike, to
excellent effect. This visual semiotic could be extended:
after the switch in act 3 characters would wear the same
clothes in a contrasting colour; the prison scene décor
could be lit contrastingly before and after the break;
Lucio's costume could be conspicuously different, so
that he appears a gallant in the beginning and a foppish
grotesque in act 4. In sum, efforts could be made, not to
slur, or to try to ignore the differences between the two
halves of the play, but precisely to foreground them.

incest' (3.1.138). However, Mariana is also, since she will double for Isabella, at one and the same time the sexual victim of Angelo's lust. This is exactly the point upon which natural-istic interpretations of Isabella's response stumble. But the unconscious knows no contradiction, as we know. The deep ambi-valences that must be denied in consciousness appear in dreams in defiant simultaneity. The role to be played by Mariana could be doubly, triply satisfying to Isabella's exacerbated imagination: she is the permitted, semi-legitimized marriage partner in a fantasy replica of Juliet's (unconsciously envied) mis-demeanour with her brother; she is sexual victim of the man who has tried to seduce her, and might well therefore have triggered the underlying masochism already observed, the more especially since in a culture of shame such as Isabella's, disguise, a kind of absence, is a potent enabling factor for sexual fantasizing. And finally, the man who has tried to seduce her is, at the censored level of intellectual and conscious values, her avowed ideal, a spiritual double. The bed-trick, stumbling block to rational or moral interpretation, thus appears as keystone in the overdetermined, poly-phonic figurations of fantasy: 'The image of it', says Isabella, 'Gives me content already, and I trust it will grow to a most prosperous perfection' (3.1.259–60).

One of the formal anomalies that have often been noticed in *Measure for Measure* – officially a comedy – is the absence of the 'other place' – the restorative, wild, or rural 'green world' in which, in so many of Shakespeare's comedies, the statutory errors and follies of the characters find their comic amendment.[20] The 'other places' in Shakespeare's 'green world' comedies create space within the play in which fantasy can function. They represent another, but available realm of the psyche where extravagant, irrational, lunatic or preposterous possibilities are entertained. But is there no such 'other place' in *Measure for Measure*?

Mariana's strangely evocative moated grange is perhaps a subliminal fragment of such a symbolic place. But listen to Isabella's descrip-tion of the passageway through the Deputy's garden to the place of assignation:

> He hath a garden circummur'd with brick,
> Whose western side is with a vineyard back'd;
> And to that vineyard is a planched gate,
> That makes his opening with this bigger key.
> This other doth command a little door,
> Which from the vineyard to the garden leads;
> There have I made my promise upon the
>   heavy
> Middle of the night to call upon him.

(4.1.28–35)

Interestingly, the new Arden editor, who makes no mention of any sexual topography in this description, notes that 'heavy middle' carries an association with 'pregnant' (p. 98, n. 35), which he relates to the play's strong 'life-affirming undertow'. I think in these hints we can make out the lineaments of a revitaliz-ing, procreatively genial 'other place' in the remedial fourth act, but it is submerged, half-suppressed, in the manner characteristic of *Measure for Measure*.

For *Measure for Measure* has its own specific 'other place', which we can now identify, as well as a particularly interesting variant of the exorcism-through-excess principle of the dual-location plays. The comic rhythm nor-mally takes us from a representation of the world of the play more or less realistically portrayed, through a preposterous or fantastic breakdown and re-creation, and back to a transfigured reality, to which the protagonists return transformed, having lost and found themselves by a species of 'regression in the service of the ego'.[21] Though they are dialecti-

---

[20] The 'green world' is a topic treated at large by North-rop Frye, *The Anatomy of Criticism* (New Jersey, 1957). My own attempt to develop a theory of exorcist comic form is in *Comic Transformations in Shakespeare* (1980).

[21] See Ernst Kris, *Psychoanalytic Explorations in Art* (New York, 1952).

cally opposed to any expansive, liberating 'green world', the prison scenes function similarly, as the alembic of unconscious and contradictory impulses. The prison sequence is correlative to the carriage of the middle scenes in Shakespeare's own best comedies, the strategy of which is to maximalize error before matters will mend. To take as a paradigmatic example *A Midsummer Night's Dream*, the delusions of the lovers and of Titania in the Athenian woods discover, enlarging as in a distorting mirror, the shadowy wishes and fears of the characters' minds, and by so doing enable the victims to enfranchise themselves of their obsessions.

Anne Barton describes the erratic, preposterous quality of the second half of the play thus: The Duke, she says, is 'a man trying to impose the order of art upon the reality which stubbornly resists such schematization. As such, he is continually being surprised by the unpredictability, not to mention the rank insubordination, of his elected cast of characters ... [who] get out of control ... [and] do things that are not in their parts as conceived by the Duke' (p. 547). In terms of the reading I am attempting, these images are a reflection of Isabella's traumatized, overwrought and hectic, but partly de-censored and therefore free-wheeling, imagination. They are therefore functionally analogous (though thematically contrary) to the 'green world', and far more significant in the dynamic of the play's unfolding than traditional interpretations allow. They contain far more than merely a representation of the seamy side of Vienna, or of the natural profanity which the fanaticism of the moral zealots does ill to ignore.

In the prison scenes of acts 3 and 4 the prison themes: illicit sexual relations, lechery and venereal disease, judgement, punishment, correction, execution – all of the play's content which has caused it to be designated a dark comedy – push to hyperbolic excess the problems and preoccupations, errors and follies of the protagonists in the first part of the play.

But these now receive a bizarre and lurid figuration, the linchpin of which is the transformation of Pompey the bawd into executioner's assistant.

Both bawd and executioner mediate a passage; the Elizabethan pun on the verb 'to die' is personified, given a dramatis dream-persona, a sado-masochistic embodiment in this transmogrification of Pompey. The Duke too, be it noted, in his plot to prevent execution, plays the role of bawd. The prison scenes can be seen as a positive saturnalia of the unconscious, an oneiric carnival of condensations and displacements – note Pompey's own equivocation on severed heads and maidenheads (v.2.1–4) – whereby the dreaming consciousness – of friar and nun, of Duke and daughter – finds ways of being both punisher and punished. The transformation of Lucio can be seen in this light too. A mocking alter ego of the Duke, as has already been observed, instigator of Isabella's reluctant mission to Angelo, he becomes now a mischief-making Adversary, an underworld Vice occupying himself in the classic Luciferian role of slanderer, liar, and prankster, spokesman for unbridled libido, underminer of fatherly authority. He makes no bones about his conviction that Angelo's icy Puritanism masks impotence,[22] insinuates sexual peccadilloes on the part of the Duke, whose identity he unmasks. And he is punished, in suitably demonic fashion, by the 'pressing to death, whipping, and hanging' of marriage to his incubus/punk.

The hectic, fevered side of distraught

---

22 See 3.2.109–12 ' . . . it is certain that when he makes water his urine is congeal'd ice, that I know to be true; and he is a motion generative, that's infallible'; and 3.2.174: 'This ungenitur'd agent'. In a footnote in *The Psychopathology of Everyday Life* (Penguin Freud Library, vol. 5, p. 90) Freud notes that 'ice is in fact a symbol by antithesis for an erection' – since it is something that becomes hard in the cold rather than in the heat of excitement. In Lucio's repeated allusions to Angelo's iciness the 'antithesis' becomes an irony.

fantasy, punitive and retaliatory at once, provides us with our clue to the meaning of the final scene. The dream repetition of events works through chaotic (but ultimately intelligible) psychic materials towards the desired escape, towards a restored equanimity. Punishment and self-punishment are an integral and necessary part of that working-through process. Isabella willed her brother's death. He it was who caused her so much suffering, threatened the whole structure of her fragile, high-strung personality. Isabella loved her brother, and Isabella was ready to let him die. Isabella loved her brother perhaps more warmly than she knew, possibly unconsciously willed his death for that very, intolerable, reason. She would be a monster if she did not suffer guilt of the acutest kind, the more especially while her repressed and newly stimulated sexuality is pressing with its insistent images upon the barriers of her consciousness. So she must, in her dream, undergo exposure and repudiation, condemnation and disbelief in the first abortive unmasking scene, and then, even when finally justified in the second, still suffer her brother's death, until finally released from the spell, so to speak, by his veritable appearance. By the same token the Duke works through the Angelo/Escalus split he was unable to resolve, seeking an Escalus way out which is repeatedly foiled, acting out Angelo's threat – 'Who will believe thee, Isabel?' (2.4.154) in his repudiation of Isabella, and his own resistance to 'the dribbling dart of love' (1.3.2) in his cruelty to her.

Seen thus, it becomes possible to perceive in Isabella's lame and mangled plea on Angelo's behalf the germ, or the adumbration, of an inchoate mixture of wish-fulfilment and self-knowledge. The wishful thinking is clear enough: '. . . As if my brother liv'd' (5.1.445). And then for the rest of the speech she takes the role, vis-à-vis Mariana's plea, of Angelo to hers, seeing the Deputy now, however, through the light of her own new knowledge of her 'bosom', of 'intents' and 'thoughts' and 'sincerities':

> Most bounteous sir:
> Look, if it please you, on this man condemn'd
> As if my brother liv'd. I partly think
> A due sincerity governed his deeds,
> Till he did look on me.
>   . . . My brother had but justice,
> In that he did the thing for which he died;
> For Angelo,
> His act did not o'ertake his bad intent,
> And must be buried but as an intent
> That perish'd by the way. Thoughts are no
>   subjects,
> Intents but merely thoughts. (5.1.443–54)

How, however, shall we see the play, retrospectively, as a totality? How shall we identify its constitutive fantasy? It is made of two impulses, one that presses towards death, one that clings to life, as in the partner speeches of the Duke and Claudio. It is not a well-formed sentence in either of the classic forms. It might have been a tragedy. It has the makings, had it only not been provided with a providential plotter. But it is so provided. With a fantastical Duke of dark corners, who hides and conceals. It might have been a comedy, had its heroine been a witty Rosalind, frankly, openly, untroubledly in love. But she is the antithesis of a Rosalind and we do not know how she feels about her unexpected betrothal. We have no way of knowing or even surmising because Isabella, at the play's end, her brother restored, her sisterhood now solely natural, her fatherly friar a husband for her bed, is impenetrably silent. Indeed, except for the Duke, none of the protagonists is given utterance in the final scene of resolutions. They fall into deathly silence, give no sign that they embrace the Eros that the play, officially, sanctifies. Expressions of happy acceptance, of joy, relief, satisfaction provide the regulation speeches of closure in Shakespearian comedies, indeed in any comedy. Here, only Lucio, the Duke's irrepressible antagonist, has a final, rueful word: 'Marrying a punk, my lord, is pressing to death, whipping, and hanging' (5.1.522–3). What can we make of so unusual a circumstance?

It is a commonplace in the criticism that a disenchantment with sex, a sexual disgust, pervades the plays of Shakespeare's middle period. But this, I think, is to give only half of the story. True, in the tragedies which follow *Measure for Measure*, the beneficence of sexuality, of procreation, is in eclipse, blacked out by a destructive fury, painful, searing, traumatic, and, in *Timon of Athens*, nearly total. It is images of women which bear the brunt of this fury. Down from the waist women are centaurs, 'there's hell, there's darkness, / There is the sulphurous pit, burning, scalding, / Stench, consumption' (*King Lear*, 4.6.127–9), and if the dream of Cordelia can still sweeten the imagination, it is only by means of a titanic struggle. *Measure for Measure* stands upon the edge of the psychological agon into which the Shakespearian *œuvre* is about to plunge, and it uneasily, uncertainly brandishes its apotropaic victory, its triad of reparative marriages which would ward off evil. But the text remains radically dual, split, in its view of the beneficence of sexuality. It affirms, and denies. Juliet, Mariana, Mistress Overdone, who brings up Lucio's child by Kate Keepdown, are powerful if peripheral figures. But in the centre is the queasy quartet: the Duke, who is,

or would be, a 'complete bosom', and 'absolute for death'; Angelo, man of congealed ice, who must be bought or bludgeoned into marriage, if at all; Claudio, easily half-convinced of the baneful, 'thirsty evil' of love; and Isabella. These characters have dramatized sexual repression and its vicissitudes. They can be seen, as has been indicated, as representing a decomposition of the central psyche, as multiples or splinters of the Duke. The enigma of their silence, an abrogation of closure, a dissolution of figure and a scandal to interpretation collapses them back into the unconscious from which they emerged, suggests their status as projective figments rather than mimetic fictions. The scapegrace, scapegoat Lucio also functions as a defence, warding off the rage and the anguish and the repulsion of the tragedies to come. Marriage to a *punk* seen as pressing to death, whipping and hanging camouflages misogyny with a socially legitimized consternation and the humour of a comic retribution. The play's formally comic dénouement affirms Eros, but its silences, its pregnant and impregnable silences, repress a corrosive doubt. Perhaps for this reason the play's language is haunted by a yearning for an unfleshed birth, parthenogenesis, or, in Christian terms, a transcendent incarnation, man new made.

ALLEGORY AND IRONY IN 'OTHELLO'

ANTOINETTE B. DAUBER

Othello is Shakespeare's Spenserian tragedy, in which the theme of slandered chastity becomes a vehicle for exploring the problems of an allegorical art. Allegory is the mode of self-conscious faith, and Spenser's corpus may be read as a portrait of the artist as allegorist, wrestling first with the burdens of self-consciousness and then with the burdens of faith.[1] In *Othello*, Shakespeare compresses and objectifies this struggle. Unlike Spenser, he is not committed to the maintenance of allegory, and so he freely dramatizes the internal weaknesses and external onslaughts that lead to its destruction.

What I am calling the 'Spenserian' quality begins with the chivalric elements in the tragedy. Truly, Othello is a kind of Savage Knight, Desdemona, the absolutely, almost miraculously, worthy lady, and Iago, something of a manipulator like Archimago.[2] But more particularly I would call attention to a specific engagement with Spenserian rhetoric. Consider Cassio's words of welcome to the disembarking Desdemona:

> Tempests themselves, high seas, and howling winds,
> The gutter'd rocks and congregated sands,
> Traitors ensteep'd to enclog the guiltless keel,
> As having sense of beauty, do omit
> Their mortal natures, letting go safely by
> The divine Desdemona.   (2.1.68–73)[3]

He sets her in the line of Spenser's heavenly allegories. As a parallel, we may recall Una, slandered by the arch-magician, abandoned by her champion, roaming the woods alone. Choosing a shady spot, she removes her fillet and stole to reveal her brilliant, sunny face for the first time. 'Did neuer mortall eye behold such heauenly grace' (4), the speaker marvels, and his hyperbolic rhetoric is literally true, until a fierce lion espies her and charges. The beast, like Cassio's high seas, is tamed by the lady's beauty: 'And with the sight amazd,

---

1 What I mean by Spenser's artistic self-consciousness is finely suggested by A. Bartlett Giamatti, 'A Prince and a Poet', *Yale Review*, 73 (1984), p. 335: 'Because he knows that words can bring forth evil as well as good, monsters as well as moral shapes, he gradually loses faith in signs, in his system of allegorical "other speech...."' By the 'burdens of faith', I refer to the poet's difficulties in maintaining his belief in the Queen who had been the centre of his work from *The Shepheardes Calendar* on. Much recent criticism, including work by Daniel Javitch, Richard Helgerson, Louis Adrian Montrose and David A. Miller, focuses on his disenchantment.

2 See Mark Rose, 'Othello's Occupation: Shakespeare and the Romance of Chivalry', *English Literary Renaissance*, 15 (1985), 293–311. Wordsworth associates Una and Desdemona in 'Personal Talk':

> Two will I mention, dearer than the rest –
> The gentle lady, married to the Moor;
> And heavenly Una with her milk-white lamb.

These lines are quoted in *The Faerie Queene, Book One, The Works of Edmund Spenser: A Variorum Edition*, eds. Edwin Greenlaw et al. (Baltimore, 1932), p. 206. The quotations below are from canto 3 of this volume. Numbers in parentheses will refer to stanzas.

3 All quotations from *Othello* and other Shakespearian works cited in passing are from *The Riverside Shakespeare*, ed. G. Blakemore Evans (Boston, 1974).

forgat his furious forse' (5). Spenser differs from Cassio, however, in that he knows his responsibility both for Una's divine beauty and for her desperate plight. The tears he weeps at her wretchedness are tears of remorse for what allegorical necessity forces upon him:

> That my fraile eyes these lines with teares do
>   steepe,
> To thinke how she through guilefull
>   handeling,
> Though true as touch, though daughter of a
>   king,
> Though faire as euer liuing wight was faire,
> Though nor in word nor deede ill meriting,
> Is from her knight diuorced in despair . . . (2)

The guileful handler is the poet himself, the lines he waters of his own composition. Judged solely on her merits, as he readily admits, Una deserves no ill, but he has a story to tell. Even as he submits to the lady's grandeur, his openly subjective stance serves as a reminder of his own authoring role:

> I, whether lately through her brightnesse
>   blind,
> Or through alleageance and fast fealtie,
> Which I do owe vnto all woman kind,
> Feele my heart perst with so great agonie,
> When such I see, that all for pittie I could die. (1)

The proximity of the blinded poet in stanza one to 'blind Deuotion', the evil character named in the Argument and developed as the sightless old woman, Corceca, would be too close for comfort did it not force us to consider the difference between the cowering, superstitious crone and the poet who allows himself to be dazzled. Even as he avows that Una's brightness blinds him and her sufferings break his heart, we are reminded that he is the author of both brightness and suffering.[4] By inoculating allegory with a dose of ironic self-consciousness, Spenser protects it from our scepticism. Yet there is nothing cynical about his insistence on his own shaping role. The truth is no less true for the fact that it needs his skill and clarifying intellect to be publicized.

On the contrary, by deliberately drawing attention to the part he plays, the poet strengthens our receptivity to his rhetoric of praise, however extravagant.

Cassio lacks this saving self-awareness. To be sure, he is familiar with one important Spenserian device for calling attention to his own imaginative powers, the ironic 'inexpressibility' topos:[5]

> . . . a maid
> That paragons description and wild fame;
> One that excels the quirks of blazoning pens,
> And in th' essential vesture of creation
> Does tire the ingener.   (2.1.61–5)

But Cassio is no Spenser, no frustrated poet whose blazoning pen reluctantly admits defeat before the spectacle of the divine maid. Spenser earns the right to use this rhetorical ploy; indeed he pays dearly for it. Cassio's words, by contrast, seem unearned, incongruous.[6] Like many second-rate versifiers of his age, he presses Spenser's exquisitely burdened stance into the service of mere compliment. But a danger lurks in the assumption that sincere admiration alone justifies the appropriation of Spenserian rhetoric. Cassio's words are snares in which he traps himself. For, if he succeeds with no other listener, he convinces himself of their truth: Desdemona's safe arrival becomes a kind of circular confirmation of his own hyperbole.

This moment is an instance of what Rosalie Colie finely calls 'unmetaphoring': 'an author who treats a conventionalized figure of speech

---

4 Cf. Thomas H. Cain's analysis of this passage in *Praise in 'The Faerie Queene'* (Lincoln, 1978), p. 64: '. . . Spenser's [narrator] takes on a predominantly passive posture. . . . At the same time, Spenser's narrator-commentator paradoxically insinuates his role as creator and omniscient author.'

5 E. R. Curtius, *European Literature in the Latin Middle Ages*, trans. Willard R. Trask, Bollingen Series, no. 36 (New York, 1953), pp. 159–62, discusses inexpressibility topoi.

6 See G. G. Sedgewick, *Of Irony, Especially in Drama* (1935; repr. Toronto, 1948), p. 106.

as if it were a description of actuality is un-metaphoring that figure'. Here the playwright brings poetic cliché to solid dramatic life, and conventional storm imagery becomes 'fictional "fact"'.[7] Shakespeare, like Spenser a self-conscious artist, both uses literary forms and breaks them in order to communicate meanings. Cassio, however, is not Shakespeare. He is as captivated by his own rhetoric as the tempests and rocks he describes. Presumably he heeds his own exaggerated commands to adore Desdemona as avidly as his humblest listener:

> O, behold,
> The riches of the ship is come on shore!
> You men of Cyprus, let her have your knees.
> Hail to thee, lady! and the grace of heaven,
> Before, behind thee, and on every hand,
> Enwheel thee round!   (2.1.82–7)

Here the deification of the lady, only a Venetian matron, after all, rivals Spenser's worship of Una or Gloriana. Because he believes in the factual truth of his poetic language, Cassio is more deeply in the grip of mystification than was Spenser, who never forgot his own shaping role. While Spenser, to the last, reserved the right to refashion the allegory, Cassio remains fixed within his.

Othello presents an even more compelling instance of the naturalization of poetic convention. In contrast to Cassio's rather cavalier bandying about of poetic forms, Othello uses them in full seriousness to define himself. He prefaces his stirring account of how he won Desdemona by his storytelling, with a poet's classic opening device, the 'affected modesty' topos:[8]

> Rude am I in my speech,
> And little bless'd with the soft phrase of
>   peace . . .
> And therefore little shall I grace my cause
> In speaking for myself.   (1.3.81–2; 88–9)

But, as with Cassio, the rhetorical commonplace seems oblivious to its literary origins. Othello speaks not as a poet feigning

modesty, but sincerely as a warrior without eloquence.

Together Cassio and Othello subject the Spenserian poetic to extreme pressure, by assuming naively that the object they portray coincides absolutely with the words they speak. Innocents who act in good faith, they lack any sense that they themselves are the authors of the cultic image of Desdemona and the rough-hewn image that the Moor projects. They resemble the hypothetical monkey who sits down at the typewriter and pounds out *Hamlet*. The irony of such a supposed 'literary' event, the way in which it would mock true art, applies to Cassio and Othello. By un-metaphoring, they deny metaphor, confuse it with fact, and mock the imagination that authored the grand allegories of the past. Their ignorant wondering use of literary topoi makes them figures of irony. Indeed Othello's modest disclaimer of rhetorical skill mocks irony itself.

Desdemona is not necessarily discredited by the naiveté of her admirers. She does nothing to put their praise in doubt. Nonetheless something of the irony rubs off on her. With no adroit mythmaker drawing off our scepticism with allusions to his shaping imagination, we may find her too good to be true.[9] By using the language of allegory unawares, as it were, Othello and Cassio rob it of its strength. They identify the figure so fully with the abstract idea that they unwittingly collapse

---

[7] *Shakespeare's Living Art* (Princeton, 1974), pp. 11 and 155.

[8] Curtius, pp. 83–5.

[9] Robert Grudin, *Mighty Opposites: Shakespeare and Renaissance Contrariety* (Berkeley, 1979), pp. 130–1, illustrates this backlash when he reluctantly observes: 'Nothing is quite so dear as innocence; but, over a period of time nothing can be so uniquely annoying. . . . Desdemona sharpens the impulse to aggression in others.' Arthur Kirsch, *Shakespeare and the Experience of Love* (Cambridge, 1981), p. 12, notes that 'there are many who do feel that she is too good to be true', though he is not of their company.

the distance between them. Their blindness falsifies allegory, making it a kind of unintentional symbolism. By so mystifying Desdemona, they leave her vulnerable to demystification once more.[10]

It is a vulnerability that Iago, the non-believer, is quick to exploit. If Othello's lack of self-consciousness damages the allegorical ideal from within the system of belief, Iago attacks from without. Hard on Cassio's high-flown praise, Iago puts Desdemona on notice that he is 'nothing if not critical'. Even when he is persuaded to paint a portrait of his ideal lady, 'She that was ever fair, and never proud,' he punctures the balloon with his deflating conclusion: 'She was a wight (if ever such wight were)— ... To suckle fools and chronicle small beer' (2.1.158–60). His attack on the ideal is two-pronged. In the parenthetical remark, he calls his own construct into question. The perfect lady is a fiction, composed of a series of near oxymora. If his auditors choose to credit the image anyway, the sinking final line insists that even if such a one existed, she would be no goddess, just an ordinary mother. And so Iago penetrates a cultural convention and discloses the universal yearning that informs it. Beneath the mystified figure of worship, he discerns man's fond and foolish hope to recover the nurturing mother. As recent criticism has shown, this is precisely the fantasy that underlies Othello's passionate idealization.[11]

Desdemona, the figure of allegory, is exposed by her admirers' unwillingness to assume the burdens of allegory and laid bare by her enemy's agnosticism about the existence of any ideal at all. This characterization of the antagonists answers to our contradictory sense that, on the one hand, the Moor and his Ancient stand in absolute opposition – the one a believer, the other a sceptic – and, on the other hand, that one is only a darker projection of the other. Either way, allegory is battered. Art emerges in *Othello* as an illusory comfort, a form whose hollowness is quickly found out,

and which, with supreme irony, mocks man's pretensions to shape reality. This note is struck clearly in the opening act. The Turks' false 'pageant' fails to take in the shrewd Senator. He simply ignores the show of the sailing vessels and relies instead on his superior reason to deduce that Cyprus, not Rhodes, must be their destination. The total failure of the Turkish pageant to persuade the Venetians is but a prelude to the persistent failures of art in this play. Admittedly, in this case we may feel that the Venetian overdignifies the Turks' trick with the name 'pageant'; perhaps the fate of art is not truly at stake. Even so, the word injects the vocabulary of art into a military context, and we fleetingly savour the Senator's superior perspective as a moment of irony.

Among Shakespeare's plays *Othello* is pre-eminently ironic. Theorists of irony frequently seize on its riches.[12] In its broad outlines it affirms certain 'general laws of inevitability', rehearsing Kenneth Burke's dictum, 'what goes forth as A returns as non-A'.[13] Specifically, passion in recoil from idealization returns as destructive furore. This formulation hints that the celebrated irony of this play devolves from the ashes of allegory. Irony is the attitude engendered by the spectacle of the ruined ideal. In the many smaller ironies that punctuate the play,[14] this dynamic interplay between allegory and the opposite force released by its breakdown shows most

---

[10] This is a good place to acknowledge my profound debt to the work of Paul de Man, especially his seminal essay, 'The Rhetoric of Temporality', in *Interpretation: Theory and Practice*, ed. Charles S. Singleton (Baltimore, 1969).

[11] See Marianne Novy, *Love's Argument: Gender Relations in Shakespeare* (Chapel Hill, 1984), ch. 7, esp. pp. 132 and 146f.

[12] See, for example, G. G. Sedgewick, *Of Irony, Especially in Drama*.

[13] *A Grammar of Motives* (1945; repr. New York, 1955), Appendix D, 'Four Master Tropes', p. 517.

[14] Bert O. States, *Irony and Drama: A Poetics* (Ithaca, 1971), pp. 28–9.

sharply, highlighting the artistic and tropological concerns of the tragedy.

The supreme foe of allegorical figuration, with his persistent denials of unseen essences, and hence the major source of irony, is Iago. When Cassio whimpers, 'Reputation, reputation, reputation! O, I have lost my reputation! I have lost the immortal part of myself, and what remains is bestial' (2.3.262–4), Iago answers devastatingly, 'As I am an honest man, I had thought you had receiv'd some bodily wound; there is more sense in that than in reputation' (ll.266–8). Cassio's self-image combines an outer physical shell with a spiritual core, much like an allegory. But Iago has no use for the spiritual centre. He credits only physical hurts. His rejoinder, like Zeno's paradox, poises the lieutenant between two contradictory possibilities. If he agrees that Iago is honest, then he must believe that reputation is illusory. Yet should he deny Iago's honesty in an effort to save reputation, he would only confirm that it is 'an idle and most false imposition; oft got without merit' (ll.268–9), for Iago's reputation for honesty, attested to by the epithet, 'honest Iago', cannot be doubted. Cassio is caught in a bind, and whichever out he chooses, his faith in one of these abstractions, which in fact are two names for the same thing, will have been shaken.

Among the critics, Iago has a reputation as a dramatic poet who turns idealization 'inside out'. He is the artist of 'real life'.[15] The differences between his attitude towards the handkerchief and Othello's illustrate the point. To Othello, it is a sacred object. He traces its origins deep into the past: from his mother who gave it to him, back to the Egyptian charmer who presented it to her, and earlier still to the 200-year-old sibyl, who fashioned it out of silk of 'hallowed' worms and the mummy of maidens' hearts. By contrast, to Iago it is an indifferent prop; any token of Desdemona's would have served the purposes of his sordid drama as well. Indeed he reminds Othello of the handkerchief to counter the Moor's own airy ideals:

> Her honor is an essence that's not seen;
> They have it very oft that have it not.
> But for the handkerchief—   (4.1.16–18)

In a virtual reprise of his reputation speech, Iago denies the essence from which an allegorical art takes its meaning, replacing it with the thing itself, whose significance is strictly circumstantial.

Midway between Othello's naive mysticism and Iago's ironic denial stand Emilia and Cassio, in this case her ally. To them, the web is a medium of exchange, something to be copied and circulated without loss. Both would have the work taken out and pass it on again to continue its mediating ways: a wifely offering from Emilia to Iago, a pretty trifle from Cassio to Bianca. Its meaning is neither inherent nor merely incidental, but as it is valued between giver and receiver. At first, perhaps, Othello might have shared this view. But pressured by his suspicions, he takes refuge in a mystifying symbolism that insists on cultic virtue. For his part, Iago is equally hostile to the middle ground of mediation. However insincerely, he claims that Othello's rejection of 'mediators' – the 'three great ones' he sent to petition for the lieutenancy on his behalf – is the cause of his implacable hatred. In retaliation, he proceeds to pervert the mediator, turning what is meant to heal and unite into its opposite.

Accordingly, he uses the embroidered handkerchief, already twice the mediator, as an instrument of divorce. Acrasia, the temptress of book two of *The Faerie Queene*, provides an

---

15 William Hazlitt, *Characters of Shakespeare's Plays*, in *The Complete Works of William Hazlitt*, ed. P. P. Howe (1930), vol. 4, pp. 207–8. See also Algernon Charles Swinburne, *A Study of Shakespeare* (1879; repr. New York, 1904), pp. 230–1; Harley Granville-Barker, *Prefaces to Shakespeare* (Princeton, 1947), vol. 2, pp. 103–12; Stanley Edgar Hyman, *Iago: Some Approaches to the Illusion of his Motivation* (New York, 1970), pp. 61–76.

instructive comparison. She, too, would orchestrate the fall of a hero, and she, too, uses the mystifying power of webs as her instrument, adorning her Bower with veils to entice Guyon. But Acrasia's tactic is to take advantage of Guyon's belief. She would beguile him into surrendering to her empty parodies, and, ultimately, it is the good faith of Spenser's own allegory that preserves the hero.[16] By contrast, Iago flaunts his anti-allegorical bias. Beyond Othello's fall, he seeks the destruction of mediation and faith, the twin premises on which a Spenserian art is founded. And so, he contrives to set Desdemona up as a mediator between Cassio and her husband that he might attack her. Entreat her to splinter the broken joint between you, he urges Cassio. Similarly, he casts doubt on Cassio's loyalty, by reminding Othello that the lieutenant frequently 'went between' the lovers in their courting days.

The grim irony of *Othello* is that whatever would 'go between' the lovers injures and finally destroys their fragile love. In *The Winter's Tale*, a play with many parallels to ours, and, not incidentally, a romance that finds Shakespeare at his most Spenserian, Leontes' self-spun allegory causes the rift, but it never entirely loses its capacity to reunite what it has sundered. Thus while Othello savagely pretends that Emilia is the keeper of a brothel, Paulina's similarly mediating role is characterized more benignly as midwifery. And Emilia's shrewd guess that Othello is being put upon by 'Some busy and insinuating rogue, / Some cogging, cozening slave' (4.2.131–2) echoes in Leontes' baseless slander of Camillo, one of the helpful mediators: 'a gross lout, a mindless slave, / Or else a hovering temporizer . . .' (1.2.301–2). Emilia is right and Leontes wrong. Middlemen in *Othello* are invariably wicked or weak, while, in the romance, mediation possesses genuine redemptive power, as is clear when it is Camillo, the temporizer, who ultimately engineers the reunion.

Not just Iago's malice, not just Othello's misprision, but it seems fair to say, the larger reality that the tragedy sponsors participates in the attack on allegory. It penetrates the texture of the play, transcending the biases of any single character. Consider the treatment of the two key abstractions, patience and jealousy. The Duke, trying to calm Desdemona's father, invokes an allegorized figure of Patience who, like the smiling victim of theft, mocks her injury:

> What cannot be preserv'd when Fortune takes,
> Patience her injury a mock'ry makes.
> The robb'd that smiles steals something from the thief;
> He robs himself that spends a bootless grief.
>
> (1.3.206–9)

Against the sorrow of ruined hopes – 'seeing the worst, which late on hopes depended' (1.203) – the Duke offers Patience. Brabantio bitterly hurls the Duke's words back on him:

> So let the Turk of Cyprus us beguile,
> We lose it not, so long as we can smile.
>
> (ll.210–11)

The allegory is inefficacious. On the contrary, Brabantio insists that the Duke's advice merely compounds the hurt:

> But he bears both the sentence and the sorrow
> That, to pay grief, must of poor patience borrow. (ll.214–15)

Moreover, words are equivocal, allegory an illusion:

> But words are words; I never yet did hear
> That the bruis'd heart was pierced through the ear. (ll.218–19)

Like Iago, Brabantio credits only physical wounds. Words that enter through the ear are powerless to assault the heart or to heal it. The Duke's Patience smiles and endures; Braban-

---

[16] See my 'The Art of Veiling in the Bower of Bliss', *Spenser Studies*, 1 (1980), 163–75.

tio's aggravates the sorrow. But both, finally, are false impositions.

A parallel allegorization and dismissal befalls jealousy. Iago cynically personifies the emotion as 'the green-ey'd monster which doth mock / The meat it feeds on' (3.3.166–7). Othello, as it were, kills off this monster with one impatient stroke: 'Think'st thou I'ld make a life of jealousy? . . . No! to be once in doubt / Is once to be resolv'd' (3.3.177–80). In the following scene, Emilia echoes her husband's language:

> They are not ever jealous for the cause,
> But jealous for they're jealous. It is a
>   monster
> Begot upon itself, born on itself.   (3.4.160–2)

But even as she retains the language of personification, 'monster', she undermines it by exposing its birth in the sick mind of the jealous man. She returns Iago's allegory to its psychological origins. Desdemona's fervent response, 'Heaven keep the monster *from Othello's mind!*' (l.163, emphasis added), indicates that she has understood Emilia properly. In these twin scenes, allegory is once more vanquished. Othello, ironically adapting Iago's stance, denies the essence altogether. He has no room for jealousy in his scheme of things. Emilia and Desdemona here are closer to the unmetaphorizers. They transmute an extravagant literary figure into the stuff of everyday reality; in Spenserian terms they turn deformed Gealosie back into Malbecco, the suspicious old husband (*Faerie Queene*, canto 3, stanza 10).

But beyond the building up and breaking down of the allegorical image, these two sets of passages, the one centring on patience, the other on jealousy, have other points in common. For, incongruously enough, Iago's Jealousy and the Duke's Patience both have mocking natures. Allegory would seem to discredit itself and words to confirm Brabantio's low opinion of them, if two such antithetical essences can be endowed with such similar traits. Furthermore, we can now see that there is something awry in this image of Patience who, unlike her resigned sisters who smile at their ills (cf. 'Patience on a monument, / Smiling at grief' *Twelfth Night*, 2.4.114–15), positively mocks. The Duke's Patience is, in short, not merely a passive suffering posture, but the superior consciousness of irony:

> When remedies are past, the griefs are ended
> By seeing the worst, which late on hopes
>   depended.
> To mourn a mischief that is past and gone
> Is the next way to draw new mischief on.
> What cannot be preserv'd when Fortune
>   takes,
> Patience her injury a mock'ry makes.
>   (1.3.202–7)

Patience emerges as the attitude of superior awareness by which man distances himself from the necessities of history. Although mislabelled, this Patience is an allegorical figure of irony. Retrospectively, then, we might see that Brabantio's ironic dissection of the Duke's allegory – 'These sentences, to sugar or to gall, / Being strong on both sides, are equivocal' (1.3.216–17) – redoubles rather than destroys the effect.

Othello, who has heard both the Duke's abortive allegory and Iago's, plays with these ideas. Had physical afflictions or poverty been his lot, he could have borne them: 'I should have found in some place of my soul / A drop of patience' (4.2.52–3), he avers. His fund of patience is too depleted to fashion a full-bodied allegory, but when his thoughts race on and he sees himself as the taunted cuckold, he allegorizes both himself and his tormentors:

> . . . but, alas, to make me
> The fixed figure for the time of scorn
> To point his slow unmoving finger at!
>   (4.2.53–5)

Public opinion is personified as time of scorn, possessed of a slow unmoving finger. Here, mockery, the unexpected common denominator between Patience and Jealousy, achieves independent allegorical status. Allegory fixes irony. But at the same time, the speaker, frozen in his humiliation, casts himself in archetypally allegorical terms: he is a 'fixed figure', a parody of allegorical figuration that mocks its own emptiness. Allegory is unmasked by irony, and irony, in turn, is re-allegorized. Bound up in each other, neither motive triumphs. On the contrary, in a gesture characteristic of the tragedy, the vexed paradox is just waved away: 'Yet could I bear that too, well, very well' (l. 56). Even as he articulates the central impasse, as he illustrates the paralysis of art, Othello simply sidesteps the difficulty. Scorn does not touch him as nearly as he had expected. He then approaches more closely to the one insupportable torture, not the jeering world, but the very private pain of losing Desdemona:

> But there, where I have garner'd up my heart,
> Where either I must live or bear no life;
> The fountain from the which my current runs
> Or else dries up: to be discarded thence!
> Or keep it as a cestern for foul toads
> To knot and gender in! Turn thy complexion there,
> Patience, thou young and rose-lipp'd cherubin—
> Ay, here look grim as hell!   (4.2.57–64)

Allegory returns, with this new personification of Patience, endowed with a young and rosy visage, Desdemona's perhaps. At any rate, it is the very antithesis of the black and ageing speaker. Yet in the act of personifying, as the puns on 'complexion' and 'Ay' suggest, Othello metamorphoses the maiden Patience into his own likeness. Rose-lipped Patience will become the thick-lipped Moor when she beholds the hideous sight. The same metamorphosis had already occurred more openly in act 3:

> I think my wife be honest, and think she is not;
> I think that thou art just, and think thou art not.

I'll have some proof. Her name, that was as fresh
As Dian's visage, is now begrim'd and black
As mine own face. If there be cords, or knives,
Poison, or fire, or suffocating streams,
I'll not endure it.   (3.3.384–90)

Here Desdemona's chaste, young face becomes as 'begrim'd' as Othello's. The final 'I'll not endure it' also hints at the figure of Patience and its dissolution into furore. Less obviously perhaps, the impasse between allegorization and irony represented in our passage in 4.2 by the paradoxical knot of images is expressed here with less strain by the first two lines. Each, self-contradictorily, by turns, affirms the validity of idealization, and Iago-like, denies it. Yet taken together and read as chiasmus – the first element joined to the fourth and the second to the third – the rejection of the unseen essence can never be total. For if Desdemona's honesty is an illusion, Iago's justness is thereby upheld, and vice versa.

But to return to our passage in act 4, the key verb 'turn' – a synonym for 'trope' – initiates the destabilization of the allegory. As Patience 'turns' to view the horror, she is assimilated to monstrous Jealousy and to 'black vengeance', the spirit Othello had conjured from 'hollow hell' (3.3.447), both twisted semblances of his own wracked mind. Once again Othello refashions his reality in line with words he has heard earlier. Iago had assured him that a husband's worst fate is to be an unwitting cuckold:

> O, 'tis the spite of hell, the fiend's arch-mock,
> To lip a wanton in a secure couch,
> And to suppose her chaste!   (4.1.70–2)

Irony can go no further than this, but presumably the Ancient's timely warnings have preserved the Moor from this ultimate disgrace. And yet Othello contrives for himself a fate even more humiliating. The decline of Othello's young cherubin inverts Iago's scheme: he lips a figure properly rosy and chaste, until his overwrought imagination supposes her black and grim. This indeed is the fiend's arch-mock, as the Moor himself ironically subverts the potentially healing allegory.

The system of mirroring figures also yields up heaven's arch-mock: 'If she be false, O then heaven mocks itself / I'll not believe't' (3.3.278–9), Othello says, as the entry of Desdemona elicits a final upsurge of faith. Malone's gloss is most suggestive: 'If she be false, Oh, then, even *heaven itself* cheats us with "unreal mockery", with false and specious appearances, intended only to deceive'.[17] Making explicit what Cassio's divinizing rhetoric had implied, Othello reads Desdemona as a figure of heavenly grace. Unmetaphoring cannot go further. Othello keeps nothing in reserve, his faith riding on Desdemona alone. Just as her virtue was taken as a sign of heaven's goodness, so her dishonesty must point to its falseness. The formulation is devastating, because it holds the universal moral order hostage to Desdemona. If she proves false, good will be proven evil, and the benevolent allegorical order that sustains the world will be devoured by irony. The divine allegorist will reveal himself to be an ironist, using a beautiful form to represent its moral opposite. Conversely, Iago, pre-eminently the ironist, will finally resist understanding by any but allegorical categories; 'I look down towards his feet; but that's a fable' (5.2.286), says Othello of his unmasked enemy. Beyond the fiend's arch-mock and heaven's, Shakespeare's arch-mock scorns both. Allegory and irony, despite their totalizing pretensions, despite the exclusion of each by the other, cannot exist independently.

The crumbling of allegory is again enacted when Iago would invoke truth in his campaign to convince Othello of Desdemona's disloyalty: 'If imputation and strong circumstances / Which lead directly to the door of truth / Will give you satisfaction, you might have't' (3.3.406–8). He conjures up a Spenserian House of Truth, where we might expect to find Desdemona as mistress. Yet the deflection of our attention from the allegorical edifice, represented by no more than a door, to the pathways which lie outside it, already belies the essential quality. Truth itself is defenceless against misappropriated allegory. The relationship between the allegorical body – the road to the house – and the spiritual abstraction – truth – is so oblique that allegory ceases to be itself and turns ironic.

A similar decomposition occurs when Desdemona exonerates her murderer with her dying gasp. Othello underscores the point: 'You heard her say herself, it was not I' (5.2.127). Emilia responds: 'She said so; I must needs report the truth' (l. 128). Here is a more poignant rehearsal of the two earlier paradoxes, Iago's 'As I am an honest man . . .' and Othello's 'I think my wife be honest.' Allegory falsifies itself, not to ensnare Cassio, nor to show Othello's confusion, but largely for the sake of the audience, which, after all, has never been given any cause to doubt Desdemona, and being neither in the camp of the sceptics (who will not believe) nor in that of the unmetaphorizers (who believe too well), probably continues to believe in allegorical idealization. Truth's last words are a barefaced lie. If Emilia repeats the truth she falsifies, but if she lies, she will be telling the truth. The thought of heaven mocking itself shook Othello's belief in idealization, and this final spectacle of lying truth is meant to shake ours.

It is inadequate to attribute the knotted embrace of allegory and irony solely to malicious cynicism or to naive unmetaphoring. Even as Emilia solemnly pronounces her verdict, the unintentional pun betrays her.

> . . I am bound to speak.
> My mistress here lies murthered in her bed—
> (5.2.184–5)

---

17 *Othello*, ed. Horace Furness, A New Variorum Edition of Shakespeare (1866; repr. New York, 1965), p. 192.

Her dead lady is simultaneously the icon of sacrificed innocence and the nay-saying voice that always gives the 'lie' to such constructions. The downward spiral of a self-invalidating art cannot be arrested. Essential truth is an illusion, and Shakespeare will not allow us to be deceived. Othello's final accusation against her, 'She's like a liar gone to burning hell' (5.2.129), brooks no denial; her protest notwithstanding, we know who killed her. Desdemona, the honest, the chaste, the true, is false, and heaven mocks itself.

Othello, always given to extremes, never learns this lesson. Released from the error foisted upon him by Iago, he immediately instals Desdemona back in the 'marble heaven' from which she fell. The execution itself prepares her for her apotheosis as a fixed figure:

> Yet I'll not shed her blood,
> Nor scar that whiter skin of hers than snow,
> And smooth as monumental alablaster,
>
> (5.2.3–5)

Once she has realized the permanence of a statue, outside the flux of life, Desdemona's unseen essence becomes manifest. The snow imagery here foreshadows the ultimate naming: 'Cold, cold, my girl? / Even like thy chastity' (5.2.275–6). Once separated from the ironic consciousness with which, in a post-Spenserian world, it is necessarily wed, allegory degenerates into something frigid and narrow, not Spenser's flexible and resilient mode, but the dead fiction that Coleridge deplored. Alternatively it is swallowed up by a kind of unthinking symbolization, as the microcosmic chrysolite, for which he would not have traded her before the recognition, reappears as the cast-out pearl after.

Howard Felperin, in a superbly supple reading, urges that Othello's famous last speech signifies a kind of wiser reallegorization that shows he has learned the dangers of previous excesses: 'He has reinvented his own earlier dramatic language with a new understanding that prior sign and present sig-nificance, conventional role and distinctive self, can never fully coincide, and creates in the process a more authentic, because more human, magic than that displayed in any of his previous rhetoric of self-definition.'[18] While the rush of images, one giving way to the next, demonstrates Othello's new flexibility in defining himself, the role-playing continues, leading Felperin to argue that the tragedy concludes on a note of endless oscillation between de- and re-mystifying: 'We are left with a character and an action "true" in their acknowledged indeterminacy and indeterminate in their presented truth.'

In my own terms we might similarly see the closing speech as Othello's understanding, at least as it pertains to himself, that allegorical projection needs its uneasy alliance with irony. Now Othello is both the deceiving Turk and the perspicacious Venetian, the pageant maker and the pageant breaker, the launcher of ships and their wrecker. Much earlier, on the occasion of his reunion with Desdemona following the stormy sea voyage, in language literally intended, yet recognizably allegorical, Othello had exclaimed grandly:

> If after every tempest come such calms,
> May the winds blow till they have waken'd
>   death!
> And let the laboring bark climb hills of seas
> Olympus-high, and duck again as low
> As hell's from heaven!   (2.1.185–9)

The tragic hero prefigures his own destiny, his climb to heaven and plunge to hell. The doughty bark sails to Olympian heights, but the remorseless sea effaces its achievement in a flood of irony. Yet as 'hills of seas' suggests, Olympus itself is built of water. Allegory and irony, heaven and hell, the cresting wave that crashes, are all products of the same watery element. 'False as water' (5.2.134), says Othello, 'More fell than ... the sea' (5.2.362),

---

[18] *Shakespearean Representation: Mimesis and Modernity in Elizabethan Tragedy* (Princeton, 1977), p. 85.

exclaims Lodovico in the final summing up. The oscillation is instantaneous, consuming itself in a dying fall.

Allegory needs the bracing effect of irony as a reminder of its fictionality. But, shaky construction that it is, it may be consumed by irony's mordancy. This tropology defines *Othello*. The conditions which enable art to credibly hold forth the promise of order and meaning are inherently unstable, and the promise is immediately retracted. 'Put out the light, and then put out the light' (5.2.7). In this phoenix of a line, our pattern of allegorical going forth and ironical return is beautifully expressed and doubled. The figure rises and burns out and rises and burns out again. Each half is a complete and simultaneous instant of flashing and quenching. The flaming mixture of incompatibles briefly yields up an instant of belief without self-deception or, alternatively construed, of scepticism willing to entertain saving fictions. It is a self-limiting moment. Left in its wake are a cold, burned-out corpse which is allegorized to the skies and, in Iago, a bleeding irony so baleful, speech itself is too affirmative.

As the fates of Desdemona and Iago show, neither unchecked allegory nor unmitigated irony offers any possibilities for further dramatic development. Perhaps, however, the almost alarming resiliency of the line, 'Put out the light, and then put out the light', does enclose a lesson. Earlier I remarked how Othello waved away the knotted paradox and started anew. Here in most concentrated form we find the same recovery, even when a strict logic would seem to rule it out. A light quenched cannot be put out again. And yet it is. Indeed Desdemona dies only to shine forth with luminous forgiveness, and Emilia dies but revives long enough to recall her mistress's song and speak the truth. Even Roderigo, it is reported, 'spake / (After long seeming dead)' (5.2.327–8), to set the record right. Othello's parting words fulfil a similar pattern: 'I kiss'd thee ere I kill'd thee. No way but this, / Killing myself, to die upon a kiss' (5.2.358–9). Kiss/kill bound fatally together once are resurrected in the hero's final gesture. If the tension of the allegorical/ironical mixture is self-limiting, it may be equally self-renewing. After all, despite their being repeatedly discredited, Patience and Jealousy have a way of reasserting themselves. Seen alone, these dying moments exemplify dramatic irony. As a reprise of an earlier moment, however, they are triumphant. At a time when essences like truth lie in ruins, Emilia confidently returns to certainty: 'she was chaste . . . / So come my soul to bliss, as I speak true' (5.2.249–50). Here Iago's 'As I am an honest man' is honestly redeemed, as is the problematic nature of Desdemona's dying words. 'Put out the light, and then put out the light.' For all its finality and despair, the repetition signals duration and hope.

CRUELTY, 'KING LEAR' AND THE SOUTH AFRICAN LAND ACT 1913

MARTIN ORKIN

Present-day South Africans read Shakespeare in a semi-industrialized, capitalist, *apartheid* state located in a condition of advanced crisis. This may prove to be a period of transition or collapse, but it is one that remains, as has been the case in the last fifty years and longer, characterized by brutal exploitation and repression. The Land Act of 1913, for instance, was one of the crucial pieces of legislation in the formation of what subsequently became the *apartheid* state. It distinguished different groups within the population of South Africa and purported to divide the land between them. In fact, as political commentators have underlined, it was to reserve less than ten per cent of the total land surface of what was then the Union of South Africa for the black inhabitants of the country. Thus the Act, in responding to the demands of white farmers to convert sharecroppers on their land into farm labourers or servants, dispossessed many black landowners and outlawed, as well, leasing or tenant farming. Commentators recognize that this Act, which came about partly as a result of the sustained thrust of mining as well as farming capital, together with other laws, ostensibly protecting black rights, actually eroded them. It destroyed 'a whole class of peasant producers, forcing them into already crowded reserves or driving them into new and arduous social relationships – as farm workers, as mine labourers, and later in the least skilled and most badly paid positions in urban industrial, municipal, and domestic employment'.[1]

Perhaps the most famous of the individual reactions to this Act was from Solomon Plaatje.[2] He recognized the extent to which loss of land ownership and land tenancy would lead to complete political subjugation. Others then and since have recorded the reaction to the passing of the Act by large numbers of the affected population. Thus Bessie Head writes that 'rather than lose their last shred of independence ... black people, tenants on the land, took to the road with their dying stock'.[3] And Plaatje describes in detail the subsequent misery and hardship thousands of old as well as young people experienced along the open road because of their refusal to stay on the now white-owned farms as servants.[4]

For the South African critic, to recall such facts as one takes up *King Lear*, a play that is in part about land, is not an indulgence. Historians working on late feudal and early capitalist England emphasize the importance of land – G. R. Elton observes that in the seventeenth-century English world the 'economic centre of gravity' was land and he stresses the extent to which status was depend-

---

[1] Tom Lodge, *Black Politics in South Africa since 1945* (Johannesburg, 1983), p. 2.

[2] Solomon T. Plaatje, *Native Life in South Africa* (1916), (Cape Town, 1982), p. 72.

[3] Bessie Head, Foreword to Plaatje, *Native Life in South Africa*, p. xi.

[4] Plaatje, pp. 78ff.

ent upon possession of land.[5] Society 'regarded only land and landed wealth as ultimately acceptable in creating status. True, there was wealth of other kinds . . . mercantile and banking fortunes . . . lawyers' incomes . . . but the only form of wealth which could gain you social recognition was land, possession of land.'[6]

More important for *King Lear*, Jonathan Dollimore has demonstrated the concern in the play with the connection between possession of land, property, and power.[7] And Robert Weimann reminds us that we are all characters in history – 'our own points of reference are, like our predecessors', products of history'.[8] He emphasizes that to re-create the mimetic and expressive dimensions of the plays is not only 'impossible without reference to Shakespeare's world . . . to reassess their affective and moral effects is impossible without reference to our audience and our world'.[9]

It is not merely the question of acquisition or possession of land which might encourage in the South African audience or reader particular recognitions in the text. The apparent awareness in the play of the impact upon the poor of the sixteenth- and seventeenth-century economy, with its systems of enclosures and vagrancy laws, must be, in South Africa, still with its notorious pass laws and influx control – albeit in new and disguised forms – of pressing interest. We know that the displacement of the poor during the enclosure movement increased the already serious problem of poverty and hardship caused in Shakespeare's day by poor harvests, the aftermath of war, and the population explosion.[10] There was a ' "savage depression of the living standard of the lower half of the population" in Shakespeare's time, a depression created by an 800 per cent increase in the value of land, an overall inflation rate of 500 per cent . . . and a fall in real wages by half'.[11] Moreover, vagrancy laws enabled the gentry, when they had a full labour supply, to remove the remainder of the poor back to the villages of

[5] G. R. Elton, *Studies in Tudor and Stuart Politics and Government*, vol. 3, Papers and Reviews 1973–1981 (Cambridge, 1983), p. 340.

[6] G. R. Elton, p. 340.

[7] Jonathan Dollimore, *Radical Tragedy* (Brighton, 1984), pp. 189–203. My indebtedness to Dollimore is everywhere evident in this article.

[8] Robert Weimann, *Structure and Society in Literary History* (Baltimore, 1984), p. 54.

[9] Weimann, p. 53.

[10] Lawrence Stone, *The Causes of the English Revolution, 1529–1642* (1972), writes: 'In the sixteenth century the combination of rapidly rising food prices and stagnant rents shifted the distribution of agricultural profits away from the landlord and towards the tenant. In the early seventeenth century rents increased more rapidly than prices and profits flowed back to the landlord and away from the tenant. This shift to economic rents was accompanied by a reorganisation of property rights by which more and more land fell into private control through enclosures of both waste and common fields. As a result of this process and of the engrossing of farms into larger units of production, there began to emerge the tripartite pattern of later English rural society, landlord, prosperous tenant farmer, and landless labourer. These changes were essential to feed the additional mouths, but tens of thousands of smallholders were driven off the land or reduced to wage labourers while others found their economic position undermined by encroachment on, or over-stocking of, the common lands by the big farmers and the landlords. The enclosure became a popular scapegoat for the dislocations inevitable in so major a redistribution and reallocation of the land, but there can be no doubt that the extra millions of Englishmen were only fed at the cost of much individual hardship suffered by many of the small peasantry.' (p. 68).

[11] Alvin B. Kernan, '*King Lear* and the Shakespearean Pageant of History', *On King Lear*, ed. Lawrence Danson (Princeton, 1981), p. 11. Carl Bridenbaugh, *Vexed and Troubled Englishmen 1590–1642* (Oxford, 1968), observes: 'the half-century after 1590 was a time of profound unprecedented and often frightening social ferment for the people of England. During these years nearly every member of the lower orders in the countryside and in the towns knew deprivation and genuinely feared insecurity; and well he might, for close to a majority of the population found themselves living perilously near the level of bare subsistence . . .' (p. 355). Christopher Hill, *The Century of Revolution 1603–1714* (Edinburgh, 1961), writes: 'To contemporaries struck by poverty and vagabondage, the overpopulation seemed absolute . . . Wage labourers did not share in the profits of industrial expansion. As prices

their birth.[12] These villages more often than not were poverty-stricken as a result of enclosures. And enclosures, we should remember, in a rather crude way also converted a tenant labour system into a wage labour system – the latter, as the South African state understands only too well, is easier to control and much cheaper.

When Shakespeare wrote *King Lear*, historians tell us, pressure against enclosures was building up in the Midlands, including Warwickshire, to break out a year or so later in rioting which was in turn brutally suppressed by the gentry. Laws to control beggars were another way in which vagrancy, a continued problematic consequence of the flux in economic conditions, was handled. When he joins that class persecuted and hounded by the state apparatus, Edgar speaks not only of Bedlam beggars and their sufferings but of that countryside through which they roam, which includes low farms, poor pelting villages, sheep-cotes and mills. The sense of the impact of the Elizabethan and Jacobean economic system upon the powerless and landless resonates when Lear speaks of 'Poor naked wretches' (3.4.28), and Gloucester, too, gives his purse to Poor Tom, as many critics note, recognizing that 'distribution should undo excess, / And each man have enough' (4.1.70–1).[13]

The ambiguities surrounding the shift of power that takes place in the play and the political cruelty that accompanies it are especially important to South Africans. Just before he has his eyes put out – in the scene which Dr Johnson described as 'too horrid to be endured in dramatick exhibition' and which even so recent a critic as Harry Levin can describe as having only a 'certain propriety as a literal climax to a whole train of metaphors involving eyesight and suggesting moral perception' – Gloucester, in reply to Regan's demand that he explain why he has sent King Lear to Dover, declares:

Because I would not see
Thy cruel nails pluck out his poor old eyes;
Nor thy fierce sister in his anointed flesh
Rash boarish fangs.   (3.7.54–7)[14]

---

rose during the sixteenth century, the purchasing power of wages had fallen by something like two thirds. Since the numbers of those permanently dependent on wages was increasing, the number of those on the margin of starving was increasing too. This fall in real wages was catastrophic for those who sold or were evicted from their plots of land and became entirely dependent on earnings . . .' (p. 24).

[12] Hill, *The Century of Revolution*, writes: 'The harsh Poor Law was breaking up the bands of roaming vagabonds which had terrorised Elizabethan England; but it could not prevent London attracting an underworld of casual labourers, unemployables, beggars and criminals. The prescribed penalty of whipping home unlicensed beggars checked freedom of movement, and detained a surplus of cheap labour in many rural areas' (p.26). Keith Wrightson, *English Society 1580–1680* (1982), notes: 'Poverty, of course, was nothing new. . . . Yet the later sixteenth and early seventeenth centuries saw the growth of a poverty which was different in both its nature and extent from that which had been known earlier. . . . By the end of the sixteenth century . . . the poor were no longer the destitute victims of misfortune or old age, but a substantial proportion of the population living in constant danger of destitution, many of them full-time waged labourers . . . the extent of the problem was frightening though it varied from area to area . . . the settled poor (were) relatively fortunate in that they had a recognised place in society and were eligible for parish relief under the Elizabethan Poor Law. . . . Beyond them and well outside the charitable consideration of the authorities, were the vagrant poor. . . . How many of them wandered the roads of the period it is impossible to say, though their numbers were undoubtedly high' (p. 141). Finally, we may note Hill again: 'although it would be wrong to think of any body of organised discontent, there is a permanent background of potential unrest throughout these decades. Given a crisis – a famine, large-scale unemployment, a breakdown of government – disorder might occur. . . . The prevention of peasant revolt was the monarchy's job; in this it had the support of the propertied class' (pp. 27–8).

[13] All references are to *King Lear*, edited by Kenneth Muir in the new Arden Shakespeare (1952).

[14] *Johnson on Shakespeare*, ed. Arthur Sherbo (New Haven and London, 1968), p. 703; Harry Levin, *Shakespeare and the Revolution of the Times* (Oxford, 1976), p. 165.

At this moment Gloucester ceases completely to deal with the *de facto* power faction or group within the ruling class. His direct statement of defiance aligns him with the hunted victims of that power – King Lear, without protection or shelter on the heath, and Edgar, proclaimed an outlaw throughout the land and disguised as Poor Tom. But the propriety of this scene to the concerns of *King Lear* is more extensive than Levin's comment admits. He in fact also remarks that the scene presents a 'deliberate and definitive' breach of classical decorum – the Greeks preferred to have Oedipus' eyes put out off stage.[15] He does not indicate that this 'breach' of decorum illustrates and embodies – in what we might call a terrifying emblematic way – one aspect of the political thrust of the play. For in this scene the whole nexus of emerging relationships that *King Lear* explores, which begins in the opening scene with a shift of power and which intensifies relentlessly in the scenes and acts to follow, comes to a point of awful clarity. Moreover, the interrogation and torture it presents set a seal on this process of change, identifying for the audience at the same time the essential nature of the *de facto* ruling power.

The phrase *de facto* is, however, in part inappropriate for the power which Goneril, Regan, and Edmund acquire in the first three acts. The text invests their possession of power with elements of legality: the daughters of the King have each received formally from their father control of most of the kingdom, the fugitive Edgar has been defined as an enemy of the state, and even the 'kangaroo' court that tries Gloucester is prompted by the Duke's communication with an invading army – foreign intruders whom he has also helped the King to join. Yet although we might note these facts we recoil from the suggestion of legitimacy; *King Lear* stresses the extent to which the shift of power within the dominant order initiated in 1.1 becomes at once also a *seizure* of power. It is sometimes forgotten that if Lear makes an appalling decision which

proves to be mistaken, what follows is only possible because the connative dissembling of his two daughters enables them to acquire for themselves most of his domain. By the end of the first scene, furthermore, they indicate their determination to deprive him of the remaining material evidence of his authority. In the acts that follow, this arrogation of power is complemented by Edmund's own frenetic activity in the displacement of brother and then father. When, then, ignoring the Fool's plea for compromise and submission to the authorities, Lear chooses the open heath he does not merely cease to be the *de facto* representative of the system of government and justice, which makes its claims for hierarchy and custom, to become its victim. He becomes also to a large degree that system's opponent and critic.

By means of this strategy the text is able to pursue the disturbing recognitions it makes from the beginning, when land is shared out with such catastrophic results, about the actual system of domination and subordination within the social order. In support of this contention, Gary Taylor's discussion of 1.4.142–66, originally in the Quarto but which does not appear in the Folio, may be cited.[16] He argues that the censor omitted the passage from the Folio because of the hints of criticism in it linking aspects of Lear's behaviour with that of James. What we know of the start of James's reign and of James personally suggests that such criticism was merited although any connection between stage and audience monarch should not be understood in a reductive way that insists upon a one-to-one equivalence, but rather in a suggestive way and one that, presumably, might have prompted reflections in Shakespeare's contemporary audience about tendencies in the court of James

---

[15] Levin, p. 165

[16] Gary Taylor, 'Monopolies, Show Trials, Disaster and Invasion: *King Lear* and Censorship', in *The Division of the Kingdoms*, eds Gary Taylor and Michael Warren (Oxford, 1983), 75–119.

and its administration.[17] Furthermore, we should recall that if the text, in certain of its parallels in the first two acts, implies criticism of James, this is balanced by other factors which, by the time the King has been removed from the ruling class, encourage in the audience an increasingly sympathetic attitude. Thus the mistake which Lear commits at the beginning of the play is presented as the result partly of faulty perception, and not the consequence of the conscious self-interest displayed by Edmund, Goneril, and Regan. Lear, furthermore, understands his mistake by the end of act 1; his later realizations may be seen as amplification of this. After the end of the second act, too, the impulse to criticism of the King is eclipsed by the presence in the text of language that directs the audience to the enormity of what is done to him.[18]

This view of Lear's role is supported as well by some suggestions Leonard Tennenhouse makes in a discussion of *Measure for Measure*.[19] He observes that at this time several comedies use a common device – 'a trickster figure, who is often but not always a monarch ... from disguise ... observes the state and witnesses both sexual misconduct and the abuses of political power'.[20] Tennenhouse points out that one of the effects of this technique of removing the ruler figure from his world to enable him to observe it is that 'being thus conceived as something separate from the monarch, the state and not the monarch becomes the object to which our attention is turned'.[21] The Duke's deputies have his auth-

seriously weakened the Crown; the Church faced an insidious and fundamental attack from the Puritan party; the House of Commons had recently grown in power and independence; the ambitions of rising classes (the gentry, the bourgeoisie) were threatening the ascendancy of the monarch and aristocracy. Altogether the traditional power of the Crown was failing in the face of a variety of discontent and criticism. All these strains became increasingly obvious in the reign of James I' (p. 157). Elton cites the inadequacy of the Stuart government as one of the main reasons why these many and varied problems intensified under James. The 'early Stuart governments ... were incompetent, sometimes corrupt, and frequently just ignorant of what was going on or needed doing.... What matters is their repeated inability, for reasons also often factious, bigoted and ill-conceived, to find a way through their problems' (p. 161). Of James's reign, particularly, Elton, *Studies* (1983), observes that it was 'a reign which was marked even more than any other you could name in (English) history as an age in which nothing happened, in which nothing was done, in which government neglected all its duties' (p.282). See also J. W. Lever, *The Tragedy of State* (1971), pp. 3–4, for the series of blows which the monarchy sustained at the end of Elizabeth's reign and during the beginning of James's reign. James's task as monarch was not made easier because of his lack of personal charisma – and he had no hope of competing with the great propaganda machine that had presented 'Gloriana' to her public. See Stephen Greenblatt, *Renaissance Self-Fashioning* (Chicago, 1980), pp. 166–9; Stone, *The Causes of the English Revolution*, p. 89.

18 Kent, who was not slow to criticize the King earlier, recognizes at the start of act 3 the 'hard rein' (3.1.27) which the King's daughters 'have borne / Against the old kind King' (3.1.27–8) and acknowledges that of 'unnatural and bemadding sorrow / The King hath cause to plain' (3.1.38–9) while Lear himself asserts 'I am a man / More sinn'd against than sinning' (3.2.59–60). The King's madness provides the opportunity for satire too. Maynard Mack, 'The Jacobean Shakespeare', *Jacobean Theatre*, Stratford-upon-Avon Studies 1 (1960), notes: 'Both (Lear) and Hamlet can be privileged in madness to say things – Hamlet about the corruption of human nature, and Lear about the corruption of the Jacobean social system ... which Shakespeare could hardly have risked apart from this licence' (p. 39).

19 Leonard Tennenhouse, 'Representing Power: *Measure for Measure* in its Time', *The Power of Forms in the English Renaissance*, ed. Stephen Greenblatt (Oklahoma, 1982), pp. 139–56.

20 Tennenhouse, p. 139.

21 Tennenhouse, p. 141.

---

17 Taylor, 'Monopolies', cites C4ᵛ–D1; 1.4.136–59. He argues that the passage refers to James's granting of monopolies, the incredible gluttony which had become a feature of the banquets at James's court, the King's wholesale dispensation of titles and his love of hunting (pp. 101–9). G. R. Elton, *Studies in Tudor and Stuart Politics and Government*, vol. 2, Papers and Reviews 1946–1972 (Cambridge, 1974) summarizes the difficulties when James came to power in this way: 'When Queen Elizabeth died, she left a system of government much debilitated by recent change. A price inflation had

ority and they represent his rule. In the same way, *King Lear* ensures that those who remain in control when Lear has been removed from power retain the aura of legitimacy. Through the vehicle of the behaviour of Edmund, Goneril, and Regan (and not through the presence of the one dramatic character who suggests the English King himself) the text may safely pursue the problems it has posed from the start of the play about the operation of state power within the dominant order. And, we may add, recent study of Elizabethan and Jacobean censorship confirms the necessity of such a tactic.[22]

For the play's depiction of an apparently legitimate but actually ruthless and cruel ruling class, the image of old age with which it begins proves especially appropriate – old age with its suggestion of the need for love, its intractability and its fallibility, presents a condition of vulnerability. But when Regan says to Lear, 'I pray you, father, being weak, seem so' (2.4.203), she voices a different demand. A great divide opens at once between those who from the beginning of the play are indifferent and cruel towards this condition in human experience, and those who offer throughout a more compassionate response. The human faculty for exploitation and persecution is registered in the language of the Fool, in the image of Poor Tom as innocent fugitive from hostile authority, in the continuing spectacle of Lear himself on the heath. Early in act 3 Lear begins to realize that power, its manifestation in land and wealth, does not automatically denote morality – beneath the semblance of order there often lies criminality. Lear's desire to plumb the depths of Regan's cruelty, find out what breeds about her heart, emerges as hopeless: the participants in the search for absolute justice in the mock-trial scene are the outcasts of the social order – a mad old King, his Fool, an exile in disguise. Against the acknowledged impotence of the seekers of absolute justice the final scene of act 3 demonstrates the extent to which the dominant order,

which controls the real apparatus of justice, may operate lawlessly when it chooses, to preserve its position: the putting out of Gloucester's eyes underlines the potential ruthlessness of rulers. The Duke too cries out for a form of providential justice, but his cries are also impotent. Instead, expelled from the dominant order and redefined as masterless, he becomes for the rulers sub-human – 'let him', says Regan, 'smell / His way to Dover' (3.7.92–3).

The treatment of Gloucester suggests the readiness of the dominant order not merely to coerce but, when faced with difference that cannot be contained, to create subversion in order to destroy it. But much earlier in the play, Gloucester's own response to an allegedly traitorous son – whom the audience knows to be innocent – has been disastrously precipitous. In an age troubled by mutinies in cities, discord in countries, and treason in palaces, Gloucester's behaviour evokes that urgent reflex in the dominant order to act punitively in order to contain possible subversion. Precisely as he acts against Edgar, Gloucester recalls the King's behaviour in the previous scene. There, Cordelia's failure to use the code her father demanded, her emphasis instead upon the contractual nature of her relationship with him, prompted the King to make an example of *her* – in his case too, anger led swiftly to fierce rejection and punishment. Lear follows the same pattern in his treatment of Kent. This suggests how, in contexts of change or uncertainty, the ruling class may move swiftly, even vindictively, ignoring its

---

[22] See Margot Heinemann, *Puritanism and the Theatre* (Cambridge, 1980), esp. pp. 36–8; Dollimore, *Radical Tragedy*, pp. 22ff; J. W. Lever, *The Tragedy of State*, pp. 1–17; Gary Taylor, 'Monopolies' pp. 75–119. I have not been able to examine Janet Clare, 'Art made tongue-tied by authority: a study of the relationship between Elizabethan and Jacobean drama and authority and the effect of censorship on the plays of the period', unpublished PhD thesis, University of Birmingham, 1981.

own complicity in or production of disorder (Lear's own culpability in his treatment of Cordelia and Kent, Gloucester's casual promiscuity, the implicit, more general responsibility of these two powerful members of the dominant order for a society apparently bedevilled by mutiny, discord, and treason) to create its enemies (Cordelia, Kent, Edgar) in order to assert, through punishment (deprivation of inheritance, banishment, the outlawed target of state persecution and oppression), its own authority. In the present state of emergency in South Africa, the government and its class, primarily responsible for the misery and suffering in the state, nevertheless denies this whilst reacting punitively against a wide range of individuals it chooses to redefine as subversive and worthy of severe punishment. Through such persecution too, its power may be entrenched. In *King Lear* these instances in the first two scenes are as disturbingly interrogative of the dominant order, of traditional notions of hierarchy and justice, as the image of Kent later in the stocks emblematically suggests, or as Regan's readiness to eliminate Gloucester blatantly illustrates.

Such episodes and language contest those episodes and that language in the play, especially in act 4, that suggest a powerful longing for the validity of a view of the human subject drawn from Christian discourse. Yet it is precisely readings of the text of this kind that traditional critics in South Africa avoid. It should be remembered that the education system in South Africa, subject to censorship and the demonizing of all forms of dissenting or alternative discourse, works to legitimate the present South African social order. Such a system not only deprives its inhabitants of an awareness of alternatives; the very capacity to analyse or envisage enabling as well as limiting counter-possibilities is severely inhibited. A use made of the Shakespeare text which encourages thoughts about the tale – generalized moral abstractions about the story of old King Lear – and thoughts about, indeed

fixation upon, character, human nature, interiority, in the South African situation has a clear political consequence in assisting in the reproduction of dominant social relations.[23] The participants in such an activity are encouraged in the belief that they too, like the text, are independent of social process. Essential truths cease to have any connection with material reality, and not yet, in South Africa, very much a matter of intertextuality – except of the most depoliticized kind – they remain other-worldly. In this, the traditionalist approach to the Shakespeare text actively reinforces in its adherents the tendency to submission.

One other aspect of traditionalist practice with the Shakespeare text in South Africa may be noted. South Africa has been perceived by English affiliated South Africans, or British academics who have always been part of the university establishment in South Africa, as an outpost on the periphery of British influence. This mental set survived long after the British empire went into decline and even after 1960 when South Africa was more or less expelled from the Commonwealth. Literary critics saw themselves as bearers of high culture to the African sub-continent. But after 1948, their struggle was not simply that of an English group within the dominant order that longed for connection with the 'mother country' and that came into contact with subordinate orders imbued with alien and what it therefore defined as inferior cultures. It was also a struggle with the emergence of a new Calvinist (Afrikaner) power group within the dominant order, one that increasingly asserted its own hegemony. Feeling doubly under attack, the bearers of civility find pluralism of meaning in any text even more unpalatable. In a world of 'racism' as well as 'savagism', in which their own participation in the existing relations of

---

[23] Cf. Kenneth Muir, 'The Betrayal of Shakespeare', *Shakespeare: Contrasts and Controversies* (Brighton, 1985), esp. p. 90.

domination and subordination is totally ignored, such critics turn to the Shakespeare text as a refuge and a retreat, as a means of personal growth, as the survival line to the metropolis.[24] As recently as 1985 one such critic offers *King Lear* as an example of a 'life-enhancing' text that communicates a 'rich social identity' and one which he contrasts with the Roman plays where the characters 'do not learn, they do not truly suffer, they do not repent, they cannot utter sentiments of human communality'.[25]

Stephen Greenblatt, noting 'the impossibility of fully reconstructing and re-entering the culture of the sixteenth century, of leaving behind one's own situation', observes that 'the questions I ask of my material and the very nature of this material are shaped by the questions I ask of myself'.[26] The study of the Shakespeare text in South Africa in one way or another reflects this fact. Significantly perhaps, the plays most frequently chosen for discussion are those likely to have been written in the period 1599–1606, and most often the tragedies. I would argue then, especially in the context of these texts, that at this moment the study of the Shakespeare text in South Africa is best assisted by the work of those critics who, engaged in recovering the political dimension of Shakespearian drama, recognize that signifying practices are located within the material struggles taking place in the social order.

From this point of view the deaths of Cordelia and Lear, despite the fact that they cherish certain traditional values, are not merely or even primarily the result of accident. What Lear and his daughter experience is the consequence not only of the acquisition and loss of power, but of political cruelty and oppression. Moreover, victims of a dominant class to which they no longer belong – one which operates as it always seems to have done, in its own interest, and which uses state power to preserve its hegemony – defeated in civil war, they face incarceration. Lear says to his daughter of their coming imprisonment, 'We two

alone will sing like birds i' th' cage' (5.3.9), and his mind, broken by persecution, envisages in the context of imprisonment a child-like fantasy of escape. His language however is no less located in the hard context of political reality. We'll 'Talk', he says, 'of court news', of

> Who loses and who wins; who's in, who's out;
> And take upon 's the mystery of things,
> As if we were God's spies   (5.3.14–17);

even as his mind comes back to the fact of oppression, the state's exercise of control through spying, he attempts to flee again. They will be the spies of God, he dreams, possessors of an omnipotent detachment free from the pressures of polity, though still, ironically, practising a form of divine surveillance. But yet again, his mind returns once more, and finally, to the 'wall'd prison' (5.3.18) around them.

It is that dominant class of which Lear was once himself part that is, then, primarily

---

[24] B. D. Cheadle, 'Hamlet at the Graveside: A Leap into Hermeneutics', *English Studies in Africa*, vol. 22, no. 2 (1979), 83–90, remarks in the course of his discussion: 'we read literature, presumably at least in part, to grow: by entering into a vision of life that is not our own we extend our awareness and our capacity and a commitment to a particular approach should not be such as to preclude the possibility of literature changing us' (p. 87). C. O. Gardner, 'Tragic Fission in *Othello*', *English Studies in Africa*, vol. 20, no. 1 (1977), 11–25, finds at the end of the play a 'loss of harmony' and 'balance' to which, he recommends, we should react with 'recognition, wonder, fear and awe ... we must learn all that we can from tragic events, we must love and admire all that is generous in thought, in feeling and in deed, but above all or beneath all we must be humble'. This final sentence strikingly suggests the use to which Shakespeare has been put in encouraging certain attitudes – a longing for instruction in particular abstractions about human behaviour, a pseudo-fatalistic or stoic resignation about the frailties of this world, acceptance of the *status quo*.

[25] Geoffrey Hughes, 'A world elsewhere: Romanitas and its Limitations in Shakespeare', *English Studies in Africa*, vol. 28, no. 1 (1985), 1–19, p. 18.

[26] Greenblatt, p. 5.

responsible for the two deaths at the play's end. When Lear re-enters the stage, we might, merely in one sense fancifully, suggest that he carries not simply the innocent murdered Cordelia, but all of those, not only in Shakespeare's day, who have died similarly. This is ostensibly the last thrust of a power group within the dominant order which ends with Edmund's death. In another sense the tendencies and characteristics the play has recognized continue beyond the last words of the text, in Shakespeare's own world and beyond that too. Dollimore observes, in this connection, that 'far from transcending in the name of an essential humanity the gulf which separates the privileged from the deprived, the play insists on it'.[27] Lear is only able to learn anything once he has lost power totally; rulers in power, the play acknowledges, never do expose themselves to 'feel what wretches feel' (3.4.34).[28] The image of Lear carrying the dead Cordelia, the image too of the powers-that-be crying, at the hint of danger, at the sound of an agonized, opposing voice, 'Shut up your doors ... 'tis a wild night ... come out o' th' storm' (2.4.310–11), and the image of that angry old man himself, deprived of power, realizing, in part confusedly, the real nature of its operation, set against the continuing indifference of that dominant class in its assertion of hegemony, perhaps more than the images in any other of Shakespeare's plays, have resonance for those of us living in South Africa.

Such realizations seem inescapable. In the same way if certain critics have found evidence in the tragedies of the assertion of bourgeois individualism, or anxiety about the ways in which traditional signifiers seem to be floating away from the signified, South Africans are located in particularly chilling versions of such processes at an advanced, critical stage. I would then, finally, also argue that many of the young men and women in South Africa, both in the townships and elsewhere, hearing Lear's identification of the materialist basis to power and justice:

> Plate sin with gold,
> And the strong lance of Justice hurtless
>   breaks;
> Arm it in rags, a pigmy's straw does pierce it
>   (4.6.167–9)

may be invited – without our betraying the Shakespeare text – to juxtapose against this, say, Solomon Plaatje's remarks about the passing of the Land Act of 1913:

Well we knew that this law was as harsh as its instigators were callous ... Lord Gladstone signed no fewer than sixteen new Acts of Parliament – some of them rather voluminous – while three days earlier, his excellency signed another batch of eight, of which the bulk was beyond the capability of any mortal to read and digest in four days ... The gods are cruel. They might have warned us that Englishmen would agree with Dutchmen to make it unlawful for black men to keep milk cows of their own ... render many poor homeless (and produce) such a rapid and widespread crash as it caused.[29]

---

[27] Dollimore, p. 192.
[28] Dollimore, pp. 191–2.
[29] Plaatje, pp. 81, 82, 22.

THE RATIONALE OF CURRENT BIBLIOGRAPHICAL METHODS: PRINTING HOUSE STUDIES, COMPUTER-AIDED COMPOSITOR STUDIES, AND THE USE OF STATISTICAL METHODS

MANFRED DRAUDT

In many respects the change in our approach to Shakespeare's text brought about by the 'new bibliography' of A. W. Pollard, R. B. McKerrow, and W. W. Greg can be compared to the scientific revolution initiated by Copernicus, Galileo, and Newton. Since the advent of these giants the strictly analytic method of inquiry, whether applied to Shakespeare's texts or to the world in general, has become *the* dominant principle.

Galileo Galilei, the father of modern science and thus also the father of analytical bibliography, was the first to use a mathematical description of nature. In order to make it possible to describe nature in these terms, he demanded that scientists should restrict themselves to studying only those properties which can be measured and quantified. His postulate was to measure those things which can be measured, and ultimately to make measurable all other things which originally were not measurable.

This approach, which has become the dominant principle of scientific examination, and of scholarly analysis emulating science, has proved extremely successful. Recently, however, not only eminent psychologists, such as R. D. Laing, but also physicists, such as Gary Zukav, Herbert Pietschmann, and Fritjof Capra,[1] have begun to voice critical warnings. They maintain that our obsession with measurement and quantification has changed our ideas of reality and truth, and thus ultimately our world, since properties which cannot be measured (values, for example, such as aesthetic ones, or feelings) tend to be regarded as less 'real'.[2]

Without intending to detract from the great achievements of Pollard, McKerrow, and Greg, to whose work I feel very much indebted, I should like to examine and question some developments in the analysis of Shakespeare's texts, where measurement and quantification recently appear to be used excessively and at the expense of other aspects. In particular I should like to point to some of

---

[1] Gary Zukav, *The Dancing Wu Li Masters: An Overview of the New Physics* (Bungay, Suffolk, 1980); Herbert Pietschmann, *Das Ende des naturwissenschaftlichen Zeitalters* (Wien, Hamburg, 1980); Fritjof Capra, *The Turning Point: Science, Society, and the Rising Culture* (Bungay, Suffolk, 1982).

[2] In spite of his pioneering achievement and his immense contribution to the overcoming of the limitations of medieval thought, Galileo was liable to preconceptions, which reflect his bias towards mathematics and rigid rationality. Although Kepler discovered during Galileo's lifetime that orbits are elliptical, Galileo continued to argue that they were circular because he wanted to maintain his belief in the perfect order of the cosmos. He also refused to entertain the idea of gravity because he considered it an 'occult' phenomenon; and he regarded sense-qualities, such as odour, for example, as totally illusory.

the problems of method which appear in highly specialized – and thus narrowly limited – studies of Shakespeare's texts.

The current flourishing of textual studies is reflected not only in the wide and intense discussion on the two texts of *King Lear* but also in the numerous bibliographical analyses of plays which until recently have been regarded as minor ones – such as *Love's Labour's Lost*, from which I should like to draw most of my examples.

Since 1978 aspects of the text of *Love's Labour's Lost* have been examined in at least ten major articles.[3] For my present purpose I should first like to recall some of the remarks made on these studies by reviewers in *Shakespeare Survey*. My main concern, however, will be with the approaches and methods employed by George Price in 'The Printing of *Love's Labour's Lost* (1598)' and particularly by Paul Werstine in the expanded version of 'Editorial Uses of Compositor Studies'. My choice of Werstine's article, on which I shall comment in greater detail, is determined not only by the fact that it is (so far) the most recent but also by the positive response it has received. The fact that it was reprinted and that the very reputable reviewer in *Shakespeare Survey* finds the argument propounded in this article, namely that the 1598 Quarto is a reprint, convincing,[4] suggests that the methods employed by Werstine are – implicitly, at least – endorsed by many modern textual scholars.

Comparing Price's and Werstine's articles of 1978, this reviewer expresses his surprise that both scholars have come to the conclusion 'that three compositors were at work', but 'Werstine's Compositors ... bear no relationship to Price's'. Furthermore, 'Werstine ... argues ... that his compositors were setting from a now lost quarto, [whereas] Price argues ... that his compositors were setting from a manuscript'. Such a 'disagreement between the two examinations must discourage the seeker after truth', observed the reviewer, who

had 'always hope[d] that scholars working independently on the identification of a compositor will reach the same conclusions'.[5]

The publication of my own article on 'Printer's Copy for the Quarto of *Love's Labour's Lost*' in 1981 made the situation even more complicated, because I argued for only one compositor but mixed copy. Hence we find the following note in *Shakespeare Survey*: 'This review in 1980 lamented the fact that two scholars working independently on the same data reached two different con-

---

3 George R. Price started the re-examination with 'The Printing of *Love's Labour's Lost* (1598)', in *Papers of the Bibliographical Society of America*, 72 (1978), 405–34. In the same year Paul Werstine, who had written a dissertation on 'William White's Printing Shop and the Printing of *Love's Labour's Lost* Q1' (1976), published his 'Editorial Uses of Compositor Studies', in *Analytical and Enumerative Bibliography*, 2 (1978), 153–65. Price and Werstine continued their studies in 1979 with 'Textual Notes on *Love's Labour's Lost*, 1598', in *Analytical and Enumerative Bibliography*, 3 (1979), 3–38, and 'Variants in the First Quarto of *Love's Labour's Lost*', in *Shakespeare Studies* 12 (1979), 35–47, respectively. In 1981 I responded to the studies of Price and Werstine in 'Printer's Copy for the Quarto of *Love's Labour's Lost* (1598)', in *Library*, vi, 3 (1981), 119–31. In 1982 Stanley Wells examined 'The Copy for the Folio text of *Love's Labour's Lost*', in *Review of English Studies*, NS, 33 (1982), 137–47; and John Kerrigan wrote on 'Shakespeare at Work: The Katharine–Rosaline Tangle in *Love's Labour's Lost*' (ibid., pp. 129–36). John Kerrigan elaborated his argument for three stages of revision in the play in '*Love's Labour's Lost* and Shakespearean Revision', in *Shakespeare Quarterly*, 33 (1982), 337–9. My response to both Wells's and Kerrigan's articles, 'The Rosaline–Katherine Tangle of *Love's Labour's Lost*', in *The Library*, vi, 4 (1982), 381–96 led to a controversy documented in the Correspondence section of *The Library*, vi, 5 (1983), 399–404. In 1982 Werstine's 'Editorial Uses of Compositor Studies' was reprinted in *Play-Texts in Old Spelling* as 'The Editorial Usefulness of Printing House and Compositor Studies' (New York, 1982), 35–64, with an 'Afterword' of more than twenty pages responding to Price's 'The Printing of *Love's Labour's Lost* (1598)' and my 'Printer's Copy for the Quarto of *Love's Labour's Lost* (1598)'.
4 See vol. 36 (1983), p. 187.
5 *Shakespeare Survey* 33 (1980), pp. 206–7.

clusions; to those two must now be added a third.'[6]

The publication of John Kerrigan's New Penguin edition and his article on the 'Katharine–Rosaline Tangle' was commented on as follows: 'We may draw two conclusions about the problem, neither of which is attractive: Kerrigan has not solved the tangle by merely cutting the knot as the Worthy did; the text does not provide enough material for a solution.'[7]

Remarking in the same volume on Stanley Wells's article, the reviewer observes: 'Wells is forced to argue that the agent preparing the Quarto was reprehensibly lazy, working thoroughly at the beginning and then giving the appearance of thoroughness at the end. He recognizes that it is not an attractive hypothesis' (p. 191).

In the next year the new textual reviewer in *Shakespeare Survey* commented on my article on the Rosaline–Katherine Tangle and on my 'Shakespeare's Unpretentious Ending to *Love's Labour's Lost*',[8] appending a critical footnote: 'For his present purposes [i.e. in the analysis of the Rosaline–Katherine tangle] Draudt minimizes the authority of F's divergences from Q, since he must repudiate F's changes to speech prefixes in 2.1. Compare the next item [where Draudt inclines to the view that the Folio addition is authentic]'.[9]

Prolonged unresolved disputes about textual matters, such as the one over *Love's Labour's Lost*, appear to result – as the reviewer in *Shakespeare Survey* came to suggest in 1983 – from the fact that 'the text does not provide enough material for a solution'. This problem is expressed even more radically by another reviewer of Shakespearian textual scholarship, Marvin Spevack:

[The] aim [of all this textual activity] is the reconstruction of what does not exist or, indeed, what may never have existed.... what is revealed is not necessarily Shakespeare but gaps achieved through surmisals. If the gaps are filled by means of inferential evidence, the whole remains in the realm of the

probable – [or, still more pessimistically, in the realm of the possible].[10]

Since in Shakespeare, in spite of our sophisticated scholarly methods, the blanks usually tend to be larger than indisputable facts about the nature or origin of the texts, scholars evolve hypotheses in order to fill in the gaps – and the reviews I have referred to suggest that these hypotheses almost always are, or at least appear to most critical readers, inconclusive or inconsistent. The only concrete support for bolstering a hypothesis is inferential evidence, such as analogous material from similar plays or texts, from the same author, compositor, printing house, etc.; but the conviction carried by such material naturally varies. What is more, analogous instances adduced in support of a particular theory are bound to reflect to a large degree a scholar's personal beliefs, his preferences, or prejudices. The textual studies of *Love's Labour's Lost* illustrate this point well: the decision to compare the Quarto of *Love's Labour's Lost* either to other reprinted books by White or to Q2 of *Hamlet* and *Romeo and Juliet* will largely determine whether one finds 'evidence' that the play is a complete reprint (as Werstine believes), or that it is based upon mixed copy (as I have argued). The problem that preconceived opinions ultimately seem to be inescapable is, however, by no means limited to bibliographical analysis alone but also applies to questions of authorship, for example. As the recent controversy over 'Shall I die?' has shown, parallel passages from Shakespeare, Spenser, Daniel, Drayton, Sidney, or any other Elizabethan poet are indicative of the conclusion to which the textual critic is predisposed rather than actual 'proof' of author-

---

[6] vol. 35 (1982), p. 186.
[7] *Shakespeare Survey 36* (1983), pp. 187.
[8] *Shakespeare Jahrbuch* (West) 1984, pp. 162–8.
[9] *Shakespeare Survey 37* (1984), pp. 216.
[10] *Shakespeare Jahrbuch* (West) 1984, pp. 233–4.

ship.[11] Since human perception and learning, and thus also the collection of 'objective' data, rely upon the mechanism of positive feedback and involve a process of filtering (according to the categories of 'relevant' and 'not relevant', for example), we ought to be aware that what traditionally is described and valued as 'objective evidence' is in fact at least partly a product of our (subjective) mental processes. Considering the scantiness of indisputable facts about Shakespeare's texts and the great variety of personalities and possible approaches, different opinions and even disagreement about the same data are inevitable.

At this point I should like to return to my initial analogy with physics, where we know that the problem whether light is to be regarded as a wave or a particle depends solely upon the kind of experiment that is undertaken. Even more pertinent to my present argument is, however, Heisenberg's uncertainty principle, which says that it is impossible to know with absolute precision both the position and the momentum of a particle, such as an electron.[12] Physicists are therefore well aware that at the subatomic level we cannot observe something without changing it; or, as Heisenberg wrote, 'What we observe is not nature itself, but nature exposed to our method of questioning.'[13]

It seems that in our analysis of Shakespeare's texts there exists an 'ambiguity barrier' similar to that described by Heisenberg. Textual scholars exclusively analysing spellings, minutiae of the text, and details of punctuation for the purpose of identifying a compositor move into something like the 'subatomic realm' of a play and thus encounter problems and difficulties which are possibly similar to those of the physicists. As Capra has pointed out, 'the patterns scientists observe in nature are intimately connected with the patterns of their minds, with their concepts, thoughts, and values. . . . Modern physics has not only invalidated the classical ideal [of an 'independent observer' and] of an objective description of nature but has also challenged the myth of a value-free science', because the distinction between objective and subjective has vanished.[14]

These commonplaces of physics should be kept in mind when we critically examine the ways in which data are collected and interpreted by textual scholars; and it might be added in parenthesis that the fact that two scholars working on the same data reach two different conclusions, which worried the *Shakespeare Survey* reviewer, would not necessarily surprise a modern physicist. While in the so-called exact sciences the traditional classic dogmas have long been modified or superseded, the methods silently accepted by most of today's textual scholars are still the old mathematical and analytical ones of Galileo and Descartes. Galileo's emphasis upon measuring and quantification and Descartes's postulate that complex phenomena can best be understood by reducing them to their constituent parts[15] (which has resulted in an ever

---

11 See Robin Robbins's and I. A. Shapiro's letters to *Times Literary Supplement* 20 and 27 December 1985, 1449–50 and 1481, 1492 respectively.

12 Heisenberg's uncertainty principle implies that as we penetrate deeper and deeper into the subatomic realm, we reach a certain point at which one part or another of our picture of nature becomes blurred, and there is no way to reclarify that part without blurring another part of the picture. This image recalls Antonioni's film *Blow Up*, in which a photographer makes bigger and bigger enlargements of a detail of his photograph until in the end he gets a meaningless haze of black dots on the paper.

13 Quoted in Zukav, *Overview of the New Physics*, p. 136.

14 Capra, *The Turning Point*, p. 77; compare also Zukav, *Overview of the New Physics*, pp. 132–6.

15 Descartes has been criticized by Heisenberg, who argues that his division between body and mind 'has penetrated deeply into the human mind . . . and it will take a long time for it to be replaced by a really different attitude toward the problem of reality' (*Physics and Philosophy* (1962), p. 81). Norman Rabkin's essay mentioned below appears to be similarly critical of Descartes.

increasing specialization) appear to underlie many textual studies.

I should now like to illustrate my points by taking Price's and Werstine's textual studies of *Love's Labour's Lost* as examples. Since I agree with some of Price's conclusions, and since it seems that, disregarding the question of the compositors, Werstine's position is not poles apart from my own (he arguing for a total reprint, I for a partial one), it should be understood that the following arguments are intended not as an attack upon these two scholars but simply as a questioning of methods which are widely accepted today and which I myself admit to having employed uncritically.

By relying heavily on large quantities of data and statistics, both Price and Werstine comply with the fallacious dogma that figures *per se* are objective, carry an overwhelming power of conviction, and are therefore best suited for finding the truth.

Since I have already commented in some detail on Price's use of data in 'Printer's Copy for the Quarto of *Love's Labour's Lost* (1598)', I shall give only one example here. Price refers to the 'number of capitals on each page as probably the strongest evidence' for the shares of individual compositors (p. 425) and therefore identifies their different stints mainly by distinguishing between different averages of capitals per page. Yet the group with an average of 26.8 capitals includes one page with only 15 capitals (D4^r), whereas the group with an average number of 17.2 includes one page with 34 capitals (C4^v).[16]

As this brief example indicates, figures and statistical data easily serve to convey subjective impressions rather than help to prove a point with objective precision.

More fundamental questions, however, are raised by Werstine's article on 'The Editorial Usefulness of Printing House and Compositor Studies'.[17] He states that his 'purpose ... is to suggest with some fresh examples that editors can benefit from researching the printing houses and compositors who produced the texts they edit'; and he continues by arguing that 'for ... an Elizabethan printer, a Shakespeare quarto is just another job of work and thus has the same status as a now long forgotten New Year's Day sermon or an almanac' (p. 35).

We may observe that the choice of analogous material from White's printing house rather than from, say, other plays by Shakespeare is bound to have some bearing on the conclusion arrived at; otherwise, however, the statement that 'for ... an Elizabethan printer, a Shakespeare quarto is just another job of work and thus has the same status as a now long forgotten New Year's Day sermon or an almanac' appears to be perfectly correct and unassailable. Only on second thoughts do we realize that it is, as Harold Pinter would say, 'both true and false'. It is true in an obvious technical sense; yet it is also false, because it neglects numerous and, it seems, very important features of a Shakespeare quarto. Shakespeare's plays, we know, were written not to be published in print but to be performed on stage, and they never reached the printing house directly from the hands of their author, as an almanac probably did. Moreover, in respect of the nature of the printer's copy such a quarto probably had very little in common with a New Year's Day sermon. Shakespeare's 'foul papers' – a hastily composed text that would in any case be copied for use in the theatre, with abbreviations for speech-headings which could easily be mistaken – as well as a prompt-book with annotations made for or during performance would pose quite different problems for a printer and compositor from those posed by the manuscript of an almanac; also, for a play a printed copy (of a 'bad quarto', for example) could have served,

---

[16] See 'The Printing of *Love's Labour's Lost* (1598)', pp. 420–3.

[17] Parenthetic page references in the text refer to this article.

either in part or in whole, as the printer's copy.

The assumption that the printing of a Shakespeare quarto is in every respect comparable to the printing of any other book by the same printer is not tenable; therefore any inferences based on this premiss can carry at best very little conviction. Although Werstine, in fact, decides to adduce most of his data from other plays, his exclusive reliance upon inferences of this kind is equally problematical. In his examination of *The Texts of 'King Lear' and their Origins* Peter W. M. Blayney has shown that the *Lear* quarto 'is exceptional not only as a quarto, a play-quarto, and a Shakespeare Quarto, but [even] as an *Okes* quarto ... *Lear* was set ... from a play-manuscript which required the compositors to impose conventions differing quite substantially from those in most of Okes's other books' (pp. 184–5).

Not only the basic premiss, the belief that the examination of other works by the same printer will necessarily elucidate the nature of a Shakespeare quarto, is untenable; Werstine's article contains also other fallacious arguments, such as that 'the *occasional* use of roman and italic for stage directions both in White's reprints and in *LLLQ*1 may suggest that *LLLQ*1 is, like the other plays White printed, *entirely* a reprint' (p. 46; my italics). The well-known fact that compositors usually (though by no means always) follow copy conventions, to which attention is drawn, neither supports the hypothesis of a complete reprint nor disproves the other possibility that the play was printed from mixed copy.

Although Werstine rightly objects 'that the data employed by Price can be shown to be irrelevant to compositor identification in the extant quarto' (p. 44), he, too, tends to interpret data (spelling patterns in his case) in a highly subjective manner and treats possibilities as probabilities, and probabilities as if they were facts.

Considering the possible contributions of the various compositors at work in White's

shop, he argues that 'since [Compositor Q's] spellings ['mee' and 'shee'] are comparatively rare in *LLLQ*1, he ... probably did no work on the play.' Yet solely on the basis that '"hir" appears ... once ... at B1' he attributes this page to 'Compositor R' (p. 37). He points out later that 'the problem of identifying compositors in *LLLQ*1 on the basis of spelling evidence [is complicated], for we can never be sure which spellings in the extant quarto may have been taken over from printed copy and which spellings may have been introduced by the compositors'; nevertheless, and despite 'the possibility that ... [these] spellings derive from printed copy', he prefers to take 'the *hir* spellings as evidence of Compositor R's hand' (p. 58).

With regard to 'Compositor S' Werstine indicates that his preferred habits 'weaken somewhat in 1599 and later', and with regard to 'Compositor T' he admits that 'he sometimes sets Compositor S's strong preferences' (p. 38). Furthermore, he finds in the respective stints of these two compositors 'some spellings Compositor S rarely or never set in his extant work' as well as 'many spellings uncharacteristic of Compositor T' (p. 38).

To a wholly dispassionate reader these facts would surely permit also other interpretations:

1. Compositor Q (whose spellings are 'comparatively rare') rather than R (whose 'hir' occurs only on B1) may have contributed to the setting of the play.

2. A distinction between Compositors S and T seems hardly possible: first, because the weakening of S's most distinctive habit, his preference for medial -y- spellings, in and after 1599, appears to preclude definite conclusions in respect of 1598, the year when *LLLQ*1 was printed; secondly, because S and T share some 'strong preferences', and because in their stints numerous spellings uncharacteristic of their work can be found.

Another issue in matters of compositor identification concerns, of course, the problem of the predictability of habits of a compositor, or of human beings in general. Although, under favourable conditions, large quantities of data may enable us to associate certain tendencies or characteristics with particular workmen, the possibility of a sudden whim, an error, or simply an unmotivated change at any given moment can never be completely excluded. The occurrence of a particular spelling on a single page only should therefore never be taken as 'evidence' of the hand of a particular compositor.

Also, a hypothesis, particularly if based upon shaky possibilities of the kind examined above, hardly serves as a reliable basis for further speculations: '*If* Compositor S did indeed set these seven [out of 74] pages of *LLLQ*1, then *LLLQ*1 was *probably* a reprint' (my italics). Similar objections need to be raised against an attempt to explain away data contradicting the original hypothesis (concerning compositor identification) by relegating them to another hypothesis: 'the mixture of these [uncharacteristic] spellings with preferential spellings of the same words on the same pages strongly suggests the influence of printed copy on *LLLQ*1' (p. 38).

If unrelated to other types of evidence and if simply taken on their own, spelling tests seem to be liable to be interpreted like Rorschach tests, namely in a highly subjective way; and almost any type of supposedly factual evidence may lend itself to supporting contrasting views. Whereas in his study of the stop-press corrections Werstine concluded that 'the extant press corrections divide neatly into two groups, for correction in sheets A and C is much lighter than in sheets D and E'[18], three years later he minimizes the distinction: 'the difference does not seem great enough' (p. 53). This example should in no way suggest that Werstine, or anybody else (and I might refer in this context also to the above-mentioned review of my own articles in *Shakespeare Survey 37*, where I was similarly criticized), deliberately 'rigs the evidence' in order to serve his particular purpose; rather, it seems that the process of selecting, analysing, and interpreting data (frequently minute details) inevitably involves not only one's own mind but is also determined, at least to some extent, by the aim or object of one's study:[19] 'Not only do we influence our reality, but, in some degree, we actually *create* it', says the physicist Zukav; 'this is very close to saying that we *create* certain properties because we choose to measure those properties'.[20]

Werstine's concluding remark to the effect that the great number of variants he analyses represent but a 'fraction' or 'sample' of the masses of data available to him is probably intended to suggest to a critical reader that his theory is trustworthy because it can be bolstered by copious additional material. However, the same type of evidence (more spelling variants) does not necessarily make a hypothesis more convincing. It is a widespread yet false belief in our present age that large quantities of data (now relatively easily available with the help of computers) more or less automatically solve complex problems. Yet problems of authorship cannot be settled merely by identifying large numbers of short parallel phrases (as the controversy over 'Shall

---

[18] 'Variants in the First Quarto of *Love's Labour's Lost*', p. 39.

[19] Compare Trevor H. Howard-Hill, who expressed similar warnings in 'Computers and Shakespearian Bibliography and Textual Criticism', in *Sprache und Datenverarbeitung*, 3 (1979), 80–8: 'In any page of the Folio, the amount of information which is not significant for compositor determination greatly exceeds that which is significant. The significant information is not known at the beginning of the analysis; it is, indeed, a goal of the procedure to identify it . . . . The computer can count the spellings but it cannot weigh them . . . . The most difficult aspect of . . . analysis techniques is to decide how to weigh categories of evidence without bringing about a programmed predisposition to certain kinds of solutions . . . . The computer's capacity to manipulate masses of data is crucial . . . although the initial perception of what evidence may be significant or relevant to a particular enquiry inevitably must be human' (pp. 84–5).

[20] *Overview of the New Physics*, pp. 53–4.

I die?' has reminded us); nor can questions concerning the compositors and the printer's copy of a play be reduced to the examination of spelling patterns alone.

Since seemingly objective data and sincerely presented hypotheses may turn out to be fallacious, any given problem needs to be approached from as many sides as possible in order to reduce the potential hazard involved in any particular theory. It is this type of comprehensiveness, coupled with an unusual awareness of the limitations of the methods employed, which appears to constitute the excellence of studies such as Peter Blayney's widely praised[21] Texts of 'King Lear' and their Origins.[22]

A final test of our nice, abstract, and very rational hypotheses is the test of common sense. We might ask ourselves how what we believe we have discovered fits into a wider context. With regard to the issue of the compositors of Love's Labour's Lost, we may ask ourselves, given the indisputable fact (accepted by Price, Werstine, and myself) that most of the play was printed with only one skeleton-forme, how likely it is that the play was set by more than one compositor? Also, inferential evidence of one kind should at least not jar with other hypotheses advanced. Thus any theory that Love's Labour's Lost was set by three compositors becomes even less convincing if two of the three reprinted plays compared to Love's Labour's Lost were set by a single compositor, the third one by two compositors, but none by three.[23]

Finally, the conclusion drawn by Werstine is questionable, and the very last sentence of his article appears to be misleading. He dismisses 'the close resemblance between the title-pages of LLLQ1 and the second quarto of Romeo and Juliet' (p. 60) as inconclusive evidence of a similarity in the histories of the publication of the two plays, but then takes a non-Shakespearian play with a distinctly dissimilar title-page formula ('Newly corrected and amended of such grosse faultes as passed in the

former impression'), White's reprint of The Spanish Tragedy, as the basis of his own speculation: 'With the possibility that an early print of LLL served as copy for the first extant quarto arises the possibility that this first printing may have provided a better, not a worse, text of the play' (p. 61). In this context, and after the refutation of the theory that Love's Labour's Lost Q1 was a 'good quarto' supplanting a 'bad' one, the unqualified use of 'better' and 'worse' is surely misleading. By simply inverting the sequence of 'good' and 'bad' and

---

21 Compare, for example, Paul Werstine's review in *Shakespeare Quarterly*, 36 (1985), 120–5, which begins, 'Once in a generation, it seems, there appears a bibliographical study of Shakespeare that changes the direction of future scholarship. . . . for this generation it will probably be Peter Blayney's . . . study'.

22 '[In spite of] the present-day preoccupation with compositors, . . . I have declined to investigate the compositorial shares of any Okes book other than *Lear* itself' (p. 11); 'the only scale in which I have found it possible to weigh the balance has been a subjective one' (p. 12); 'In the study of a quarto, as distinct from a folio, it is rather more difficult to cope with a number of limitations which are inherent in [the method itself]; "identification" [of compositors] is a potentially (and, in some cases, demonstrably) misleading description of what the methods can actually do' (p. 151); 'to assume that each group of identified pages can be treated as a unit . . . introduces an element of circularity. The only phenomena which are likely to be judged significant after that point are those that support the already-suggested division' (p. 152); 'it is possible for the most plausible of such deductions to be disastrously wrong' (p. 291). Similarly aware of the limitations inherent in the methods of modern textual criticism is T. H. Howard-Hill in 'Computers and Shakespearian Bibliography': 'Distinctive spellings often do not occur in sufficient numbers on a particular page to enable distinctions to be made . . . spellings may be taken as compositor discriminants which are in fact characteristic of the particular copy from which a play was set' (p. 83).

23 The basis of Werstine's evaluation of the data of *Love's Labour's Lost* Q1 is a comparison with data from three reprinted plays from White's shop, *The Famous Chronicle of king Edwarde the first* (1599), *The Spanish Tragedie* (1599) and *The True Tragedie of Richarde Duke of Yorke* (1600); the numbers of the compositors involved in their setting are given by Werstine (see p. 44).

thus neglecting the fundamental differences in quality between reprints and different versions of a text, this statement seems to suggest that in the case of *Love's Labour's Lost* the extant quarto (which allegedly supplanted a 'good' one) is comparable to a 'bad quarto'. Although such a hypothesis is, of course, theoretically conceivable, all the facts we know speak against it: not a single 'bad quarto' of a Shakespeare play was ever published *after* a 'good' one had been printed. Because Werstine is surely aware of this circumstance, I take it that he means the gradual deterioration of texts in the course of being reprinted. Such a process, in which many – largely insubstantial – errors are introduced but the the text is preserved essentially intact, is, however, fundamentally different from, and therefore should not be compared to, the replacement of a 'bad' text by a 'good' one (which happened in the cases of *Romeo and Juliet* and *Hamlet*, for example). The other hypothesis, that *Love's Labour's Lost* Q1 is an inferior reprint of a 'good quarto' – though equally conceivable in theory – is hardly compatible with the nonsensical confusions in act 4, scene 1, and, furthermore, contradicts Werstine's earlier arguments. Since this 'massive corruption ... is unlikely to originate with the compositor ... [but] must be assumed [to have] ... derived from the compositor's copy, which [was] a print' (pp. 38–9), both the possibility that the printer's copy was a 'good quarto' and the explanation that 'such massive corruption' happened in the course of reprinting are ruled out.

I have tried to suggest that we ought to weigh more carefully what is commonly accepted as 'factual evidence' or 'objective data', and that the increasing concern with measuring, quantification, and statistical methods in the study of Shakespeare's texts does not necessarily bring us closer to the 'truth'. Such warnings have, however, already been voiced earlier, and by much greater men than myself.[24] In a paper delivered to the International Shakespeare Congress at Vancouver in 1971, Norman Rabkin said, 'My guess is that our troubles stem in good part from the value we have put on reductiveness. We have been betrayed by a bias toward what can be set out in rational argument.'[25] Similar thoughts have been expressed by Sir Karl Popper, who repeatedly criticizes our 'misplaced faith in formalization or precision'. Still more pertinent to the present argument appears to be the warning of another Austrian, the physicist Capra: 'Modern physics can show the other sciences that scientific thinking does not necessarily have to be reductive or mechanistic; ... [since] physicists have gone far beyond [the Cartesian] model, it is time for the other sciences to expand their underlying philosophies.'[26]

---

[24] Compare E. A. J. Honigmann's *The Stability of Shakespeare's Text* (1965), which concludes with a critical remark on 'The "Optimism" of the New Bibliography': 'It is as well to recognise that though we have learnt much from the closer study of Shakespeare's text, we have wasted our time if we have not also learnt caution.... the optimists are at their most dangerous precisely when they offer the world new "bibliographical facts"' (pp. 169–70).

[25] 'Meaning and Shakespeare', *Shakespeare 1971*, ed. Clifford Leech and J. M. R. Margeson (Toronto, 1972), 89–106, p. 99.

[26] *The Turning Point*, pp. 32–3.

SHAKESPEARE'S LATE PLAYS AT STRATFORD, ONTARIO

ROGER WARREN

John Hirsch, Artistic Director of the Shakespeare Festival at Stratford, Ontario from 1981 to 1985, had hoped to stage all four of Shakespeare's late plays in a single season but felt unable to run the financial risks, and it was left to his successor, John Neville, to take the plunge and base the 1986 season on three of them: *Pericles*, *Cymbeline*, and *The Winter's Tale*. It is a pity that Mr Hirsch could not realize his ambition, for his 1982 production of *The Tempest* there was the only coherent version of the play I have seen, and whatever the virtues of Mr Neville's season, coherence was not among them.[1] He aimed instead at diversity within unity, engaging three different directors. Each avoided a generalized fairy-tale setting, and located the action within a specific period, but of widely different kinds: *Pericles* was set in the eighth century Byzantine empire, *Cymbeline* in the late 1930s, *The Winter's Tale* in the nineteenth century.

Of course, several connections emerged even so. One involved the theatre's huge thrust stage. It is often suggested that these are intimate plays intended for the Blackfriars Theatre. Yet *Pericles* and *The Winter's Tale* certainly, and *Cymbeline* presumably, were also given at the Globe, and the staging of several scenes here – Cerimon's revival of Thaisa, the battle in the narrow lane in *Cymbeline*, the trial of Hermione – demonstrated that these are big scenes for all their intimate verbal detail. The combination of wide, far-flung staging with a close scrutiny of psychological motive also stressed how in several scenes there is an intimate, private action going on within a more public one. Most interesting of all, the moments of extreme theatrical virtuosity – the bedroom, burial, and Jupiter scenes in *Cymbeline*, the statue scene in *The Winter's Tale* – emerged as an externalization of the characters' inner experiences, including their dreams.

There were more specific parallels too. When seen side by side, the painful spiritual process by which Pericles moves from despair to new life ('I am great with woe, and shall deliver weeping', 'Give me a gash, put me to present pain', 'I am wild in my beholding') seemed very close to Leontes' painful sixteen-year recovery. The pain of these spiritual journeys was one aspect of a more general darkness, even sadism, that kept surfacing in performance, especially in intimate relationships: Marina maltreated by Boult, Lysimachus, *and Pericles*; Leontes' extraordinary brutality to Hermione and the baby Perdita; Polixenes' correspondingly furious attack on Florizel and Perdita; the sexual violence lurking beneath the relationships of Innogen,

---

[1] I have described this production of *The Tempest* in *Shakespeare Survey 39* (Cambridge, 1987), pp. 179–81. My visits to Canada were made possible by awards from the British Academy and from the Research Board, University of Leicester.

Posthumus, and Giacomo.[2] This darkness came to seem an essential aspect of the writing: forgiveness, reconciliation, and renewal were hard-won.

I

Since the pagan world of *Pericles* also includes a tournament from the Christian era, Richard Ouzounian's production drew upon a visual style that included both elements, the art of Byzantine Christianity. This worked particularly well for the blaze of purple and gold splendour at Pentapolis, and contributed to an opening scene of tremendous impact as Geraint Wyn Davies's fair-haired hero in golden armour faced Nicholas Pennell's sinister blood-red Antiochus. And there was some excellent detail here. Commentators have wondered why the previous suitors couldn't solve a riddle so transparent. Mr Pennell's fearsome authority suggested why: they couldn't face admitting the truth to so ferocious an adversary, even at the cost of their lives. The difficulty of the riddle lay not in deciphering what it meant but in finding a way of telling the king: here Pericles won a stay of execution by taking Antiochus downstage and confidentially hinting at the truth out of earshot, without shaming the king in front of his entire court.

An especially interesting aspect of this production was that during its rehearsal period the radical reconstruction of the text prepared by Gary Taylor and MacDonald P. Jackson for the Oxford Shakespeare became available to the company, and they incorporated extensive passages into their version. The Oxford text draws upon the verse 'fossils' embedded in the prose of George Wilkins's novel *The Painful Adventures of Pericles* to fill gaps in the Quarto text or to emend much of its corruption. What this production made quite clear was that this text makes it possible to play some scenes which had seemed unplayable, and increases the theatrical impact of others. One example of

each kind of improvement must serve for many.

Modern productions often omit scene 2 altogether because it seems so corrupt in the Quarto. By inserting a mere six lines drawn from Wilkins, Oxford makes complete sense of the scene at a stroke. In the Quarto, there is no reason for Helicanus to accuse his fellow councillors of flattery, or for Pericles to be so angry with Helicanus later in the scene. The new speech provides the missing motivation. First, Helicanus roundly criticizes Pericles, thus motivating his subsequent anger:

> You do not well so to abuse yourself,
> To waste your body here with pining sorrow,
> Upon whose safety doth depend the lives
> And the prosperity of a whole kingdom.
> 'Tis ill in you to do it,

then, turning to the lords, he continues:

>   and no less
> Ill in your council not to contradict it.

This leads seamlessly into the hitherto unmotivated Quarto line:

> They do abuse the King that flatter him.

The sensation of hearing this speech in performance for the first time was extraordinary: the scene came immediately into focus. Helicanus' new, or recovered, speech helped the actor to create a character of real authority, 'a figure of truth, of faith, of loyalty', instead of the cipher he seems when the scene is omitted in the mistaken belief that it is irretrievably corrupt.

Another example of an underwritten character in the Quarto text is Thaisa, who has no direct declaration of her love to Pericles; she reveals it in a letter to her father. But the Oxford text gives her an eleven-line speech

---

[2] All references are to *William Shakespeare: The Complete Works*, eds. Stanley Wells, Gary Taylor, John Jowett, and William Montgomery (Oxford, 1986).

10   *Pericles*. Stratford, Ontario Festival, 1986.
Pericles (Geraint Wyn Davies) dances with Thaisa (Goldie Semple). King Simonides (William Needles) looks on

drawn from Wilkins in which she does declare her love, concluding:

> What with my pen I have in secret written
> With my tongue now I openly confirm,
> Which is I have no life but in his love,
> Nor any being but in joying of his worth.

Thaisa was played by Goldie Semple, the most versatile member of the company, and she made much of the opportunities offered by this speech, modulating from edged criticism of her father for showing Pericles the letter ('what . . . I have *in secret* written') to heartfelt tenderness: 'I have no life but in his love.' Both this restored speech and the Helicanus one made important contributions to the impact of the first two acts. But there is this difference: Helicanus' speech made sense of a scene that didn't make sense before, Thaisa's enriched her role rather than filling a demonstrable gap. For although Thaisa has no *verbal* declaration of love in the Quarto, she can express it by other theatrical means, as this production also suggested: the dance at Pentapolis between Pericles and Thaisa, at once sensuous and graceful, became a ritual of courtship; they declared their love through the traditional symbolism of the dance.

While the Oxford text has contributed decisively to modern staging of the play, problems remain. The new text recovers sense, not necessarily great drama or poetry. The reconstructed speeches are at best vigorous and serviceable, and there is still a huge gulf in quality between Thaisa's declaration of love and Pericles' lament for her apparent death in the next scene, a gulf this production widened by playing Simonides as bumbling rather than formidable: the shift from the near-farce of his changes of mood in scene 9 to Thaisa's 'death' in childbirth in scene 11 was even more jarring than usual: it was like moving into another play.

Although Cerimon's revival of Thaisa made its customary impact, it becomes a different kind of scene on this huge open stage than, say, in The Other Place at Stratford-upon-Avon. The medical detail, 'the boxes . . . fire and cloths', that were such a feature of The Other Place version[3] were important here, too, but the shape and size of this stage stressed that this is also a large-scale scene. Attendants with flaming torches alternately advanced in radial movements to surround the chest containing Thaisa's body and retreated first in alarm at discovering the 'dead' body and then in amazement as it revived. These re-groupings intensified the sense of natural magic as Thaisa asked wonderingly 'What world is this?' Here the production touched the heart of the play and of the romances: it was at once simple yet strange, magical yet familiar and movingly human.

The brothel scenes were vilely funny but dangerous too: these brothel-keepers meant business. So, even more, did Joseph Ziegler's Lysimachus. His offhand practical inquiry, 'wholesome iniquity have you, that a man may deal withal and defy the surgeon?' was chilling, as was the ruthlessly matter-of-fact way he manoeuvred Marina on to the cushions, a mere perfunctory prelude to intercourse. Kim Horsman's Marina was in real danger, and needed every syllable of her eloquence to defend herself from this Lysimachus. She also needed, therefore, Wilkins's version of the scene, which provides that eloquence. Lysimachus' Quarto response, 'I did not think / Thou couldst have spoke so well' then made perfect sense: her integrity had shamed and converted a tough whoremonger. She converted Nicholas Pennell's Boult not just by eloquence but by bribing him with the gold Lysimachus had given her. Her grim experiences had made her wise in the ways of this world. The scene, superbly taken by all three

---

3 Described in *Shakespeare Survey 33* (Cambridge, 1980), pp. 171–3.

actors, was by far the best in the production, its climax and turning point.

Marina then found herself assaulted by yet another violently predatory man as Pericles alternated between an animal-like state of despairing self-abasement and violent outbursts, initially roughly pushing her away and later seizing her equally roughly to interrogate her. But the scene was an anti-climax because Geraint Wyn Davies failed to rise to its final overwhelming ecstasy. He could express the 'present pain' but not the 'great sea of joys rushing upon' him. For the first time in my experience the scene was not at all moving. But what most hampered the production's success was the treatment of Gower, played by a female jazz singer. Gower's couplets were largely replaced by sub-literate drivel ('wanna tell ya a story', 'we love to entertain ya', 'When the news of this / Got around Pentapolis') set to music of breathtaking banality and so massively amplified as to obscure any hope of following the narrative. It seemed paradoxical that a staging which restored much of the text should jettison an entire area of it, but such contradictions summarized the uncertainty of an uneven production.

II

There was nothing uncertain about Robin Phillips's astonishing view of *Cymbeline*, set in the late 1930s. The theatre's publicity caught the tone: 'as the skies over Europe darken with approaching war, a commoner wins the heart of the heir to the British throne' – a kind of Edward VIII and Mrs Simpson in reverse. The aim was to place the events of the play, and particularly the war between Britain and Rome, in a context the audience could recognize, and it gave help to the characters most in need of it.

Cymbeline and the Queen are mere figureheads, and Robin Phillips helped us to accept them as such by providing them with instantly recognizable 1930s equivalents. Cymbeline

was clearly George V, wearing a variety of naval uniforms and shooting outfits, attended by grooms and gamekeepers on his country estates. The Queen was Janus-faced: on public occasions she was the very image of Queen Mary; but in private, she was a blue-stocking lady doctor in a white lab coat, rather like the eccentric sanatorium owner in Dürrenmatt's *The Physicists*. The advantage of these striking images was that they enabled Eric Donkin and Susan Wright simply to play the scenes as they came: they were images of royalty, 'givens' about whom questions of motive or psychological consistency did not arise.

Robin Phillips caught with uncanny precision the stultifying atmosphere of faded, musty English country house society between the wars. A decadent English aristocracy was set against a different kind of decadence in Italy: the civilians lounged indolently in clubs or on the lido, the military were fascist stormtroopers in trench-coats. This cool, clear, rational daylight world, observed in fastidious detail, was then boldly contrasted with the scenes in Wales, where the exiled princes were near-naked savages, images of natural man uncorrupted by the clothes and institutions of twentieth-century 'civilization', a contrast vividly, even violently, made when Innogen barged into their world disguised in a tin hat and uniform of a British 'Tommy', pushing a bicycle. The incongruity was played for maximum humorous effect: Innogen and the princes were amazed at each other's appearance, and the friendly punches they exchanged, which drew much laughter from the audience, made the securely Shakespearian point that it is often through humour that warmth and affection are expressed. An image like 'the night to th' owl and morn to th' lark less welcome' came naturally from these princes – but so did the other side of the natural man's spontaneity, the violence and brutality, even bestiality, which emerges in phrases like 'we are beastly . . . like warlike as the wolf', and which culminates in the killing of Cloten.

11 *Cymbeline*. Stratford, Ontario Festival, 1986.
The Wager Scene. Foreground: Giacomo (Colm Feore) and Posthumus (Joseph Ziegler)

12   *Cymbeline*. Stratford, Ontario Festival, 1986. Innogen (Martha Burns) and Giacomo (Colm Feore)

The new period worked on two levels. The public nightmare of a world rushing headlong into a cataclysmic war was reflected on the private level by the personal nightmares of Innogen and Posthumus, with Giacomo as the catalyst in each case. The scenes between these three were presented with great psychological complexity and conviction; and the conscious theatricality of Robin Phillips's staging of the three dreams / visions / nightmares – Giacomo emerging from the trunk, Innogen waking by the headless corpse, and the descent of Jupiter – brought out Shakespeare's own technique in these scenes, using shock effect to jolt the audience into extra awareness of extreme emotional states.

Their early scenes gained from the production's realism. The wager took place in an Italian gentlemen's club. Giacomo was partly an embodiment of this lounging, indolent world, partly something more sinister, psychotic beneath his contained exterior. He and Posthumus inevitably clashed, for Posthumus was a stiff-backed English prig, thoroughly ill at ease both with this casual society and, more important, with himself. He burned on the shortest of fuses, exploding very early in the scene at the slightest hint that Innogen might be imperfect: his trust in her was less than absolute. But if he was rash and priggish, he was also vulnerable. The cynicism of his soliloquy after Giacomo's 'proof' of Innogen's disloyalty was played as the utterance of a man whose precarious self-confidence was shattered and who, on the brink of tears, was finding conventional phrases to save himself from complete collapse. It was very cleverly thought out and movingly performed by Joseph Ziegler: the audience took all the points and responded to the soliloquy with applause.

Vulnerability was also an important element of Martha Burns's Innogen, not through any insecurity about herself or her partner, but because of Giacomo's threatening sexuality. Their encounter was superbly detailed on both sides. She was mettlesome and quick-witted as well as vulnerable, on her guard throughout: 'My lord, I fear, / Has forgot Britain' was a sharp, suspicious question rather than a gullible acceptance of his insinuations. Colm Feore handled Giacomo's tortuous speeches in this scene with a suave ease that fully communicated their suggestive, loaded sexuality, and he took this much further in the bedroom scene, the first theatrical *tour de force* of the production. Giacomo whispered the entire speech, using a throat microphone. This might have distracted attention from the text to the device, had it not been performed with such bravura. As the scene progressed, Innogen seemed in greater and greater danger: there was always the sense that she might in fact be raped. He even drew the bedclothes off her and straddled her before *kissing* the mole on her breast (as he subsequently tells Posthumus he did). She almost woke; her sleep was troubled. Perhaps she was dreaming about Tereus and Philomel, whose story she had been reading earlier. The scene carried a very strong suggestion that this near-rape was an externalizing of her nightmare. The audience listened throughout with engrossed, breathless attention, and then applauded Mr Feore, who had caught both the sophisticated theatricality and the emotional realities that it expresses – desire, obsessive sexuality, a rape that is not quite a rape.

There was a link between the intensely physical treatment of this scene and that of Innogen's second nightmare, beside Cloten's decapitated corpse. Mr Phillips aimed for a surreal effect here. Autumn leaves floated from the roof; wailing, unearthly voices filled the air; the princes chanted the dirge like some strange primitive rite. But it lacked the heart-catching simplicity of the text, and the actors lacked the technique to bring it off. So the scene sagged, and Martha Burns had difficulty in sustaining the waking soliloquy; but when, at the end, she put her leg over the 'Martial thigh' she takes to be Posthumus', the weird necrophilic embrace recalled Giacomo's physical intimacy with her in the bedroom. So both these theatrically sensational scenes were linked together; and the nightmare effect recurred in the battle sequence, culminating in the most sensational moment of all, the descent of Jupiter.

This sequence was centred firmly on Posthumus. The thrust stage itself became the 'narrow lane' in which he and the princes, aided by some very atmospheric lighting, acted out the battle in all its ferocity, as the text requires. And then Posthumus' account of what we have already seen, which is for that reason usually drastically shortened or cut altogether, was included almost intact, and was another *tour de force*: Joseph Ziegler delivered it with a sophisticated virtuosity which also brought out the underlying emotional reality: Posthumus was badly shell-shocked, as shaken by the violence of war as he had earlier been by his uncertainty about Innogen. He grew up before our eyes, maturing from a rash, callow youth to a man chastened by grim experience. The Jupiter scene then emerged as the exhausted sleep of someone who had just been through a violent battle.

The doggerel of the apparitions was overlapped, and interpreted as the confused, incoherent babble of a nightmare; at its climax, 'eagle' was the name of a Second World War bomber, a 'thunderer' with two huge propellers; Jupiter himself was a pilot 'whose bolt . . . / Sky-planted, batters all rebelling coasts'. And that public military violence was related to Posthumus' private violence towards Innogen which was on his conscience, but from which he dreamed he might be freed:

> He shall be lord of lady Innogen,
>   And happier much by his affliction made.

The extreme sensationalism of the staging, a modern equivalent of the baroque extravagance of the descending god, ran the risk of drawing attention from the lines, but that is always a danger with the eagle anyway, and I thought the risk worth taking. There were several important advantages. This vision focused attention on the returned, maturing Posthumus in a way that few productions do because it seemed so obviously an externalization of his dream and of his shaken mental state. It connected with the other two theatrical 'dreams': it picked up the earlier suggestion that Giacomo's near-rape may be an externalizing of Innogen's dream; and because Posthumus lay in exactly the same place on stage as Innogen had done by Cloten's corpse, in similar ghostly light, the point was made that husband and wife were undergoing similar traumatic, purgative experiences. And finally, the ferocious apparition emphasized how 'affliction' is inseparable from happiness and human relationships in this as in the other late plays.

This point was reinforced in the final scene when Posthumus – not deliberately but nevertheless significantly – strikes Innogen when they are reunited. Their chastened, silent response to one another during the multiple revelations was the more moving because the rigours which they had experienced had been so graphically staged. The ending was not wholly dark, despite the gigantic cannon under which it took place. The emotional reunion of Innogen and her brothers was achieved through laughter at their recollection of those comradely blows they had exchanged earlier on. But in general it was a strong, clear reading rather than one which dwelt on the lyrical beauty of the play.

III

The clarity of David William's production of *The Winter's Tale* was of a fundamentally different kind, despite superficial similarities in the staging. The first act took place during a European court reception in the 1830s. The evening dress and chandeliers evoked a world of glittering protocol whose civilized, sophis-

13 *Cymbeline*. Stratford, Ontario Festival, 1986. Posthumus (Joseph Ziegler), Innogen (Martha Burns),
and Cymbeline (Eric Donkin)

14   *The Winter's Tale*. Stratford, Ontario Festival, 1986. Polixenes (Stephen Russell) tells Hermione (Goldie Semple) about his childhood with Leontes

ticated values were embodied in Hermione. During an elegant court game, she laughingly indicated to Leontes that he should usher the court offstage so that she could be alone with Polixenes to persuade him to stay. Goldie Semple's natural poise and grace, and her delightful sense of humour, exactly caught the exquisite blend of playfulness and tenderness in Hermione; and Stephen Russell as Polixenes matched her in warmth and wit as he lay stretched out languorously on the ground beside her, reliving his boyhood with Leontes as he described it. This passage was filled with a terrifying pathos, a sense that precious things were about to be destroyed – not just Polixenes' friendship since boyhood with Leontes

but his new friendship with Hermione. The easy familiarity with which their mutual understanding was expressed could however be misinterpreted: as Leontes returned to the stage slightly ahead of the court, he heard his wife say to his best friend 'Th'offences we have made you do we'll answer, / If you first sinned with us' – and the damage was done. He interpreted their laughing familiarity as sexual intimacy, and embarked on the disastrous course of distorting everything he saw.

David William's evocation of the 1830s had nothing like the precision of Robin Phillips's re-creation of the 1930s, largely because he was less concerned with period authenticity as such than with differentiating sharply between the public aspect of a scene and the private relationships embedded within it. In the Folio text, act 1 scene 2 is not a public scene at all: the stage direction brings on only the three principals, Mamillius, and Camillo, without attendants, and the Oxford Shakespeare's new text follows its example and that of several modern productions. The scene then becomes a domestic one: the three chief characters are not presented primarily as kings and a queen; they are chiefly significant on another and possibly deeper, archetypal level. What struck this Leontes to the heart was that his wife had apparently betrayed him, not just with any lover, but with his best friend.

As in most recent productions, a drastic change of light marked Leontes' 'Too hot, too hot', indicating the gap between what was actually happening on stage and the view that Leontes takes of it. A little later, Hermione felt her baby kick, and Polixenes' hand instinctively, solicitously, moved to the place. This was bound to inflame Leontes, to seem evidence of 'affection' in the sense of sexual instinct; but his next lines unconsciously expressed how far removed his interpretation was from the facts: 'With *what's unreal* thou coactive art, / And *fellow'st nothing*'. They seemed to define the mental illness, the paranoia, that was rapidly taking hold of him. Once the jealous obsession was established, his fantasies assumed a terrifying certainty and clarity in his mind; the convoluted syntax of the jealous speeches was the logical expression of his twisted mental state, and Colm Feore delivered them with exceptional fluency and clarity.

This did not, however, involve any diminution of his sadistic cruelty, expecially in the trial scene. At the start he was enthroned on the upper level, the visual embodiment of the unjust judge. The court assembled from all sides of the thrust stage to convey a sense of awesome, oppressive occasion, and to focus attention upon Hermione as she moved slowly, painfully to the centre of the stage immediately below Leontes. She presented a shocking sight. In the most absolute contrast to her elegance earlier, she was barefoot and in prison rags, her hair crudely cropped and her hands manacled, and her face was ashen. Her defence was unbearably moving, not least because the experience was almost unbearable for her. She almost broke down as she spoke of his 'immodest hatred', and he demonstrated this most of all as he denied the truth of the oracle, his face distorted with an insane hatred so obsessive that he was heedless of everything else, even blasphemy. A flash of lightning and another drastic lighting change expressed both Apollo's anger and the departure of Leontes' mental disease as suddenly as it had come. And in that change of light he thought he saw Hermione fall dead.

The most original and striking episode in the production followed. It had never occurred to me before that when Paulina describes Hermione's death she might think that it was the truth. Most actresses interpret Paulina's exaggerated hyperboles as a deliberate attempt to deceive Leontes in a parody of his own extravagant language and so to begin his cure; but Susan Wright delivered them with a near-crazed grief that made it plain that she thought Hermione dead. 'Betake thee / To nothing but despair' was her spontaneous reaction before, moved by his genuine anguish, she decided then and there to help him. He lay prostrate on the floor, hands outstretched; she knelt and extended her hand to his; slowly she helped him to rise. It was an image of the process of the next sixteen years. She would guide his painful 're-creation' by experiencing it with him, and she began literally from the ground up. From these depths, literal and psychological, both Leontes and the play had to rise.

The play only did so spasmodically in Bohemia, which as usual had nothing like the charge of the Leontes scenes. The period was now 1846, and a Hardyesque rural community, in the browns and yellows of 'middle summer', certainly provided a context for the

15   *The Winter's Tale*. Stratford, Ontario Festival, 1986. Paulina (Susan Wright) with Perdita

flower dialogues, registering agreement or otherwise with Perdita or Polixenes, and developing the courting dance of Florizel and Perdita into a full-blooded fertility ritual, watched over by a corn-dolly image of Proserpina. But Martha Burns was a high-pitched, over-insistent Perdita, and the scenes were only partly successful despite vigorous playing from Joseph Ziegler's wolfish Autolycus and Nicholas Pennell's energetic Camillo. What did work completely was the volcanic fury which Stephen Russell unleashed upon Florizel and Perdita. His threat to scratch her beauty with briars, and to devise 'a death as cruel for thee / As thou art tender to't' was unmistakably a replay of Leontes' violent cruelty to Hermione. There is sadism even in Arcadia.

But as always full dramatic interest was restored only with the re-appearance of Leontes, who was discovered as a penitent, prostrated on the sarcophagi of Hermione and Mamillius, a position echoing his prostration when last seen, watched over now as then by Paulina. He spent the whole scene learning, as it were, to get up, nerving himself to exorcize the ghosts of the past when Florizel and Perdita arrived. It was a psychologically dangerous business that might, as he puts it, 'unfurnish me of reason'. This possibility remained dangerously present throughout the statue scene which, like the opening act, was clearly taking place on two levels, public and private.

The shape and size of the Ontario stage contributed substantially to this impression. The statue was at the centre of the thrust stage, while on the steps at the front of it the others moved wonderingly backwards and forwards,

a hypnotic effect which intensified the sense of Paulina's 'lawful spell'. She and Leontes remained by the statue: this was the culmination of their sixteen-year relationship. And in order to ensure a genuine reconciliation between Leontes and Hermione, she had to risk everything, even the possibility that the experience might in fact 'unfurnish [him] of reason'. Affliction was central to this purgative process right to the end, as it had been to Pericles' 'present pain' and Posthumus' vision of Jupiter: 'I could afflict you farther.' Leontes accepted this, 'For this affliction has a taste as sweet / As any cordial comfort'. Much more was involved in the statue's coming to life than a theatrical trick: it was the final stage in his 're-creation'. 'It is required / You do awake your faith': since Leontes was spiritually ready, the miracle could happen. It took place within him, and outside too, for Goldie Semple vividly expressed the fact that so much was at stake in human terms that her gradual return to life could not be hurried.

The impact was overwhelming; yet Irving Wardle spoke condescendingly of 'Canadian acting at its most bouncily extrovert'.[4] A more positive way of putting it would be that these Canadian actors gave greatly daring performances which most other companies would not have risked, in order to do full justice to the enormous human potential of the play. And so it was the finest *The Winter's Tale* I have seen, and the crown of an uneven but fascinating and invaluable trilogy.

---

[4] *The Times*, 23 June, 1986.

SHAKESPEARE PERFORMANCES IN LONDON, MANCHESTER AND STRATFORD-UPON-AVON 1985–6

NICHOLAS SHRIMPTON

Is Shakespeare getting too expensive? Even with simple sets and ruthless doubling, his plays are beginning to pose formidable financial problems for regional repertory theatres. Rehearsing and retaining a company of fifteen or more actors, and making a profit, seems not to have been difficult in Jacobean London. Today a single production on this scale can distort the budget of an entire season. Shakespeare has hitherto met the shifting demands of modern performance with surprising ease. The growth of the one-set-and-three-actors formula may yet banish his work from all but the grandest national stages.

Given this melancholy consequence of the labour-intensive nature of Jacobean drama, it is heartening to be able to report that this year the plays have, in fact, been bursting out all over – often in the most unlikely places. *As You Like It*, for example, was performed by the London Theatre of the Imagination in Heaven, the gay night club under Charing Cross Station. *The Two Noble Kinsmen*, never previously included in a Royal Shakespeare Company repertoire, appeared in the astonishing circumstances of The Swan – a brand new theatre, created entirely by private generosity, at Stratford-upon-Avon. And theatre-goers really infected with a hunger for improbable texts in unfamiliar settings could, in April 1986, actually have gone to a converted school hall in Battersea and seen *Edmund Ironside*.

Almost as surprising today, it must be said,

is the presence of Shakespeare in the commercial West End. Yet, in June and July 1986, Triumph Apollo Ltd brought Toby Robertson's Theatr Clwyd productions of *The Taming of the Shrew* and *Antony and Cleopatra* to the Theatre Royal, Haymarket for an eight-week season. In a thin summer for tourists, Vanessa Redgrave and Timothy Dalton (named, just after the run had ended, as the new James Bond) played to substantial houses. Meanwhile, down the road in the Law Courts, another London Shakespeare project took a small but crucial step towards fulfilment. Mr Justice Harman announced a settlement of the dispute over the agreement, originally made in 1981, whereby Southwark Council were to provide land for Sam Wanamaker's replica of the Bankside Globe. Under the terms of the settlement Southwark will not only compensate Derno, the developers, but will give the Globe Trust a 125-year lease on the one-acre site at a peppercorn rent. Wanamaker left immediately for America, to get on with the job of raising money.

My theatre-going year began, appropriately enough, in a brewery warehouse on the northern outskirts of Stratford. Here, in the last two weeks of 1985, the RSC brought their small-scale touring production of *The Taming of the Shrew* back home for a well-deserved encore. The show had spent fourteen weeks on the road, playing in rooms and halls from Workington to the Isle of Wight. It celebrated this vagabond role by adopting the manners

16   *The Taming of the Shrew.* Royal Shakespeare Company Small-Scale Tour, 1985. Alfred Molina as Petruchio

and appearance of a troupe of early nineteenth-century strolling players. A beguiling cross between the limelit braggadocio of Vincent Crummles and the genteel pastoral of Mary Russell Mitford, it made subtle and intelligent use of its elaborate period style.

The director, Di Trevis, was fully aware of the problems which make this play currently both the most difficult and the most exciting in the canon. Her strolling players entered with a vast sackcloth banner, bearing as its strange device the words 'The Taming of the Shrew, A Kind of History'. The unfamiliar quotation (Induction 2.138) was clearly intended to remind us, in Shakespeare's own words, of the feminist argument that history is all too often 'his story'. *The Taming of the Shrew* must today make sense in the light of this claim if it is to make sense at all, and Trevis made it do so with a striking combination of good sense, high spirits and delicate originality.

At the simplest level, she placed unusual stress on the text's play-within-a-play status. Every director nowadays adds extra Christopher Sly material from the 1594 *Taming of A Shrew* and draws attention to the action's conscious theatricality. Few, however, use it as anything more than an excuse for a pantomimic extravagance of comic effect. Trevis used it, with exceptional cunning, to keep our dispassionate judgement of the play alive at those moments when the emotional potency of the plot most tempts us to drift into uncritically realist assumptions. Thus, at the end of act 3, after Petruchio's assertion that he will be master of what is his own ('She is my goods, my chattels'), Tranio and Bianca led the company in a triumphant country dance. What we were watching, however, was not real events in a real Padua, but their enaction at an English country fair. Katharina, off stage for the dance scene, crept back on to watch it, nursing a baby. Sian Thomas was playing a Regency actress (with a young family) who was, in turn, playing the just married Katharina Minola. Instead of the customary

need either to reject or to be swept away by the taming plot, we were offered a third and more discriminating possibility.

Within this aesthetic *cordon sanitaire* the issue of taming was treated with seriousness and sympathy. Casting an Anglo-Italian actor, Alfred Molina, as Petruchio made it possible to invest the *commedia dell'arte* Padua of the play with a genuinely Latin *machismo*. When Kate slaps him at 2.1.216, for example, his reply ('I swear I'll cuff you, if you strike again') had the cool menace of a man more likely to reach for a stiletto than a hairbrush. At the same time, his treatment of his wife was, if not tentative exactly, at least pondered and conscientiously discussed. 'Say that she rail' (2.1.169–80) was nervous self-inquiry. And 'Thus have I politicly begun my reign' (4.1.172–95) was, for once, less the boasting of a successful know-all than a scrupulous clinical debriefing. Its climax – 'He that knows better how to tame a shrew, /Now let him speak' – was a genuine challenge: quiet, authoritative, and deliberately designed to draw the audience into a shared therapeutic inquiry.

This willingness to take the exemplary function of the play seriously, while insulating it from contemporary prejudice within a double layer of artifice, did not exhaust the originality of this production. On the contrary, these very qualities made possible a coherent reading of Katharina. Sian Thomas played her, with unusual single-mindedness, as a rejected child, fiercely distressed by the experience of being locked out of the familial conspiracy of mutual love and humour. Offered an alternative conspiracy by Petruchio, she grasped it hungrily just as soon as she realized what it was. In case this sounds too neat, I should perhaps add that her transition was charted with exceptional care. Her husband's threat to deny her a sight of her sister's wedding was clearly a far more potent inducement than any mere matter of food or clothing, and her self-abasing final speech was cunningly explained by allowing her to linger on stage after 5.2.48 long enough

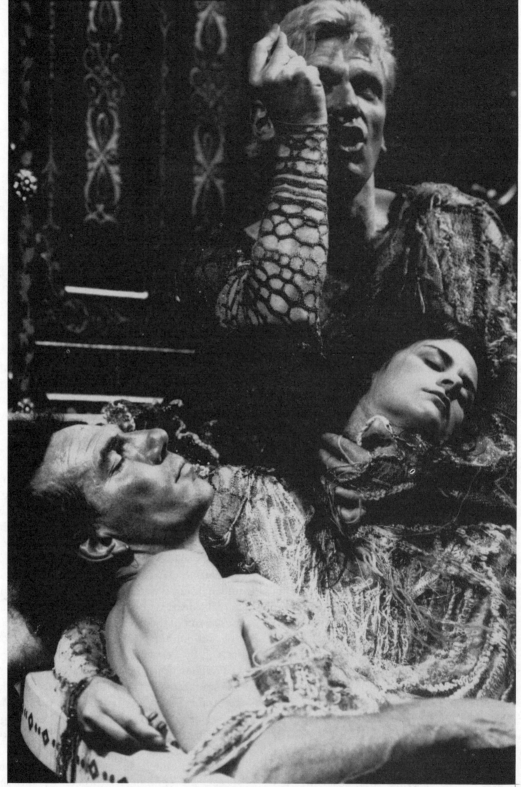

17 *A Midsummer Night's Dream*. Royal Shakespeare Theatre, 1986. Bottom (Pete Postlethwaite),
Oberon (Gerard Murphy, standing), and Titania (Janet McTeer)

172

to overhear the terms of the bet. This exceptionally thoughtful production was also extremely funny, beautiful to look at, and punctuated with marvellous music from a pair of female gipsy fiddlers.

The production of *The Taming of the Shrew* at the Haymarket, directed by Toby Robertson and Christopher Selbie, confirmed one's sense that the RSC production showed how the play must now be handled. It did so, however, only in the form of an unhappy contrast. The one genuinely new idea on offer was some elaborate and (to me at least) impenetrable business whereby the Lord of the Induction was, in the words of the programme, 'possibly Mr W.H.', and Ken Bones doubled the part of Vincentio with the new role of 'The Author (probably Mr W.S.)'. All this presumably had something to do with the fact that the players entered carrying a large head of Shakespeare on a stick. Quite what it was, however, remained obscure.

Otherwise the production offered a dashingly romantic Petruchio from Timothy Dalton, a persistent (but not in any way pointed) stress on the players as players, and an exceptionally undisciplined, not to say vulgar, Tranio. The costume was Jacobean, the interpretation commonplace. Quite what an actress with the known political interests of Vanessa Redgrave was doing in so complacent a reading of this controversial play is hard to fathom. Her Katharina sported trousers and a Lancashire accent. But without any real opportunity for violent or comic business she seemed more brow-beaten and downcast than wounded and shrewish. Her taming, as a consequence, was routine, and her final speech appeared without explanation, qualification, or apology. The production simply had no ideas about it, and no ambition to be anything more subtle than a romp.

A contrast as pronounced as this between the RSC and a West End production might tempt one to rash judgements about the difference in quality between subsidized and commercial theatre. The temptation should be resisted. Working on a larger scale, and in their own main theatre, the RSC proved this year that they are as capable of wrong-headed or routine work as anybody else in the business. *A Midsummer Night's Dream*, directed by Bill Alexander, opened in Stratford in July 1986. William Dudley's designs placed the court of Theseus in 1930s Mayfair, took the mechanicals from a 1950s beatnik espresso bar, and (despite lip-service to Arthur Rackham) based the fairy scenes on what Henry Woudhuysen shrewdly identified as 'Cicely M. Barker's saccharine *Flower Fairies*'.[1] The style was as obtrusive as it was inconsistent, swamping the action with grandiose transformation scenes, unhelpful detail (giant flowers, for example, make the actors playing fairies look tiny, but unfortunately make the lovers and mechanicals look tiny as well), and unnecessary scene-changes.

Behind this eclectic extravagance lay a reading of the play as Hippolyta's dream. While Oberon and Theseus were played by different actors, Janet McTeer doubled the parts of Hippolyta and Titania. A woman forced into respectable marriage with a dull bureaucrat, in other words, fantasized about alternative relationships – first with a glamorous cad and then with a rough plebeian. The director ignored difficulties in the text (such as Oberon's complaint of Titania's 'love to Theseus' at 2.1.76), not even bothering to cut them, and solved the problem of the play's benign ending by implying that once Hippolyta has had her satisfying piece of rough-trade (albeit in a dream) she is reconciled to the thought of marriage. The triteness of this interpretation was summed up by the fact that the production actually failed to leave any space for the dreaming, since Hippolyta entered for the dawn scene, in 4.1, having apparently been up all night at a party.

---

[1] *Times Literary Supplement*, 18 July 1986.

Incompetent verse speaking, uncertain accents, and a determination to substitute elaborate business for the play's verbal humour reinforced this air of incoherence. Peter Postlethwaite, as Bottom, suffered from the double handicap of being made to wear a furry balaclava helmet with rabbit ears instead of an ass's head, and being made to behave as a sympathetic sex-object rather than a buffoon. As a result, an actor who elsewhere gave two of the finest comic performances of the season (as Bobadill in *Everyman in His Humour* and Roughman in *The Fair Maid of the West*, both at the Swan) here gave one of the most dismal.

Janet McTeer had a similarly mixed year, preceding this unmemorable Hippolyta with an outstanding Rosalind in the Royal Exchange's splendid *As You Like It*. Nicholas Hytner's production opened in Manchester in January and set off on a tour of sports halls and community centres in April and May. I saw it at the Bletchley Leisure Centre, in its mobile theatre-in-the-round (actually a tented heptagon), and can only say that it made even Milton Keynes seem briefly magical.

The setting appeared to be Russia in the years after the revolution, with the usurping Duke Frederick as a bony-headed, wire-spectacled Bolshevik tyrant. Grim commissars in grey uniforms scuttled obsequiously about his gloomy Kremlin. Military commands and stamping feet came echoing down offstage corridors. The party chairman issued his orders with mechanical impersonality, yet himself jumped nervously at an unexpected movement from Charles the wrestler (a potential assassin) and squirmed when obliged to interrogate his daughter under the cold gaze of the politburo. Meanwhile Touchstone was a clown from the Ballets Russes production of *Petrushka*, and the exiled court a band of Czarist counter-revolutionaries huddled around a Siberian camp-fire.

Not every critic, it should be said, shared my sense that the environment was specifically Russian. Michael Ratcliffe saw it as 'a place of

fascistic repression and conspiracy',[2] Michael Coveney as grey and Arctic but 'non-committal'.[3] In my view the daring decision to use so hostile an image of the Russian Revolution (unthinkable in the English theatre twenty years ago) produced immensely valuable consequences for the outer narrative structure of the play. The praise of 'The constant service of the antique world' (2.3.57), for example, has far more force and substance when placed in the context of a recognizable, modern instance of nostalgia for feudalism. Adam was here not an anomalously emblematic figure but a realistic cousin of Chekhov's Feers, who mourned a social change as poignant as the felling of the cherry orchard, and shook with loyal amazement when, at the end of 2.7, he realized that it was his monarch who was embracing him.

Within this stimulating framework Janet McTeer offered a tender, witty, and touching Rosalind. Her friendship with Celia was fully and carefully observed, her cross-dressed courtship of Orlando alive with real erotic tension. To her role as a boy she brought a persuasively gruff bravado. Yet the emotional vulnerability suggested in the splendid nervous giggle of her opening scenes never disappeared, and her eventual arrangement of the lovers' destinies was as delicate as it was stylishly imperious.

Richard McCabe, as Touchstone, was slightly too eager and nervous to seem a natural clown, and Raad Rawi's Jaques was sharp, forceful, and striking, but insufficiently melancholy. Otherwise it was hard to fault a production which did equal justice to the humour of the emotional complexity of the play. Less lavish, less disturbing, and less intellectually innovative than Adrian Noble's 1985 production (which was still playing, at the Barbican, when Hytner's version opened), it was at the same time clearer, truer, and ultimately more effective.

---

[2] *Observer*, 12 January 1986.
[3] *Financial Times*, 13 January 1986.

18   *As You Like It*. Royal Exchange Theatre, Manchester, 1986. Rosalind (Janet McTeer) and Celia (Suzanne Burden)

The gulf between the RSC's incisive production of *The Taming of the Shrew* and their inept *A Midsummer Night's Dream* suggested that, with comedies at least, they were this season happier on small stages. This impression was confirmed when they turned to the late plays. One reason, of course, might simply have been the creative excitement generated by the acquisition of a new, small-scale theatre. The Swan, a 440-seat auditorium arranged in three tiers of balconies around a long, thin thrust stage, opened on 8 May 1986 with Barry Kyle's production of *The Two Noble Kinsmen*. The text was trimmed (both Prologue and Epilogue, for example, disappeared), rearranged, and in places judiciously re-written. More significant, however, than such minor verbal changes was the deliberate imposition of an exotic dramatic style. Nervous, perhaps, about staging an

unfamiliar play in an unknown setting, Kyle and his designer Bob Crowley transported its action to medieval Japan and borrowed many of the conventions of the Kabuki theatre.

The kinsmen were samurai, and their battles involved the costumes, ritual, and movements of kendo fighting. Theseus, accordingly, was a slit-eyed oriental warlord and the symbolic messages from the gods in 5.1 were staged as pieces of Bunraku conjuring. More subtly, characters walked once around a pole to indicate an exit, Palamon's hiding place in a 'bush' could be shown by four upright rods, and a green cord stretched down the centre of the stage in 2.1 told us that Emilia was walking in a garden. Some of these Japanese imports were more useful than others. The historical setting helped to make sense of the chilly autocracy of Theseus and the docility of his women. The formalized action solved both some small

19   *The Two Noble Kinsmen*. Swan Theatre, 1986. Arcite (Hugh Quarshie) and Palamon (Gerard Murphy), the two
kinsmen

worries about the need to get actors on and off stage quickly in an exceptionally elongated theatre, and some large ones about the unusually mannered quality of the Shakespeare-and-Fletcher romance style. *The Two Noble Kinsmen*, with its stark clash between love and duty, anticipates the seventeenth-century Heroic Drama. Encasing the play in a set of alien conventions which we do recognize and respect helped modern audiences to accept a theatrical code which, though part of our own native tradition, is today profoundly unfamiliar.

That said, it was hard with hindsight not to feel that Kyle had over-compensated. Ebullient productions later in the season of *Everyman in His Humour*, *The Rover*, and *The Fair Maid of the West* (all profiting from this example) showed that the Swan was more

flexible, and neglected seventeenth-century plays more accessible, than had originally been assumed. The Japanese detail frequently cluttered rather than clarified the play. It could not be stretched, for example, to the morris-dancing countrymen, and failed to help with the crucial matter of the relationship between Palamon and Arcite. Gerard Murphy and Hugh Quarshie gave thoughtful and athletic performances as the kinsmen, and in 2.1 (suspended from the roof in a swaying bamboo cage) conveyed a vivid sense of close male friendship. Thereafter, as the strains upon that friendship become more and more the subject of the play, the samurai convention froze its expression into ritual gestures.

The result was a production which seemed rather chilly at what one might reasonably expect to be its heart, and which compensated

20 *The Winter's Tale*. Royal Shakespeare Theatre, 1986. Polixenes (Paul Greenwood) and Hermione (Penny Downie); Leontes (Jeremy Irons) looks on

by emphasizing more marginal material. The morris-dancing was uproariously phallic, the Gaoler's Daughter breath-takingly acrobatic (Imogen Stubbs delivered an entire speech while walking on her hands), and the play ended with an unexpected tableau of mourning women as Hippolyta, Emilia and the Gaoler's Daughter simultaneously mimed disapproval of their spouses. Such choices were odd, but not wilfully or self-indulgently so, and the production succeeded in giving this heterogeneous text a high degree of narrative and thematic coherence.

The same could not, alas, be said of the late play which opened the week before on what will henceforth have to be called the main Stratford stage. Terry Hands' production of *The Winter's Tale*, anticipating the same

theatre's *A Midsummer Night's Dream* in its stress on show at the expense of substance, based its reading on the notion that political tyranny re-enacts the egotism of a spoilt childhood. Jeremy Irons was, accordingly, made to play Leontes as a monster of the nursery, a fractious brat whose jealousy expressed itself in tears and tantrums. For the trial of Hermione in 3.2, for example, he sported a child's paper crown and perched himself on a giant alphabet brick, swaying the while in a rocking chair draped in a cot-blanket. At 2.1.103 he could not mention 'A school-boy's top' without playing with one. And just in case we missed the point, he spoke his lines throughout with infantile exaggeration. This bizarre combination of verbal and physical excesses was best summed up in the explanation of his jealousy to Camillo at 1.2.207–8: 'Why, he that wears her like a medal' (drapes self around Camillo's neck) 'hanging / About his neck, Bo – heem – ee – arrh'.

Such symbolic and emotional extravagance might have made more sense had it been placed in a coherent context. But Hands, quite bafflingly, seemed at the same time to be suggesting that Hermione and Polixenes were indeed lovers. Penny Downie offered an exceptionally flirtatious and ingratiating Hermione in a décolletée maternity dress. Paul Greenwood's Polixenes lavished cuddles, back-rubs, and love-lorn gazes upon her so ostentatiously that Camillo's 'Come, sir, away' (1.2.465) became a desperate attempt to avoid public scandal. You did not, in these circumstances, need to be a jealous child to think that something might be going on between them.

This deep confusion was in no way helped by the other outstanding feature of the production. *The Winter's Tale* contains Shakespeare's most famous, and in some ways most difficult, stage direction: '*Exit, pursued by a bear*'. Directors and designers are professionally obliged, at an early stage of their preparations, to decide how they will handle it. Terry Hands and his designers, Gerard Howland and Alexander Reid, unfortunately confused technical difficulty (their business) with dramatic significance (our interest) and elevated this momentary sensation into a predominant motif. The bear haunted the entire play. In Sicily a gigantic polar bear rug lay on the floor of Leontes' palace, its huge eyes gazing balefully at the audience. In 3.3 the rug suddenly rose thirty feet into the air, like some huge and malevolent glove-puppet, to smother a startled Antigonus. Even at this point it was possible to think that one had had too much of a good thing. But the bear returned, somewhat shrunken, after the interval in the form of Autolycus' winter coat. My best guess as to the point of all this complicated scenic business was that it was an attempt to make much of the Clown's observation, at 4.4.791, that 'authority be a stubborn bear', thus putting the ursine bad temper of Leontes (and subsequently Polixenes) in symbolic perspective. If so, I can only say that the simple game was not worth the expensive candle.

Elsewhere the production offered emotional effects closer to melodrama than fairy tale, the most vulgar version of pastoral I have ever seen (disco music, eccentric dancing, and costumes which hovered indecisively between Jacobean sheep-shearing and a Hawaiian beach party), a laborious Autolycus, and a pointless doubling of the parts of Hermione and Perdita. It rarely offered more than spectacle, and even as that undermined its effects by the carelessness and incoherence of its detail.

Much the same note had already been struck on the main stage at Stratford when the first tragedy of the season, Michael Bogdanov's production of *Romeo and Juliet*, opened on 8 April. Bogdanov is often spoken of as a director of Shakespeare for audiences which dislike Shakespeare, and particularly for schoolchildren who come to the theatre resenting a dreary set-text. Confronting such antipathetic expectations is a valuable role, but also a limiting one – at least if it involves your giving the impression that you dislike Shakespeare yourself. That was certainly the effect on this occasion. The text was cut to ribbons (everything after Juliet's suicide disappeared, for example, and was replaced with the first eight lines of the Prologue, rewritten in the past tense and delivered as a press statement by a lounge-suited Escalus). What remained was buried beneath a torrent of noisy modernity. Verona was the fashionable glossy magazine Italy of Fiorucci, Benetton, and Gaggi, and the (unmentioned) two hours' traffic of the stage became on this occasion a procession of real motor-bikes and sports cars. Michael Billington summed it up as 'Alfa-Romeo and Juliet'.[4]

---

[4] *Guardian*, 10 April 1986.

21 *Romeo and Juliet*. Royal Shakespeare Theatre, 1986. Tybalt (Hugh Quarshie) and Mercutio (Michael Kitchen)

Within this flashy carapace, Bogdanov attempted to develop two ideas. One was a suggestion that the feud was an episode in the class war, with nouveaux-riches Capulets threatening the old-money Montagues. Inconsistent accents and a simple lack of appropriate material in the text brought this to nothing. The other was a determination to relate the action to the experience of modern adolescents. Roller-skates, rock-music (with Mercutio on lead guitar), a swimming pool, telephones, Alka-Seltzer, and romantic suicide by shooting-up with a hypodermic were duly imported. At the same time the artifice of the play was ruthlessly suppressed. The Chorus, with his stuffy old sonnets, was abolished and soliloquies were cut to a minimum. The result was a context in which young actors could perform as if they were in an episode of *East Enders*.

The trouble with such an approach is that it makes Shakespeare's text look like an intrusive nuisance. A single intractable word, like Juliet's 'banishèd' in 3.2.112–13, can throw out a whole scene with its awkward reminder that this is verse, not soap-operatic prose, and the medium something other than cinematic naturalism. Michael Kitchen, as an engagingly drunk Mercutio, could perhaps be said to have rescued the Queen Mab speech from the danger of whimsy by speaking it with the fixed scorn of a teenager sending up a soppy bedtime story. Elsewhere the playing sank the characters beneath the level of the ordinary (which was intended) to the level of the unmemorable (which was not). Above all, the

22 *Richard II*. Royal Shakespeare Theatre, 1986. Jeremy Irons as King Richard

production lacked a real sense of either love or death. It offered instead a busy slice of life, full of tricks and tableaux, but void of tragic purpose.

It was not until the autumn of 1986, in fact, that work on the main stage at Stratford recovered the ability to combine such lavish scenic effect with coherent and complex interpretation. Barry Kyle's production of *Richard II* opened in September, with designs by William Dudley which marked an epoch in the staging of the history plays. Twenty years ago Peter Hall and John Bury dressed the Wars of the Roses in sackcloth and steel, thereby transforming the image of Shakespeare's Middle Ages for a generation. Now the wheel of taste has come full-circle. The subdued Gothic splendours which Dudley provided for Bill

Alexander's *Richard III* in 1984 blossomed in *Richard II* into a shimmering illuminated page from the *Très riches heures du Duc de Berry*. Courtiers bright with jewels and heraldry walked in an intricate walled garden, under an emblematic sky-scape of blazing blue and gold.

This visual feast was not gratuitous. On the contrary, it was an essential image of the cultural richness of the Ricardian court. In place of the customary dialectical understanding of the play, sympathetic to both Richard's legitimacy and Bolingbroke's efficiency, touched by a personal tragedy yet conscious of the political needs which make it inevitable, Barry Kyle offered a controversially single-minded reading. His Richard, in the person of Jeremy Irons, was a witty, supercilious, and sophisticated king whose avant-garde views had led him to a proper, if impolitic, scorn of his reactionary barons. His high-taxing, high-spending regime was presented as the necessary prop of a lavish arts policy (impossible not to sense tendentiously topical implications here, despite the elaborately medieval setting). His favourites were neither crooks nor pretty boys but serious intellectuals.

Bolingbroke, by contrast, was a brutal philistine. Michael Kitchen played him as a venomous Uriah Heep, unctuously hypocritical before he achieved power, sadistically ruthless thereafter. Speaking with the mannerisms of a man still two or three grappas the worse from his spell as a dipsomaniac Mercutio, Kitchen stalked the stage at the head of a band of militaristic gangsters, snarling, wheedling and viciously befuddled. What such acting suggested, the staging reinforced. Bolingbroke's kind thoughts about the Queen at 3.1.36, for example, were here carefully undermined by offstage chopping noises, as his hooded prisoners were cruelly and audibly dispatched.

The play's sympathies, in other words, were for once entirely slanted towards Richard. As history it became an orthodox episode of the Tudor myth, a sternly legitimist parable. The Bishop of Carlisle's speech in 4.1 was, as a consequence, given unusual resonance, and its claims were echoed by a closing tableau in which gardeners with sickles scattered the red and white roses of imminent civil war. In fact, however, the result was really less a history play than something more wholeheartedly a tragedy than we expect of *Richard II*. Degrading Bolingbroke so totally made Richard an object of empathy from the very first scene, rather than merely from the moment of his fall. The play was always his play, and his fortunes were consistently lamentable.

Jeremy Irons rose to this challenge with an energy and intelligence which his Leontes had never suggested. He could perhaps be said to have acted better than he spoke, since his

soliloquies rarely achieved the true Richard music and their obsessive sense of mortality remained elusive. The compulsively self-destructive quality of Richard's fall was, however, brilliantly conveyed and he made the deposition scene a masterpiece of fatalistic taunting. Occasionally the production was carried away by its lavish stage-machinery. It remained original, elegant, and rigorously consistent.

Tragedy of this quality was, fortunately, also to be seen on the commercial stage where Vanessa Redgrave and Timothy Dalton achieved in their Haymarket *Antony and Cleopatra* the distinction which eluded them in their attempt at comedy. The production (again by Toby Robertson and Christopher Selbie) lacked the extravagantly symbolic settings of the RSC, making do with two tiers of Roman arches and some sombre Jacobean costumes. Within these austere limits it offered both a splendid narrative clarity and an uncluttered space for powerful acting.

Historical event was calmly and lucidly unfolded. As a consequence, details which are normally passed over in haste were here given an unusual prominence. Antony's practical value to Cleopatra, for example, in the struggles of Middle Eastern power politics ('That Herod's head / I'll have. But how, when Antony is gone, / Through whom I might command it?') emerged very clearly. When, sixteen scenes later at 4.6.12-14, a remorseful Enobarbus referred in passing to the same rival monarch ('Alexas ... did dissuade / Great Herod to incline himself to Caesar') we knew, for once, exactly where we were on a complex geo-political map.

This sense of Egypt as a power, rather than merely a playground, had of course much to do with the maturity of its monarch. Vanessa Redgrave played Cleopatra as an imperious older woman, more 'grizzled' (3.13.17) than her youthful Antony. Witty, decisive, sometimes almost matronly, the performance generated a powerful effect of dramatic sur-

23   *Antony and Cleopatra*. Theatre Royal, Haymarket, 1986. Cleopatra (Vanessa Redgrave) and
Antony (Timothy Dalton)

prise at the discovery that this worldly-wise and unillusioned creature was willing to die for love. The result was a striking tragic symmetry. It here seemed every bit as remarkable for Cleopatra to think the world well lost as it did for the soldier and statesman Antony.

Some areas of the play were understated to make room for this central study. A subdued Enobarbus, an anonymous Caesar, and a lightweight Pompey (the last played by Sylvester McCoy as a diminutive Glaswegian thug) were allowed to make little impact. The minor preliminary tragedy of Octavia's diplomatic marriage was, however, given unusual weight in a moving performance by Kika Markham. Timothy Dalton's Antony suffered briefly from a piece of overblown staging when, in 4.15, he was hoisted on to the monument, bleeding and naked but for a loin cloth, by a crane which gave him the appearance of the crucified Christ. Elsewhere he was brisk, direct and powerful. The heart of the production remained Vanessa Redgrave's remarkable Cleopatra – a performance not sexy or desolating like Helen Mirren's in 1982, but marked by a splendid vocal command and by a certain, admirably traditional, grandeur of scale and manner.

In a year of worry about Shakespeare's survival in regional repertory, it is perhaps appropriate to conclude with a glimpse of how tragedy is faring in those circumstances. The Oxford Playhouse Company's *Hamlet*, directed by Richard Williams, is scarcely a typical example, having opened at Elsinore Castle (in August 1986) and then set off, via the Edinburgh Festival, on an international tour. By the time it got back to its home-base in Beaumont Street it had lost both its original Prince (David Threlfall) and its original Gertrude. It still offered an instructive example of the expedients to which a company which is neither grandly national nor unembarrassedly small-scale is likely to be driven.

Williams chose to set the play in *ancien-régime* France. A few masks and costumes, and a great deal of ritual gesture, gave the effect of an elaborately interpretative décor. Courtiers in frock coats and tricorn hats abased themselves before a glittering *roi soleil* and greeted every regal utterance with a flutter of gloves and fans. The set meanwhile was merely black drapes. The ghost was a spotlight. Fortinbras's army was the rest of the cast cheerfully shouldering spears.

Some characters flourished in this context. Richard Kay offered a marvellously sinister Polonius, and Colin Bruce was a brusquely heroic Laertes. But elsewhere the production hovered awkwardly between effects of grandeur and effects of intimacy, and Hamlet himself was lost somewhere in the gap. A Shakespearian style larger than studio performance yet smaller than the magnificently reinterpretative procedures of the Royal Shakespeare Company is something which seems increasingly elusive. We may yet have need of it.

THE YEAR'S CONTRIBUTIONS TO SHAKESPEARIAN STUDY

I. CRITICAL STUDIES
reviewed by R. S. WHITE

'Shakespeare' is being thoroughly overhauled as more critics come to practise recent theoretical approaches. His (its?) status as a national institution is being systematically scrutinized by structuralists, deconstructionists, Marxists, and feminists, and there are enough books in this field this year, for the first time, for us to assess their contribution as a whole. No longer can we assume that Shakespeare speaks from an innate grasp of 'the human condition', and we are advised to examine coolly the texts, and critics of other persuasions, for their underlying structures and value systems. Meanwhile, and somewhat ironically, the Chinese have chosen 1986 to reinstate Shakespeare as part of their own cultural heritage, with large festivals in his honour in Beijing and Shanghai.

Terence Hawkes's subject in *That Shakespehearian Rag: Essays on a Critical Process*[1] is, as the title implies, not Shakespeare directly but his critics. An examination of the critical statements of some influential critics of this century such as Raleigh (mainly the twentieth-century one, though his earlier namesake makes some entertaining appearances), Bradley, Eliot, and Dover Wilson, demonstrates the appropriation of Shakespeare to particular causes and educational policies which require close examination. Recent literary theory, Hawkes

argues, threatens the 'establishment' views represented by these writers by presupposing that all analysis, particularly that which is justified by appeals to 'objectivity' or 'impartiality', is in practice underpinned by ideological frameworks which should be brought into the open. In the post-structuralist future, the hope is that

'English' would consist, not of a supposedly innocent encounter with literary texts, but of an analysis of the ways in which the meanings of those texts have been produced and used: the study of how readings of them arise, operate, conflict and clash, of the social and political positions which they embody and on behalf of which they function.

(p. 123)

If the centre of attention should be not 'the text' (which is 'an orthographical blank, a vacancy, a disconcerting sign which invites a dialogical "improvised" response' [p. 89]) but 'the process of mediation', then new critics who do not owe allegiance to dominant English cultural assumptions from the past may, reading like Coleridge's 'active, creative being', make new readings of Shakespeare from their own points of view. Stated like this it sounds surprisingly close to the 'bourgeois pluralism' which has been so derided, the

---

[1] Methuen, London and New York, 1986.

radical difference lying in the explicit admission of guiding attitudes rather than a pretence of impartiality. The theme is taken up by other books reviewed below. Hawkes presents the case entertainingly and shrewdly, but his best points are made through old-fashioned metaphor rather than the hard precision of language claimed by many of the new theorists. Sometimes we are asked to make some intellectual backward somersaults in following the logic. We first see Bradley as a young radical at Balliol, threatening to bring down the citadel of educational values. After becoming the first 'professional' literary critic, he is transformed, we are told, into the force for conservatism itself. Next, all the old attacks are mounted on him as a post-Romantic, reading plays as if they were novels, imposing his own emotional needs on the text; *and yet* he suddenly appears to be confronting 'the central issues of textuality' now associated with the names of Barthes, Derrida and Lévi-Strauss. Hawkes then uses a rather lyrical image for Bradley's mode of reading – the sea-shell at the ear brings us not the sound of the sea but of our own pulse – only to reveal later that Bradley gave him the initial image in an early poem. Finally, the 'argument' is wrapped up in a deconstructive reading of undergraduate clerihews on Bradley's name. Hawkes cannot have it *all* ways at once. Similarly it is distasteful to represent the work, radical in its own time, of Wilson Knight by a long quotation written in old age during the Falklands conflict. The chapter on Eliot is persuasive, and the most valuable insights of the book emerge here. In this chapter, Hawkes seems more confident of his argument, and hovers on saying that there have been critics who have been radical in their times but whose words have been themselves distorted and 'mediated' by a later educational hegemony. The worst of the new literary theorists, in contrast, seem to think that not a word of sense was ever spoken by anybody before Derrida, and that not a single line of decent commentary was written before 1980.

In *Signifying Nothing: Truth's True Contents in Shakespeare's Text*,[2] Malcolm Evans attempts to release the text from the 'incrustations' of a critical tradition. In giving 'free play to the signifier', stressing the primacy of the fluidity of dramatic speech over the fixedness of the written text (a central issue in *Love's Labour's Lost*, for example), we are led away from stultifying thematic studies. We are encouraged to revel in the multiple layers of wordplay in *As You Like It* without trying to impose a rigid pattern on them, and we should accept that *Macbeth* is a thoroughly 'equivocating' text from start to finish. The writer seeks to give the Shakespearian texts 'a positively *enabling* function' (p. 264, quoted out of context) in the creation of new meanings. Evans is at pains to distinguish this perspective from the dominant 'humanist pluralism' of other critics who claim to accommodate different readings while in fact neutralizing them within an overriding preoccupation with unity, 'total meaning', and ideologies based on western individualism. The book is exuberant and valuable, despite a great amount early on of fictive playfulness which I found irritating rather than revealing. Although largely in sympathy with the book's thesis, I have some doubts about the execution. One senses that although Evans skilfully 'deconstructs' traditional critical approaches, when he comes to look at the texts he may owe more than he thinks to them. The whole notion of responsibility to and for language raised in *Love's Labour's Lost* has been explored by other critics (however tendentious their conclusions may be), there has been much virtue in 'if' in *As You Like It* for quite a long time, the account of *Macbeth* merely gestures towards the significance of 'equivocating' interpretations of *Macbeth*, again by drawing upon earlier readings which are not always acknowledged (or known about?), while *The Tempest* has had

---

[2] The Harvester Press, Brighton, 1986.

more searching readers than Frank Kermode in dealing with neo-colonialism. It is hard to see why Evans should be quite so unqualifiedly scathing about Empson and Rabkin (and almost silent on Brecht), while hailing Weimann for his originality, when there is some connection between the demotic impulses in these writers and Evans himself. This is not to fudge the issue and push Evans himself into the abhorred position of eclectic unifier of diverse views, but to say that when the top layer of the argument is dealing with other critics, some diversity should be acknowledged in their practices. It is not quite fair to deride critics under some blanket term like 'mimetic' at the level of theory while ransacking their local perceptions in detailed analysis. Secondly, and perhaps more seriously, by trying to draw upon several new critical theories (Derrida, Marx, Bakhtin, feminism, and so on), Evans paradoxically runs the risk of creating a new synthesis, a bogus unity, between ideologies which do contain genuine differences and tensions between them. A Marxist may be poles apart from a feminist to the point of complete non-agreement on fundamental issues, a structuralist can be opposed to both on the issue of the validity of firmly held beliefs. The differences should not be blandly ignored. Where I realize I sound thoroughly naïve is in my plea for less tricks, less defensive irony and private jokes, more straightforward assertions of the central points which may make this book a refreshing force.

In Catherine Belsey's book, *The Subject of Tragedy: Identity and Difference in Renaissance Drama*,[3] I do find the level of seriousness which the argument as a whole deserves. Renaissance drama, including Shakespeare but not making him a priority, it is argued, expressed, helped to determine, and also criticized modern cultural assumptions of 'liberal humanism, the consensual orthodoxy of the west' (p. ix). The orthodoxy boils down to a belief that human nature is universal and mirrors male, English, bourgeois values, expressing the unchallenged

supremacy of notions like unity, empirical knowledge, subjectivity and autonomy of the individual, all presented through illusionist drama. The book takes fire when the subject is gender, and in particular misogyny, which the evidence convincingly shows is attacked as well as confirmed in some plays. The 'silent endurance of patriarchal tyranny', the lot of Grissel, is analysed, as are the contradictions in patriarchy in many texts which are not so well known these days, including *The Tragedy of Mariann*, 'the only play of the earlier seventeenth century we know to have been written by a woman' (pp. 164–5). Shakespeare is treated, without portentous reverence, as a dramatist who in many ways is close to his contemporaries in his attitudes, if more influential than others upon succeeding centuries. The book, I warn, is not an easy read, and I feel sure that such intrinsically interesting ideas could be presented with more compelling clarity. I know that such a statement 'foregrounds the signifying process . . . at the expense of meaning' (p. 60), but my plea stands.

Graham Holderness's *Shakespeare's History*[4] has the virtue of being written with relative lucidity, apart from the Introductions which may have been composed after the main body of the text, in an attempt to incorporate all the diferent ideas in the book. It is interesting, if uneven. Demolishing the critical stances of Tillyard, Traversi, and Dover Wilson may not be as daring an enterprise as once it would have been, but the concentration upon influential films based on Shakespeare's plays, and upon critics writing during the Second World War, does pay dividends. We come to realize that many assumptions about the 'patriotic' nature of the history plays do originate – at least in England – from this period of criticism, and owe their currency to nationalistic ideologies

---

[3] Methuen, London and New York, 1985.
[4] Gill and Macmillan, Dublin; St Martin's Press, New York, 1985.

prevailing at the time which have never been rigorously questioned. In opposition, Holderness presents his own interpretations of the chronicle plays from *Richard II* to *Henry V* as progressive and grounded in Elizabethan historiography, since he chooses to emphasize the existence of alternative patterns in the texts. He sees Bolingbroke as a figure who embodies the historical contradictions prevalent in an age when royal authority conflicted with feudal tribalism reflected through chivalric codes. Drawing upon Barber and Bakhtin, he sees Falstaff as a wholehearted subversive, a republican presence which cannot be easily rejected or accommodated. The general claim is that Shakespeare does not simplemindedly reflect the political assumptions of his own day, but that he had a genuine and radical understanding of states of political transition in the fourteenth century, yoked with an apprehension that centralized monarchy was not an inevitable development. The readings of each play seem rather tame (the rendering of Falstaff, for example, has been anticipated), when judged against the claims for progressivism in the opening and closing sections of the book, but there is subtlety and the presence of a mind willing to look afresh at points of detail. The analysis of post-war representations of Shakespeare, such as Olivier's *Henry V*, in the latter half of the book is impressive. The overall perspective has the great advantage of wresting 'Shakespeare' away from jingoistic prime ministers who seek to enlist him in any war effort designed to 'busy giddy minds with foreign quarrels'.

Terry Eagleton seems to be smoothly effecting a transition from *enfant terrible* of the critical world to *éminence grise* among those who employ radical approaches (perhaps signalled by the metamorphosis from Terence to the more relaxed Terry?). It might be an inevitable change for those who undertake General Editorship of a new series. His *William Shakespeare*, the first volume in the promising Rereading Literature series from Blackwell,[5] is

an argument drawing upon both Derrida and Marx. Unlike Malcolm Evans, Eagleton does recognize that the linking requires justification, and he argues that where the two converge is in a common scrutiny of 'value'. Both money and words are based on 'ideological dilemmas' (p. 101) concerning value and valuelessness, significance and arbitrariness. The analysis of each play is always intelligent and lucid, and the book's cryptic brevity makes it the only one in this section that one would wish longer rather than shorter. The distinctiveness of Eagleton's approach is that no matter how provocative and self-consciously perverse he may be on occasions, there is no meretricious joking, and there is a feeling (dare we say it?) that he regards the plays as mimetic. In speaking of Shakespeare's texts, Eagleton is not indulging in whimsical 'freeplay of the signifier', but he is taking language, and the activity of interpretation, seriously. He is speaking of 'life', at least as it is perceived as a complex set of ideological positions that have a profound bearing on the arrangement of the societies in which Shakespeare-readers live. A kind of love-hate relationship seems to exist between the socialist critic and the 'conservative patriarch' who gives the palpable impression that 'he was almost certainly familiar with the writings of Hegel, Marx, Nietzsche, Freud, Wittgenstein and Derrida' (pp. ix–x). For Eagleton, Shakespeare is an old and trusted antagonist, a worthy Aufidius. Shakespeare is seen as a writer who, while legitimizing aristocratic power in the comedies, can equally demolish its *raison d'être* in some tragedies; who, while remaining callously uncritical of manipulations of money and law, can appeal fundamentally to concepts of mercy and justice. He is one who, while disposing of the rights of 'the exploited and dispossessed', can out of the blue give a powerful voice to their genuine

---

[5] Basil Blackwell, Oxford, 1986.

grievances. Eagleton can be glib and intellectually reckless when he focuses solely on language or desire, but he is genuinely enlightening when he becomes passionate about social justice. He gives the strong and refreshing impression that Shakespeare still *matters*.

So does Joel Fineman, whose profuse acknowledgments to the work of Derrida probably mean he would like to be placed among the new theorists. I have not made my peace with *Shakespeare's Perjured Eye: The Invention of Poetic Subjectivity in the Sonnets.*[6] At times I felt it is a profound book. At other times, struggling with the style, observant of repetitions, I suspected that an idea had not quite crystallized in the author's mind, and that he was in the process of groping for something which would eventually form a short, lucid essay. Anybody who can write in an 'Introduction' in this fashion may not deserve a reader patient enough to wade through over 350 pages:

This is to deny, however, or not to take seriously, the linguistic idealization that informs such reflexive reflection when it is either theorized or thematized. At least ideally, there is activated in praise an effective correspondence or reciprocity between objective reference and subjective self-reference, a correspondence that, at least ideally, erases the difference between objective and subjective discursive indication. (p. 6)

(Even *in* context it is difficult.) Sometimes the writer cheers us up by saying 'This point . . . is not really very complicated', but it certainly sounds it when words like 'hendiadistically', 'epideictic logos' and 'scotomized occlusion' reel off his pen. The fog lifts for an instant when we reach the first quotation, '"fair," "kind," and "true," is all my argument', but closes relentlessly behind us as we go on. This is, of course, unfair (although the writer must have *some* responsibility for the sharing of meaning), not only because Fineman often apologizes for being 'heavy-handed', but also because the argument has genuine conceptual complexity in its analysis of multiple paradoxes. My summary may not capture the subtleties, but at least I can give some indication for the reader who may be interested. The 'young man sonnets' give us traditional panegyric, expressed in the older poetics of praise. The 'dark lady sonnets' innovate 'a poetry of praise paradox', expressing praise for what is unpraiseworthy, desire for the undesirable. Alongside these contrasts runs a parallel set, the one based upon 'a poetics of silent, visual similitude', the other 'a poetics of verbal disjunctions' (p. 183). In juxtaposing and merging these contrasts, Shakespeare gives us through his persona 'the very first "person" of our literary tradition' (p. 184), demonstrating a radically new concept of subjectivity which has become 'the governing model for subjectivity in literature after Shakespeare' (p. 299). Some brief comments relate these findings to a 'characterological psychology' to be found in the plays. The book is one to wrestle with rather than read, but again, like Eagleton (though for very different reasons), Fineman leaves us in some awe at the profound importance of Shakespeare to him and, by implication at least, to us.

Shakespeare and the Question of Theory,[7] edited by Patricia Parker and Geoffrey Hartman, is this year's American team's contribution to post-structuralist debate. (The only British essay in the volume comes from Terence Hawkes, who must be so fond of 'Telmah' that he has reproduced it a third time. The hapless Dover Wilson, flaunting his political bias on his briefcase, once again rides on that unfortunate train to Sunderland, like some endlessly repeatable video.) There is a difference in tone when we compare these essays with their British counterparts, though I am not sure whether this is because the Americans have absorbed so deeply the modes of reason-

---

[6] University of California Press, Berkeley, Los Angeles and London, 1985.
[7] Methuen, New York and London, 1985.

ing of Derrida, Lacan, and Foucault that they can express their ideas without recourse to an arcane, specialist vocabulary, or whether, more cynically, they merely use some handy new critical theory to kick off yet another formula essay delivered in the oracular style of Bloom and Frye. There are certainly some big names wheeled out – Hartman, Greenblatt, Fineman, Harry Berger Jr, Weimann, all names to make the English academic envious of the glamour of the English professor's status in the USA – and they for the most part eschew tricksy wordplay and in-jokes in favour of dense, text-centred argument, addressing the wide world rather than their friends. There is, however, a sense in which the essays could well form a *festschrift* for some elderly traditionalist without offending him, rather than a volume claiming theoretical innovativeness. Whatever the particular stance of the writer, we are encouraged to admire the complexity of the Shakespearian text rather than the shortcomings of liberal humanist critics (several of whom, in modern disguise, appear in this book). Howard Felperin's elegant piece on *The Winter's Tale*, admitting the limitlessness and limitations of self-referentiality in drama, accepting 'the inescapable mediacy of language' (p. 16), could largely have been written without reference to the Derridaean 'Deconstruction of Presence' in its title. When Hartman exuberantly celebrates wordplay in *Twelfth Night* (with some majestic results, admittedly), we might even recall the words of that incongruously pre-structuralist, Virginia Woolf, as the real source:

For Shakespeare is writing, it seems, not with the whole of his mind mobilized and under control but with the feelers left flying that sport and play with words so that the trail of a chance word is caught and followed recklessly. . . . [8]

In five essays grouped under the heading 'Politics, economy, history', we look in vain for argument dealing with such things as Protestant politics, and class structure of Eliza-bethan England, or the state of capitalism in the period with its consequential social implications. We find, instead, the *PMLA* formula, with its familiar, sober exegesis of text. In Nancy Vickers's long essay on Lucrece, we find the kind of thematic study of 'heraldry in Lucrece's face' that could even have been acceptable in polite, pre-feminist society. Elaine Showalter has more to say on pictorial and dramatic representations of Ophelia than on the theoretical issue of 'the responsibilities of feminist criticism' of her title. The book is intellectually impressive, and shows some of the best American critics writing at their formidable best, but I remain unconvinced that 'The Question of Theory' has been addressed, and suspect that older conventions of essay-writing, dealing mainly with themes, analogues, and structure, have prevailed.

Upon encountering the British collections of essays based on new literary theory, even the most ardent supporter might wince just a little. *Political Shakespeare: New Essays in Cultural Materialism*[9] edited by Jonathan Dollimore and Alan Sinfield, and *Alternative Shakespeares*[10] edited by John Drakakis, give many signs of having been thrown together to catch a fashion rather than to present and advance the cause of a genuinely important movement of mind. After reading essay after essay (each writer gratefully acknowledging the help of the others) on the iniquities of the Newbolt Report on Education in 1921 and its social consequences, we feel that we are, in rather smug fashion, witnessing the creation of a new cliché rather than exploration of a serious issue. After getting undiluted Derrida in large

---

[8] Quoted in Stanley Wells, *Twelfth Night: Critical Essays* (Garland Publishing Inc., New York and London, 1986), 79, reviewed below. Hartman proves in his essay that 'alternative' criticism can be written with comprehensible grace.

[9] Manchester University Press, Manchester, 1985.

[10] Methuen, London and New York, 1985, New Accents Series.

doses, we increasingly suspect that this writer's idiosyncratic vocabulary and open, tentative responsiveness have somehow been ossified rather than respected, applied, or assimilated. Some of the essays are presented with a self-gratulatory cleverness, while others are totally incomprehensible. There are, however, some exceptional pieces which advance serious issues in a form which they deserve. Margot Heinemann's 'How Brecht Read Shakespeare' in *Political Shakespeare* is a model of real historical research employed in the service of progressive ideas, while Catherine Belsey's 'Disrupting Sexual Difference: Meaning and Gender in the Comedies' in *Alternative Shakespeares* is a sparkling example of taking an old subject and making it new.

Some works, while being 'alternative' in taking inspiration from unorthodox or innovative sources, do not focus so directly on recent literary theory.

With its female-centred subject, and its indebtedness to modern psychological theories rather than traditional literary criticism, *Domination and Defiance: Fathers and Daughters in Shakespeare*[11] by Diane Elizabeth Dreher probably belongs in this section. It works in a disarmingly effective way. At first the central perception seems too simple:

Repeatedly, Shakespeare's plays depict the father at middle life, reluctant to release his daughter into adulthood and face his own decline, while she stands at the threshold of adult commitment in marriage. The passionate conflicts, fears, and insecurities as each faces a crucial challenge of adulthood cast a new light on questions of moral development, male and female sex roles, traditional and progressive social norms.   (p. 1)

The application of principles from Freud, Jung, and Erikson seems to take us back to the bad old days when characters in Shakespeare were seen as 'real people', case-studies rather than dramatic constructs trapped in their linguistic contexts. However, as the argument develops it inspires trust, and the reader

wonders why she or he never noticed such central patterns in the plays before. We are given a Renaissance view to counteract any sense of anachronism in the modern psychological perspective which dwells on paternal domination and the daughter's need to escape its fetters. Shakespeare's fathers are divided into different manifestations of patriarchy; apt quotation neatly pins down Brabantio as 'Reactionary', unable to release his daughter into adulthood by refusing to acknowledge that Desdemona has grown up; Portia's father, Capulet and Polonius as 'Mercenary' who treat their daughters like property; Leonato and Prospero as 'Egocentric', unable to see their daughters as other than parts of themselves (a wickedly chosen passage shows Leonato using variants of the words 'I' and 'myself' seventeen times in fifteen lines when talking of Hero); Cymbeline and Egeus as 'Jealous' of their daughters' dawning sexuality. Lear is 'A Father in Turmoil', representing all of these negative feelings towards his daughters. The analysis then turns to the responses of the daughter. Dreher argues that Ophelia, Hero and Desdemona all exhibit 'innocence, obedience, and submission to authority' (p. 76); but Ophelia eventually escapes in her own way, Hero could hardly do other than she does, while Desdemona is remarkably assertive, before facing an appalling misunderstanding. We might agree, however, that all are victimized by the power structure. Other daughters are seen as defiant (many in this category, pre-eminently Cordelia), and others as 'Androgynous' in their responses, mostly in the comedies, and mainly fatherless, interestingly enough. The romances are interpreted from the point of view that the fathers reach balance and integration largely through the redemptive love and harmony represented by their respective daughters – a more specified version of the traditional approach which

---

[11] The University Press of Kentucky, Lexington, 1986.

stresses the myth of rebirth. If one sometimes wishes the book a little less schematic, it is overall a convincing account of a subject which has been treated either from the male point of view or with partiality.

At this stage, the present reviewer might be forgiven the indulgence of mentioning *Innocent Victims: Poetic Injustice in Shakespearean Tragedy*.[12] The book seeks to interpret the existence of characters in the tragedies who 'do not deserve to die', such as Lucrece, Lavinia, children, Ophelia, Cordelia and Desdemona. The argument, which involves a certain amount of Brechtian de-familiarization in its inevitable questioning of tragic heroes and critics alike, argues for a morally educative design behind the plays, suggesting that the dramatic significance of the violent deaths of these characters forces us to judge the world in which they must act. Before readers begin to think of Victorian habits of sentimentalizing the tragic heroines, it should be said that the perspective stresses 'innocence does not mean weakness' (p. 112). Innocence is used in opposition to guilt, not to experience.

H. R. Coursen's *The Compensatory Psyche: A Jungian Approach to Shakespeare*[13] is a kind of maverick, 'alternative' approach which, in theoretical terms, shares ground with new literary theory only to the extent of making explicit the set of principles guiding the analysis. Plenty of 'non-aligned' critics bandy words like 'selfhood' and 'identity', but at least Coursen has strict definitions taken from Jung. Fortunately, there is rarely anything but insistence upon characters as fictional and dramatic creations rather than living case-studies. Coursen attempts to escape the charge of anachronism in his use of Jung, first by suggesting that, in the same way that any theoretical starting point (thematic or structural) can do, 'Jung's abstraction of human personality can inform the fictions Shakespeare creates' (p. xxi). Secondly, he argues that in fact there are analogies between Jung's 'self-compensating psyche' (the premises of a person's being

which, if ignored or violated, will effect a 'punishment') and concepts of the 'soul' in medieval theology and mysticism exemplified by St Augustine and St Bernard. It is further argued that Jung's theories of transference and transformation – the bringing of unconscious elements into consciousness – can give a technical vocabulary to explain the significance of dreams and blurred states of consciousness in Shakespeare. Where the book becomes reductive and unhelpful (and even Jung might have disagreed with the judgements) is when Coursen divides tragic characters into introverts and extroverts. The book is interesting for the sake of the ideas, and it is more consistently Jungian than its recent competitor, James P. Driscoll's *Identity in Shakespearean Drama*,[14] but those who do not believe in using modern psychological theories to analyse Shakespeare should keep their distance.

And those who still believe that a Shakespearian text can be seen 'as in itself it really is', using Eliot's 'intuitive activity of the civilized mind' and Leavis's 'maturity' and 'intelligence', should beware of all the books in this section.

All but one. On the occasion of the posthumous publication of *Essays on Shakespeare*,[15] William Empson must be honoured as the most dazzling and readable representative of the rogue tradition in Shakespearian criticism. Before the word deconstruction was coined, before the probing of underlying ideologies held by Dover Wilson and Tillyard were attempted, Empson apparently casually and with perfect temperance saw through their royalist politics and understood the patriotic contexts which shaped their ideas (see pp. 35–7). Terry Eagleton might be envious of

---

[12] The Athlone Press, London, 1986. This is the second edition of a book first published in 1982.
[13] University Press of America, Lanham, New York and London, 1986.
[14] Louisburg, London and Toronto, 1983.
[15] Cambridge University Press, Cambridge, 1986.

the swift unmasking of the patrician editors of the New Arden, with Empson's 'deconstruction' of the editor of *A Midsummer Night's Dream*:

The real feeling of Brooks, I submit, is: thank God we don't have to watch a lady actually giving herself to a stinking hairy worker. 'Even a controlled suggestion of carnal bestiality is surely impossible', he remarks. (p. 224)

(Such a suggestion is certainly not impossible to the imagination of Empson, who sees carnality as the real point of the liaison between Titania and Bottom.) Empson's wit always has an element of gravity, his gravity a streak of puckishness. He soberly speculates about the strange precision of the velocity at which Puck travels, observing that it is almost exactly the speed of Major Gagarin when he took the first trip in space. If we laugh at this, we are not laughing at Empson but at the parody of a certain method of scholarship which makes whole books out of lesser coincidences. In his adopted stance of wise jester, he is close to the character whom he helped to liberate from the restrictions of moralistic critics, Falstaff (again, before anybody had heard of Mikhail Bakhtin). He achieved the feat by employing the terms (not totally inappropriate for the 'new pluralists') which made him famous as a young man – 'Dramatic Ambiguity' (p. 37). Those capital letters are a little unnerving. Does it imply that *Seven Types of Ambiguity* was all the time intended as a pre-emptive parody of what mainstream criticism has taken so dearly to its heart? A demolition elaborately prepared, no less whimsically perpetrated than that carried out in 'Hunt the Symbol'? In speaking of 'the inhumanity and wrongheadedness' of his own adversaries in his generation, 'Pound, Wyndham Lewis, Eliot, etc.' (p. 243), Empson reveals his own deep concern for a humanitarian basis for criticism. Of an earlier critic's suggestion about a line in *Macbeth* having 'no sense', he can confidently say 'Here one must lose

patience, I think; no one who had experienced civil war could say it had no sense' (p. 157). Empson's logic may not always be clear in its lateral leaps, but his heart is in the right place and his judgement firm. This entertaining volume contains, amongst those already adverted to, essays on the narrative poems, *Hamlet*, and the Globe Theatre.

ORTHODOXIES

Well, relatively orthodox, in the sense that recent literary theory is not so much in evidence in general books and thematic studies.

Germaine Greer's *Shakespeare*[16] is fresh and unpretentious in spirit, a surprising feat when her brief was a contribution to the Past Masters series which aims to present 'introductions to the thought of leading intellectual figures of the past whose ideas still influence the way we think today'. The book packs into its 136 pages a lot of brisk, no-nonsense points, made with touches of waspishness and dry humour. Greer stresses 'Shakespeare's invisibility', seeing the plays as dialectical in form. 'Shakespeare seldom, if ever, spoke in his own person' (p. 17). Apparently forgetting this, the writer occasionally slips casually into phrases like 'in Shakespeare's view' (e.g. p. 51), but overall it is the mode of impersonal, dialectical reasoning, particularly suited to the form of drama, which is presented as Shakespeare's contribution to a series that includes Freud, Marx, and Wittgenstein. Perhaps Greer kept her Wittgenstein on the desk while she wrote, since his influence is detected at various points, but in an argument on dialectical drama surely Brecht should have been a little more openly acknowledged. The approach highlights the amount of egalitarianism and frank anti-authoritarianism (balanced as these are by fascination with power) we can find in Shakespeare's work, and Greer's own early research

---

[16] Oxford University Press, Oxford and New York, 1986.

interests surface in her thoughts on Shake-speare's introduction of concepts of companionship and love into marriage. It is Shakespeare for the common person, and avoids being patronizing. Unfortunately I cannot write in quite the same terms about Philip Edwards's *Shakespeare: A Writer's Progress*,[17] much as I admire other work by this scholar. It lacks unifying threads, and although it, too, is a volume in an 'introductory' series, it is hard to envisage its readership. The accounts of plays and themes are so brief and watered down that even a schoolchild encountering Shakespeare for the first time might find it lacking in interest and sometimes condescending: 'Prospero is a theatre person. He puts on shows' (p. 175); 'So Bully Bottom ascends to the bed of the fairy queen' (p. 89). Oddly enough, it is only by knowing a lot that the reader can appreciate the skill with which problems are skated around. The writer, from his professorial summit, may have underestimated the amount of complexity that can be tolerated by students if ideas are presented to them with clarity rather than oversimplification. He may have felt constrained by the introductory nature of the OPUS series, but the example of Marilyn Butler's volume on the Romantics[18] shows that even in such a context one can be challenging and original. I can imagine a reader being stimulated by Greer's book to read Shakespeare. After reading Edwards's book the same person might wonder what all the fuss is about.

A couple of meatier books have been presented for the scholar, dealing with Shakespeare's poetics. Diana Akers Rhoads's *Shakespeare's Defense of Poetry*[19] is a solidly documented demonstration of how *A Midsummer Night's Dream* and *The Tempest* draw on Renaissance justifications for poetry. The book does a service in reminding us that Shakespeare's concept of the imagination was not the same as Coleridge's. She shows that the Elizabethans, with their adherence to notions of imitation and the ethical utility of

literature (rather than originality and political non-alignment), could understand more easily than we the potential of poetry for challenging authority, supporting the imperatives of desire and social justice above the need for order, rather than being set apart from social concerns as an imaginative construct. Fictiveness and social comment could co-exist in the Elizabethan's attitude to poetry and drama. Secondly wonder (as epitomized in Browne's work, although he is not mentioned) was not considered an uncritical or escapist state of mind, a Romantic daydream, but an experience which could excite people to seek knowledge through rational inquiry. Such reassessments at the level of theory are presented convincingly, and they are important. This said, however, it must be added that the actual treatment of the detail of plays is often heavy-handed, uncritical, and reductive:

A Midsummer Night's Dream most clearly indicates a conflict between poetry and politics by keeping the poet and the politician separate, whereas *The Tempest* resolves the conflict by joining the two in a poetical philosopher-king.　　　　(p. 183).

The analysis of the *Dream* is tougher than that of *The Tempest*, but given the potential of the argument it could have been applied with more finesse and less schematism – with the strategy of Elizabethan 'wonder', in fact.

By contrast, Ekbert Faas's *Shakespeare's Poetics*[20] is not so revisionist in its theoretical approach, but the level of critical commentary is considerably more sophisticated. It is a great pleasure to read, and has the virtues that stem from a wide and deep knowledge of Shakespeare's texts and a humane outlook, even

[17] Oxford University Press, Oxford and New York, 1986.
[18] *Romantics, Rebels and Reactionaries: English Literature and its Background, 1760–1830*, Oxford University Press, Oxford, New York, Toronto and Melbourne, 1981.
[19] University Press of America, Lanham, New York and London, 1985.
[20] Cambridge University Press, Cambridge, 1986.

though we do not find any startling new discoveries. The emphasis is on Shakespeare's lack of a dogmatic theory of poetry. At times he can use conventions, at other times ridicule them in apparently opportunistic fashion. For example, in terms of his attitude to the audience:

What we find, then, is a paradox. While consistently disrupting the illusion of the stage action, Shakespeare, with equal deliberateness, tried, at least temporarily, to make the spectators lose themselves in the spectacle. (p. 65).

The theoretical centre of the book itself lies in the middle chapters, where Faas compares Shakespeare with Montaigne and Bacon, arguing that all three were philosophically involved in a systematic 'dismantling of essentialist discourse', an 'inverted platonism', seeing language itself as having immediacy of content and not existing as a code or conduit for spiritual truths or abstractions. Poetry is seen as having its own experiential authority and not as merely a branch of 'knowledge'. Here, presumably, Rhoads would part company, for her analysis dwells on the attitude that poetry *is* a form of knowledge for the Renaissance mind, initiating us into political and moral truths. By stressing Sidney and Plato we come to Rhoads's position, by stressing Bacon and Montaigne, we come to Faas's. The conclusion which so maddeningly recurs in Shakespeare studies is that the same evidence of his plays themselves can justify both approaches. Faas's argument is probably the more comfortable since it does not force us to think in a disagreeably alien way, to retrieve, as Butterfield said, a historical imagination for the Renaissance. Montaigne and Bacon, more even than Shakespeare, were themselves instrumental in shaping a modern consciousness of the advantages of individualism, empiricism and pluralist tolerance. Faas does not raise complicated issues like poetic justice with any rigour, and his conclusion which returns us to Shakespeare as the poet of 'Nature'

involved in creating 'The Theatre of Multiple Response' is too safe to rock anybody's boat. Fortunately, the plays of Shakespeare emerge free of the nets of partially pursued theory, retaining some enigma for the rest of us to work upon.

Three books take the theatrical experience as the central plank upon which to base critical perceptions. I am put a little on the defensive by the tone of Anthony Brennan's *Shakespeare's Dramatic Structures*[21] when he refers to the chilly influence of academic criticism and proclaims his approach to be unrepentantly stage-centred. The division between stage and closet always seems an unnecessary nuisance. My feeling that the scholar-critic is dealing with potential meanings which can be helpful to the director and performer who must make actual decisions does not seem to make the groups naturally antagonistic. I take heart from Harry Berger Jr's distinction between 'latent' and 'manifest' meanings[22] which amounts to the same thing. The 'Structures' which Brennan analyses are twofold: 'Pattern and Variation' between incidents (repetition, scene-linkages, variations on similar incidents), and 'relative weighting of material' (how much stage-time is devoted to certain characters and relationships as opposed to others; strategies of continuity and separation, the linking of some characters while separating others). Although the account gives the impression of a scientific empiricism, using charts and diagrams to clarify the structures, it is philosophically difficult to see these patterns as anywhere but in the writer's mind rather than 'there' in the text. Another critic might take the poetry as a structural and dramatic unit, locating the ebb and flow of intense engagement, disengagement between people, and soliloquy. It would be neither more nor less provable than any other kind of abstraction

---

[21] Routledge and Kegan Paul, London, Boston and Henley, 1986.
[22] *Shakespeare and the Question of Theory* (above), p. 214.

one might use to 'discover' patterns. This would not matter so much (and there is plenty of local insight to keep us reading), if only the tone did not banish critics who think poetry and language are central, to the position of woolly subjectivists. There is a risk too that Brennan, no matter how sincerely he wants to reveal theatrical fluidity of the living moment on the stage, might in fact sometimes identify a 'structure' in such a way that it pins the play down to a static singleness. Is Shakespeare 'keeping us waiting' for Lear's reconciliation simply to intensify the moment when it comes, as Brennan asserts (p. 121), or is the dramatist artfully distracting us from this thread of the plot as he appears to be doing at other times ('Great thing of us forgot!')? There is no way of knowing, and both can be productive starting points for discussion or performance, but it is injudicious to choose one as *the* structural effect. Brennan's book could have been richer in suggestion if the findings had been presented more provisionally and if he had not set himself so prescriptively against academic criticism.

Where Brennan has a concept of structure as something fixed, measurable, and 'in' the text, Philip C. McGuire in *Speechless Dialect: Shakespeare's Open Silences*[23] tries to embrace the multiple opportunities available to the actor and director in actualizing the playtext. His book takes an initially unlikely starting point, and one that could easily lend itself to parody: it had to happen; after all the sound and fury, a book on what a character is doing or thinking when *not* speaking. But the argument is developed thoughtfully through full consideration of exemplary scenes towards a long and interesting theoretical section. Here McGuire in 'A Different Paradigm' takes his cue from Norman Rabkin's still pertinent *Shakespeare and the Common Understanding*[24] in exploring the theory of 'complementarity', the idea that a text is multiple in potential meaning. The 'new paradigm' is the theory lying behind quantum physics and Heisenberg's uncertainty principle, that causality and abstract notions of unity are mocked by the unpredictability of physical reality and, besides, influenced by the presence of an observer. The 'text' merely 'establishes a range, a distribution of possible events during a performance, including acts of speaking, but it does not determine in minute and complete detail all the events that happen during a specific performance' (p. 139) or, we should add, during a specific reading. The evidence is concentrated upon moments of a character's silence because this takes drama at its most indefinable point. What the actress playing Hippolyta does while she is not speaking can shape our attitude to Theseus and the rest of the action. The same goes for Barnardine, the non-speaking ensemble in the last moments of *King Lear*, and so on. The book gives a refreshing urgency to Prospero's plea that we should set him free, and it could stand for all Shakespeare's dramatic personages. An unsympathetic reader might say that few of McGuire's points are really new, but they are put together in a spirited and persuasive manner. It would be valuable to get a book which takes the implications into the reader's experience (both more and less limited than a theatre-audience's) following the theories of reader-response critics in Germany and others like Norman Holland in America.

Kent T. van den Berg's *Playhouse and Cosmos: Shakespearean Theater as Metaphor*[25] begins from the interesting proposition that Elizabethan theatre architecture mirrors the world-view of the plays, but we find that it gradually returns us to a set of familiar concepts like 'reality and play', and some metadramatic theory.

---

[23] University of California Press, Berkeley, Los Angeles and London, 1985.
[24] The Free Press, New York, 1967.
[25] University of Delaware Press, London and Toronto, 1985.

D. K. C. Todd in *Shakespeare's Agincourt*[26] attempts to mediate between audience and reader, theatre and seminar. It is a project which some of us thought could never be done: a book-length, close study of *Henry V*. It turns out that the play does sustain such intense scrutiny, mainly because of Mr Todd's subtlety of explication, picking his way graciously through the shoals of epic and burlesque, sincerity and irony, moral idealism and political expediency, without programmatic presuppositions. It is, in a term given us by computing studies which actually has some utility, a 'user-friendly' book, as we are always aware of the writer's presence, politely guiding, giving us credit for having other views, cajoling, expressing self-doubt, and gliding off into personal anecdote which disarmingly returns us to the issue in hand. The learning is held lightly, and at the end of the book we have some shrewd observations first about the function of language in drama and secondly about the teaching of Shakespeare in the classroom. Mr Todd implicitly tests the integrity of us all in his final statement:

... I was recently in a theatre when I caught myself wondering, 'Do I really believe all that stuff in my book?' I found to my horror that I didn't know.

(p. 174)

It is a book for the reader who has time to relax into it, and the humanistic impulse to contemplate more than just 'the words on the page'.

There is, as in most years, a rump of books published on 'themes', studies which follow through a particular subject-matter. This year there are some fairly sensational themes ranging from love to suicide, despair, and death.

Richard A. Levin wrote *Love and Society in Shakespearean Comedy: A Study of Dramatic Form and Content*[27] as a corrective to the 'festive' approach which, since it has had quite a bashing in recent years, can no longer be taken as the dominant view. The 'anti-romantic' elements that particularly interest Levin are social pressures in the form of wealth and status. Lovers are seen to compromise ideals, collude in malice against socially unrespectable 'losers', and they generally reveal a streak of dark individualism in their competition to reach the top. Characters like Shylock, Don John and Malvolio (representing the three plays chosen for close analysis) are seen to be little worse than the lovers, and they are 'shaped by the same social forces that mould others' (p. 93). Interesting points are made about particular issues, like Antonio's weeping as it is parodied by Solanio and Salerio, and Margaret's reasons for being resentful enough of Hero to abet her shaming, and we are asked to find new respect for the coherence of each play-world, and Shakespeare's understanding of the ways social units work upon the individual. Sometimes we get the strong impression we are witnessing contemporary *American* society as we read Levin's account. As the bright young executive fights his way to a company directorship he reveals cut-throat business ethics, the breezy sophomore beats off envious competitors to win her phi-beta-kappa man, and the killjoy, partly shaped by the very social forces he resents, is firmly put in his place *outside* the smart set. Anybody who thinks Levin makes the comedies a little too mercenary in their concerns should try the essay by Lars Engle, "Thrift is Blessing": Exchange and Explanation in *The Merchant of Venice*',[28] which makes Profesor Levin seem like an ingénu in such matters. Engle claims to examine financial transactions in the play 'with something of

---

26 The New Century Press, Durham, 1985. This is a new publishing venture from Durham University, which promises interesting material for a minority, academic audience.

27 University of Delaware Press, London and Toronto, 1985.

28 *Shakespeare Quarterly*, 37 (1986), 20–37. See also David Bady, 'The Sum of Something: Arithmetic in *The Merchant of Venice*', *Shakespeare Quarterly*, 36 (1985), 10–30.

an accountant's eye for cash flows, unpaid balances, and the like' (p. 21). He concludes that 'love and money reflect and express each other' in the play.

William C. Carroll in *The Metamorphoses of Shakespearean Comedy*[29] returns us to brighter things. In an urbane and lucid study he traces the motif of metamorphosis through the early comedies, *The Merry Wives of Windsor* and, more allusively, the last plays. In dealing with such a subject the critic could use several areas to give theoretical support – Ovid, romance conventions, or even Elizabethan attitudes to dreams and figurative language. Carroll's springboard is Elizabethan attitudes to witchcraft, a fairly arbitrary choice and one that does not lead as far as he seems to expect. But the commentary on the plays is often perceptive.

Since the work of Weimann and Bevington in particular, some historians of the drama have concentrated upon popular and theatrical sources for Shakespeare, rather than classical and literary backgrounds, what Raymond Williams calls 'the culture of the selective tradition'. Romance as a dominant popular mode has been claimed as a major force behind all of Shakespeare's works and not just the late plays,[30] while Latin New Comedy and its Italian Renaissance legacy have been considered less significant than was previously believed.[31] Now Alan C. Dessen in *Shakespeare and the Late Moral Plays*[32] assesses the importance to Shakespeare of a neglected kind of drama, the 'Moral Play', which, it is argued, was popular not only before Shakespeare wrote but during his career. Indeed, Dessen's research suggests that this kind of drama was more rather than less popular after 1600, and that it remained influential. This form Dessen carefully distinguishes from the better known Morality tradition with its Everyman figure. Moral plays such as Robert Wilson's *The Three Ladies of London* are didactic and allegorical in presentation, often socially satirical and presenting attacks on authority and materialism. Dessen argues cogently that we are wrong to impose upon the Elizabethans our modern distaste for didacticism, and points as evidence to the enormous appeal of the popular sermon at the time. Within this framework the analysis of such figures as the Vice in relation to Falstaff becomes less conventional than it sounds post-Spivack, and it is rooted in the Moral Play of the time. The application of the Moral device of following the fortunes of two protagonists rather than one works interestingly when applied to the 'two-phased structure' in *Richard II* and *Henry IV*. Bertram's 'conversion' in *All's Well That Ends Well* is explained not in terms that assume either 'unification in a central character' (p. 65, quoting R. G. Hunter) or psychological realism, but as a confrontation between hero and vice figure, in a way that is implicitly allegorical and didactic. Given his claims for the central influence of the Moral Play, I really wanted Professor Dessen to get his teeth into, say, *King Lear* rather than paddle about in the shallows. His book has the strengths and limitations of a carefully defined historicism, and though it will not set the world alight it makes its claims soundly.

The title of Richard Marienstras' *New Perspectives on the Shakespearean World*[33] is in some ways misleading. It is not 'new' either in the sense of not having been published before or in the sense that it draws on recent critical theory. It does, however, offer perspectives, mainly on 'aspects of Elizabethan ideology' described more accurately in the 1981 French title, *Le*

---

[29] Princeton University Press, Princeton, New Jersey, 1985.

[30] See R. S. White, '*Let Wonder Seem Familiar': Endings in Shakespeare's Romance Vision*, The Athlone Press, London, 1985.

[31] But compare L. G. Salingar, *Shakespeare and the Traditions of Comedy* (Cambridge University Press, 1974).

[32] University of Nebraska Press, Lincoln and London, 1986.

[33] Translated from the French by Janet Lloyd, Cambridge University Press, Cambridge, and Éditions de la Maison des Sciences de l'Homme, Paris, 1985.

Proche et le lointain, ideas of the familiar and the foreign as represented in Elizabethan documents of various kinds, and allusively applied to some of Shakespeare's plays. Subjects include the symbolism of the forest to the Elizabethans, attitudes to sacrifice, the status of foreigners under James I, travel literature, incest and social relations, all studied with scrupulous historical reference. The information can be intrinsically fascinating, but I feel the sections remain self-sufficient essays rather than making a book. The commentary on the plays, *Titus Andronicus, Julius Caesar* and *Macbeth, Othello, The Tempest*, and *'Tis Pity She's a Whore* do not fully mesh with the historical material, which in turn often overburdens the literary text. On the other hand, the book contains one of the soundest essays we have on *Othello*. It locates the real problem of the play as one of 'discourse', the way Othello and Desdemona are talked about rather than as they present themselves, and the way Othello's foreignness is perceived rather than as it is *per se*. In other sections there is enough material of interest to stimulate ideas, but the Shakespearian applications are often disappointing.

Another book of essays is by Leo Salingar, who collects his various published contributions on, for example, *The Merchant of Venice*, Falstaff, *Twelfth Night*, 'Shakespeare and the Ventriloquists', and two on *King Lear* (amongst other non-Shakespearian pieces) under the title *Dramatic Form in Shakespeare and the Jacobeans*.[34] The 'theme' is said to be various aspects of dramatic form, but so diverse are the essays that such a statement is a little unnecessary and perhaps misleading. Overall, the volume is a welcome one, and makes one wonder when Salingar's promised sequel to his book on Shakespearian comedy will appear.

The shades are drawn for the gloomy finale to thematic studies of the year. Rowland Wymer's *Suicide and Despair in the Jacobean Drama*[35] has all the virtues and few of the vices of the thesis turned into a book. The research is thorough, conclusions emerge from the information and are expressed with firmness but without overstatement. The central argument is driven about as far as one would wish, with individual variations in the material duly noted. The Renaissance attitude to suicide was apparently radically ambivalent, a symptom of moral resolution or of despair.

The way in which individual dramatists incorporated the different implications of suicide into their plays tells us much about their art, less about their ethical viewpoint. Of the better-known playwrights, only Massinger and Chapman have a clearly detectable 'ethical bias', the former towards an orthodox Christian horror of suicide, the latter towards a neo-Stoic approval of it. In general, dramatic treatments of suicide are governed by a pragmatic awareness of its capacity to symbolise nobility as well as guilt and despair.   (p. 25)

Shakespeare is the one who 'appears most alert to the many different dramatic nuances of suicide' (p. xi). There is a full analysis of *Hamlet*, suggesting that suicide presented in this play as 'a form of "resolute" action which springs from despair and which conscience checks' (p. 34) is a source for the 'moral doubt and uncertainty' which surrounds revenge and runs through the play. The poetic and dramatic accounts of Lucrece and other 'chastity-suicides' (p. 104) take account of the political dimension given by the Renaissance to the myth: 'From very early on, the Lucrece story was being shaped as a political myth of republicanism and evolution' (p. 104). The end of *Othello* brings together themes of 'repentance and despair, honour and shame' (p. 90), while 'the death of Brutus has been carefully made to imply not simply nobility, but despairing failure – the failure of a man divided against himself' (p. 155). Self-division and duality are seen as a key in many plays to

---

[34] Cambridge University Press, Cambridge, 1986.
[35] The Harvester Press, Brighton, 1986.

Shakespeare's use of suicide as a theme. The dualities are precariously resolved in the love suicides of Antony and Cleopatra, since events epitomize 'the contradictory urges of the lovers towards both erotic self-annihilation and worldly self-assertion' (p. 131).

In contrast, Harry Morris's *Last Things in Shakespeare*[36] has the virtues and the vices of the coffee-table book. It is certainly the most handsomely presented of this year's offerings, printed on glossy paper with a wealth of Renaissance woodcuts nicely reproduced as a feast for the eyes. It is written in a breezy style which might even attract those who may want to give a specialist book of almost 350 pages on death in Shakespeare to a relative at Christmas. The trouble lies in the text. The level of analysis reveals the sage and subtle discrimination of a person sorting potatoes into good, bad, and those with eyes. When dealing with the tragic heroes, Morris confidently speculates on their eternal fates. *Hamlet* sets up the categories. Some are damned (for the record, Claudius, Rosencrantz and Guildenstern), some are saved through repentance (Ophelia, Polonius), and one dies in grace (Hamlet). This job done, we wash our hands and move briskly on to other plays. 'Othello, then, is the good man who does not have the defenses to defeat the evil' (p. 82); Lear is 'a man bad at the outset' (p. 115) but he circumspectly repents for his rejection of Cordelia and assures himself of salvation in the nick of time. 'That Macbeth is evil at play's beginning needs no demonstration' (p. 163). Really? What are all those people who squabble about his equivocating conscience on about? He is 'a bad man at the outset', gets worse, does not repent at the end, and thoroughly deserves damnation. A canter through *As You Like It* and *A Midsummer Night's Dream* turns up quite a few 'memento mori images' and 'the et-in-Arcadia theme', while time chimes through 'the Henry plays' (*Henry IV*, that is), and we all know this means curtains for Falstaff – read the book to find out what happens to him. The interesting

pictures are there really to look at, rather than to relate closely to the text, and the commentary is full of critical commonplaces and assertions delivered in a genial voice and substantiated by reference in footnotes to a bevy of critical authorities.

INFLUENCE AND COMPARISON

Boris Pasternak, when he undertook translations for an anthology of English poetry from a Russian point of view, reflected that he and his co-editors had detected an 'enigma', that the fascination of Byron, Keats, Shelley, Swinburne and their Russian counterparts 'was not accounted for by the attraction they themselves exerted'. There was an 'elusive foundation' which at first they attributed to the English language itself:

We were wrong. The secret additional something that gives a supplementary charm to every English line is the invisible presence of Shakespeare and his influence in a whole host of the most effective and typical devices and turns of phrase in English.[37]

The quotation is not used by Jonathan Bate but it could well stand as epigraph to *Shakespeare and the Romantic Imagination*.[38] This excellent book, written as 'a study of Shakespeare's influence on the minds and works of the major English Romantic Poets', is a pioneering work which sets new standards for 'influence' studies. After a general chapter which summarizes eighteenth- and nineteenth-century critical appropriations of Shakespeare, we are asked to contemplate the influence of Shakespeare's poetry upon Coleridge, Wordsworth, Blake, Keats, Shelley and Byron in turn. It is potentially an enormous enterprise, and Bate is wise in not claiming to be exhaustive, and in insisting that he is not combing poems for

---

[36] Florida State University Press, Tallahassee, 1985.
[37] 'Notes of a Translator', from *Russian Poets on Poetry* ed. Carl J. Proffer (Ann Arbor, 1976), 97.
[38] Clarendon Press, Oxford, 1986.

'sources'. Instead, he establishes the importance of Shakespeare to the general poetics of the particular poet (perhaps most satisfactorily in the cases of Coleridge and Wordsworth, more compactly for Blake and Keats, not very thoroughly for Shelley and Byron though here he is at the mercy of the material), and then attempts a brief account of the general influence of Shakespeare on that writer's imaginative work. The analysis presents general impressions illustrated by specific examples when their effect is telling. Bloomian concepts of 'Oedipal relationship' are treated with discretion:

> The identifications of poet-figure as Hamlet, ghostly father as Shakespeare, the older Wordsworth as a self-conscious Lear, are suggestive rather than definitive. (p. 105)

Every third thought is a quotation so apt that it seems at times as though the poet had written it deliberately with such a book as this in mind. The other way to describe this impression is to say that the research is thorough, the author sensitive to the material. (At times, though, we do catch sight of a very large shoe-box full of index-cards.) The influence of Shakespeare on the Romantics does not often lie in the way a quotation is used or adapted as a 'source'. It is located rather in Pasternak's 'invisible presence' behind the individual style and imaginative temper of each poet. It is an odd phenomenon that in echo and even quotation each poet chooses from Shakespeare what we feel uncannily 'could' have been written by the recipient. Othello's 'moving accidents by flood and field' has a Wordsworthian ring to it, could have been uttered by Michael, and indeed did influence the poet (p. 115). The phrase 'Bound upon a wheel of fire' would surely have been coined by Blake if Shakespeare had not got there first. Shelley was no doubt imaginatively predisposed to take note of the 'gilded butterflies' (p. 206). 'I 'gin to be a-weary of the sun' struck the writer of *Don Juan* (p. 229). Keats's own taste for 'fine Phrases', language which is itself mimetic of sensation and intensity without overt abstract connotation, is reflected in the markings he made on Shakespeare's plays and in the lines he chose half-consciously to echo in his poetry. (In the case of Keats Bate argues convincingly that 'the idea of *echo*' is most potent' [p. 177], and he reaches tentatively towards a new vocabulary of 'influence' which is suggestive without being impossibly vague.) The whole subject has a deeper importance, since it is easy to forget that however historically-minded a critic may be, we all live now, for better or worse, in a post-Romantic age of criticism, and at least we can try to be aware of the multiple channels of 'influence' operating shadily upon our own interests and choices in Shakespeare.

Although written without presupposing specialist knowledge on the reader's part, *Shakespeare and Southern Writers: A Study in Influence*,[39] edited by Philip C. Kolin, is of more regional interest. Essays by different scholars deal with the influence of Shakespeare upon eight writers from the south of North America. For Shakespeare critics the essays on John Crowe Ransom and Robert Penn Warren are interesting for their demonstration that academic theories fed into and were partly created from creative literary endeavours. For the 'general reader' (who may or may not read this section of *Shakespeare Survey*), Mark Twain and William Faulkner are the recognizable names, and these two essays are accessible and informative. One is struck throughout by the adoration the south maintained for Shakespeare (documented further in the sister-volume, *Shakespeare in the South: Essays in Performance*, also edited by Kolin),[40] and also by the bold colonial refusal to be intimidated by tradition. The irrepressible determination not to be overawed or merely truculently aggressive, so difficult to sustain in England's class system, is most memorably pictured in

---

39 University Press of Mississippi, Jackson, 1985.
40 University Press of Mississippi, Jackson, 1983.

the case of Twain and in the glimpse of the young Faulkner at a gathering of artists in 1921:

Finally the conversation turned to Shakespeare and to *Hamlet*. It was only then that the little man in the corner spoke.

'I could write a play like *Hamlet* if I wanted to,' he said, and then lapsed back into silence. (p. 83)

Shakespeare and his Contemporaries: Essays in Comparison[41] edited by E. A. J. Honigmann does not consistently justify the editor's enthusiasm for a set of essays each of which looks at a play by Shakespeare beside a comparable play by a contemporary. Somehow the enterprise never escapes the inhibiting weight of an examination paper made up of a set of 'compare and contrast' questions. In line with the levelling tendency of exams of this sort, we get a series of B+ essays, and quite a few in the category 'does not perform up to standard'. One or two are decidedly thin. There are exceptions. K. Tetzeli von Rosader gives an admirably detailed and far-reaching study of temptation and its proximity to imagination in Renaissance thought and drama. What might have made it complete would be some mention of the specific contribution of Protestant thought to these considerations: Milton did not come out of the blue, after all, and he himself drew on *Macbeth* and *Dr Faustus* quite substantially in his relentless studies of temptation. Edward Pechter, writing on *Julius Caesar* and *Sejanus*, makes some perceptive, general points both about, and also utilizing, metadramatic theory. G. K. Hunter applies his familiar, muscular style to produce some briefly searching remarks about class in *The Merry Wives of Windsor* and *The Shoemakers' Holiday*, compelling assent by hitting nails firmly on the head. Too many of the other essays are hazily uncertain about whether they are speaking of sources, influences, or shared attitudes, and they do not take the occasion to focus on important, general issues that preoccupy dramatists. But one does not begrudge such an international gathering its moments of indulgence, especially in a volume dedicated to the former general editors of the indispensable Revels Plays series.

Finally, the most ambitious book in scope, and one of the best. Shakespeare gets only one chapter to himself in Matthew H. Wikander's *The Play of Truth and State: Historical Drama from Shakespeare to Brecht*,[42] but his presence looms large throughout. The author speaks of 'the question of imitation of Shakespeare that unites this study' (p. 239), and the description is apt. It is not just a survey but an argument about the dramatic presentation of history. Shakespeare is seen as 'a touchstone for historical drama . . . in terms of the equal footing he takes with his sources' (p. 7), presenting history through human agencies, changing his sources if it fits his sense of historical 'truth' (as in the death of Cordelia), and above all not dictating a ready-made moral or pattern. Through the multi-layered action, revealed through people's responses, plays like the *Henry IV* sequence force the audience to become historians in making sense of it all. However, the achievement was fragile, and in *Henry VIII*, perhaps due to the ethos in which it was written, Shakespeare shows himself more at the mercy of an orthodox interpretation of the past, more providential and passivist, finding little freedom for the individual and allowing little freedom for the audience. No matter how much subsequent dramatists admired Shakespeare's earlier stance, they could not escape the sense of 'history's horrid fatalism, its ineluctable laws' (p. 6), and the frustration is traced through English writers to the Restoration and through Schiller, Strindberg, Musset, and Büchner. 'The Pathos of Power' is what we observe in them. All until Brecht, who discovered, partly through

---

[41] Revels Plays Companion Library, Manchester University Press, Manchester, 1986.
[42] The Johns Hopkins University Press, Baltimore and London, 1986.

Shakespeare and partly through Marx, the secret that Shakespeare had tapped. He, like Shakespeare, places himself on an equal footing with the historian, shaking cherished expectations (for example, 'motherhood' in Brecht, 'kingship' in Shakespeare), sees history as residing in the actions of people (communities in Brecht, individuals in Shakespeare), and he does not allow himself to be restricted within a circumscribed world-view or received pattern. He too, particularly in *Galileo* (and as in Shakespeare's case the achievement was short-lived), forces the audience to make sense out of the action:

Brecht's and Shakespeare's lessons thus are critiques of the processes by which we derive lessons from the past. What distinguishes Brecht and Shakespeare from run-of-the-mill dramatists like Rowe is that they engage their audiences in their own passionate scrutiny of the imaginative activity of understanding the past. The tension between the chaos of life, as we experience it, and the order of history, as we reflectively learn from it, is at the surface of their drama. Politics is the area of experience where this tension is greatest, where the human capacity for imposing order is most severely tested. Political action, for both, is the paradigm of human action. (p. 237)

ARTICLES AND COLLECTIONS

It is pleasant to note that journals devoted to Shakespeare have this year emanated from at least six countries.

The Sydney Studies in English series has presented *Studies in Shakespeare*[43] as its theme for a 1985 issue. Michael Orange in '*Hamlet*: A Cry of Players' contributes to the metadramatic approach to that most metadramatic of plays. Christina Mangala Frost begins '"Who dares do more?": *Macbeth* and Metaphysical Dread' by considering the puzzling scene, 4.3, the encounter between Malcolm and Macduff, to institute a study of the workings of the moral imagination both within and in judging the play. I find it a pity that she does not throw caution to the winds (as Malcolm Evans

almost does) and actually question the almost universal interpretation of that scene, rather than conceding that 'Admittedly, Malcolm's self-detraction is a shrewd political move, to test Macduff's integrity and ensure his loyalty' (p. 57). Stressing the possible authenticity of Malcolm's vision of his own potential evil gives force to the parallel with Macbeth's earlier 'raptness', makes more sense of why the scene is so long and why Macduff's response is one of bewilderment, and opens up an altogether more interesting interpretation of the play as a whole than we normally find. I am not quite sure why the orthodox reading of 4.3 has never been systematically demolished. Alan Brissenden in 'Three Gardens in Shakespeare' contributes towards an underrated but useful area that might be labelled 'non-verbal iconology', in dealing with the significance of the gardens in *Richard II, Much Ado About Nothing* and *Twelfth Night*. A source that he might well have considered is the Elizabethan pictorial tapestry, which often includes a garden 'inside', a hunting scene 'outside' the social setting. Derick R. C. Marsh's piece on the 'lords and owners of their faces', Octavius Caesar and Prince Hal, contrasted with those who do not husband their feelings, Antony and Falstaff, has a somewhat faded air about its mode of analysis, as has A. P. Reimer's 'The *Othello* Music'. If Reimer's intention is really to return us to 'an older, possibly more naive, view' of the tragedies, 'before they are entirely disjointed by exegetical endeavour' (p. 44), I rather hope he fails. He prefers *Otello* to *Othello*. For some reasons so do I, for some reasons not. To use 'The methods and practices of musical (specifically operatic) criticism and analysis' (p. 35) seems designed to ensure that a relative opinion is destined to turn into a truth. Opera and plays are surely *different*. In the present instance Verdi may well idealize

---

[43] Vol. 10 (1985), Department of English, University of Sydney.

and heroicize the effect, but by excluding the racism, very real drunkenness, the seedy clown, Emilia's bawdy and moral outrage (all the things which Reimer might in truth be objecting to), we are discarding all the lateral atmosphere which makes the play so much a strangely uneasy juxtaposing of the beautiful and the sinister. D. H. Craig produces some tantalizing problems about the scenes in which people introduce themselves in *King Lear*. Howard Felperin gives an impressive display in unravelling the 'metamimic art' of the Sonnets, although I should be tempted to play chiasmically with his title: 'Towards a Post-structuralist Practice: A Reading of Shakespeare's Sonnets'. A good deal more sprightly and supple in his playful deconstruction than Joel Fineman (above), he at least acknowledges the irony of having to use so many words, so much intricacy of mind, to explain the simplicity of something like 'Why is my verse so barren of new pride,/So far from variation and quick change?' (Sonnet 76, ll. 1–2). In the subsequent issue of *Sydney Studies*, Anthony Miller, in considering the 'movements' of revenge in *Hamlet*, finds Shakespeare parodying and also 'ethically sophisticat[ing] the convention', through 'the dramatic pattern by which expectations are aroused and disappointed'.[44]

Still Hamlet, but this time from India. Now coming up to its seventh volume, *Hamlet Studies*[45] has established the principle that the potential for new ideas on this one play is endless. The latest volume to hand presents a generous selection of articles and notes on diverse and eclectic subjects, as well as a useful review of periodical literature on *Hamlet* by W. Hutchings. So confident is the journal of the fruitfulness of the play's complexity that it can even afford a little self-parody in R. F. Fleissner's '*Princeps Arte Ambulandi*: The Pace of Hamlet' – at least I hope this article is intended as a joke – dwelling on the density of references to walking hither and thither in the play. In more serious vein, Robert R. Wilson

untangles the different levels of narration, in an article which could be a companion piece for Orange's in *Sydney Studies in English*. John Hutton Landis sees Poland in the play as a 'strongly functioning symbol', representing male violence, while Vincent F. Petronella moves further afield, looking at 'a Norwegian prince with a French name' in Fortinbras, 'the embodiment of internationalism ... instrumental in wiping out the Danish royal family'; "Denmark is indeed swamped by the World"' (p. 5). The two articles together form an interesting supplement to, different in some ways from, Ralph Berry's more comprehensive chapter on the presentation of different nations, published in his *Shakespearean Structures*.[46] Prem Nath gives us a valuable and thorough survey of '*Hamlet* in the Eighteenth Century, 1701–1750: from John Dennis to Arthur Murphy'. In the Notes Shanti Padhi suggests that the notorious book of slanders that Hamlet reads may be a famous *picaro* novel called *The Rogue*, one of the best-sellers after 1599 and full of anti-marital bias which suits the *Hamlet* context. Greg Bentley looks at the motifs of madness and syphilis as contributing to the play's central theme. Although the information is from contemporary sources, the writer might have been interested to know that D. H. Lawrence in various places identifies syphilis not only as the theme of *Hamlet* but of the post-*Hamlet* age. Robert E. Burkhart is bringing good news in concluding that the critical tide is quietly flowing against those who feel that Hamlet procrastinates. The fact that almost all articles claim to have found a 'central theme', each of them differing from the others, might mean that we should start revising our use of this phrase, or else some-

---

[44] '*Hamlet*: Mirrors of Revenge', *Sydney Studies in English*, 11 (1985–6), 3–22.

[45] The latest volume, 6 (1984) is, it is advised, one year behind schedule.

[46] Macmillan, London, 1981, Chapter 3 '*Hamlet*, Nationalism and Identity'.

body should present a fuller article on the theories that might account for such a polyphonic structure in one play.

From Italy we have almost a whole number of *Analysis: Quaderni di Anglistica*[47] devoted to Shakespeare, and the essays show that the Bard's industry is still a growth area in that country. Fernando Cioni gives close attention to Enobarbus and his dramatic discourse, arguing for (that word again, more euphoniously) 'la centralità' of the character's contrasting visions, and Francesco Marroni writes interestingly on 'La Teatralizzazione della Violenza' in *Titus Andronicus*, a subject which few would deny *is* central. Paola Pugliatti gives a rather diagrammatic account of presentation of individuals, groups, and situations on the stage, using mainly *Richard II* for exemplification. Leo Marchetti examines the existence in *Richard III* of a train of imagery taken from the natural world, arguing that it builds into 'una estetica sostanzialmente allegorica', giving a mythic quality to the narrative. Laura Spaggiari analyses the structural implications of misunderstanding in *The Comedy of Errors* while Anthony L. Johnson (this time in English) counts up the twofold and threefold patterns in *Macbeth*, concluding that there is some correspondence between number symbolism and thematic concerns. (Briefly, *threes* mean co-operation and *twos* disjunction.)

Most journals have a house-style of their own, and West Germany's *Shakespeare Jahrbuch* has one of the more identifiable. The rules seem to be, ask a very modest question which ought to be readily answerable, set out as many bits of evidence, both internal and external, preferably in numbered sections to give the air of logical organization, include if possible some historical facts, and come to a firm conclusion. The formula is a godsend to a harassed reviewer, since everything is so structured, even though there may be some absence of the excitement of speculation and the headiness of asking an unanswerable question. The

1985 volume[48] contains many such essays. When William E. Stewart asks 'Does Iago Die?' he answers 'no', after an argument that Iago is 'motivated by his addiction to survival' (p. 79). Karl P. Wentersdorf concludes that the 'Time Problem in *Othello*' can actually be solved: Othello and Desdemona were married through 'exchange of *de praesenti* vows in a clandestine ceremony' (p. 74) during the many weeks when Othello visited Brabantio's house in Venice. The amount of critical reference here is extensive, but the writer does not mention Emrys Jones, whose views on the subject seem to me the most sensible available.[49] The 'pattern' of 'frustrated pattern' found in *King Lear* by Peter Bilton has been probed by many critics, while Ann Jennalie Cook comes to the conclusion, after surveying Shakespeare's 'gentlemen' (and some cads) that 'he reveals what it does and does not mean to be a gentleman' (p. 27). In examining Shakespeare's *Richard III* beside Hall's Chronicles, R. Chris Hassel Jr finds 'that Shakespeare diminishes the attractiveness of Hall's Richard and enhances that of his Richmond' (p. 197). Wolfgang Riehle argues that the Shakespearian soliloquy is a development from the aside which he first used in adapting Plautus into *The Comedy of Errors*: 'So hat das Drama Shakespeares auch viele Impulse aus der römischen Komödie aufgegriffen, weiterentwickelt und verfeinert' (p. 44). Werner v. Koppenfels studies the protagonist's loss of sense of self, through language and deeds, in *Othello* and *Macbeth*, arguing that by the end of each play 'Sie selbst bieten damit dem Proze ihrer Selbstenfremdung Einhalt, bewahren sich so vor dem letzten Selbstverlust' (p. 62).

The North American *Shakespeare Quarterly* seems to prefer a hard-nosed, worldly

---

[47] Vol. 4 (1986), published by the Associazione de Anglistica, University of Pisa.

[48] *Deutsche Shakespeare-Gesellschaft West Jahrbuch 1985*.

[49] *Scenic Form in Shakespeare*, Oxford University Press, Oxford, 1971.

approach, sceptical of the workings of drama-tic illusion, and essays that are readily categori-zable, usually into structural studies (prefer-ably metadramatic) or linguistic analysis. James L. Calderwood has a field day with his chosen field of metadrama in finding 'Creative Uncreation in *King Lear*', as he sees the play virtually demolishing itself from the inside: 'Thus if the play begins with an uncreating act of abdication, it ends with another – uncreat-ing its own fictional reality by abdicating to a sterner successor outside.'[50] A. Lynne Mag-nusson follows this up by discovering a remarkable number of breaks of pattern in *The Tempest*, interruptions in plot and language, which appear curious in such a 'well-made play'. Her conclusion is close to Calder-wood's, that the play is 'confessional', decon-structing itself, confessing 'the unmaking and the "being made of" that are the perpetual conditions of making' (p. 65). Katharine Eisaman Maus chooses the linguistic slot, arguing that the problems of *The Rape of Lucrece* lie not in the field of characterization but that of language and rhetoric: problems of linguistic *decorum* and 'the dangers of meta-phor'. A theme-tune of each of these essays (which may or may not be significant in itself) is 'frustration' which is located in the texts: 'an acute and profoundly uneasy self-conscious-ness about poetic techniques and resources' (Maus, p. 82).

There is not much of that in *Shakespeare Survey*, in which sweetness and light tend to reign. While its house-style is harder to pin down, its taste more catholic, there tends to be a preference for an urbanely historical approach, without earnestness or over-subtlety. After all, a number of its contri-butions every other year start life as spoken papers at the International Conference at Strat-ford. It seems unnecessary to repeat all over again what papers appeared in last year's volume, largely devoted to 'Shakespeare and History',[51] but I might mention that I found particularly profitable Gary Taylor's 'The For-tunes of Oldcastle', while Jonathan Bate's 'Hal and the Regent' forms an interesting *coda* to his book on Shakespeare's influence on the Romantics reviewed above. The New Literary Theorists will be aghast to see that a whole volume on history does not get down to examining what precisely that term means in the context of drama, although in defence of the essay-writers, each gives some indication of how that question *might* be answered.

If pressed to state a personal preference about articles this year, I should bracket together G. K. Hunter on *The Merry Wives* (above) and Barbara Everett on *Twelfth Night* as the two I most enjoyed reading. Everett's 'Or What You Will'[52] gives full weight to the phrase in the title as 'the play's image of the pursuit of a kind of wholeness beyond expression and perhaps even beyond possibility' (p. 313). It is wrong to describe summarily the essay from this busy, intense critic who has the gift for preserving lightness within seriousness, since the piece hangs together weightlessly. The two keys lie in music, as the medium so admired by the symbolist poets, and dignity, discovered in a play full of 'sheer adult social consideration, of people's steady and reflective judgment of each other' (p. 306). In all her essays on the comedies, Everett is particularly acute and suggestive about the kind of *society* portrayed, an identity both made up of and overarching the individual characters, which is surely a clue to the fragile but tensile strength of this group of plays. In this essay the secret of Illyria is glimpsed in its 'fine exclusiveness' (p. 303) which at first holds at bay Viola and her brother, those who 'have no ideals and no illusions because they have nothing'. Within this world a Malvolio can be contained and even, up to a point, protected: 'the fact is he is more ambitious than lecherous, and more day-

---

[50] *Shakespeare Quarterly*, 37 (Spring 1986), 18.
[51] Cambridge University Press, Cambridge, 1985.
[52] *Essays in Criticism*, 35 (1985), 294–314.

dreamily, touchingly and absurdly vain than he is ambitious' (p. 30). Barbara Everett has contributed another article which, although primarily an exercise in textual criticism, is worth reading for its incidental critical insight into *Othello* and *Twelfth Night*.[53]

Alice Goodman's 'Falstaff and Socrates'[54] is one of those articles which initially look like being pedantic but end up opening fascinating windows. It begins with the teasing similarity between Socrates' symptoms of death (ascending paralysis, induced by conium, I am informed), and those of Falstaff. Using Jowett's translation of the *Phaedo*, Goodman demonstrates the ambiguity of Socrates himself as wise fool: 'he is at one and the same time the Silenus and the divine image inside it'. She then goes on to argue cautiously that Shakespeare 'recreates the truth of Socrates' in Falstaff, a suggestion that might shock the fat knight on one level, while flattering his immense ego on another. It is easy to credit Shakespeare himself with such a private joke, when he put the words of Saint Paul into Bottom's mouth, and allowed Glendower to speak for Merlin.

Although academic journals are notoriously conservative, some are now devoted to new approaches, and other older ones are willing to flirt with the danger of an essay or two based on literary theory.

New Literary History: A Journal of Theory and Interpretation is where we look for the *au courant*. However, two essays on Shakespeare do not have to be seen as particularly radical. Yves Bonnefoy in 'Readiness, Ripeness: *Hamlet, Lear*'[55] sets Hamlet's 'readiness is all' and Edgar's 'ripeness is all' in a historicist reading of the period in which the plays were written. Taken together, they are said to reveal Shakespeare's understanding of his own historical moment. Respectively, 'readiness' is for change from a God-centred, medieval world-view to a more modern, human-centred one; 'ripeness' is the death-knell for the old, an acceptance that some values must die

before the new ones can prevail. Johannes Birringer in 'Rhapsodies of Words: "Trapicality" in Shakespeare's Theater' observes stylistic variations, 'linguistic mutability' and 'the rhetoric of ... duplicity', which are said to have important implications for the interactive processes involved either in performance or in the act of reading. The analysis is mainly concentrated on *Hamlet, Troilus and Cressida* and *King Lear*. The two essays might be slotted into recent theoretical categories – the new historicism and reception theory respectively, but their final court of appeal is the good old text.

David Simpson takes the bull by the horns in *Critical Quarterly*, questioning whether the old text is so good after all.[56] In '"Great things of us forgot": Seeing *Lear* Better' he examines the 'privileging of Shakespeare' in the English and North American educational system as a questionable phenomenon. Dwelling on the death of Cordelia, he speaks 'rather strongly, of Lear as a figure who might be blamed for what happens' (p. 21), and challenges our traditional complacency in exercising 'empathy, feeling, or compassion' for Lear. Fine, but why necessarily tar Shakespeare with the critics' brush? Why not turn such observations into a new reading of *King Lear*, one that suggests the play itself can have the effect of shocking us into a radically moral frame of mind by using Brechtian techniques of consciously foreclosing the easy paths? In the same issue of *Critical Quarterly* Jacqueline Rose launches a possibly more potent salvo against the text. In '*Hamlet* – the *Mona Lisa* of Literature'[57] (a title based on Eliot's famous phrase), Rose examines, from a feminist direction, the question of femininity as reflected in Eliot's

---

53 'Two Damned Cruces: *Othello* and *Twelfth Night*', *Review of English Studies*, 37 (1986), 184–97.
54 *English*, 34 (1985), 97–112.
55 17 (Spring, 1986), 477–91.
56 28 (Spring/Summer 1986), 15–31.
57 Ibid, 35–49.

version of the play, modern psychoanalytic theory, and the play itself:

> ... what does it mean to us that one of the most elevated and generally esteemed works of our Western literary tradition should enact such a negative representation of femininity, or even such a violent repudiation of the femininity in man?

Well, yes again, if it were only Eliot and Freud we are considering. To add *Hamlet* itself to the consideration, we ought to consider the way the issue is presented in the play. Hamlet is surely seen to be simply *wrong* in his assessment and treatment of Ophelia, and lacking in basic understanding in his treatment of Gertrude. Add to this the fact that Shakespeare was showing in other plays of the time, *Othello*, *Much Ado About Nothing* and (arguably) *Troilus and Cressida*, and the Dark Lady Sonnets which may have been written as late as this, the simplifying, stereotyping nature of male perceptions of woman. In all of these works the man is shown to be just as wrong, and we may feel that male weaknesses are on parade and being savagely attacked, rather than there being an attempt to portray 'women as they really are'. The interest of Shakespeare here may reveal an uncomfortably male priority, but that is surely a different argument.

Carol Cook in her essay in *PMLA*, ' "The sign and semblance of her honor": Reading Gender Difference in *Much Ado About Nothing*',[58] takes an equally sceptical view of her chosen play. She examines sexual aggression, and argues that the play cleverly confirms rather than undermines patriarchal values. Cook concludes that the play is dominated by the phallus; that Beatrice, far from being a 'profess'd tyrant' to men, swings it as vigorously as they: 'She usurps the masculine prerogative of language and phallic wit.' The other image of femininity, Hero, is a 'blank'. 'She is the "nothing" that generates so much ado.' The essay not only presents a challenge to male critics but represents some internecine warfare, since the idea of the specifically

feminine dominance in *Much Ado About Nothing* has come as much from women (such as Barbara Everett[59]) as from men.

Just to mention an opinion on the same controversial subject, James L. Hill in ' "What, are they children?": Shakespeare's Tragic Women and the Boy Actors'[60] suggests rather tentatively that the female characters do not reveal centrally Shakespeare's conception of femininity, but they are responses from a practising dramatist to the acting limitations of his boy actors:

> What we see of Lady Macbeth or Cleopatra may well be a result of having to write for a boy actor; that does not mean, of course, that it is completely at odds with what Shakespeare thought of women, but it does mean that whatever he thought can be glimpsed only through the limiting filter of the boy actor's art. (p. 256)

Not so exciting, but it is worth considering at least.

Thomas Cartelli, in 'Ideology and Subversion in the Shakespearean Set Speech'[61] concentrates on particular episodes involving Henry V, Ulysses and Portia, concluding,

> Shakespearean drama challenges dominant ideological structures in the very act of *being used* by them.

Speeches and speakers are placed in dramatic contexts that subvert what is being said. Again, the terminology is 'recent' but the perceptions are not, though perhaps the more confirmation of Ulysses' politic hypocrisy we have, the better, if only to counteract the influence of English Government ministers who use Ulysses' speech on 'order' as evidence that 'Shakespeare was a Tory, without any doubt' (interview with Nigel Lawson in the *Guardian*, 5 September 1983, pertinently rebutted in correspondence

---

[58] 101 (1986), 186–202.
[59] *Critical Quarterly*, 3 (1961), 319–35.
[60] *Studies in English Literature, 1500–1900*, 26 (1986), 235–58.
[61] *ELH*, 53 (Spring 1986), 1–26.

by Kenneth Muir, quoted by Margot Heinemann in her essay mentioned above).

The University of Toronto Quarterly has three Shakespearian essays in one issue, two on *The Tempest*. Ellen R. Belton in '"When no man was his own": Magic and Self-Discovery in *The Tempest*'[62] argues that Prospero uses his magic not to heal nor directly to create, but to *test* each character and group of characters, to reveal the true nature of each with his rational perceptions. Richard Hillman discusses '*The Tempest* as Romance and Anti-Romance'. 'The world of the play is premised on a complex romance pattern' (p. 145), *but* 'the requisite romance symbolism ... is violently interrupted' (p. 156) with a sense of mortality and the meaninglessness of life. Prospero's great speech is recognizably a tragic one, with no analogue in the romances nearly so close as Macbeth's 'To-morrow' soliloquy (5.5.19ff.) or Lear's 'Is man no more than this?' (pp. 156–7). Peter Hyland in 'Disguise and Renaissance Tragedy' finds that disguise used in tragedy (including *Lear*, which gets lengthy consideration) is a sign of 'degradation', indicating an anarchic world of reversed values. The dramatists 'were fully aware of what ambiguous and disturbing effects would be created from the employment in a tragic play of what is essentially a comic device' (p. 170).

The Renaissance issue of *Studies in English Literature: 1500–1900* also has three relevant essays. I have already quoted from James L. Hill's article on 'Tragic Women and the Boy Actors',[63] and there is another essay on a characterological topic – '"The weight of Antony": Staging "Character" in *Antony and Cleopatra*' by W. B. Worthen. Lawrence Danson contributes to a similar area of discussion in 'Continuity and Character in Shakespeare and Marlowe', where he considers 'the stability of individual identity' in dramatic characters as imitations of person. After beginning with the unlikely comparison between Shakespeare's Kate and Marlowe's Edward II, he goes on to examine the wider questions raised:

What happens when a character acts from one moment to the next in ways so radically different that the transformation challenges our ordinary standards, if not for authorial competence, then for the integrity of the self? (p. 217).

In *Comparative Drama* we have two essays which raise equally theoretical questions. The scene in *Richard III* when Richard descends from the throne (4.2) is examined by Peggy Endel[64] as a 'Profane Icon', a stage image which is disturbing in its associations with demonism. Where the article is of theoretical interest is in the implications about the complexity of audience response to an apparently straightforward scene. Richard Fly in 'The Evolution of Shakespearean Metadrama: Abel, Burckhardt and Calderwood' (pp. 124–39) efficiently charts the territory indicated in his title, ending with some thoughts about the future of Shakespearian metadrama as a methodology. Do we see the start of a whole new field? Metacriticism of Metadramatic Theorists?

There are other articles on single tragedies. Y. B. Olsson in 'Edmund and Lear (A Study in the Structure of *King Lear*)'[65] examines the intricate processes and their implications as Lear falls from power and Edmund rises. The presentation is a little stiff, concentrating on the familiar territory of 'order' and 'nature' rather than presenting anything really new, but the argument is efficiently conducted. Mark Rose is more innovative in interpreting *Othello* in the context of the Elizabethan revival of chivalry.[66] While other dramatists felt able to burlesque the revival, Shakespeare does something more fundamental. Unable to

---

[62] 55 (Winter 1985/6), 127–40.
[63] Note 60, above.
[64] 'Profane Icon: The Throne Scene of Shakespeare's *Richard III*', *Comparative Drama*, 20 (Summer 1986), 115–23.
[65] *Durham University Journal*, NS 47 (June 1986), 251–8.
[66] *English Literary Renaissance*, 15 (Autumn 1985), 293–311.

leave entirely 'the absolute world of fidelity' found in romance, he turns romance into an 'intermediate' form, tragedy, which 'rebukes romance' without killing off its inner values. The transitional quality of the achievement is seen from the fact that although at the end Desdemona remains 'a miracle of fidelity' and Othello 'dies reasserting his allegiance to his heroic self', yet the old world does not reassert itself because these characters die. We are left with 'a mere vacancy, or, rather, a tableau of corpses and a disconcerting promise that Iago too will be tortured'.

Modern Drama brings the story of Shakespeare's influence right up to the present day in two essays that fit together neatly. Michael Hays ends his essay 'On Maeterlinck Reading Shakespeare'[67] with these words:

Shakespeare [for Maeterlinck] served to name a process of self-inscription belonging much more to Maeterlinck than to the Bard of Avon. It would not surprise me if the same were true for many of the early modern dramatists who turned to 'Shakespeare' and the 'Classics' in order to define a dramatic space of their own. (p. 58)

This speculation inadvertently informs the next essay, 'Bond, Shakespeare and the Absurd' (pp. 60–70), where James C. Bulman examines Bond's *Lear, Bingo* and Bond's shorter writings on Shakespeare. For all his antagonism to the lack of committed moral stance in Shakespeare, Bond is in part using Shakespeare to define a dramatic space of his own, and one that is most strongly opposed to the political evasiveness of Beckett and the Absurd. Bond's approach to Shakespeare is of great interest and subtlety, and deserves close reading.

Finally, a word on casebooks, which may provide a route to stardom for some essays and books, a descent to oblivion for the others which are not chosen. I could happily recommend Stanley Wells's *Twelfth Night: Critical Essays*[68] to students as a reliable guide to the best essays available on the play. They are not chosen for any flashy polemics or dazzling prose, but for their soundness and intrinsic interest. It is an imaginative choice to include accounts by J. B. Priestley, Henry Morley (on 'Samuel Phelps as Malvolio', 1857), Max Beerbohm, Virginia Woolf, and a review of Peter Hall's 1958 production. Most of the more academic pieces more or less choose themselves.

With over 600 pages per volume (and prices to match), *Shakespearean Criticism*,[69] part of the Gale Literary Criticism Series, is unlikely to sit on the tables of many students, waiting for rapid reference. It is really destined to be an aid to professional critics who want quick access to commentary on each play, with periods represented from the eighteenth century to the present day. Three volumes have so far appeared of a projected seven (by my calculations) and each one deals with a major tragedy, a major comedy and a handful of other plays. (We presumably cannot blame the editors for publicity which classes *Troilus and Cressida* as 'a minor comedy'.) We are given extracts from early and out-of-the-way critics, most uniquely from Europe, but for more modern criticism we are at the mercy of sometimes idiosyncratic, and very American choices. The 'Additional Bibliography' for each play, although helpful in giving short abstracts of books and articles, is extremely selective, and although one could never wish for completeness, the editors had such an enviable amount of room to play with that they could have been a bit more comprehensive. Repro-

---

67 29 (March 1986), 49–59.
68 Cited above, in Note 8.
69 Laurie Lanzen Harris and Mark W. Scott (eds), *Shakespearean Criticism: Excerpts from the Criticism of William Shakespeare's Plays and Poetry, from the First Published Appraisals to Current Evaluations* (Gale Research Company, Detroit, Michigan). Vol. 2 (1985) covers *Henry VIII, Lear, Love's Labour's Lost, Measure, Pericles*; vol. 3 (1986) covers *1, 2, 3 Henry VI, Macbeth, Dream, Troilus*.

ductions of paintings based on the plays make the tomes a little less formidable.

For those who like to keep their fingers on the pulse of critical fashion, my impression is that *Hamlet* wins in the popularity stakes. This seems something to do with the absorption into critical discourse of metadramatic theory. Its acceptance may be promising to the newer approaches, which have yet to shed an image of voguishness. It will be interesting, in particular, to find how fundamentally feminism will cause us to rethink many plays, since it is the movement most decisively moral in its orientation. Already, *The Taming of the Shrew* is taking on a new life. For the sake of *Hamlet* (and perhaps Shakespeare in general), I hope Jacqueline Rose's view is not the one that wins ascendancy, but we must wait and see. With all this reassessment going on, Martin Dodsworth's *Hamlet Closely Observed*[70] may even be the last of its kind – a meticulous, traditional,

humanist approach to the play. Meanwhile, the history plays seem to be on the way up (with a fairly unillusioned, political approach beginning to dominate), apparently meeting the last plays on the way down in critical popularity. The romantic comedies maintain a steady group of disciples.[71]

---

[70] The Athlone Press, London, 1985.

[71] For the sake of comprehensiveness if not completeness, I should mention that in compiling this review I am aware of, but have not included comment on, R. Stamm, 'The First Meeting of the Lovers in Shakespeare's *Romeo and Juliet*' in *English Studies*, 67 (1986), 2–13; Werner Brönimann, 'Shakespeare's Tragic Practice' in *English Studies*, 67 (1986), 211–15 (really a review, not an article); K. Chellappan, *Shakespeare and Ilango as Tragedians: A Comparative Study* (Tamil University Thanjavur, Tamil Nadu, India, 1985); Visvanath Chatterjee, 'Shakespeare's Tragic Heroines' in *Journal* of the Department of English (Rabindra Bharati University, Calcutta, 1, 1983–4, publ. 1985). I did not have access to the most recent volume of *Shakespeare Studies*.

2. SHAKESPEARE'S LIFE, TIMES, AND STAGE
reviewed by RICHARD DUTTON

William Shakespeare: His World, His Work, His Influence,[1] edited by John F. Andrews, is, like its subject, almost too vast to contemplate in its entirety: a collection of 60 essays by leading scholars and notable creative and interpretative artists, covering most conceivable aspects of the phenomenon that is Shakespeare and running, in three volumes, to some 950 elegantly presented double-column folio pages. It is a monument and, at (I am told) £180, an expensive one; like most monuments, I fear, it will not lack for detractors. I hope I shall not be seen as one of those, since I want to stress that there is much here that is valuable, as one would expect from an undertaking supervised by the former editor of *Shakespeare Quarterly*. But there are bound to be doubts about the style and substance of volumes like these, centring on the question of the readership to

which they are addressed and the sumptuousness of their presentation. Dr Andrews says they are 'designed to provide a multifaceted twentieth-century view of Shakespeare for the same kind of audience the compilers of the First Folio addressed in 1623 as "the great variety of readers" ' (p. viii), and I suppose it may be argued that that estimable volume was not published cheaply either. But the force of his rationale is for an exercise in popular publishing, something along the lines of the Pelican or Sphere Guides to English Literature though focusing exclusively on Shakespeare and Shakespeariana. Indeed, in terms of content, that is not far from what he has achieved, and I mean no derogation in saying

---

[1] 3 vols, Charles Scribner's Sons, New York, 1985.

so. The essays here are not, and do not pretend to be, works of original research or scholarship; nor are they bibliographical reviews of such works, though most of them come with useful selected bibliographies attached. They offer, rather, condensed surveys of subject-areas on which their authors are almost invariably acknowledged experts. It is invidious in this context to single out individuals but if I mention G. R. Elton on 'The State: Government and Politics Under Elizabeth and James', Andrew Gurr on 'Theaters and the Dramatic Profession', and Wylie Sypher on 'Painting and Other Fine Arts' (in Volume 1, *His World*), S. Schoenbaum on 'The Life: A Survey', M. C. Bradbrook on 'Shakespeare and His Contemporaries', and Arthur Kirsch on 'Shakespeare's Tragedies' (Vol. 2, *His Work*), and G. E. Bentley on 'Shakespeare's Reputation – Then Till Now', W. Moelwyn Merchant on 'Shakespeare and the Painter and Illustrator', and Jonathan Miller on 'Shakespeare and the Modern Director' (Vol. 3, *His Influence*), readers will get some idea of the calibre of contributors. And it is difficult to believe that what they (that is, all of them) have produced, as introductions for 'the great variety of readers', could be better informed, more authoritative or, for the most part, more lucidly written. One might quibble about the inclusion or exclusion of certain items, particularly in Volumes 1 and 3. There is no essay specifically on the City of London or the Court, for example, in the former; and, while Anthony Burgess (on 'Shakespeare and the Modern Writer') and Peter Ustinov (on 'Shakespeare and the Modern Playwright') are characteristically shrewd and witty in the latter, their allotted themes are too nebulous for comfort. But one can have no such doubts about the great majority of the material here. More then the pity that 'the great variety of readers' are only going to have access to these volumes in libraries.

There remains a further worry. The editor expresses the hope that the 'awareness and appreciation', of Shakespeare that should derive from reading the essays 'will carry with it the impulse to pursue the quest for Shakespeare beyond the confines of these pages' (p. x). The risk is that such weighty tomes, carrying such illustrious names, may have exactly the opposite effect and be seen, as it were, as a distillation, if not of all knowledge, at least of all knowledge that *matters*. It is a danger that perhaps attends any kind of popularization, but it might have been kept more at bay if contributors had been given a stronger direction to highlight the main lines of scholarly cut-and-thrust in relation to their subject-areas – to keep reminding readers that *nothing* about Shakespeare is settled beyond debate. There is something of this in most essays, and this is where they are most valuable to established scholars (Patrick Collinson on 'The Church: Religion and Its Manifestations', for instance, is exemplary); but it might have been made a more central element. Here again, one cannot help thinking that the sheer elegance of the books is their own worst enemy, an invitation to think of them as coffee-table volumes. In this form they run the risk of doing a disservice to the liberal humanist tradition of Shakespearian scholarship, criticism, and production which they in effect champion; they may well be taken to embody what some would call, and see as the real enemy, 'establishment Shakespeare' and 'the Shakespeare industry' (witness Ralph Berry's survey of 'Major Shakespearean Institutions', among which he includes this venerable periodical). The names of Stephen Greenblatt, Louis Montrose, Jonathan Goldberg, and Jonathan Dollimore just squeeze into the last two sides of the last essay, Maurice Charney on 'Contemporary Issues in Shakespearean Interpretation'; others like Terry Eagleton, Alan Sinfield, Gary Waller and John Drakakis do not appear at all. One wonders whether another compendium such as this will be possible, indeed thinkable, in another twenty years, when their contributions to the subject have been fully absorbed. Shakespeare as the cornerstone of literary studies in the English-speaking world is, ironically, more vulnerable than he has ever been, just as this monument to his pre-eminence appears. It would be a service to its subject, and to the values he is taken here to represent, if this work could be made genuinely available to 'the great variety of readers' for whom it was written.

Speaking of the new critical approaches to Renaissance literature that have mushroomed this decade, there are two timely articles in the most recent number of *English Literary Renaissance*. Louis Montrose himself considers the development of what he categorizes as the New Historicism in America and Cultural Materialism in Britain, suggesting that 'interpreters of Tudor–Stuart literature ... find themselves now particularly well placed to rearticulate literature as a social practice; and by so doing to rearticulate criticism as a social practice'.[2] Jean E. Howard insists that 'the historically-minded critic must increasingly be willing to acknowledge the non-objectivity of his or her own stance and the inevitably political nature of interpretive and even descriptive acts'; she reviews the works of Montrose and Greenblatt, and comes close to accusing them of lacking the courage of their own convictions.[3] Both are required reading for anyone still unsure about the aims and implications of this recent criticism. Richard Levin has not yet, to my knowledge, addressed this new-style criticism in his self-appointed role as arch-critic of the criticism of Renaissance drama (*vide* his *New Readings vs. Old Plays*, 1979), but he seems to be getting there. In 'The New Refutation of Shakespeare' ('refutation' in the sense of managing to find in Shakespeare something different from, even possibly opposite to, what he seems to say) he takes a hatchet with his usual relish to an article on 'Text against Performance' in *Macbeth* in order to demolish the ultra-ironic style of criticism, which finds nuances and implications that could never be apparent in performance.[4] He

then broadens the debate in 'Performance-Critics vs. Close Readers in the Study of English Renaissance Drama', with an analysis of the whole argument between those who approach plays primarily as performance-texts and those who treat them as works of literature;[5] he reviews the evidence of Renaissance opinions on the question, concludes that they fall between the two extremes, and calls a plague on modern extremists in both houses.

Readers will recognize in Leo Salingar's collection of essays, *Dramatic Form in Shakespeare and the Jacobeans*,[6] criticism of a more traditional complexion than any of this. Most of the essays are devoted to detailed readings of individual works (*The Merchant of Venice*, *1 & 2 Henry IV*, *Twelfth Night*, *Hamlet* and *King Lear* by Shakespeare; *Volpone*, *The Silent Woman*, *Bartholomew Fair*, *The Revenger's Tragedy*, and *The Changeling* by major contemporaries) though there are also two general essays on the key Renaissance terms, 'art' and 'wit', and a small anomaly, a discussion of *Don Quixote*. Though most of these essays belong to the last ten years, the tone is perhaps set by the *Scrutiny* piece on '*The Revenger's Tragedy* and the Morality Tradition': close attention to the verse, character types, and dramatic structures, informed by a broad knowledge of intellectual and theatrical traditions. All of these pieces have been published before – *Shakespeare Survey* readers will know from 1981 'Shakespeare and the Ventriloquists', on the nature of Shakespearian characterization, focusing on *Hamlet* – but it is fitting that these sober and undogmatic pieces should be collected as a considered view of some of the major achievements of Elizabethan and Jacobean drama.

---

[2] *English Literary Renaissance*, 16 (1986), 5–12.
[3] ibid., 13–43.
[4] *Modern Philology*, 83 (1985), 123–41.
[5] *Modern Language Review*, 81 (1986), 545–59.
[6] Cambridge University Press, Cambridge, 1986.

Herbert Berry's *The Boar's Head Playhouse*[7] is a painstaking study of all the known documentation (mainly legal depositions, though with some corroboration from maps) relating to the theatres associated with the Boar's Head Inn and Yard 'without Aldgate' during the sixteenth and seventeenth centuries. The main bulk of the book traces the ownership and disposition of the buildings involved from the 1530s to the present day (even pinpointing the spot where a plaque might commemorate the stage of 'the third theatrical enterprise in the brightest day of the English theatre'), but concentrates on the interminable legal wrangles of 1598–1603 when Oliver Woodliffe and successive partners (including Francis Langley, looking to recoup his lossess from the Swan) built a tentative inn-yard theatre which was quickly translated into a much more substantial rival to the Globe and Fortune, and then proceeded to sue each other to maximize their profits. Professor Berry pursues these matters single-mindedly, and anyone not conversant with the Elizabethan legal system may find this heavy going (J. H. Baker on 'Law and Legal Institutions' in *William Shakespeare: His World, His Work, His Influence* would be useful here). But Chapters 11–13, in which he applies the evidence to the nature of the successive theatres, will be of immediate interest and value to anyone concerned with the Elizabethan stage. Berry establishes, for example, that the original stage was like a boxing-ring, detached from the buildings around it and without a covering, but was later moved to abut the tiring-house and acquired a 'heavens', though it is not clear if these were substantial enough to contain machinery; also that the audience stood in the galleries of the earlier theatre but were seated in the later one. He makes a good case for the theatre being a settled base for the Earl of Derby's Men, when the Globe and the Fortune were the only public theatres officially sanctioned around London. He even establishes to his own satisfaction that the galleries above the tiring-house at the rear

of the later stage were for spectators, and were not used during performances by actors or musicians, who would thus require scaffolding of some sort on the stage itself for activities 'above'. Twelve illustrations by the indefatigable C. Walter Hodges, while inevitably containing much hypothetical detail, are extremely illuminating and useful. The book must be said in many respects to supersede C. J. Sisson's posthumous *The Boar's Head Theatre* (1972, edited by Stanley Wells) about whom and which Professor Berry has several unkind things to say. It is odd that, while being so meticulous about other matters, he accepts uncritically Leslie Hotson's thesis about *Twelfth Night* being first performed at Court on 6 January 1601 (doubted by the Arden editors among others). It seems a gratuitous attempt to associate the Boar's Head with The Bard, in line with a slight tendency to inflate the significance of this theatrical enterprise: yes, it existed and operated at the same time as the first Globe and Fortune, but only briefly, and we still know far too little about the companies that played there and their repertoires.

Another with whom Berry crosses swords is Willem Schrickx who, in *Foreign Envoys and Travelling Players in the Age of Jonson*,[8] pulls together many of the threads of his long archival research in Brussels, London, The Hague, and elsewhere, to create a book that charts many facets of the diplomatic, military, and theatrical relations between England and the Spanish Netherlands from 1598 to 1621. Those who know his many articles, published in *Shakespeare Survey* and elsewhere, will recognize much of this material, though it is substantially recast. But there is also much previously unpublished, including some especially interesting discoveries/speculations

---

[7] Folger Books, Washington: Folger Shakespeare Library, and Associated University Presses, London and Toronto, 1986.
[8] Universa, R.U.G., Gent, 1986.

about the life and career of Cyril Tourneur (including some support for the now unfashionable assumption that he *did* write *The Revenger's Tragedy*), and some suggestive reflections on the works of Marston, particularly relating to the staging of *The Malcontent* by the King's Men. The book, dense with information and inferences, is not always easy to follow, but there is much to reward a reader's patience, including further thoughts on the naming of Polonius (pp. 107–9) and details of performances of *Dr Faustus* at Strasburg in the 1590s which, as he observes, editors of the play have ignored. (Ormerod and Wortham have indeed perpetuated the omission; see below). The appendices offer useful texts of several notable manuscripts in continental archives, including a Spanish account of Campion's *Masque of Squires* and part of *An Apologie of the Earl of Essex*.

A measure of the difficulties involved in the researches of Professors Berry and Schrickx is to be found in the figure or figures of 'Robert Browne'. Berry is mainly concerned with the 'Browne of the Boar's Head', whose death Edward Alleyn's wife announced in a letter of October 1603; Schrickx with the one who led a notable troupe of actors on the continent from c. 1591–c. 1621. As both admit, there is inevitable confusion about which records relate to which actor. Berry convincingly reviews a good deal of the evidence (though not all) in his Appendix 9, and accuses Schrickx (in an earlier article) of particular confusions: 'His most important assertions for our purposes are that the Browne of the foreign tours led Derby's men at court in the winters of 1599–1600 and 1600–1601 and that, by implication, the company had nothing to do with the Boar's Head' (p. 193). Whether because he has himself come to doubt these assertions, or because they are not to his purpose here, Schrickx does not repeat them in his book, but he does adduce some new information on the family of (apparently) the continental-based actor. Reading these books in

succession, the mind boggles at all the Brownes. If I have read them aright (though neither actually draws this connection), Susan Browne, the widow of Robert Browne of the Boar's Head, married Thomas Greene of Queen Anne's Men, who (according to Schrickx) may well have been the brother of John Green, who was the principal partner of the continental-based Robert Browne ... the mind begins to spin.

Professor Schrickx recently retired, and his friends, colleagues, and students have produced a *festschrift*: *Elizabethan and Modern Studies, Presented to Professor Willem Schrickx on the Occasion of his Retirement* (ed. J. P. Vander Motten).[9] Fittingly, a good half of the short pieces here relate to Renaissance subjects: A. G. H. Bachrach considers in some detail the storm with which *The Tempest* opens;[10] W. L. Brackman has edited for the first time an undistinguished 'Mournefull Dittie' on the death of Essex, usefully comparing it with parallel works;[11] John Briley briefly re-thinks the early life of Mary Sidney (his title is rather misleading);[12] Walter Colman looks at some of Gabriel Harvey's extensive marginalia in relation to his enthusiasm for the study of Greek;[13] Marysa Demoor helpfully reviews the Victorian Andrew Lang's response to the Shakespearian issues of his day, such as the authorship question, and reproduces a delightful skit on objections to the 'history' in *Richard III*;[14] Joseph de Vos looks at the Shakespearian performances (particularly Hamlet) of Jan Dilis;[15]

---

[9] Seminarie Voor Engelse en Amerikaanse Literatuur, R.U.G., Gent, 1985.

[10] 'Shakespeare, the Sea and the Weather', 9–20.

[11] 'A "mournefull dittie" on the Death of the Earl of Essex, Queen Elizabeth's Favourite', 21–36.

[12] 'Mary Sidney – a 20th Century Reappraisal', 47–56.

[13] 'Gabriel Harvey's Holograph Notes in his Copy of *Gnomologiæ*', 57–66.

[14] 'The Trumpets Sound. Enter Andrew Lang, Victorian Critic, in Armour', 97–108.

[15] 'Jan Dilis, the First Shakespeare Performer in Flanders (1852–1918)', 109–118.

Julian Hilton offers a lively survey of the Pickleherring question, plausibly tracing the whole tradition back to the famous clown, Richard Tarlton;[16] E. A. J. Honigmann pursues Shakespeare in his known and suspected relations with foreigners living in London, including Peter Street (the builder of the Globe and Fortune), the Droeshouts (one of whom was responsible for the First Folio portrait), Gheerart Janssen (who carved the Stratford bust), and the Mountjoys, with whom he apparently lodged – an intriguing line of inquiry, surely worth following up;[17] (elsewhere, incidentally, Sidney Thomas adduces a redundant stage direction in *King John* to rebut Honigmann's use of that play in *Shakespeare: the Lost Years*, where it is central to his argument for an 'early start' to Shakespeare's career (see this column last year));[18] Veselin Kostic ponders over the mixture of particular and universal elements in Shakespearian characterization;[19] Kenneth Muir considers three dramatic adaptations of the same work, Cervantes' exemplary novel, *La Fuerza de la Sangre*, including Middleton and Rowley's *The Spanish Gipsy*;[20] Nicole Rowan adds to the growing body of criticism anxious to establish the inherent value of the *Henry VI* plays;[21] the late Jürgen Schaefer examines the limits of current thinking about synonymy as part of the richness of Shakespearian language and suggests directions that future study might take;[22] Gustav Ungerer reconsiders a crux in *The Merchant of Venice*, where Shylock mentions that some people 'love not a gaping pig', 4.1.40ff: with a wealth of convincing iconographic evidence (not for weak stomachs) he suggests that this is a reference to a traditional association of heresy with the living animal, rather than to a dead, cooked one;[23] and Stanley Wells offers some of the fruits of his editing of the Sonnets for the Oxford Shakespeare.[24]

Kent T. van den Berg's *Playhouse and Cosmos: Shakespearean Theater as Metaphor*[25] is a significant addition to the extensive literature on the Elizabethan-playhouse-as-symbol. Admirably, though unostentatiously, conversant with Renaissance fictive theory, with the psychology of 'play', and with current research into the Elizabethan stage, Professor van den Berg argues that 'the playhouse itself defined the place of performance as a subjective world, corresponding to the Renaissance concept of the poem as second nature created in the mind. The concept . . . reflects a new view of poetry derived from reading and writing: a view of the poem as a thing or place, an enclosure or interior containing fictive experiences, a theater of the mind' (p. 15). He rejects both the idea of the commercial playhouses as deliberate, Vitruvian architectural symbols (Frances Yates, *Theatre of the World*) and the suggestion that metadramatic self-consciousness within Shakespeare's drama implies infinite recessions of doubting about the nature of 'reality' itself (Anne Righter Barton, *Shakespeare and the Idea of the Play*), insisting with what may seem an unfashionable reliance on common sense on 'metaphor's mimetic capacity to restore within subjectivity itself a viable sense of objective reality' (p. 53). He grounds this argument in detailed readings of *As You Like It*, *Henry V*, and *Macbeth*, deliberately spanning the genres. The book as a whole champions the study of

---

[16] 'Pickelhering, Pickleherring and What You Will', 131–42.

[17] 'Shakespeare and London's Immigrant Community, circa 1600', 143–54.

[18] '"Enter a Sheriffe": Shakespeare's *King John* and *The Troublesome Raigne*', *Shakespeare Quarterly*, 37 (1986), 98–100.

[19] 'The Suppression of Motivation in Shakespeare's Characters', 167–72.

[20] 'Hardy, Middleton, Calderón and Cervantes' *La Fuerza de la Sangre*', 181–90.

[21] 'Shakespeare's Henry VI-trilogy: A Reconsideration', 191–202.

[22] 'Shakespeare's Synonymy Re-examined', 203–10.

[23] 'Shylock's Gaping Pig', 267–76.

[24] 'New Readings in Shakespeare's Sonnets', 317–22.

[25] University of Delaware Press, Newark, and Associated University Presses, London and Toronto, 1985.

the playhouses not as an end in itself but as the best way of informing our *reading* of Shakespeare; it is a sane and lucid demonstration of his conclusion that: 'The generosity of Shakespearean imagination flows from the vitality of the theatrical event. To recover this value in and for the act of reading is the best reason for studying the plays in their original theatrical context' (p. 151).

Professor van den Berg's book contains the most persuasive explanation I have read of what the 'sign' of the Globe might mean, assuming it existed (pp. 36–38); G. Blakemore Evans[26] offers further corroboration that it did exist, in the 'Elegy on Richard Burbage' (though I think his main point has been made before, by J. C. Adams),[27] and also that 'nunnery' had the colloquial secondary sense of 'brothel' when *Hamlet* was written. Barbara Everett takes two more cruces – Iago's description of Cassio as 'almost ? in a fair wife' and Sir Andrew's admiration of his own leg 'in a ? colour'd stock' – as a starting point for a sustained imaginative exploration of the verbal texture of *Othello* and *Twelfth Night*.[28] René Graziani finds associations in the name of Marcadé, who announces the death of the princess's father in *Love's Labour's Lost*, with the Dance of Death rather than Mercury, as some have argued.[29] John Boe has proposed a new and undoubtedly plausible (if unexciting) 'Mr. W.H.' – William Hall, father of Shakespeare's son-in-law, John Hall.[30]

It is pleasant to welcome another volume in the Records of Early English Drama series. I reviewed *Norwich, 1540–1642* here last year, and everything I said there about the selfless scholarship and high publishing standards of the series holds good for Audrey Douglas and Peter Greenfield's volume covering *Cumberland, Westmorland, Gloucestershire*.[31] This volume represents a new departure for the series: publication of the records in county (or even multiple-county), rather than borough, collections where the relative paucity of the material warrants it. This will apparently lead, as here, to strange bedfellows occupying the same volume, depending on when the materials became available, and it does mean that the records lack the simple chronological sequence or the appearance of an unfolding historical pageant found in some of the earlier volumes. Anyone consulting this volume, even casually, would be well advised to read the Contents and Preface pages first, where the arrangement of materials is explained. For example, anyone pursuing Shakespearian references might well want to know if Lord Strange's Men toured Cumberland and Westmorland, just north of the Stanleys' principal fiefs: if we look up 'Strange' in the Index we are directed to 'Derby' and thence to 'Stanley' and thence to 'Patrons and Travelling Companies', which last item does not appear in the Index at all. The explanation of this conundrum is that 'Patrons and Travelling Companies' is a separate section in the book, as the Contents reveal. It might be helpful in subsequent volumes, if a similar principle is to be followed, to set such index entries in a distinctive type-face or simply to include the first page-number of the section. (The answer to the initial query, incidentally, is that Strange's Men were never in Cumberland or Westmorland, though they visited Shallow's Gloucestershire in 1591/2). Of other companies with plausible Shakespearian connections, the Queen's and Leicester's Men both visited Gloucester when he could have been with them, and the Queen's reached Carlisle (Cumberland) in 1588/9 and

---

26 'Two Notes on *Hamlet*: II.2.357–8; III.1.121–31', *Modern Language Review*, 81 (1986), 34–6.

27 *The Globe Playhouse*, 2nd ed. (New York, 1961), p. 31.

28 'Two Damned Cruces: *Othello* and *Twelfth Night*', *Review of English Studies*, NS 37 (1986), 184–97.

29 'M. Marcadé and the Dance of Death: *Love's Labour's Lost*, V.ii.705–11', *Review of English Studies*, NS 37 (1986), 392–5.

30 'Mr. W.H.: A New Candidate', *Shakespeare Quarterly*, 37 (1986), 97–8.

31 University of Toronto Press, Toronto, Buffalo and London, 1986.

Kendal (Westmorland) in 1592/3. But Pembroke's, the Lord Chamberlain's, and the King's Men do not appear in these pages at all. Direct Shakespearian connections, then, are apparently few, but there is a wealth of details about royal visits, local festivities, and such matters as the survival of the *Corpus Christi* play at Kendal into the reign of King James; there is also full documentation of the even more scandalous 1621 play at Kendal that satirized local dignitaries and became a Star Chamber matter. Other theatrical connections with the central government seem to have been very few. The 'players of the Master of the Revelles' who were rewarded at Gloucester in 1583/4 were (according to E. K. Chambers) probably not Tilney's own troupe but an unauthorized company who had stolen a licence; apart from them, the Master of the Revels is not mentioned in these pages prior to 1624, when Sir Henry Herbert made his authority felt as far afield as Gloucester – which tends to confirm the picture that has been appearing in earlier volumes of the Records of Early English Drama. Quibbles about the indexing apart, these are immensely valuable works. An earnest of the kind of insights which the whole project is eventually likely to afford us is provided by J. A. B. Somerset, who is currently at work on the Records volume on Shrewsbury, where his study of the local playing-place, a quarry adapted to be a semi-circular amphitheatre, challenges previous assumptions that all fixed outdoor playing-places were circular or for performances 'in the round'.[32]

I should, incidentally, offer a belated welcome to *Medieval and Renaissance Drama in England*, an annual volume of essays edited by J. Leeds Barroll III, in the second issue of which Professor Somerset's article appears. Although material on Shakespeare is specifically excluded (I think we can concede that he is adequately catered for elsewhere), it is a publication that Shakespearians will want to keep an eye on, if not for the critical pieces on Shakespeare's predecessors and contemporaries (which strike me as of an excellent standard, though it is beyond my brief to comment on them here) then certainly for the papers relating to the Elizabethan stage, the theatrical profession and the editing of Renaissance plays. In the most recent volume, for example, William B. Long focuses on an apparently innocuous marginal note in the manuscript of *Woodstock* to demonstrate the dangers of leaning uncritically on the assumptions of great scholars of the past, like Chambers and Greg, about prompters, bookholders, and the processes of adaptation/revision that a script might go through before it was used in the playhouse;[33] John H. Astington argues that descent machinery in our period was relatively unsophisticated and inexpensive and would have been available in all purpose-built Elizabethan theatres, even those without a 'heavens', which challenges Glynne Wickham's recent assertion that it was something only introduced with the investment in more opulent theatres in the 1590s;[34] William Ingram 'explore(s) the current state of our knowledge, add(s) a few new facts and essay(s) a few conjectures' on the question of the Whitefriars private playhouse which seems to have operated between 1607 and 1614, a useful exercise which certainly makes sense of what little we do know, though he tantalizes us at the end with piquant details from the unedifying subsequent career of Thomas Woodford, the man at the centre of the enterprise, about which we must wait to hear more.[35] (Leaving *Medieval and Renaissance Drama in England* for a moment), S. P. Cerasano has unearthed four

---

[32] 'Local Drama and Playing Places at Shrewsbury', *Medieval and Renaissance Drama in England*, 2 (AMS Press, New York, 1985), 1–29.

[33] '"A bed / for woodstock": A Warning for the Unwary', 91–118.

[34] 'Descent Machinery in the Playhouse', 119–34.

[35] 'The Playhouse as an Investment, 1607–1614; Thomas Woodford and the Whitefriars', 209–30.

new wills by Elizabethan/Jacobean actors (William Bird, *alias* Bourne, Francis Grace, John Robinson, Ellis Worth), and printed them with a minimum of commentary;[36] the author follows this up in *Medieval and Renaissance Drama in England* with a re-think of the whole question of share-holding in the public playhouses, prompted by one of the wills, that of Francis Grace (1623), an actor and shareholder in the Lord Palsgrave's Men: it was clearly a more variable business than has been suspected, and one that changed over the Elizabethan-Jacobean period.[37] This is all presumably a spin-off from Cerasano's review of our knowledge of Philip Henslowe, announced here last year. David McPherson looks specifically and in detail at some of the accusations levelled at Renaissance dramatists – libel, bawdy, and blasphemy – tracing their provenance and identifying why they mattered in different degrees to different parties.[38] Lee Bliss's piece in the volume falls into a different category, but will interest those concerned with Shakespeare's impact on his contemporaries: she sees *Philaster* as a reworking not only of *Hamlet* (as argued by J. F. Danby) but also of *Othello* and *Twelfth Night*, reworkings which were not lazy plagiarisms but helped Beaumont and Fletcher define for the first time their own distinctive tragicomic mode.[39]

One of the indispensable aids to our appreciation of Shakespeare, *A Shakespeare Glossary*, has appeared in a new edition.[40] C. T. Onions compiled the first two editions of the *Glossary* with the aim of 'supplying definitions and illustrations of words or senses of words which are now obsolete or which survive only in archaic or provincial use'. Robert D. Eagleson retains this aim in the first new edition for almost seventy years, which incorporates much of the new thinking on Shakespeare's language in that time and has been helped in particular by the existence of two computer-generated concordances to Shakespeare's works (Howard-Hill and Spevack). Every

entry is now accompanied by at least one citation from the works and, wherever possible, by two other references to allow for comparisons; different parts of speech have been listed under a single head-word; foreign words have been brought into the main alphabetical listing; special symbols have been regularized and reduced. The result is a reference-book that is extremely easy to use, either casually or systematically; it is neatly printed and a good advertisement for the use of computers in the compilation of such works.

New editions of two plays will also be of interest. *A Yorkshire Tragedy*[41] has perhaps the strongest claim of any of the plays in the Shakespeare Apocrypha to have been at least partly written by Shakespeare himself; it was ascribed to him in both the 1608 and 1619 quartos (though the printer, Thomas Pavier, was none too scrupulous in such matters), and was adopted in the third and fourth Shakespeare folios. A. C. Cawley and Barry Gaines, the editors of this Revels edition (it is good to see volumes still coming out in the series) review the question of authorship, including recent strong claims for Middleton, but remain agnostic; the edition itself is admirably up to the Arden-style standards set by the series, though its brevity (the play was written to be performed in tandem with three others) makes one rather gulp at the price of £25. Sad

---

36 'New Renaissance Players' Wills', *Modern Philology*, 82 (1985), 299–304.

37 'The "Business" of Shareholding, the Fortune Playhouses, and Francis Grace's Will', 231–51.

38 'Three Charges against Sixteenth- and Seventeenth-Century Playwrights: Libel, Bawdy, and Blasphemy', 269–82.

39 'Three Plays in One: Shakespeare and *Philaster*', 153–70.

40 C. T. Onions, *A Shakespeare Glossary*, enlarged and revised throughout by Robert D. Eagleson (Clarendon Press, Oxford, 1986).

41 A. C. Cawley and Barry Gaines, eds, *A Yorkshire Tragedy*, The Revels Plays (Manchester University Press, Manchester and Dover, New Hampshire, 1986).

to relate, the copy I was sent to review was blank on pp. 81, 84–5, 88–9, 92–3 and 96, which I should not like to have found had I spent all that money. (The genre of 'domestic tragedy', to which the play belongs, is the subject of a piece by Lena Cowen Orlin which, though focused on *Arden of Feversham*, has wider perspectives;[42] she looks at the play in the context of Renaissance conceptions of the 'house' – and not just the great house, like Penshurst – as a microcosm of social order, emphasizing that Thomas Arden and later protagonists of 'domestic tragedy' were 'gentlemen', and not bourgeois or citizen heroes as is often loosely asserted). *Dr Faustus* is probably compared more often with the works of Shakespeare than any other single play. David Ormerod and Christopher Wortham have taken note of the shift in scholarly opinion, which now considers the 1604 (A-text) quarto closer to Marlowe's original script than the 1616 (B-text) quarto, which has held sway most of this century.[43] Their text is in modern spelling but retains the original lack of act and scene divisions; it is clearly printed, with copious notes *en regard* to the text; there is a detailed introduction which synthesizes much recent thinking about the play (though the emphasis is markedly on its intellectual content and context rather than its theatrical history or potential); and there is a useful bibliography.

Winifred Maynard's *Elizabethan Lyric Poetry and Its Music*,[44] establishes its credentials by analysing the variety of lyric forms and their settings in the great miscellanies and song-books of Elizabethan England, distinguishing between such forms as ballads, ayres, madrigals, consort-pieces, and songs for royal entertainments in their marriage of words and music (much of the latter having only recently been identified and published). On this foundation she looks with fresh eyes at the achievements of Sidney, Campion, and Jonson, against a detailed musicological account of Byrd, Gibbons, Ferrabosco, Dowland,

Morley, Lanier, Robert Johnson and others. The last third of the book examines the dramatic and literary uses of lyric in the works of Shakespeare, whom the author describes as 'the playwright who exploited the dramatic potentialities of song most variously and most fully and functionally' – a large claim, here well substantiated. The book is deeply learned without being over-technical, and is aptly illustrated from manuscripts and first editions. There are more detailed studies of many topics covered here (Jonson's dramatic lyrics, for example), but this is likely to remain for some time the standard scholarly overview of the Elizabethan lyric and of what its author sees as both its 'summation and summit' in the plays of Shakespeare. It was, unfortunately, published too late for anything more than a brief advance notice in Louise Schleiner's 'Recent Studies in Poetry and Music of the English Renaissance',[45] one of *English Literary Renaissance*'s invaluable review articles.

Jerzy Limon's *Dangerous Matter: English Drama and Politics 1623/24*[46] is a stimulating discussion of the politically charged theatrical season, 1623/4, in the wake of Prince Charles's unmarried and humiliated return from Spain, when the Prince and the Duke of Buckingham turned against King James's policy of friendship with Catholic Spain and favoured war with the old enemy. Dr Limon considers all the extant plays associated with this critical period, including Drue's *The Life of the Duchess of Suffolk*, Massinger's *The Bondman* and Middleton's *A Game at Chess*,

---

42 'Man's House as His Castle in *Arden of Feversham*', *Medieval and Renaissance Drama in England*, 2 (1985), 57–90.

43 David Ormerod and Christopher Wortham, eds, *Christopher Marlowe, Dr Faustus: the A-text* (University of Western Australia Press, Nedlands, Western Australia, 1985).

44 Clarendon Press, Oxford, 1986.

45 *English Literary Renaissance*, 16 (1986), 253–68.

46 Cambridge University Press, Cambridge, 1986.

and Jonson's unperformed masque, *Neptune's Triumph for the Return of Albion*, seeing them all as part of a campaign to promote the policies now espoused by the Prince and the Duke. This is not an old-fashioned exercise in allusion-spotting but a considered analysis of drama-as-propaganda, with a sophisticated theoretical rationale for how works of art relate to the political environment that creates them and how these dramatic works in particular alert their audiences to that relationship. I cannot agree with all of Dr Limon's emphases. I think, for example, that he underplays the role of the Earl of Pembroke who was both kinsman and immediate superior (as Lord Chamberlain) to Sir Henry Herbert, the Master of the Revels, the key figure in the censorship of the drama; it was at his estate, Wilton, that Sir Henry obtained the King's (apparently belated) consent to his purchase of the Mastership from the incumbent, Sir John Astley – in the midst of the religio-political agitation Dr Limon outlines so well. Pembroke had formerly been one of the staunchest opponents of Spain, though his attitude to war wavered when the Prince and the Duke adopted that policy. Might this have something to do with what some have suspected as satire aimed at Buckingham in the otherwise forthrightly anti-Spanish *A Game at Chess*? More generally, Dr Limon's conventional insistence on the 'severe censorship' of the day ought to be set alongside Philip J. Finkelpearl's important and persuasive rethinking of the censorship mechanisms that related to the Jacobean stage, in which he argues that they were neither as efficient nor in practice as daunting as they are often made out to be[47] – though this was published too late for Limon to have consulted it. But this remains an intelligent, challenging, and engaged book, written by someone for whom censorship is anything but an abstract academic issue. The whole discussion of drama in terms of its radical or subversive influence sits interestingly alongside Jonathan V. Crewe's analysis

of George Puttenham's rather neglected views on theatre in his *Arte of English Poesie* (1589): 'In Puttenham's terms, an unbreakable reciprocity exists between the public institutions of theater and the possibility of "good government", and no other theoretical or practical possibility exists for that theater.'[48]

Joseph P. Roach's *The Player's Passion: Studies in the Science of Acting*[49] is what the author calls a 'history of the theatricalization of the human body', looking at acting styles from the seventeenth century to the twentieth in relation to prevalent theories about the human body and its workings, particularly explanations of emotion and its manifestations; in an application of the history of science to the quasi-science of acting Professor Roach offers a resolution to the 'tiresome debate over the relative formalism or naturalism of seventeenth-century acting style' and insights into all major theories of acting since then, paying particular attention to Diderot. James L. Hill looks in detail at the demands placed on those playing the mature female roles in Shakespeare's tragedies, as compared with the male roles around them, in relation to their having been written for 'boy' actors.[50] Thomas Hyde is concerned with the heightened or artificial modes of self-representation employed in the tragic endings of some Elizabethan plays, notably *The Spanish Tragedy*, *Richard II*, *Richard III*, *Othello*, and *Hamlet*.[51] Davenant is a key figure in the seventeenth-century theatre and specifically in the transmission and adapt-

---

[47] '"The Comedians' Liberty": Censorship of the Jacobean Stage Reconsidered', *English Literary Renaissance*, 16 (1986), 123–38.

[48] 'The Hegemonic Theater of George Puttenham', *English Literary Renaissance*, 16 (1986), 71–85.

[49] University of Delaware Press, Newark, and Associated University Presses, London and Toronto, 1986.

[50] '"What, are they children?": Shakespeare's Tragic Women and the Boy Actors', *Studies in English Literature 1500–1900*, 26 (1986), 235–58.

[51] 'Identity and Acting in Elizabethan Tragedy', *Renaissance Drama*, NS 25 (1984), 93–114.

ation of Shakespeare's plays. Sophia B. Blaydes and Philip Bordinant have produced a comprehensive and user-friendly bibliography of works both by and on him.[52] Annotations are descriptive rather than critical, though there is some cross-referencing of scholarly debates; entries are arranged chronologically, but a detailed index allows for easy topical investigations. Students of Shakespeare's self-styled son will find this a useful tool, more helpful in many respects than the same authors' rather unsatisfactory volume on Davenant in the Twayne's English Authors series.

The chronicling of major Shakespearian productions and performances continues apace. One of the most curious by-products of the 'star' system in the nineteenth-century theatre was the phenomenon of international performers like the Italians Adelaide Ristori, Tomasso Salvini, and Ernesto Rossi,[53] most of whose performances in Britain and America were given in their native language; their appeal must have been akin to that of modern operatic stars, focused on technique almost for its own sake – a parallel reinforced by one photograph of the portly Rossi as Romeo, whose performance in that role must have demanded a considerable suspension of disbelief. The intensity with which they prepared for their star roles – in styles often markedly at odds with those in vogue in the English-speaking world – and their undoubted success in some of the virtuoso tragic roles, at least in some venues, is well charted by Marvin Carlson from contemporary reviews and accounts. Salvini's performance as Othello is one of the examples that James R. Siemon mentions in his analysis of how popular sentiment forced actors in the eighteenth and nineteenth centuries to alter the ending of Othello, and particularly the killing of Desdemona.[54] This might usefully be compared with Wilfred Harrison's day-by-day account of his own recent experience, as an English director, of preparing Polish actors to play Othello in

Polish, which he seems to have found taxing but rewarding.[55] Similarly, Karen Newman's feminist account of The Taming of the Shrew,[56] in which she looks at the play in the context of an actual skimmington on Plough Monday, 1604, and suggests that its 'patriarchal master narrative' is exposed as neither natural nor divinely ordained but culturally constructed, might illuminatingly be read alongside Geraldine Cousin's comparison of two recent productions of The Taming of the Shrew 'performed in non-conventional playing spaces', those of the Medieval Players in New College, Oxford and the RSC touring version.[57] Mary Hamer, in 'Shakespeare's Rosalind and Her Public Image', has reviewed the history of this particularly challenging proto-feminist role in the theatre.[58]

I conclude with two major studies of directors central to the history of Shakespearian production this century (as may be seen in Stanley Wells's overview of 'Shakespeare on the English Stage' in William Shakespeare: His World, His Work, His Influence). Dennis Kennedy's Granville-Barker and The Dream of Theatre[59] is the first full-length account of the earlier phase of Granville-Barker's engagement with the theatre, when he was actively involved as an actor, playwright, manager and

---

[52] Sir William Davenant: An Annotated Bibliography, 1629–1985 (Garland Publishing, Inc., New York, 1986).

[53] Marvin Carlson, The Italian Shakespearians (Folger Books, Washington: Folger Shakespeare Library, and Associated University Presses, London and Toronto, 1985).

[54] '"Nay, that's not the text": Othello, V.ii. in Performance 1766–1900', Shakespeare Quarterly, 37 (1986), 38–51.

[55] 'Othello in Poland: Notes from a Director's Diary', New Theatre Quarterly, 2 (1986), 154–74.

[56] 'Renaissance Family Politics and Shakespeare's The Taming of the Shrew', English Literary Renaissance, 16 (1986), 86–100.

[57] 'The Touring of the Shrew', New Theatre Quarterly, 2 (1986), 275–81.

[58] Theatre Research International, 11 (1986), 105–18.

[59] Cambridge University Press, Cambridge, 1985.

(though the term was not then current) director. Though it helps to put his later scholarly achievements (notably the *Prefaces to Shakespeare*) in context, it is mainly concerned to trace his practical contributions towards the development of a new style of theatre – a non-commercial repertory system acting plays of substance, with a proper regard for the integrity of the text, as against the established Victorian/Edwardian 'business' of dominant actor-managers, over-elaborate and time-consuming sets, and 'the long run'. That is, it sees Granville-Barker as a (or rather *the*) direct precursor of what finally emerged as the National Theatre. Professor Kennedy does this most convincingly by reconstructing all the productions in which Granville-Barker was involved – including his own plays, those of Shaw and the new Europeans, Euripides and Shakespeare – from eye-witness accounts, correspondence, account-books and prompt-copies. Perhaps the most telling 'proof' of his thesis is that everything emerges as so seamlessly modern, so much what we now expect of both the National Theatre and the Royal Shakespeare Company, that we have to keep reminding ourselves how revolutionary it was at the time. Shakespearians will find a good deal of specific interest, from comments on Granville-Barker's playing of the title role in William Poel's 1899 *Richard II* (he learned a lot from Poel but did not confuse respecting the integrity of the text with antiquarianism) to his uncredited direction with Lewis Casson of John Gielgud's 1940 *King Lear*, a rare re-emergence into practical theatre late in his career. But most attention will focus on the three remarkable Savoy productions of Shakespeare: *The Winter's Tale* and *Twelfth Night* (1912) and *A Midsummer Night's Dream* (1914), played with virtually uncut texts, no naturalistic scenery, orchestra pit, or footlights, and breaking out of the proscenium arch with suggestions of what scholars then thought the Elizabethan stage was like (including a raised 'inner stage') but without antiquarian severity

– indeed, some of the sets, costumes and back-drops were described as 'Post-Impressionist'. The text is supported with over forty photographs which, though 'posed', give a vivid impression of what must have seemed so unusual to audiences of the time, none more so than the frontispiece, rare colour photographs of the stunning 'golden fairies' of *A Midsummer Night's Dream*.

Michael L. Greenwald's *Directions by Indirections: John Barton of the Royal Shakespeare Company*[60] is about a distinguished Shakespearian director still very much with us. Barton's reputation has always languished behind that of Peter Hall and Trevor Nunn, partly because of his own reticence about giving interviews, and Professor Greenwald has performed a valuable service in documenting this distinctive career from its roots in Cambridge (though both he and Barton are anxious to dismiss the 'scholar' label that has dogged him), through his establishment of a verse-speaking style with the RSC, his famous-notorious 'adaptations' of Shakespeare and others (including *The Taming of the Shrew*, the *Wars of the Roses* cycle, *King John*, *Dr Faustus*, *The Greeks* and *The Vikings*), his most notable successes (including the Judi Dench/Donald Sinden *Twelfth Night*, the Richard Pasco/Ian Richardson *Richard II*, the 'problem plays' – *All's Well That Ends Well* and *Troilus and Cressida*, the Victorian *Much Ado About Nothing* and *Othello*, the myth/magic *Merchant of Venice* and *The Winter's Tale*) to his recent work with more modern playwrights (including Schnitzler and Whiting). The style and method of the book, however, are not always what one might have wished. I am not sure that it helps even an American readership to describe the RSC as 'prestigious' or the Prospect Theatre Company as 'acclaimed' or to keep talking of Cambridge as having a campus. Barton, we

---

60 University of Delaware Press, Newark, and Associated University Presses, London and Toronto, 1986.

are assured, was 'the most respected theater figure on campus'; and it is difficult not to wince for other reasons when told that 'throughout his Cambridge days Barton was a man of uncommon vision'. To be fair, there is less of this once Barton is safely established with the RSC but then another problem takes over. Professor Greenwald has been most assiduous about interviewing people who have worked with or around his subject, and Barton himself (with a tape-recorder, I suspect). Much of the substance of the book is derived from these interviews, spliced and re-arranged; some of those he spoke to (including Barton) do not emerge from this process as notably articulate, while with others candour is naturally always debatable, and the author rarely makes allowances for either problem. The result is an over-deferential book without a strong or convincing thesis about its subject.

Perhaps this is appropriate for a career still in progress and I must not give the impression that there is not here a good deal of solid information and analysis, because there is; but not all readers will welcome the style in which it is conveyed.

Speaking of the RSC, an endnote. Paul Bertram and Frank Cossa reopen the question of the authenticity of the 'Flower Portrait' of Shakespeare (which hangs in the galleries of the RSC's Royal Shakespeare Theatre at Stratford) in the light of its 1979 restoration. Long thought of as an eighteenth-century copy (or a fake, in view of its '1609' inscription), they are not now so sure.[61] Could we really have been looking at a portrait of the man, from the life, all this time?

---

[61] '"Willm Shakespeare 1609": The Flower Portrait Revisited', *Shakespeare Quarterly*, 37 (1986), 83–96.

3. EDITIONS AND TEXTUAL STUDIES
reviewed by MacDonald P. Jackson

'No longer the tiresome repetitions: "Who is the real author?" "Have we proof of his authenticity and originality?"', urges Michel Foucault. However, theorists who share his views continue to publish books under their own names – and to collect their royalties. And questions of authorship still arouse widespread interest. When they concern Shakespeare the stakes are high. For admission to the Shakespeare canon confers status on a work, guaranteeing sympathetic attention from critics, producers, readers, and playgoers. Had *1 Henry VI* been excluded from the First Folio, would it have appeared quite the unified product of youthful genius that commentators find it today? And had the anonymous chronicle play *Edmund Ironside*, preserved in a manuscript of the late-sixteenth or early-seventeenth century, been included in the First Folio, would everyone have accepted its authenticity? Eric Sams believes so, and has published a modern-

spelling edition with introduction and elaborate commentary designed to convince us that *Edmund Ironside* was written by Shakespeare at the beginning of his career as a dramatist.[1]

There is a right way to go about confirming such a theory. Supposing he has established a date of around 1588 for the composition of *Edmund Ironside*, the investigator must seek quantifiable variables of style, diction, orthography, and so on, that can in combination serve to discriminate each early play undoubtedly Shakespeare's from all extant plays known to have been written for the public stage by other dramatists during the period 1585–95 (let us say), and then show that application of the distinguishing criteria to *Edmund Ironside* associates it unequivocally

---

[1] *Shakespeare's Lost Play Edmund Ironside*, ed. Eric Sams (Fourth Estate, London, 1985).

with the Shakespearian plays.[2] Eric Sams does not attempt this arduous task. Instead he cites a multitude of parallels in phraseology, dramatic technique, concatenation of images, and the like, between *Edmund Ironside* and the earliest Folio plays, especially *Titus Andronicus* and *1 Henry VI*. His argument thus rests on the assumption that a similar range of links could not be found between *Edmund Ironside* and any non-Shakespearian play. But since parallel-hunters of the late nineteenth and early twentieth centuries, using Sams's methods, were wildly at variance with one another in their attributions of anonymous Renaissance plays, this assumption cannot be the self-evident truth Sams believes it to be.

Sams (p. 2) likens his procedures to those of R. W. Chambers in his famous essay on Hand D's contribution to *Sir Thomas More*, and quotes Chambers's analogy: 'You have to meet in a crowd a Mr. Harris, hitherto unknown to you, but who, you are informed, has red hair, wears a monocle and walks with a limp. You address with some confidence a stranger possessing these characteristics; and if he responded to the name of Harris, you would accept the identification, without brooding over the fact that there are nearly a thousand Harrises in the London Telephone Directory alone.' True enough, but while the proportion of the total population who wear a monocle, have red hair, walk with a limp, or answer to the name of Harris is undoubtedly low, Elizabethan plays which, like *Edmund Ironside*, contain the idea of 'hammering in the brain', for example, are much less scarce. Sams (p. 308) points to three early Shakespearian instances, but in Thomas Lodge's *The Wounds of Civil War* no fewer than four hammerings in the brain, head, or heart are associated with plots and revenge. Likewise, a 'special trick' exhibited in *Edmund Ironside* and said to characterize Shakespeare 'in his early *Titus* phase' – the setting of a vocative between repeated words, as in 'stay, Edmund, stay' – occurs at least sixteen times in Henry Porter's *Two Angry Women of Abingdon*. Sams would doubtless reply that the significance of the links between *Edmund Ironside* and *1 Henry VI* (or *Titus Andronicus*) lies in their multiplicity, but the number of resemblances between any two plays is potentially infinite. In the identification of 'Harris' a limited set of rare attributes has been specified in advance, whereas Sams's procedure leaves him free to make a *post hoc* inventory of any similarities at all. Stand Harris beside any man in the street and the pair will turn out to have many of their innumerable characteristics in common, over and above those that declare them to be human: both wear black shoes, are left-handed, have moustaches, carry umbrellas, are six feet tall, and answer to 'Hey, you!' We might even reckon probabilities – one in ten men is left-handed, one in eight wears a moustache, and so on – and enlarge the list to the point where multiplying the separate odds would produce a billion-to-one coincidence. Harris must have met his *doppelgänger*! No, the passer-by is a stout Caucasian and Harris is a slim West Indian. The total absence of constraints on our search for resemblances renders the calculations meaningless.[3]

One further argument advanced by Sams deserves comment. Drawing on the admirable work of Eliot Slater, who proved that Shake-

---

[2] Strictly speaking, both the Shakespearian and the non-Shakespearian plays should be randomly divided into two groups, one being used to generate the criteria for Shakespearian authorship and the other to test their reliability. This is because of the 'regression effect', described by statisticians Frederick Mosteller and David L. Wallace, *Inference and Disputed Authorship: The Federalist* (Addison Wesley, Reading, Mass., 1964), 200.

[3] Compare Richard Levin's chapter on 'Fluellenism' in *New Readings vs. Old Plays* (University of Chicago Press, 1979), 209–29. Chambers's claims were buttressed by other scholars' evidence from handwriting and from bibliographical and orthographical links between Hand D and the Shakespearian good quartos. Moreover, to anyone familiar with Shakespeare's style the *More* attribution has a strong *prima facie* plausibility, whereas the *Edmund Ironside* attribution does not.

spearian plays written at about the same time shared more of their rare-word vocabulary than Shakespeare plays written at different times, Sams shows that the rarer words in *Edmund Ironside* occur much more frequently in the earliest Shakespeare plays than in the later ones, and claims that since the association cannot have arisen by chance Shakespeare must have written *Edmund Ironside*.[4] His argument thus takes the form of a fallacy: all Shakespeare plays display a certain relationship between vocabulary and the date of composition; *Edmund Ironside* displays such a relationship; therefore *Edmund Ironside* is a Shakespeare play. In fact, we would expect the vocabulary of most non-Shakespearian plays written between 1585 and 1605 to be more closely connected to the vocabulary of the early Shakespeare than to that of the far more distinctive later Shakespeare. It is virtually certain that *The Spanish Tragedy, James IV, Edward II*, and *Locrine*, for example, share significantly more of their rare words with *1 Henry VI* and *Titus Andronicus* than with *Antony and Cleopatra* and *The Winter's Tale*.

Despite the flaws in his methodology, Sams may nevertheless be right. Certainly the verse of *Edmund Ironside* is not markedly worse than that of many scenes in *1 Henry VI*. The value of Sams's book is that it raises vital questions about Shakespeare's beginnings as dramatist. Accepting *1 Henry VI* and *Titus Andronicus* as wholly Shakespeare's and as the first-composed of the Folio plays, Sams regards *Edmund Ironside* as their immediate predecessor. His evidence for dating *Edmund Ironside* about 1588 is inconclusive, and in the Oxford Shakespeare's *Complete Works Titus Andronicus* and *1 Henry VI* are placed fifth and sixth in the chronological sequence, while the latter is judged to be only partially Shakespeare's.[5] The case for disintegrating *1 Henry VI* (and attributing act 1 to Thomas Nashe) seems to me strong.[6] What we need now is a thorough statistical survey of the idiosyncrasies of the various Tudor dramatists, conducted along the same lines as the investigations of Cyrus Hoy, David Lake, and others into problems of authorship in Jacobean and Caroline drama.[7]

Even less persuasive than Sams's case is Mark Dominik's for giving credence to the title-page ascription of *The Birth of Merlin* (1662) to William Shakespeare and William Rowley.[8] While few scholars have doubted Rowley's participation in the play, fewer still have seen signs of Shakespeare's. But Dominik, dating the composition around 1613–15, after the late romances, believes *The Birth of Merlin* to be 'not part-Shakespeare and part-Rowley' but 'entirely Shakespeare-and-Rowley' (p. 10). He posits a process of 'dilution', as though Rowley were the water in Shakespeare's whisky, but how this analogy translates into the business of putting dialogue

---

[4] The fullest account of Slater's work is in his 'The Problem of *The Reign of King Edward III*, 1596: A Statistical Approach' (PhD dissertation, University of London, 1981), but he also published a series of articles in *Notes and Queries* from 1975 to 1978.

[5] William Shakespeare, *The Complete Works*, eds. Stanley Wells, Gary Taylor, John Jowett, and William Montgomery (Clarendon Press, Oxford, 1986). This modern-spelling volume is briefly noticed at the end of this review and will be examined in detail in *Shakespeare Survey 41*.

[6] It has been made in an article by Gary Taylor, 'Shakespeare and Others: The Composition of *Henry the Sixth Part One*', forthcoming in *Medieval and Renaissance Drama in England*.

[7] Hoy's studies of the Beaumont and Fletcher canon appeared in *Studies in Bibliography* from 1956 to 1962; see also Lake, *The Canon of Thomas Middleton's Plays* (Cambridge University Press, 1975); MacD. P. Jackson, *Studies in Attribution: Middleton and Shakespeare* (University of Salzburg, 1979); R. V. Holdsworth, *Middleton and Shakespeare: The Case for Middleton's Hand in 'Timon of Athens'* (Clarendon Press, Oxford, forthcoming). A possible clue to the authorship of *Edmund Ironside* is the frequency of 'whenas' meaning 'when': there are at least eleven examples, considerably more than in the whole Shakespeare canon. The many instances of 'ye' also tell against Shakespeare's authorship.

[8] *William Shakespeare and 'The Birth of Merlin'* (Philosophical Library, New York, 1985).

on to paper is never explained. Elsewhere Dominik writes of an 'intimate collaboration' (p. 151), but since this is said to have 'obscured' the familiar lustre of Shakespeare's style (p. 103), we would have to suppose that Rowley was arrogant or stupid enough to re-write a Shakespearian script, while somehow contriving to retain those turns of phrase and clusters of images that Dominik considers typically Shakespearian. But for Dominik almost any expression is 'reminiscent of Shakespeare': so 'blunt and rude' in *The Birth of Merlin* reminds him of Shakespeare's 'blunt and saucy', 'blunt and ill', 'rude and savage', and 'rude and merciless' (p. 73). He compiles lists of such 'evidence'. His chapter on spellings and linguistic forms (pp. 43–56) is very naive. He does make some interesting comments on the play, which contains several powerful passages. Like most seventeenth-century plays, it bears traces of Shakespeare's influence. To be taken seriously, Dominik needs to discover reliable discriminators between the works of Shakespeare's final period and the works of Rowley and every other potential contributor to *The Birth of Merlin*, and then find them in the doubtful play.

The most widely publicized recent attempt to add to the Shakespeare canon is the most difficult to assess. A lyric of ninety short lines allows little scope for valid stylistic or linguistic tests. Gary Taylor's claim for 'Shall I die?' is thus heavily dependent on the external evidence – the unequivocal ascription to Shakespeare in a manuscript miscellany compiled in the late 1630s and preserved in the Bodleian Library.[9]

Certain points emerge from scholarly debate on the subject. A substantial majority of the Bodleian compilation's fifty-four other ascriptions are unquestionably correct, and of the four that are highly suspect three were widely credited in the 1630s; and early seventeenth-century manuscript ascriptions of poems to Shakespeare are, unlike those to

Donne and Jonson, generally accurate. So the external evidence deserves respect. Taylor cites many verbal parallels between the poem and Shakespeare's acknowledged works. Theoretical objections to Sams's evidence are equally applicable here. The Shakespeare canon is large, consisting mainly of drama, and any comparison with the number of parallels between 'Shall I die?' and the canons of other poets is complicated not only by the different size and generic make-up of the comparative material but also by the difficulty of maintaining consistent standards in defining parallels. Taylor points out that some twenty-two of his Shakespearian parallels survive a 'negative check' in the available concordances to the poems of Spenser, Sidney, Jonson, Donne, and Marvell, and to the works of Marlowe, Herbert, Herrick, and Crashaw. This is encouraging, but were we to begin with a long list of parallels between 'Shall I die?' and the poems of Spenser, for example, it is likely enough that after we had checked the concordances to Shakespeare and others a residue of distinctively 'Spenserian' phrases would

---

[9] There is a variant text in another miscellany in the Beinecke Library at Yale University; there the poem is unascribed. See Taylor's 'A new Shakespeare poem? The evidence . . .', *Times Literary Supplement*, 20 December 1985, pp. 1447–8, followed by Robin Robbins, '. . . and the counter-arguments', pp. 1449–50; Taylor's article also appeared in the *New York Times Book Review*, 15 December 1985, pp. 11–14. Correspondence followed in both journals, the most significant being that of Peter Beal in the *Times Literary Supplement*, 3 January 1986, p. 13. Taylor answered his critics in ' "Shall I die?" immortalized?', *Times Literary Supplement*, 31 January 1986, pp. 123–4. Two further articles on studies of the Shakespeare canon may be mentioned here: G. Harold Metz, 'Disputed Shakespearean Texts and Stylometric Analysis', *Text: Transactions of the Society for Textual Scholarship 2*, ed. D. C. Greetham and W. Speed Hill (AMS Press, New York 1985), 149–71; M. W. A. Smith, 'An Investigation of the Basis of Morton's Method for the Determination of Authorship', *Style*, 19 (1985), 341–68. Metz expounds Morton's methods, while Smith exposes flaws in the ways they have been used.

remain.[10] Little significance can be attached to the fact that the Shakespearian parallels with 'Shall I die?' are mainly in early works (especially *Venus and Adonis, Romeo and Juliet,* and *The Taming of the Shrew*), as are links in rare words. I should expect most madrigals, lute songs, and lyrics of the late-Elizabethan, Jacobean, and even Caroline periods to yield a similar pattern.

One promising line of inquiry comes from Bradley Efron and Ronald Thisted, who, with the help of sophisticated statistical techniques, were able to predict, from data in Spevack's Shakespeare concordance, the number of words never used in the canonical works, and the number used once, twice, three times, and so on, that would turn up in any newly discovered Shakespearian work of a specified size.[11] 'Shall I die?' affords a remarkably good match to the estimates. Poems by Donne, Marlowe, and Jonson do not. If in a large sample of non-Shakespearian lyrics similar in kind to 'Shall I die?' none or few were to meet the expectations of the Efron and Thisted model, the case for Shakespeare's authorship of the piece would be greatly strengthened. Taylor promises further analysis of the Bodleian miscellany. The poem's status remains doubtful. It is an ingenious and lively piece of rhyming, and seems by no means out of place among the Oxford Shakespeare's 'Various Poems', alongside stray epitaphs and epigrams and winnowings from *The Passionate Pilgrim.*

No doubts over authorship need trouble readers of the two comedies now added to the New Cambridge series, but minor irritations may be caused by cruxes in the First Folio, on which modern texts of *All's Well That Ends Well,* and *Twelfth Night* must be based.[12] Russell Fraser brings little relief. His edition of *All's Well That Ends Well* is doggedly conservative. He retains F's 'I see that men make rope's in such a scarre,/That we'll forsake ourselves' at 4.2.38–9, regarding the text as 'irrecoverably corrupt'. Daniel's conjecture,

adopted by Sisson – 'may rope's in such a snare' – provides a plausible alternative. At least Shakespeare *might* have written it, which is more than one can say for F's utter nonsense. At 2.4.27 Fraser recognizes that a short speech by Parolles has probably dropped out, but does not record conjectural restorations in his collation notes, though it is not hard to see that something like Nicholson's 'In myself', adopted by Dover Wilson, is required. Among other sensible emendations that he rejects are: 'e'en' (F 'in') at 1.3.33, 'fits' (F 'shifts') at 2.1.140, 'coacher' (F 'torcher') at 2.1.158, 'nay' (F 'ne') at 2.1.169, 'heaven' (F 'help') at 2.1.188, 'when' (F 'whence') at 2.3.117, 'fortunes' (F 'fortune') at 2.4.12, 'or wit or will' (F 'or will') at 2.5.41, 'think not' (F 'think') at 2.5.44, 'heard' (F 'hear') at 3.2.37, 'still-piecing' (F 'still-peering', F2 'still-piercing') at 3.2.102, 'are you' (F 'are') at 3.5.26, 'warrant' (F 'write') at 3.5.59, 'mute' (F 'mule') at 4.1.33, 'name' (F 'maine') at 4.5.30, 'inf'nite' or possibly 'ancient' (F 'insuite') at 5.3.214. Fraser admits that no other instance of 'torcher' (2.1.158), meaning torch-bearer, is recorded by *OED*, but regards Hunter's 'coacher' (charioteer) as 'a needless improvement'. But it makes little sense to have the

---

[10] To return to 'Harris', the long list of attributes he shares with Smith will dwindle as we subtract those that he also shares with Brown and Jones. But some will remain. However, if we begin by listing similarities between Harris and Jones, we will likewise be left with a residue after eliminating those that also link Harris to Smith and Brown.

[11] 'Estimating the number of unseen species: How many words did Shakespeare know?', *Biometrika*, 63 (1976), 435; their research on 'Shall I die?' is reported by Gina Kolata, 'Shakespeare's New Poem: An Ode to Statistics', *Science*, 231 (24 January 1986), 335–6.

[12] *All's Well That Ends Well*, ed. Russell Fraser, and *Twelfth Night*, ed. Elizabeth Story Donno, both published by Cambridge University Press, 1985. My line references are to the editions reviewed, or, in comments on articles, notes, and other books, to *The Riverside Shakespeare*, ed. G. Blakemore Evans (Boston, 1974).

sun-god (Phoebus or Helios) as torch-bearer to his own horses, which 'bring' him along his daily course; their 'torcher' would be 'bringing' them. And since all seventeenth-century torches are 'fiery', 'coacher', which could easily be misread as 'torcher', has the further advantage of removing a pleonasm.

Alice Walker's transposition of 'not to find' to 'to find not' so markedly improves the metre of 1.3.188 that it must surely restore Shakespeare's original. Transposition of 'have' and 'by the great'st', to give 'When miracles by th' great'st have been denied', would similarly regularize 2.1.137.[13] Some of the names listed by Parolles at 4.3.136–9 seem too bizarre to be correct: 'Guiltian' looks like an error for Guilliam, and 'Chitopher' for Christopher. Commas might helpfully have enclosed 'hourly' in 'call her hourly mistress' at 3.2.75. At 1.1.30–1 Fraser's punctuation ('promises. Her') makes for less pregnant sense than 'I have those hopes of her good that her education promises her dispositions she inherits, which makes fair gifts fairer', where 'her dispositions she inherits' means 'the dispositions that she inherits'.

There are at least two trivial errors in Fraser's text. At 2.3.20 F has 'shall read' not 'will read', and at 2.3.66 F has 'nere' ('ne'er') not 'never'. The Italian *capriccio* and *coraggio* anomalously appear as 'caprichio' (taken over from F) and 'corragio' (F 'Coragio') at 2.3.270 and 2.5.86. This is nit-picking. A more substantial complaint is that, like most editors, Fraser fails to mark asides in the scenes in which Parolles is gulled, 4.1 and 4.3.

Fraser's 'Textual Analysis' concludes that behind the Folio lay Shakespeare's own papers, containing 'authorial inconsistencies or changes of mind' (p. 152). His account of the Folio compositors ignores Howard-Hill's demonstration, supported by O'Connor, that signatures V3 and V3v were set by Compositor D.[14] His commentary is excellent: this is the most helpfully annotated edition available. But his note on 'mites' at 1.1.123 misses the point of Parolles's delightfully paradoxical 'Virginity breeds mites, much like a cheese; consumes itself to the very paring, and so dies with feeding his own stomach.' Fraser says: 'These tiny spiders carry disease and are therefore inimical to the host.' Disease is irrelevant, or at best incidental: the point is that the more the cheese-mites flourish and multiply, the more quickly they devour the cheese that is the source of their vitality, and so hasten their own death by starvation. The application of this image of a hyperactive closed system to 'virginity', which commits a form of genocide through its passive failure to 'breed', complicates the paradoxes to the point where Parolles is in danger of deconstructing his own rhetoric.

The mingling of contrasting styles in *All's Well That Ends Well* has sometimes been taken to indicate that it was composed in the sixteenth century and revised in the seventeenth. Fraser, in a subtle analysis, sees the variations as functional, rightly stresses the play's affinities with the late romances, and dates it about 1605, as offering 'a sceptical recension' of material deployed in *Measure for Measure*. His critical account of the play is a densely, and at times obliquely, written investigation of its *chiaroscuro*. For him, the 'swapping back and forth of goodness and badness, faults and virtues, thorns and leaves – disparate things on

---

[13] The unemended line would be a good hexameter if 'great'st' were allowed the unelided 'est' ending, but the Folio compositors were much less inclined to introduce elisions than to expand them, and 'great'st' does not appear within a full ('justified') line of print. Besides, a rhymed pentameter couplet seems to be intended. Fraser calls 2.3.50, which also rhymes with a normal pentameter, a hexameter line: 'Thou hast power to choose, and they none to forsake.' But the metre is much more natural if 'Thou hast' is elided in pronunciation ('Thou'st') and 'power' taken as monosyllabic.

[14] T. H. Howard-Hill, 'The Compositors of Shakespeare's Folio Comedies', *Studies in Bibliography*, 26 (1973), 61–106; John S. O'Connor, 'Compositors D and F of the Shakespeare First Folio', *Studies in Bibliography*, 28 (1975), 81–117.

any conventional reading – affords the central insight of *All's Well That Ends Well*, a 'great play whose time has come round' (pp. 26, 8). He detects in its many structural and verbal echoes a blurring of moral distinctions that suggests 'the radical sameness of characters who differ superficially' (p. 14). In illustrating this process of homogenization he often distorts theatrical effects and the dialogue's plain sense. 'Shakespeare's readiness to withhold powers of perception' even from characters as mature and sagacious as the Countess (p. 17) cannot reasonably be inferred from her avowal that she has 'no skill in sense / To make distinction' (3.4.39–40). Returned to their context, the Countess's words are a simple and moving declaration that she loves Helen and Bertram equally. I think that Fraser reads too much into Helen's gnomic rhymes at the end of 1.1, where she determines to take the initiative: they are not overweening, just plucky. Fraser's valuable section on the play's stage history ends with the observation that while 'the television cameras in recent years have given us an *All's Well* that does indeed end well, the theatre has left us a touch more sceptical – "All yet seems well" '. 'Seems' is the operative word for Fraser. But the more complicated, questioning presentation is not necessarily the more Shakespearian, or the more profound.

A persistent strain of melancholy does darken the riot and romance of *Twelfth Night*, including its ending, with Feste's infinitely evocative song. Elizabeth Story Donno's critical introduction to this most perfect of Shakespeare's comedies disappointingly fails to convey, or even suggest, its 'bitter-sweet' essence. The Penguin and Riverside editors seem more fully attuned to the play. Donno is another critic keen to note occasions 'when an attitude or an action or situation relating to one character is duplicated by another', to the point where it seems that 'many touches of nature make the whole world kin' (p. 17). No doubt similarities exist between Olivia and Malvolio

(pp. 17–18), but so what? This is Sams's 'salmons in both' parallel-hunting applied to criticism. There are incidental points of interest in Donno's account – her stress on the youth of the main characters, a pertinent quotation from Donne, and another from a young nobleman, Anthony Browne, on the duties of stewards – and the many illustrations, from engravings and production photographs, brighten the volume. The general editor of the series, Philip Brockbank, has brought up-to-date Donno's stage history, which outlines the various ways in which Malvolio's part has been acted. In the section on the play's date of composition Donno points to the consistency of its seasonal allusions (late spring or early summer) as confirming 'the metaphorical nature of the title *Twelfth Night*' (p. 4); she inclines to a date about the middle of 1601.

Donno gives a full and lucid account of the textual situation for the play, agreeing with Robert K. Turner that copy for the Folio was a scribal transcript from Shakespeare's foul papers; she argues that evidence so far adduced does not rule out Ralph Crane as possible scribe. She appears to be unaware of Paul Werstine's partial vindication of Folio Compositor B, who set *Twelfth Night*, from charges of extreme high-handedness with his copy.[15] Her own handling of the text is, in the main, admirable. She is judicious in drawing on the emendations of her predecessors, and in defending her decisions she gets straight to the point. Several errors have, however, survived the proof-reading: 'yet' has been omitted from 2.1.6, and 'to' from 2.3.6; at 3.4.271 'comes' should be 'come', and at 5.1.148 'th'' is an accidental interpolation. The commentary is very full and helpful. Musical settings for the songs are not included in the volume.

---

[15] See Werstine's essay, 'Folio Editors, Folio Compositors, and the Folio Text of *King Lear*', in *The Division of the Kingdoms*, eds. Gary Taylor and Michael Warren (Clarendon Press, Oxford, 1983), 247–312.

A well-known crux in *Twelfth Night* is Sir Andrew Aguecheek's coy boast that his leg 'does indifferent well in a dam'd colour'd stocke' (1.3.109–10). Donno accepts Collier's emendation to 'dun-coloured', pointing out that, though some editors consider dun too drab for Sir Andrew, Shakespeare's fellow actor-sharer in the King's Company, Augustine Phillips, bequeathed to his apprentice his 'mouse coloured Velvit hose'. Stanley Wells proposed 'divers-coloured'.[16] Barbara Everett, after a subtle examination of the equivocal social overtones that yellow stockings (such as those Malvolio is duped into wearing) had acquired by 1601, makes out a strong case for seeing Sir Andrew's hose as 'lemon-coloured'; she posits misreading of 'limond' as 'damnd', which is undoubtedly possible.[17] Her concern in a long and elegantly written article is with '*two* damned cruces' – the other occurring in Iago's notorious denigration of Cassio as 'A Fellow almost damn'd in a faire Wife' (F, 1.1.21). Her thorough discussion of the crux produces the solution 'almost *limned* in a fair wife', meaning that Cassio is 'almost describable as', 'the virtual equivalent of' a fair wife: Iago is calling Cassio a cissy. Everett shows how 'textual problems may take us into the depths of a writer's work' (p. 97).

David Amneus has a very different explanation for Iago's scornful words.[18] For him they are vestiges of an earlier state of *Othello* in which Cassio was married and Iago was not. In fact, the gist of the argument of his book is that the *Othello* we know from the Quarto of 1622 and the First Folio of 1623 is a twice revised version of what had originally been a more coherent play, one without the famous 'double time' scheme, without Roderigo, and with a far more credibly motivated hero and villain. *Othello-I* he assigns to 1602, *Othello-II* to 1606 or later, and *Othello-III* to 1612. His case rests on anomalies within the play as it has come down to us and on discrepancies between the extant *Othello* and a twenty-six-

stanza ballad which he believes to have been based on the lost *Othello-I*. This ballad, preserved in a British Library manuscript and entitled 'The Tragedie of Othello the Moore', has been dismissed as a Collier forgery, but Amneus judges it to be a genuine composition of around 1620 that Collier merely transcribed. As he recognizes, his theory requires that the King's Men chose to revive the hypothetical earliest version of *Othello*, recalled by the balladeer, at about the same time as two of the company's members, Heminges and Condell, were arranging to put *Othello-III* into print, in the First Folio. This is, on the face of it, unlikely.

Amneus sometimes sees clear discrepancies between the ballad and the extant tragedy where others might consider the ballad vague or elliptical, as ballads often are, and he tends also to exaggerate the obtrusiveness of the play's anomalies. But he manages to fit the complementary items of evidence neatly together, and he has obviously thought long and hard about the play. The evidence adduced is inadequate to sustain his hypothesis, but there is one means by which it might be confirmed. Amneus seems confident that he can, at least roughly, separate the play's three strata. If he is right about the dates of composition and revision, the three strata ought, on Eliot Slater's rare-vocabulary tests, to show markedly different distributions of links with Shakespeare's other plays; the vocabulary of passages introduced into *Othello-III* should be demonstrably later than that belonging to the original script.

Amneus also discusses the relationship between the Quarto and Folio texts. His

---

[16] *Re-editing Shakespeare for the Modern Reader* (Clarendon Press, Oxford, 1984), 34.

[17] 'Two Damned Cruces: *Othello* and *Twelfth Night*', *Review of English Studies*, NS 37 (1986), 184–97.

[18] *The Three 'Othellos'* (Primrose Press, Alhambra, Ca., 1986). My brief quotation of Amneus's findings is from the book's cover.

findings are that copy for Q 'consisted of the *Othello-II* promptbook plus Shakespeare's own autograph *Othello-III* alterations made in its margins and on interleaves', and that the copy for F was a transcript of this document, edited, expurgated, and sophisticated by a careless and pedantic scribe. He concludes that Q should form the basis of a modern edition. He is often perceptive about Q/F variants. Editors might profitably take account of his observations. Few will grant that the whole theoretical edifice rests on solid foundations.

While speculations about lost stages of a play's evolution as theatrical script have been unfashionable since the days of John Dover Wilson, belief that major divergences between Quarto and Folio are for some plays the result of revision by Shakespeare is steadily gaining ground. In 'Shakespeare as Reviser', E. A. J. Honigmann, whose *The Stability of Shakespeare's Text* (Edward Arnold, London, 1965) pioneered the new developments, looks yet again at certain Q/F variants in *Othello* and *King Lear*, especially, and argues that evidence that Shakespeare changed the ending or the planned ending of these two plays and of *Troilus and Cressida*, *1 Henry IV*, and *The Rape of Lucrece* 'is both textual and literary, both internal and external, and this evidence is mutually supportive' (p. 11).[19] Like Everett, he is excited by the potential interchange between the disciplines of textual and literary criticism: 'The new work on Shakespeare's "revisions" is of the first importance to his literary critics and editors. It carries us far beyond the limited horizons of "The Disintegration of Shakespeare" and opens up new critical territories: strategies of revision, the adjustable ending, radically different editions' (pp. 21–2).

In another paper Honigmann re-examines the puzzling case of *Troilus and Cressida*.[20] His conclusions may be summarized as follows: The play was written in the early months of 1601. Though not performed on the public stage, because of its dangerous, though un-

intended echoing of the Essex story, it was given a private performance, perhaps at Cambridge. Shakespeare conceived the play as a tragedy, but changed his plans while writing the last act, which anticipates a sequel that never eventuated. Since the play could not be viewed at the Globe, an influential admirer wanted to read it. So Shakespeare wrote out a fair copy, into which he introduced revisions. This manuscript was printed as Q. Shakespeare made his fair copy from his own foul papers, which, with some tidying up in which the playwright himself assisted, also formed the basis for the private production and, via a scribal copy, reached print as the Folio text (pp. 53–4). This is a complex hypothesis about complex data. Honigmann inclines to reject Gary Taylor's simpler view (outlined in *Shakespeare Survey 37*, p. 205) that Q *Troilus and Cressida* transmits the foul papers, F a later text prepared for the theatre. At least Honigmann and Taylor agree that revision has taken place.

Steven Urkowitz is an even more thoroughgoing revisionist.[21] Having argued for two *King Lears*, he now turns his attention to the three versions of *Hamlet* preserved in Q1 (1603), Q2 (1604/5), and F, and notes that when the texts are examined for theatrical 'cues encoded on the page', differences that seem purposeful rather than accidental appear in the presentation of certain key moments. He believes that Shakespeare himself was respon-

---

[19] *Textual Criticism and Literary Interpretation*, ed. Jerome J. McGann (University of Chicago Press, 1985), 1–22.

[20] 'The Date and Revision of *Troilus and Cressida*', *Textual Criticism and Literary Interpretation*, pp. 38–54.

[21] ' "Well-sayd olde Mole": Burying Three *Hamlets* in Modern Editions', *Shakespeare Study Today*, ed. Georgianna Ziegler (AMS Press, New York, 1986), pp. 37–70. Revision is also the theme of Gary Taylor's 'Some Manuscripts of Shakespeare's Sonnets', *Bulletin of the John Rylands University Library of Manchester*, 68 (1985), 210–46; this provides the full data on which his *Times Literary Supplement* piece, noticed last year (*Shakespeare Survey 39*, p. 250), was based.

sible for these 'theatrical variants' (p. 67), disapproves of modern editorial attempts to conflate Q1, Q2 and F into a single 'text that Shakespeare intended', and is convinced that 'present-day students, actors, and directors would be interested in trying out the alternative versions' of sequences of action and business 'if editors could only find a way to inform their readers of the richness of the scripts underlying their eclectic texts' (p. 63).

Further illustration of this last point is furnished in S. P. Zitner's witty cogitations over a choice of stage business in *Hamlet* that affects understanding of character and plot. In 5.1 should Hamlet leap into Ophelia's grave after Laertes (as directed by Q1), or should only Laertes leap (as in F), or should neither of them do so (as allowed by Q2)? Zitner's sympathies are with editors who print a stage direction for a single leap, but he would prefer even less editorial legislation within the text itself and more ample commentary on the possibilities for staging and their critical implications.[22]

Michael J. Warren takes up Urkowitz's theme.[23] He 'can conceive of a book of *Hamlet*, for instance, that involves the reproduction of the first and second quartos and the folio text', with all commentary banished to a separate volume (pp. 35–6). At present, as he says, even academic critics are apt to rely uncritically on edited, modernized texts, of which examples proliferate. Scrutinizing instances of editorial intervention in *King Lear* and other plays – where unavoidable decisions have limited the possible interpretation of a word or stage event – he pleads for 'a new format for the scholarly study of individual plays' that would encourage an 'encounter with the earliest versions in photographic reproduction with their original confusions and corruptions unobscured by the interferences of later sophistication' (p. 35).

Homer Swander also wants less editorial tampering with an early printed text.[24] He concentrates on the role of Menas in Folio *Antony and Cleopatra*, arguing that if 'we submit ourselves to an editorial discipline that arises directly out of the nature of the material to be edited, and if we thus get beyond the literary curtain that modern editors still drop between us and the script, we suddenly discover a Menas – and much else – that looks and sounds like theatre, the theatre of Shakespeare' (p. 187). I think that his analysis of F is over-ingenious, and that he underestimates the disorderliness and incompleteness of Shakespearian foul papers – in which asides, for example, would seldom be clearly indicated – and the vagaries of compositors.

The preparation of critical editions still seems a worthwhile activity to Fredson Bowers. In 'Authority, Copy, and Transmission in Shakespeare's Text' he classifies the kinds of genealogical relationship obtaining between variant early printed texts of Shakespeare's plays, reconsiders the question of the manuscripts used as copy or in its preparation, and takes stock of achievements and desiderata in the study of compositors and printing techniques.[25] Among the most important of his opinions is that since use as printer's copy would have spoilt a manuscript, probably 'no Shakespeare play was set directly from the promptbook' (p. 25).

One crucial question of relationship mentioned by Bowers concerns the good Quarto (Q2) and Folio texts of *Hamlet*. Was F printed from a marked-up copy of Q2, or from a transcript of a marked-up copy of Q2, or from a completely independent manuscript? May Q2 have been consulted occasionally by the Folio compositors or by the person who prepared copy for them? Examining the shared Q2 F

---

[22] 'Four Feet in the Grave: Some Stage Directions in *Hamlet*, V.i', *Text: Transactions of the Society for Textual Scholarship 2*, ed. D. C. Greetham and W. Speed Hill (AMS Press, New York, 1985), pp. 139–48.

[23] 'Textual Problems, Editorial Assertions in Editions of Shakespeare', *Textual Criticism and Literary Interpretation*, pp. 23–37.

[24] 'Menas and the Editors: A Folio Script Unscripted', *Shakespeare Quarterly*, 36 (1985), 165–87.

[25] *Shakespeare Study Today*, pp. 7–36.

errors, unusual spellings, and other oddities that have been supposed to establish F's direct or indirect dependence on Q2, G. R. Hibbard pronounces the combined evidence indecisive.[26]

While Hibbard explains away apparent errors common to Q2 and F, Jeffrey Rayner Myers ferrets out another.[27] Where both texts read (substantially): 'As peace should still her wheaten garland weare / And stand a Comma tweene their amities' (Q2, 5.2.41–2), Myers would revive Theobald's forgotten conjecture 'enmities' for 'amities', on the grounds that a comma is normally thought of as separating, not linking, two items, and emendations of 'comma' itself have been unconvincing. Though suitable glosses of the text as it stands in Q2 and F are possible, Myers makes out a fair case. In the same issue of *Notes and Queries*, R. J. C. Watt proposes 'trust', where Q has 'crush' and F 'trace', in Iago's reference to Roderigo as 'this poore Trash of Venice, whom I trace / For his quicke hunting' (F, 2.1.303–4).[28]

It has long been recognized that the 1609 Quarto of *Pericles*, from which all later editions derive, is seriously corrupt, most probably containing some form of reported text. Gary Taylor seeks to identify the agents responsible for the report.[29] Philip Edwards had suggested that two reporters adopted contrasting methods in reconstructing the play, one composing a virtual paraphrase of acts 1 and 2, the other more faithfully setting down his fragmentary memories of acts 3–5. After a devastating rebuttal of this hypothesis, Taylor searches for clues that, like other 'bad quartos', *Pericles* was memorially reconstructed by two or three actors who had taken part in stage productions. Fluctuations in the apparent quality of the text and limitations on the possibilities for doubling encourage him to put forward the theory that the main reporter was a boy who had doubled Lychorida and Marina, that he may have have been apprenticed to the actor-sharer who played Gower and have gained access to Gower's 'part', and that one of the hired men who had taken minor roles probably lent further aid.

Elsewhere, in an exchange with Jennifer Krauss about Pistol's title in *Henry V*, Taylor ably defends his decision to modernize to 'Ensign', rather than the familiar 'Ancient'.[30]

Matters of principle are also the subject of Taylor's 'Inventing Shakespeare', an exhilarating discussion of how editors have reacted and ought to react to their copy-text's omissions.[31] As he insists, the task of repairing lacunae is 'primarily creative and critical, rather than bibliographical' (p. 34), the ideal gap-filler will be not neutral but unmistakably characteristic of the author, and the art of emendation requires in its exponent not only critical acumen but 'a facility in and an inclination toward *playing* with words' (p. 43) – a due combination of those faculties that the eighteenth century knew as 'wit' and 'judgement'. Taylor's article, which deals with several specific examples of probable omission in Shakespearian texts, redirects us towards a goal that in all our prodigious labours to analyse press-work, identify compositors, and determine the nature of copy we sometimes lose sight of – the solution of cruxes.

---

[26] 'Common Errors and Unusual Spellings in *Hamlet* Q2 and F', *Review of English Studies*, 37 (1986), 55–61.

[27] 'A Neglected Emendation of *Hamlet* V.ii.42', *Notes and Queries*, NS 32 (1985), 474–6.

[28] ' "This Poor Trash of Venice": A Crux in *Othello*', *Notes and Queries*, NS 32 (1985), 476–8. In 'Armado's *fadge not* in *Love's Labour's Lost*: The Case against Emendation', *Notes and Queries*, NS 33 (1986), 349–50, Watt argues against emending 'fadge not' to 'fadge now' in *Love's Labour's Lost*, 5.1.147; this issue of *Notes and Queries* contains several glosses on passages in Shakespeare's plays.

[29] 'The Transmission of *Pericles*', *Papers of the Bibliographical Society of America*, 80 (1986), 193–217.

[30] Jennifer Krauss, 'Name-Calling and the New Oxford *Henry V*', *Shakespeare Quarterly*, 36 (1985), 523–5; Gary Taylor, 'Ancients and Moderns', 525–7.

[31] *Deutsche Shakespeare-Gesellschaft West: Jahrbuch 1986*, pp. 26–44.

Information about the conditions under which Shakespeare's plays were put into print remains nonetheless desirable. George Walton Williams has written a readable introductory guide to the development of the craft of printing till Shakespeare's time, to the publication history of his poems and plays, and to the techniques of analytical bibliography that have been applied to them.[32] His monograph is well illustrated and includes a seven-page classified list of pertinent books and articles. One ingenious application of knowledge of printing house practices to a Shakespearian textual problem is Eric Rasmussen's note making the point that in books set by formes compositorial 'space-wasting' may sometimes have been necessitated not by inaccurate casting-off of copy but by a compositor's accidental omission of lines at an earlier point in his copy.[33] This observation is shown to throw light on at least one divergence between Q2 and F *Hamlet*.

Principles of bibliographical investigation are a concern of Susan Zimmerman.[34] In 1982 I demonstrated to my own satisfaction that two compositors set the 1598 Quarto of *1 Henry IV* and Peter Short's section of the 1597 Quarto of *Richard III*.[35] Invoking D. F. McKenzie's scepticism about the utility of headline analysis, and of spacing evidence for the determination of compositors' stints, Zimmerman attacks these conclusions. She raises questions of procedure and interpretation. Naturally, my own view is that I was right and she is wrong. But this is not the place to carry on a debate.[36] *1 Henry IV* Q1 (1598) was printed by Short from a quarto, known as Q0, which originated in the same shop, and of which only a fragment survives. In my 1982 article I gave grounds for thinking that the manuscript copy for Q0 was scribal, not authorial. In a recent note I adduce an item of evidence that further confirms this view.[37]

'Line division, as an editorial problem, has received only sporadic attention from modern Shakespeareans' – so Paul Werstine begins a

long and detailed article in which he makes good the deficiency.[38] By comparing certain Folio plays with the quartos from which they were reprinted and relating changes made in lineation to the stints of the various Folio compositors, he is able to show 'that distinctive kinds of mislineation ... are associated with individual compositors and that therefore Harrison and Bertram have been too hasty in tracing metrical irregularities to Shakespeare's hand' (p. 111). The tendency of Werstine's thorough and thoughtful study is to vindicate traditional arrangements of Shakespeare's blank verse.

Stanley Wells proposes some 'New Readings in Shakespeare's Sonnets', such as 'spoiled by' for 'My sinfull earth' in 146.2, 'ensilvered o'er' for 'or siluer'd ore' in 12.4, 'rein' (or

---

[32] *The Craft of Printing and the Publication of Shakespeare's Works* (Folger Shakespeare Library, Washington, and Associated University Presses, London and Toronto, 1985). Williams has been criticized for his cautious statements about proofing methods; there is a balanced discussion of this contentious issue by James P. Hammersmith, 'Early Proofing: The Evidence of Extant Proof-Sheets', *Analytical and Enumerative Bibliography*, 7 (1983), 188–215.

[33] 'The Relevance of Cast-off Copy in Determining the Nature of Omissions: Q2 *Hamlet*', *Studies in Bibliography*, 39 (1986), 133–5.

[34] 'The Uses of Headlines: Peter Short's Shakespearian Quartos *1 Henry IV* and *Richard III*', *The Library*, 7 (1985), 218–55.

[35] MacD. P. Jackson, 'Two Shakespeare Quartos: *Richard III* (1597) and *1 Henry IV* (1598)', *Studies in Bibliography*, 35 (1982), 173–90.

[36] A thorough treatment of the points at issue is forthcoming.

[37] MacD. P. Jackson, 'The Manuscript Copy for the Quarto (1598) of Shakespeare's *1 Henry IV*', *Notes and Queries*, NS 33 (1986), 353–4.

[38] 'Line Division in Shakespeare's Dramatic Verse: An Editorial Problem', *Analytical and Enumerative Bibliography*, 8 (1984), 73–125. See also Werstine's 'Edward Capell and Metrically Linked Speeches in Shakespeare', *The Library*, 7 (1985), 259–61. In 'The Hickmott-Dartmouth Copy of *Love's Labour's Lost* Q1 (1598)' *Notes and Queries*, NS 32 (1985), 473, Werstine notes that collation reveals no new variants.

'raign') for 'naigh' in 51.11, and 'these' for 'the' in 82.8.[39] The last three of these are incorporated in his attractively printed edition of the *Sonnets*.[40] 'Ensilvered' is especially compelling.

Richard Corballis writes on 'Copy-text for Theobald's "Shakespeare"', and William C. Woodson on 'Isaac Reed's 1785 Variorum Shakespeare'.[41] Robert F. Fleissner supports 'sullied' against 'solid' in *Hamlet*, and 'Indian' against 'Judean' in *Othello*, and weighs the merits of 'confined fast in fires' against Q2 F 'confin'd to fast in fires' in *Hamlet*, 1.5.11.[42] And John W. Velz and Frances N. Teague have edited a selection of letters by nineteenth-century American Shakespeare scholar Joseph Crosby; these are mostly about Shakespearian matters, including textual obscurities, and reveal Crosby's 'sharp intelligence, ... excellent philological education, energy, and ... open mind' (p. 28).[43]

The major publishing event of 1986 occurred too late to be adequately noticed in this review. The Oxford Shakespeare's modern-spelling edition of *The Complete Works* will be followed by the old-spelling edition and a textual companion in which readings are fully defended. Meanwhile, it must suffice to note that the magnificent new volume amply fulfils expectations aroused by the Oxford *Henry V* (reviewed in *Shakespeare Survey 37*, pp. 202–3). The approach to a single crux may whet the appetite: I mentioned that in his New Cambridge *All's Well That Ends Well* Russell Fraser has Diana say to her would-be seducer, Bertram, 'I see that men make rope's in such a scarre, / That we'll forsake ourselves'

(4.2.38–9), which follows F but makes no sense; and I called Daniel's conjecture, 'may rope's in such a snare' (where 'rope's' means 'rope us') a distinct improvement. Recognizing that 'in' may represent 'e'en' (as it may do at 1.3.42), the Oxford editors come up with 'I see that men make toys e'en such a surance / That we'll forsake ourselves' (4.2.40–1). This comes as a shock, but it sounds remarkably like Shakespeare![44]

---

[39] *Elizabethan and Modern Studies Presented to Professor Willem Schrickx on the Occasion of his Retirement*, ed. J. P. Vander Motten (Ghent, 1985), pp. 317–22.

[40] *Shakespeare Sonnets and A Lover's Complaint*, ed. Stanley Wells (Clarendon Press, Oxford, 1985).

[41] Corballis, *The Library*, 8 (1986), 156–9; Woodson, *Studies in Bibliography*, 39 (1986), 220–9.

[42] 'Hamlet's Flesh Revisited', *Hamlet Studies*, 7 (1985), 101–5; 'The Case of the "Base Judean" Revisited', *The Upstart Crow*, 6 (1986), 44–52; '*Hamlet* and *The Supplication of Souls* Reconvened', *Notes and Queries*, NS 32 (1985), 49–51. Fleissner has more to say about the *Hamlet* crux in *The Prince and the Professor: The Wittenberg Connection in Marlowe, Shakespeare, Goethe, and Frost* (Carl Winter, Universitätsverlag, Heidelberg, 1986), which also takes yet another look at the 'dram of eale'.

[43] *One Touch of Shakespeare: Letters of Joseph Crosby to Joseph Parker Norris, 1875–1878* (Folger Shakespeare Library, Washington, and Associated University Presses, London and Toronto, 1986).

[44] Many general works on the theory and practice of editing have appeared. G. Thomas Tanselle's 'Historicism and Critical Editing', *Studies in Bibliography*, 39 (1986), is a characteristically trenchant and comprehensive survey. Also to be noted is that editors have a new aid to annotation in C. T. Onions, *A Shakespeare Glossary* (Clarendon Press, Oxford, 1986), enlarged and revised by Robert D. Eagleson.

Editor's note. We should also note the appearance of the first two volumes (1983, 1985) of a five-volume edition of the Complete Works translated for the first time into Georgian. The translations are by various hands; there is an Introduction by Nico Kiasashvili, who also supplies notes. The volumes include a remarkable series of highly imaginative illustrations, many of them in colour, by living Georgian artists.

INDEX

INDEX

CAMBRIDGE

The Cambridge Companion to Shakespeare Studies
Edited by **STANLEY WELLS**

This comprehensive introduction to the study of Shakespeare offers a series of essays specially written by an international team of leading scholars. Particular attention is given to new critical approaches and the plays on film and television. Thus the book forms an indispensable companion to anyone with a serious interest in Shakespeare.

'... invaluable to all students of the plays and their presentation.'   *The Times Education Supplement*

340 pp. 0 521 26737 4 **Hard covers £27.50 net**
        0 521 31841 6   **Paperback £8.95 net**

The Merchant of Venice
M. M. MAHOOD

In this latest addition to *The New Cambridge Shakespeare* series Professor Mahood pays special attention to the expectations of the play's first audience, and to our modern experience of seeing and hearing the play. She explores the Englishman's myth of Venice, Elizabethan notions of equity, the position of Jews in society and attitudes towards them.

206 pp. 0 521 22156 0 **Hard covers £15.00 net**
        0 521 29371 5   **Paperback £2.95 net**

The New Cambridge Shakespeare

For a full list of titles available in The New Cambridge Shakespeare series, please contact The Publicity Department at Cambridge University Press

Shakespeare's Tragedies: An Introduction
DIETER MEHL

This is an introduction for the student and general reader to Shakespeare's tragedies and to many of the problems, both old and new, of interpreting them. Traditional questions and answers about the texts and their realisation in performance are freshly examined and it is shown how the plays do not offer easy or final solutions to the tragic dilemmas presented, but engage the reader or spectator in a debate with more than one possible outcome.

282 pp. 0 521 30423 7 **Hard covers £27.50 net**
        0 521 31690 0   **Paperback £9.95 net**

Playgoing in Shakespeare's London
ANDREW GURR

This book refines upon previous oversimplified accounts of Shakespeare's audience. Professor Gurr assembles all the evidence from the writings of the time and describes the structure of the playhouses, the cost of entry, the size of the crowds, the smells, the pickpockets, identifying who went to which plays and at which theatre.

302 pp.   0 521 25336 5   £27.50 net

Stage Images and Traditions: Shakespeare to Ford
MARION LOMAX

This book looks at the traditions behind some of the common images that appeared on stage in the early seventeenth century. Dr Lomax discusses in particular the years 1607-1614, which were important both because of the developments taking place in the playhouses and also because of the variety of drama on offer.

215 pp.   0 521 32659 1   £22.50 net

Shakespeare's Clown
Actor and Text in the Elizabethan Playhouse
DAVID WILES

This book argues that a professional Elizabethan Theatre company always contained one actor known as 'the clown'. Its focus is Will Kemp, clown to the Chamberlain's men from 1594 to 1599 and famed for his solo dance from London to Norwich in 1600.

260 pp.   0 521 32840 3   £25.00 net

Cambridge University Press
The Edinburgh Building, Shaftesbury Road, Cambridge CB2 2RU, England